Lecture Notes in Computer Science **16625**

The series Lecture Notes in Computer Science (LNCS), including its subseries Lecture Notes in Artificial Intelligence (LNAI) and Lecture Notes in Bioinformatics (LNBI), has established itself as a medium for the publication of new developments in computer science and information technology research, teaching, and education.

LNCS enjoys close cooperation with the computer science R & D community, the series counts many renowned academics among its volume editors and paper authors, and collaborates with prestigious societies. Its mission is to serve this international community by providing an invaluable service, mainly focused on the publication of conference and workshop proceedings and postproceedings. LNCS commenced publication in 1973.

Andrea Mauri · Lola Burgueño ·
Riccardo Tommasini
Editors

Web Engineering

26th International Conference, ICWE 2026
Lyon, France, June 9–12, 2026
Proceedings

Editors
Andrea Mauri
Lyon 1 University
Villeurbanne, France

Lola Burgueño
University of Malaga
Málaga, Spain

Riccardo Tommasini
INSA Lyon
Villeurbanne, France

ISSN 0302-9743 ISSN 1611-3349 (electronic)
Lecture Notes in Computer Science
ISBN 978-3-032-29371-8 ISBN 978-3-032-29372-5 (eBook)
https://doi.org/10.1007/978-3-032-29372-5

This Springer imprint is published by the registered company Springer Nature Switzerland AG
The registered company address is: Gewerbestrasse 11, 6330 Cham, Switzerland

Preface

Welcome to the Proceedings of the 26th INTERNATIONAL CONFERENCE on WEB ENGINEERING, ICWE 2026.

ICWE aims to promote research and scientific exchange related to Web engineering, and to bring together researchers and practitioners from various disciplines in academia and industry to tackle emerging challenges in the engineering of Web applications and associated technologies, as well as to assess the impact of these technologies on society, media, and culture. Supported by the INTERNATIONAL SOCIETY OF WEB ENGINEERING (ISWE), since 2001, ICWE has served as the leading annual conference for the Web Engineering community.

This volume collects the full research papers, New Ideas and Emerging Results (NIER) papers, tool demonstrations, posters, and tutorials presented at the 26th International Conference on Web Engineering (ICWE 2026), held in Lyon, France, from June 9 to 12, 2026.

The ICWE 2026 theme, "Agentic & Autonomous Web: Design, Trust, Accessibility, Sustainability, and Performance," invited discussions on the design of web systems not just for humans but for and in collaboration with autonomous agents. This theme encouraged discussions on how to balance trust and security, as well as visions and ideas on how agents can make web engineering more sustainable and accessible. For instance, it aimed to address the environmental impact of web technologies and how emerging AI-assisted coding paradigms (e.g., vibe coding) may open web engineering to a less technical audience. Last but not least, it welcomed discussions AI support for web engineering in performance-critical environments (e.g., edge-cloud continuum).

This year's Call for Papers attracted 75 submissions worldwide, distributed across several tracks. The selection process was rigorous, and facilitated by a Program Committee (PC) of distinguished experts. Each submission was single-blind reviewed by at least three PC members, with final decisions made through thorough discussions. The research track received 49 submissions–31 full papers, 9 NIER papers and 3 short papers. Six full papers were desk-rejected. Eight full papers were accepted, reflecting an acceptance rate of 26%; as well as 4 NIER papers and 3 short papers.

The conference also featured competitive sessions for short papers, industrial contributions, demonstrations, posters, as well as a Ph.D. symposium with 8 accepted proposals, 1 leading-edge tutorial, and 4 workshops. The final program featured innovative approaches, novel findings, and thought-provoking ideas. It covered various topics related to Web infrastructures; the human-centered Web; LLMs, search, and knowledge; security, safety, and privacy; inclusion and the accessible Web; and security, safety, and inclusion on the Web.

We extend our deepest gratitude to everyone who contributed to the organization of the conference, especially the track chairs: UJJWAL SHARMA & YEN-CHIA HSU (Industry Track), DANIELE DELL'AGLIO & SERGIO FIRMENICH (Posters and Demonstrations), SEBASTIAN HEIL & IN-YOUNG KO (Ph.D. Symposium), ABEL GOMEZ & JAVIER

L. CÁNOVAS IZQUIERDO (Tutorials), STEFANIA DUMBRAVA & JAVIER A. ESPINOSA-OVIEDO (Workshops), GIANPAOLO IULIANO & ROBERTO STANZIONE (Proceedings), AMEDEO PACHERA & GIANLUCA ROSSI (Web and Publicity).

Our thanks also go to JORDI CABOT *(Luxembourg Institute of Science and Technology*, SENJUTI BASU ROY *(New Jersey Institute of Technology*, and EFTHYMIA TSAMOURA *(Huawei Labs)* who agreed to be our keynote speakers.

We appreciate the invaluable support of the Université Claude Bernard Lyon 1 & INSA Lyon, LyonTech-La Doua Campus. We are also grateful to *Springer* and *River Publishers* for sponsoring the ICWE 2026 best paper awards, and to *Springer* for publishing these proceedings. Our sincere thanks go to the PC members, additional reviewers, and student volunteers whose dedication ensured the success of ICWE 2026, both academically and practically.

Finally, we thank all the authors and members of the ICWE community for their contributions and participation in making ICWE 2026 a successful event.

June 2026

Andrea Mauri
Lola Burgueño
Riccardo Tommasini

Organization

General Chairs

Andrea Mauri	Claude Bernard University Lyon 1, France

Program Chairs

Lola Burgueño	University of Málaga, Spain
Riccardo Tommasini	INSA Lyon, France

Industry Track Chairs

Ujjwal Sharma	University of Amsterdam, Netherlands
Yen-Chia Hsu	University of Amsterdam, Netherlands

Poster and Demo Chairs

Daniele dell'Aglio	Aalborg University, Denmark
Sergio Firmenich	National University of La Plata, Argentina

PhD Symposium Chairs

Sebastian Heil	Chemnitz University of Technology, Germany
In-Young Ko	Korea Advanced Institute of Science and Technology, South Korea

Tutorial Chairs

Abel Gomez	Universitat Politècnica de València, Spain
Javier L. Cánovas Izquierdo	Universitat Oberta de Catalunya, Spain

Workshop Chairs

Stefania Dumbrava	ENSIIE & Inria & Télécom SudParis, France
Javier A. Espinosa-Oviedo	Claude Bernard University Lyon 1, France

Proceedings Chairs

Gianpaolo Iuliano	University of Salerno, Italy
Roberto Stanzione	Inria, École normale supérieure, France

Web and Publicity Chairs

Ameodeo Pachera	Claude Bernard University Lyon 1, France
Gianluca Rossi	Claude Bernard University Lyon 1, France

Program Committee

Sören Auer	TIB Leibniz Information Center Science & Technology and University of Hannover, Germany
Mohamed-Amine Baazizi	Sorbonne Université, France
Marcos Baez	Bielefeld University of Applied Sciences, Germany
Maxim Bakaev	Novosibirsk State Technical University, Russia
Luciano Baresi	Politecnico di Milano, Italy
Javier Berrocal	University of Extremadura, Spain
Juan Boubeta-Puig	University of Cádiz, Spain
Antonio Brogi	Università di Pisa, Italy
Radek Burget	Brno University of Technology, Czech Republic
Christoph Bussler	Mistral AI, France
Carlos Canal	University of Málaga, Spain
Javier L. Canovas Izquierdo	Universitat Oberta de Catalunya, Spain
Cinzia Cappiello	Politecnico di Milano, Italy
Sven Casteleyn	Universitat Jaume I, Spain
Richard Chbeir	Université de Pau et des pays de l'Adour, France
Stefania Dumbrava	Institut Polytechnique de Paris, France
Pablo Fernandez	University of Seville, Spain
Flavius Frasincar	Erasmus University Rotterdam, Netherlands
Martin Gaedke	Chemnitz University of Technology, Germany

Alejandra Garrido	Universidad Nacional de La Plata, Argentina
Irene Garrigos	University of Alicante, Spain
Cesar Gonzalez Mora	University of Alicante, Spain
Vijay Govindarajan	Expedia Group, USA
Julián Grigera	Universidad Nacional de La Plata, Argentina
Sebastian Heil	Technische Universität Chemnitz, Germany
Radu Tudor Ionescu	University of Bucharest, Romania
Gianpaolo Iuliano	University of Salerno, Italy
Stefan Klikovits	Johannes Kepler University Linz, Austria
István Koren	Eötvös Loránd University, Hungary
Nathalie Moreno	Universidad de Málaga, Spain
Radka Nacheva	University of Economics – Varna, Bulgaria
Elena Navarro	University of Castilla-La Mancha, Spain
Guadalupe Ortiz	University of Cádiz, Spain
Oscar Pastor	Universidad Politécnica de Valencia, Spain
Mohamed Ragab	Nahda University in Beni Suef, Egypt
Werner Retschitzegger	Johannes Kepler University Linz, Austria
Thomas Richter	Rhein-Waal University of Applied Sciences, Germany
António Rito Silva	Universidade de Lisboa, Portugal
Gustavo Rossi	Universidad Nacional de La Plata, Argentina
Hrishikesh Terdalkar	BITS Pilani, India
William Van Woensel	University of Ottawa, Canada
Markel Vigo	University of Manchester, UK
Manuel Wimmer	Johannes Kepler University Linz, Austria
Yeliz Yesilada	Middle East Technical University NCC, Northern Cyprus
Peide Zhu	Delft University of Technology, Netherlands
Shubhangi Agarwal	Indian Institute of Technology Kanpur, India

External Reviewers

Paula Garcia-Tapia-Mateo	Universidad de Alicante, Spain

ICWE 2026 Partners

Contents

Research and Industrial Tracks

Tutorials

Research and Industrial Tracks

Web of Things-Driven On-Device Automation for Resource-Constrained Energy Devices

Leonhard Esterbauer[1], Max Thoma[1](✉), Tobias Schwarzinger[1](✉), Thomas I. Strasser[1,2](✉), and Wolfgang Kastner[1](✉)

[1] TU Wien, Vienna, Austria
{leonhard.esterbauer,max.thoma,tobias.schwarzinger,thomas.strasser, wolfgang.kastner}@tuwien.ac.at

[2] AIT Austrian Institute of Technology, Vienna, Austria
thomas.strasser@ait.ac.at

https://www.tuwien.at/, https://www.ait.ac.at/

Abstract. Energy-related Internet of Things (IoT) devices such as inverters, storage systems, heat pumps, and Electric Vehicle (EV) chargers are increasingly connected and remotely controllable, yet their integration logic is often tightly coupled to specific standards, service providers, or vendor clouds. As protocols and business processes evolve, this coupling can lead to vendor lock-ins or complex gateway-based compatibility layers, which make local fallbacks or user-defined automation difficult. At the same time, most residential energy automations are conceptually simple and follow a consistent pattern: ingest a signal (e.g., dynamic tariffs or local PV surplus), evaluate it against a policy, and actuate a device accordingly.

In this paper, we explore how these automations can be enabled on resource-constrained hardware using standardized, machine-readable interfaces. To this end, we present a software architecture that realizes a consumer-side subset of the Web of Things (WoT) Scripting API on embedded devices, including `consume`, `readProperty`, `writeProperty`, and `invokeAction`. The architecture supports asynchronous I/O via an on-device JavaScript executor and exposes additional device functionality to scripts through host bindings. To quantify the limits of our approach, we evaluate practical resource costs on an ESP32 using an energy automation scenario and report on firmware footprint and memory usage. Overall, the results indicate manageable firmware and memory overhead, demonstrating the feasibility of deploying standards-based automation logic directly on constrained IoT devices.

Keywords: Web of Things · Energy Automation · Scripting API · Embedded Computing · Resource-Constrained

A. Mauri et al. (Eds.): ICWE 2026, LNCS 16625, pp. 3–17, 2026.
https://doi.org/10.1007/978-3-032-29372-5_1

1 Introduction

The energy domain is undergoing a rapid transition toward more dynamic and distributed operation. Devices such as inverters, batteries, heat pumps, and Electric Vehicle (EV) chargers increasingly expose network interfaces and are expected to react to external signals such as energy prices, local surplus, or grid capacity. In practice, the integration needs are often captured in domain-specific protocols and standards such as EEBUS, OpenADR, or OCPP and directly implemented in the device firmware or in vendor-specific ecosystems. Although this approach enables immediate functionality, it also creates a coupling between device behavior and the current assumptions of markets, processes, and protocols. When the ecosystem changes, the effort required to maintain interoperability is typically shifted into additional layers such as gateways, middleware, or cloud backends, which obscure system behavior and make the overall setup intransparent to end users.

One way of reducing integration effort for consumers is to provide devices with built-in automations that operate out of the box without requiring a dedicated gateway, for example by reacting to a dynamic price signal. However, in many current products, such built-in automations are implemented as predefined control strategies tied to one specific signal or optimization objective, which limits their composability with additional local context (e.g., local photovoltaic (PV) generation surplus, household constraints, or other devices). Widely used alternatives are central local controllers and cloud-based orchestration through vendor backends or service platforms that coordinate monitoring, control, and optimization remotely. While local controllers introduce additional system complexity and hardware or maintenance overhead, cloud-based orchestration increases dependency on third parties, requires external data access, and makes user-defined fallback behavior more difficult.

At the same time, most residential energy automations are conceptually simple and follow a consistent pattern: ingest a signal (e.g., dynamic tariffs or local PV surplus), evaluate it against a policy, and actuate a device accordingly. Such policies are conceptually understandable to users and can often be expressed in a few lines of code. Enabling these automations directly on devices would improve locality (no mandatory external data access), reduce single points of failure, and allow domain logic to evolve without requiring changes to the device firmware. However, achieving this requires a runtime where users can deploy custom automations.

The W3C Web of Things (WoT) standard offers a strong basis for this scenario: Thing Descriptions (TDs) [8] specify device interactions in a machine-readable format, while the WoT Scripting API [14] provides a standardized API for developing automation scripts. However, existing WoT Scripting API implementations primarily target mid- to high-resource environments such as gateways or servers.

In this work, we investigate the feasibility of realizing a consumer-side subset of the WoT Scripting API on resource-constrained hardware. Our goal is to enable users to deploy custom automation scripts directly on their Internet of

Things (IoT) devices, shifting decision-making closer to the edge. The present prototype focuses on periodic, polling-based automations and assumes trusted local deployment. Push-based interactions and a full security model for untrusted third-party scripts are outside the current scope. To assess feasibility, we implement and evaluate the approach on an ESP32 microcontroller unit (MCU) using a representative energy-automation scenario.

This leads to the following research questions: **RQ1:** What software architecture components are required to realize consumer-side use of the WoT Scripting API on MCU-class devices while supporting its Promise-based programming model? **RQ2:** What is the performance overhead of executing these automations on MCU-class hardware, and what are the practical limits for a typical residential energy-optimization scenario?

The remainder of the paper is organized as follows. Section 2 outlines the background and related work, while Sect. 3 introduces the motivating use case related to EV charging optimization. Section 4 presents a software architecture and related implementation that realizes parts of the WoT Scripting API on embedded devices. The evaluation is presented in Sect. 5, followed by a discussion of the results in Sect. 6. Finally, Sect. 7 concludes the paper with a summary of the main findings and an outlook on potential future work.

2 Background and Related Work

The WoT ecosystem spans a wide range of IoT devices, from powerful cloud servers to resource-constrained MCUs. To categorize such resource-constrained devices, the IETF defines three classes in RFC 7228 [3]. These classes depend on the device's Random Access Memory (RAM) and Read-Only Memory (ROM) sizes. The WoT Architecture extends this definition to eight device categories (C0 to C7). Table 1 summarizes these categories and their different hardware capabilities.

Table 1. The eight device categories as defined in the WoT Architecture. Adapted from the official specification [10]

Category	Data size (RAM)	Code size (Flash, ROM, ...)
C0	<< 10 KiB	<< 100 KiB
C1	~10 KiB	~100 KiB
C2	~64 KiB	~256 KiB
C3	~64–256 KiB	~256 KiB - several MB
C4	~256 KiB - several MB	~1 MB - several MB
C5	~1–8 GB	~1–16 GB
C6	~several GB	~several GB
C7	~several GB	~several GB

Furthermore, the WoT Architecture specification recommends that the deployment target for the Scripting API be devices in category C5 and above [10]. Correspondingly, the reference implementation of the WoT Scripting API `node-wot` [1] relies on the Node.js [2] JavaScript runtime, which is too resource-intensive for embedded devices in C4 or lower categories.

Resource-constrained devices in the categories C0 to C4 (MCUs) are expected to implement the Native WoT API to integrate with the WoT ecosystem [10]. In contrast, the WoT Scripting API primarily targets higher-resource platforms. Because it models interactions with Things through asynchronous interfaces, its direct adoption on MCU-class devices is non-trivial and creates a gap between devices in categories ≤C4 and the higher-resource platforms in categories ≥C5. Many MCU platforms do not readily support asynchronous programming, so the Scripting API interfaces must be approximated and adapted for such resource-constrained environments.

However, transforming asynchronous semantics to synchronous is not trivial. An example of porting the Scripting API to native platform code is presented in [12]. The authors propose a template-based CLI tool to generate native WoT Servient-like code for MCUs. Their work focuses on the `expose` functionality of the WoT Scripting API and does not implement `consume` interfaces. Moreover, no dynamic scripting support is offered, and affordance handler logic is implemented in native code.

While the WoT Scripting API specifies how scripts interact with Things, it leaves the runtime specification to the implementer [14]. Nevertheless, the Scripting API's interface definitions are specified in WebIDL, which maps naturally to ECMAScript. At the same time, embedded software development is increasingly shifting beyond bare-metal programming toward modern IoT runtimes that improve developer experience and introduce innovative concepts to the embedded domain [13]. These runtimes facilitate the use of higher-level languages, shorten iteration cycles, and provide mechanisms for application isolation. As a result, running ECMAScript runtimes on devices in the C2–C4 range has become feasible [6,7].

However, these advances in IoT runtime development have not been fully exploited by the WoT community. As an example, the Moddable SDK demonstrated the early feasibility of embedded ECMAScript-based Thing interactions, but its WoT library saw limited adoption and was deprecated soon thereafter. As a result, it remains limited to the legacy Web Thing API rather than the current WoT specifications [11]. More recently, the authors in [9] proposed using WebAssembly as a WoT runtime. Their approach departs from the current WoT specifications by requiring extensions to the TD, and does not provide scripting support.

In summary, deploying automations to high-resource devices is common practice, but there is still little support for executing them on resource-constrained hardware. The approaches presented in this section either exceed typical embedded resource budgets or require a different development workflow that is incompatible with the convenient methods used on more capable devices. Although embedded ECMAScript runtimes offer the potential to broaden the set of supported devices, their use within the WoT ecosystem remains underexplored. As a result, many WoT deployments rely on gateways or other translation layers to host automation logic, increasing architectural complexity and maintenance effort. We address these limitations by proposing and evaluating an approach for running automations directly on resource-constrained hardware, thereby extending the benefits of the WoT Scripting API to embedded devices.

3 Motivating Use Case: EV Charging Optimization

With the increasing prevalence of EVs, optimizing their charging behavior has become a critical area of research. Particularly in Vehicle-to-Grid (V2G) scenarios, where an EV can also be discharged to provide energy, this problem is non-trivial and requires different strategies depending on the objective.

Figure 1 shows an overview of the most prominent implementations of EV charging optimization and a desired approach without a dedicated gateway.

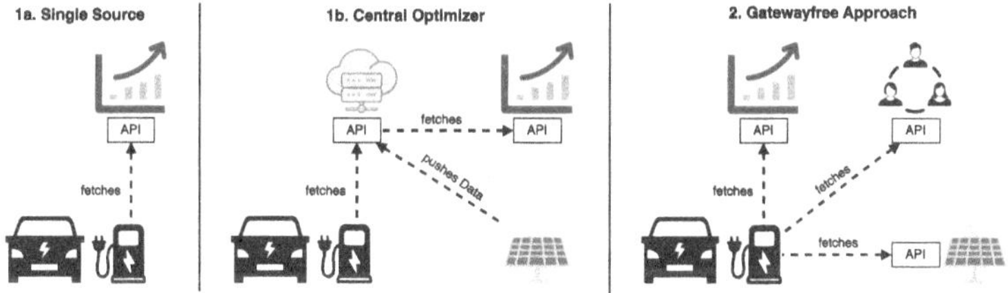

Fig. 1. Three implementations of EV charging optimizations.

In contemporary deployments, EV charging optimization is typically implemented using one of two approaches: either the charger supports only a single source or optimization strategy (1a), or it relies on a central optimizer (1b). A primary limitation of approach (1a) is its inflexibility, as it prevents users from easily combining multiple strategies. For example, a user might wish to optimize simultaneously for electricity market prices and the surplus energy in their local energy community. Approach (1b), on the other hand, requires additional computing platforms. In the case of a local controller, this introduces either extra hardware costs or, in the case of a cloud-based controller, it introduces significant privacy and data sovereignty concerns.

Approach (2) mitigates the drawbacks of the approaches mentioned above by aggregating all necessary data directly on the device. This eliminates the need to transmit and store sensitive local information (e.g., power consumption) to an external cloud, and it avoids the costs associated with additional local hardware. Furthermore, it supports sophisticated optimization strategies, but at the expense of requiring more capable processing hardware within the charging device itself. Assuming there are sufficient hardware capabilities, this localized approach presents a flexible and future-proof solution for many scenarios.

However, it also introduces a significant challenge, as the optimization strategy cannot be easily modified by flashing a new firmware version due to considerable safety and reliability risks. Consequently, the device requires a dedicated environment in which users can safely deploy custom optimization strategies without altering the core firmware. The approach presented in the next section enables this deployment model on resource-constrained hardware commonly found in residential IoT devices.

4 Approach

The WoT standard describes multiple ways of hosting applications. One of the primary deployment architectures involves fixed-function IoT devices that are controlled by a sufficiently powerful gateway. This gateway runs a full-fledged WoT runtime with scripting support, such as `node-wot` [1] and is called a WoT servient.

Running on the gateway, the WoT servient can host applications that interact with IoT devices through their WoT affordances. As discussed in Sect. 3, the requirement for a separate gateway device often introduces additional hardware costs and maintenance overhead, even though the overall setup can be robust. In contrast, extending IoT devices by hosting a WoT runtime directly on the device itself is often infeasible due to hardware limitations. In this section, we therefore present the design and implementation of an embedded servient that enables deploying and running automations on MCU-class hardware making fixed-function devices more flexible.

4.1 Embedded Servient Architecture

Based on the *Abstract Servient Architecture* [10], Fig. 2 illustrates an embedded servient architecture. The servient is logically divided into four major components: the HTTP Server, the Script Store, the Scripting Runtime, and the Automation Scripts themselves. Additionally, the architecture includes system-provided libraries. Each of these components is described in the following.

The *HTTP Server* provides the primary interface for interacting with the servient. It achieves this by exposing TDs at well-known URLs, a web-based user interface for manual script development, and the device's affordance APIs. In the proposed architecture, the device is modeled using two distinct Things. The first one (EV Charger Thing) provides access to the actual hardware affordances of the device, while the second one (Script Manager Thing) is dedicated entirely to managing the *Scripting Runtime*. The Script Manager Thing provides common affordances for managing deployed automations, including operations to install, uninstall, list, start, and stop them. This Script Manager API is based on [4] and the WoT Script Manager Thing proposal[1]. Because the EV Charger Thing's affordances are inherently use-case specific, we do not detail them further here.

[1] https://github.com/w3c/wot-scripting-api/tree/main/applications/script-manager.

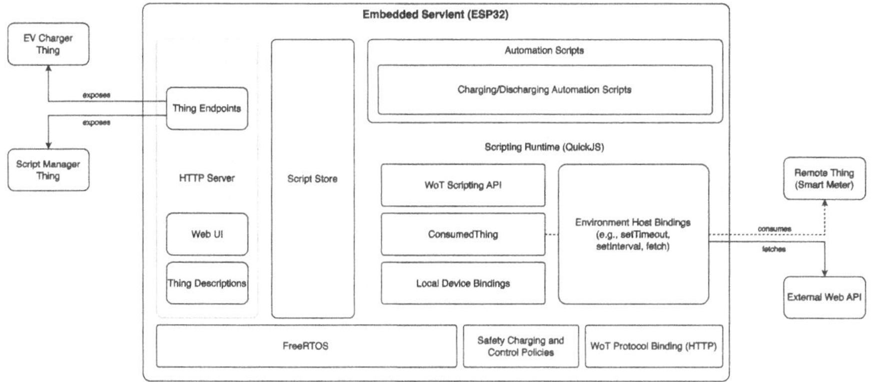

Fig. 2. Overview of the embedded servient architecture.

Since the main memory of embedded devices is typically volatile, deployed scripts must be saved to persistent storage to survive a system restart. The *Script Store* component fulfills this crucial role. During startup, the servient queries the Script Store to determine which scripts must be loaded and executed. The Script Manager Thing implementation directly uses this component to store and remove scripts. If the original script source is no longer needed on the device after deployment, minification can be used to reduce the required script storage space.

The *Scripting Runtime* forms the core of the servient and is responsible for executing automations. It is built around the QuickJS ECMAScript engine. We selected QuickJS because the WoT Scripting API is inherently asynchronous and benefits from native `async`/`await`. At the same time, QuickJS remains lightweight enough for MCU-class devices while supporting modern ECMAScript features (ES2023). This combination is important because most Scripting API methods return a `Promise` representing an asynchronous result. Without native `async`/`await` support, managing these promises quickly becomes cumbersome. For interacting with the runtime, the system employs the WoT Scripting API alongside additional host bindings. This environment allows scripts to act as consumers of other things, typically by fetching and consuming a TD. Once consumed, the `ConsumedThing` interface allows automations to interact with exposed affordances without requiring knowledge of the underlying communication protocols. Section 4.3 details the implementation of the WoT Scripting API and the available host bindings.

Finally, many important components are provided by the real-time operating system (FreeRTOS) and the accompanying platform-specific libraries. These encompass essential network components, such as the HTTP client and server.

4.2 Runtime Integration

Figure 3 presents a schematic of a running servient instance hosting the Scripting Runtime. The system is distributed across two independent tasks scheduled by the operating system. While the HTTP Task handles incoming requests for user interaction, the Runtime Task hosts the Scripting Runtime responsible for executing automations.

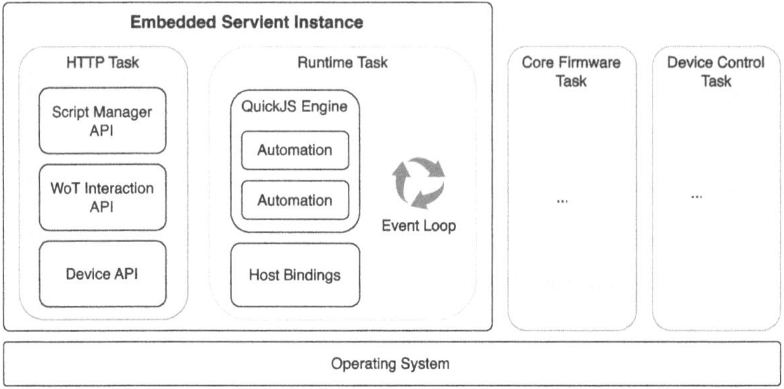

Fig. 3. Conceptual view of a running embedded servient instance.

In addition to these two WoT-specific tasks, the operating system concurrently executes core firmware tasks that implement the device's primary functionality (e.g., a control loop for battery management). These core tasks encapsulate the critical logic required to ensure safe and sustainable operation. Deployed automations can only influence these processes by providing setpoints or similar target values, as the automations cannot directly access the available hardware. The final decision of whether an action is safe to execute remains strictly with the device's core firmware, thereby enforcing the same safety guarantees applied to external actors controlling the device via its exposed affordances.

To support asynchronous behavior, the runtime uses an event-driven design with dedicated FreeRTOS queues (request, response, script, and timer queues). The JavaScript runtime task waits on these queues, processes incoming events, and executes pending jobs in QuickJS. Automations do not run continuously. A script is executed when it is enqueued via the script queue. HTTP completions and timer expirations then produce follow-up events that resume promise callbacks or invoke timer handlers.

The queues also implement inter-task communication: when JavaScript starts an HTTP request, the request is placed on the request queue. The HTTP worker task performs the network call and pushes the result to the response queue. The JavaScript runtime task consumes that response, resolves or rejects the stored Promise, and continues execution in the next event-loop cycle. Subsequent automation activity (for example periodic logic via `setInterval`) is triggered by new timer events.

In the current prototype iteration, the consumer core is not yet fully implemented. For example, the `observeProperty` method remains unsupported because it requires a mechanism to repeatedly poll an HTTP endpoint. Nevertheless, the foundational event queue architecture discussed above is well-equipped to support these asynchronous APIs in future development.

4.3 Host and Protocol Bindings

To interact with the host environment, the Scripting Runtime can register global JavaScript objects and functions that can be called from automation scripts. This includes the WoT Scripting API itself, which is registered under the global `WOT` object. In addition, because many automations rely on them, common bindings for managing timers are provided (e.g., `setTimeout`, `setInterval`) and primitives for requesting data from a web server (e.g., `fetch`). These additional host bindings are not part of the WoT Scripting API, but they fulfill requirements that are often needed in automations.

Ideally, interactions with other devices happen primarily through the WoT Scripting API instead of `fetch`, as this keeps scripts protocol-agnostic. When an affordance of a `ConsumedThing` is called, the Scripting Runtime will select and use one of the available forms. For example, in the case of an HTTP form, this involves reading the `href` and issuing an HTTP request. For an automation running inside the runtime, it does not matter how the form is realized. If the form changes to a different protocol (e.g., MQTT), the automation can remain the same.

Lastly, as one of the primary use cases of our approach is interacting with the host device, a local dispatch path is implemented. If an automation consumes an affordance of the host device, the runtime automatically redirects the request to a native implementation. This implementation can directly interact with the hardware and thus avoid the overhead of setting up an HTTP request and response. Affordances supporting this mechanism feature a specialized `wot+local://` form in their definition.

5 Evaluation

5.1 Experimental Setup

We evaluated the use case on an ESP32-C6-WROOM-1 with a total of 500 KiB of available SRAM, using the ESP-IDF (v5.5.2), QuickJS (v2024-01-13), and riscv32-esp-elf-gcc v14.2.0. All experiments use a local Wi-Fi network with line-of-sight to the access point. A laptop hosts the HTTP endpoint and captures device diagnostics (e.g., heap high-water marks). The source code required to compile the firmware image, along with the automation scripts used in the scenario-based evaluation, is publicly available on Zenodo [5].

The automation that implements the motivating use case of Sect. 3 is based on a rule-based control strategy. The desired behavior of the charging strategy was provided to an Artificial Intelligence (AI) agent as a task description.

The agent (*Gemini 3 Flash Preview* via the `gemini-cli`) implemented the described rule behavior and created a deployment script that uploads the automation via the Script Manager API.

5.2 Storage Usage

This section evaluates the extent to which the flash storage capacities of resource-constrained devices can meet the demands of an embedded WoT runtime. We used the ESP-IDF tool `size-components` to determine the sizes of compiled objects within the flashed firmware image.

Figure 4 illustrates the flash storage consumption of the deployed firmware image. The firmware image itself was compiled with size optimizations enabled, resulting in an image approximately 14% smaller than a performance-optimized build. These measurements exclude automation scripts as they are dynamically deployed at runtime.

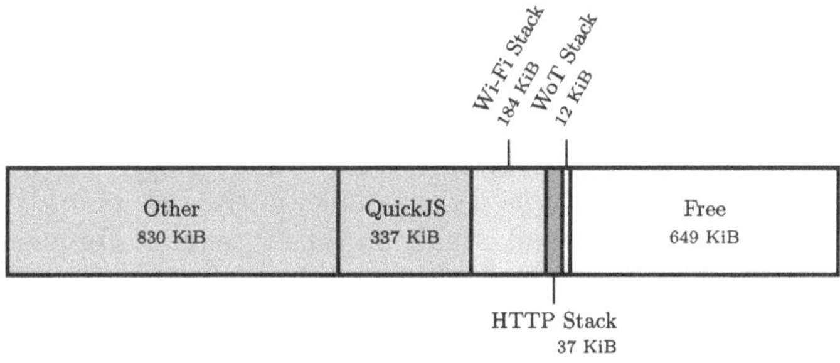

Fig. 4. Amount of flash storage consumed by individual parts of the flashed image. (Size-optimized build)

The largest single component in the final firmware image is QuickJS, which occupies approximately 337 KiB. Together, however, foundational elements such as the Wi-Fi stack and protocol providers consume the majority of the storage footprint. Since the WoT stack (WoT binding and runtime management) itself requires only about 12 KiB, free flash memory remains available to integrate additional device capabilities.

5.3 Memory Usage

In addition to the flash storage consumption, we evaluated the dynamic heap utilization of our implementation during execution. To obtain the device's heap metrics, we utilized the diagnostic tools provided by the underlying operating system. These tools report the minimum free heap observed during execution. Subtracting this value from the initial free heap yields the peak heap usage. It is important to note that the heap constitutes only a fraction of the total available memory since a portion of the main memory is reserved for other tasks.

Table 2 presents the results of these experiments in four scenarios. The Base Usage scenario accounts for the system's baseline memory footprint without the HTTP server or the Scripting Runtime active. Two intermediate scenarios evaluate the system with only one of these respective components running. Although this is not a practical operational mode, it effectively isolates and attributes memory consumption to each component. Finally, the Full Setup scenario executes both components concurrently while deploying and running the automation script from the motivating use case. In general, after automation has been loaded and executed, approximately 114 KiB of heap memory remains available on the device.

Table 2. Heap usage under different scenarios, reporting the initial free heap, the minimum free heap observed during execution, and the derived peak heap usage.

Scenario	Initial Free	Minimum Free	Peak Heap
Base Usage	380 KiB	308 KiB	72 KiB
HTTP Server Only	367 KiB	272 KiB	95 KiB
Scripting Runtime Only	362 KiB	171 KiB	191 KiB
Full Setup	360 KiB	114 KiB	246 KiB

Additionally, two exploratory tests provided rough reference points for script complexity and size on the target device. A synthetic script with around 100 JavaScript object definitions and 100 function definitions could still be deployed and executed, but was already close to the practically usable memory limits, while a second test yielded a maximum script size of about 31 KiB. These values are only indicative, as they depend on the specific structure and size of the language constructs used. In practice, script size can often be reduced by minifying scripts before uploading them to the MCU.

5.4 Runtime Overhead

This experiment aims to quantify the computational overhead introduced by the event loop and the JavaScript runtime. To this end, we implemented four microbenchmarks that sequentially issue HTTP requests. Specifically, these benchmarks evaluate the latency of executing the JavaScript code that dispatches the request, as well as the processing required to handle request completion. The corresponding HTTP target server was hosted on a laptop, as stated in Sect. 5.1.

Figure 5 plots the achieved requests per second for each benchmark. Two benchmarks were implemented natively on the platform, one of them reusing the HTTP client instance between calls, while the other does not. Reusing the instance more than doubles the achievable number of requests. The other two benchmarks use the JavaScript runtimes QuickJS and Moddable SDK, respectively.

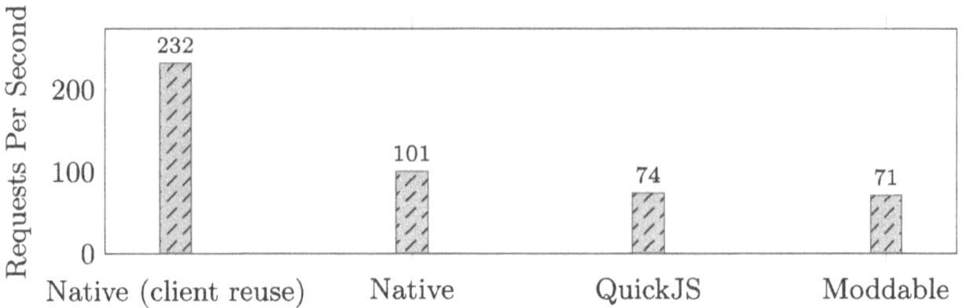

Fig. 5. Comparison of achievable requests per second in microbenchmarks across different request loop implementations.

6 Discussion

Our results indicate that a WoT-driven, consumer-side scripting interface can be realized on MCU-class hardware for reasonably-sized automations. Below, the main findings, trade-offs against existing integration patterns and limitations of the current prototype are discussed.

6.1 Findings

The evaluation shows that representative on-device energy automations can be expressed compactly using `consume` and `ConsumedThing` interactions while executed within the resource budgets of modern MCU-class devices. In particular, the approach is well-suited for periodic control loops that combine a small number of signals (e.g., tariffs and PV surplus) and translate them into device setpoints. The practical implication is that a device can remain adaptable to evolving data sources and strategies without requiring firmware-level reimplementation of new (domain-)standards or service-provider integrations.

Moreover, a central benefit of grounding the approach in WoT TDs is the use of machine-readable contracts to describe capabilities and interaction endpoints. This improves interoperability because automation logic targets contracts rather than proprietary APIs and provides a natural entry point for automated tooling. In particular, a tool or agent can discover the availability of an on-device runtime via TDs, derive the interaction surface like properties and actions, and generate or adapt scripts accordingly. While this work does not evaluate agentic deployment workflows in detail, it establishes the architectural prerequisite: a standardized, discoverable, and deployable execution environment on the device.

However, on-device scripting is not a replacement for gateway- or cloud-centric orchestration. Gateways remain advantageous for global optimization across many devices, richer user interfaces, and compute-heavy analytics. In contrast, on-device execution reduces dependence on a central component and can improve resilience during connectivity or platform outages. It may also reduce integration overhead for narrow local tasks by eliminating mandatory intermediaries. Nevertheless, distributing logic across devices introduces operational questions such as deployment, updates and observability that are typically better supported in centralized controller architectures.

Apart from that, existing ecosystems already support local automation through device-specific integrations and gateway-level platforms, e.g., rule engines or home automation hubs. In addition, some consumer devices even already expose embedded scripting environments. Compared to these platform-specific automation stacks, the distinguishing aspect of our approach is the use of the WoT Scripting API as a standardized contract layer. This choice aims to improve portability of automation logic and reduce vendor lock-in at the interface level.

Taken together, these results provide a direct answer to our research questions. Regarding **RQ1**, the prototype shows that consumer-side WoT scripting on MCU-class devices mainly requires a dedicated runtime task, an event-driven queue-based integration model for asynchronous I/O, persistent script management, and protocol or host bindings that map WoT affordances to native functionality. These components were sufficient to approximate the Promise-based programming model of the WoT Scripting API on constrained hardware. Regarding **RQ2**, the evaluation shows that the resulting overhead is noticeable but manageable for the targeted class of applications. Although the JavaScript runtime and event-loop integration consume a relevant share of flash and heap memory and are slower than native request handling, the motivating automation scenario could still be executed successfully on the evaluated ESP32 with remaining resource headroom. This suggests that the approach is practical for small, periodic, rule-based energy automations.

6.2 Limitations and Prototype Scope

The evaluation only targets periodic, low complexity energy control loops with modest communication demands and does not cover compute-heavy or high-rate streaming workloads. Additionally, the prototype intentionally targets only the minimal subset of functionality that is required for our demo scenarios, which leaves several aspects out of scope. Extending the prototype in the future will require additional device resources such as more flash for larger program code. However, the evaluation indicates that memory and storage headroom remain available for further extensions.

Apart from that, our approach intentionally focuses only on a consumer-side subset of the WoT Scripting API such as the `consume` and `ConsumedThing` interactions (`readProperty`, `writeProperty`, `invokeAction`). Support for the `ExposedThing` API is out of scope for the present work. Additionally, push-based interactions such as `observeProperty` and `subscribeEvent` are not implemented. Supporting these would require subscription lifecycle management and push-capable bindings (e.g., WS/MQTT/SSE).

Regarding security, the prototype does not yet implement a complete security model for third-party scripts. Without additional controls, the Script Manager API could allow unauthorized code deployment, the unrestricted host bindings could enable data exfiltration or unintended actuation, and missing resource enforcement could result in denial-of-service through runaway scripts. Even so, the architecture provides clear enforcement points for mitigating these risks, for example by protecting Script Manager operations through authentication and authorization, optionally complemented by signature checks. Host bindings can be constrained through per-script capability policies, for example by allowlisting endpoints and permitted local operations with timeout limits. Runtime execution can be bounded through measures such as memory caps and watchdog-style interruption, optionally extended with fine-grained quotas for multi-script settings. In this paper, however, we focus on feasibility and resource costs under a safe local-deployment assumption.

7 Conclusion and Future Work

This paper investigated how small on-device automations can be enabled on MCU-class hardware using standardized, machine-readable interfaces. We presented an embedded execution architecture that realizes a consumer-side subset of the WoT Scripting API on MCU-class devices and demonstrated how automations can be deployed in an on-device JavaScript runtime. Furthermore, we quantified the overhead of our approach and reported on firmware footprint, RAM usage and script size. The findings indicate that deployable interfaces can be practical for common automations on modern IoT devices while reducing vendor lock-ins and providing a mechanism for device individualization.

However, future work is required to fully implement this vision. First, a secure deployment and trust model is needed, including authentication and authorization for Script Manager operations, script provenance, and credential/secrets handling. Second, we plan to introduce a machine-readable capability description for the embedded runtime (e.g., a TD extension) so tools and agents can discover supported APIs, built-in libraries, host bindings, and resource budgets. Third, we will investigate agent-assisted workflows that use this capability description to generate and deploy scripts. Lastly, WebAssembly gains momentum in IoT and is therefore a promising candidate for constrained devices. However, the use of WebAssembly would require significant adjustments to the WoT Scripting API.

Acknowledgments. This work was supported in part by the Austrian Research Promotion Agency FFG through the research project ICBC under Grant 54899325.

Disclosure of Interests. The authors have no competing interests to declare that are relevant to the content of this article.

References

1. eclipse-thingweb/node-wot, February 2026. https://github.com/eclipse-thingweb/node-wot. Original-date 2018-06-04T19:15:06Z
2. nodejs/node, February 2026. https://github.com/nodejs/node. Original-date: 2014-11-26T19:57:11Z

3. Bormann, C., Ersue, M., Keränen, A.: Terminology for Constrained-Node Networks. Request for Comments RFC 7228, Internet Engineering Task Force, p. 17, May 2014. https://doi.org/10.17487/RFC7228, https://datatracker.ietf.org/doc/rfc7228
4. Esterbauer, L., Steindl, G., Kastner, W.: Improving energy community interoperability by utilizing Web of Things. e & i Elektrotechnik und Informationstechnik **140**(5), 425–431 (2023). https://doi.org/10.1007/s00502-023-01152-2
5. Esterbauer, L., Thoma, M., Schwarzinger, T., Strasser, T.I., Kastner, W.: Proof-of-concept implementation: web of things-driven on-device automation for resource-constrained energy devices, February 2026. https://doi.org/10.5281/ZENODO.18721677, https://zenodo.org/doi/10.5281/zenodo.18721677
6. Gavrin, E., Lee, S.J., Ayrapetyan, R., Shitov, A.: Ultra lightweight JavaScript engine for internet of things. In: Companion Proceedings of the 2015 ACM SIGPLAN International Conference on Systems, Programming, Languages and Applications: Software for Humanity, Pittsburgh, PA, USA, October 2015, pp. 19–20. ACM (2015). https://doi.org/10.1145/2814189.2816270, https://dl.acm.org/doi/10.1145/2814189.2816270
7. Grunert, K.: Overview of JavaScript engines for resource-constrained microcontrollers. In: 2020 5th International Conference on Smart and Sustainable Technologies (SpliTech), Split, Croatia, September 2020, pp. 1–7. IEEE (2020). https://doi.org/10.23919/SpliTech49282.2020.9243749, https://ieeexplore.ieee.org/document/9243749/
8. Kaebisch, S., McCool, M., Korkan, E., Kamiya, T., Charpenay, V., Kovatsch, M.: Web of Things (WoT) Thing Description 1.1. Tech. rep., W3C, December 2023. https://www.w3.org/TR/wot-thing-description/
9. Li, B., Fan, H., Gao, Y., Dong, W.: WaWoT: towards flexible and efficient web of things services via web assembly on resource-constrained IoT devices. IEEE Trans. Comput. **74**(3), 1094–1108 (2025). https://doi.org/10.1109/TC.2024.3500385, https://ieeexplore.ieee.org/abstract/document/10756513
10. Lagally, M., Matsukura, R., McCool, M., Toumura, K.: Web of Things (WoT) Architecture 1.1. Tech. rep., W3C, December 2023. https://www.w3.org/TR/wot-architecture11/
11. Moddable Tech, Inc.: Moddable Documentation: Web Things. https://www.moddable.com/documentation/network/webthings
12. Sciullo, L., Zyrianoff, I.D.R., Trotta, A., Felice, M.D.: WoT micro servient: bringing the W3C web of things to resource constrained edge devices. In: 2021 IEEE International Conference on Smart Computing (SMARTCOMP), Irvine, CA, USA, August 2021, pp. 161–168. IEEE (2021). https://doi.org/10.1109/SMARTCOMP52413.2021.00042, https://ieeexplore.ieee.org/document/9556223/
13. Taivalsaari, A., Mikkonen, T.: A taxonomy of IoT client architectures. IEEE Softw. **35**(3), 83–88 (2018). https://doi.org/10.1109/MS.2018.2141019, https://ieeexplore.ieee.org/document/8354417/
14. Kis, Z., Peintner, D., Aguzzi, C., Hund, J., Nimura, K.: Web of Things (WoT) scripting API. Tech. rep., W3C, October 2023. https://www.w3.org/TR/wot-scripting-api/

SBAC: A Shape-Based Access Control Model for Knowledge Graphs

Christoph Göpfert(✉), Jan Ingo Haas, and Martin Gaedke

Technische Universität Chemnitz, 09111 Chemnitz, Germany
{christoph.goepfert,martin.gaedke}@informatik.tu-chemnitz.de

Abstract. Access control for knowledge graphs is commonly implemented at dataset, graph, or triple granularity, or via query-time filtering and rewriting. The number of required access control rules increases with the granularity of the access control model, thereby increasing the administrative burden. Current approaches suffer from a linear increase in the number of rules with increasing granularity, as well as from the inability to express policies at intermediate granularity levels. This paper introduces a novel access control model, the Shape-Based Access Control (SBAC) model, targeting an intermediate granularity level. In this model, access is granted over declarative shapes that define the parts of the graph that can be accessed. SBAC derives the corresponding subgraph for each shape that a user has access to. By merging these subgraphs, we obtain the graph of accessible shapes, against which queries are executed. Before executing a query, an authorization policy checks whether the query can be answered safely using this graph. If it cannot, the query is rejected. We evaluate the effectiveness of SBAC and its impact on query performance in a university setting using the LUBM benchmark.

Keywords: Access Control Model · Knowledge Graph · RDF · SPARQL · Shapes · SBAC

1 Introduction

Knowledge graphs have been widely adopted across many disciplines, such as life sciences, linguistics, and geography [1]. At their core lies the Resource Description Framework (RDF) [12], which provides an expressive graph-based data model for describing entities and their relationships. However, that expressiveness comes at a cost, introducing complexity that also affects access control.

In practice, knowledge graphs often include sensitive data that should be accessible only to certain principals, i.e., specific users or groups. Traditional access control mechanisms in triplestores often build on role-based access control (RBAC), sometimes in combination with further restrictions, such as graph-level restrictions or fine-grained policies realized through query rewriting. Graph-level approaches typically operate on named graphs, restricting access at the

A. Mauri et al. (Eds.): ICWE 2026, LNCS 16625, pp. 18–31, 2026.
https://doi.org/10.1007/978-3-032-29372-5_2

granularity of entire subgraphs. Although straightforward, these mechanisms are typically coarser-grained than desired, or require manual partitioning of the dataset into multiple named graphs. This complicates data management and deployment.

Fine-grained policies, on the other hand, typically require a large number of access control rules in complex scenarios. A set of access control rules is commonly referred to as an access control policy. Maintaining these rules becomes increasingly difficult as the number of protected entities and properties increases. Moreover, enforcing access restrictions in RDF is inherently challenging because information about a single logical entity is often spread across multiple nodes in the graph, which are linked via nested relationships. For instance, a resource representing a person entity might be connected to a digital business card node, which is connected to a literal representing the person's family name. Consequently, a single subject's set of triples does not necessarily include all relevant properties of the represented entity. Protecting such data requires information about structural patterns in the graph.

To address these challenges, we introduce a shape-based access control (SBAC) approach that leverages shape definition schemas to control query execution. The core concept is to treat shape definitions as access boundaries. SBAC determines whether a SPARQL query's Basic Graph Patterns (BGP) are structurally compatible with the set of shapes accessible to a principal. Then, a structural query satisfiability check is performed to ensure that the query patterns can be embedded into the accessible shapes graph. This subgraph of the knowledge graph contains exclusively the shape instances that the principal is permitted to access. If the query is structurally compatible, it is executed against this subgraph; otherwise, access is rejected.

SBAC offers three main benefits: First, policy evaluation relies solely on shape definitions, so it remains efficient regardless of the knowledge graph size. Second, expressing access control declaratively at the schema level simplifies rule management, eliminating the need for complex instance-level rules. Third, structural validation ensures that access decisions respect the nested, path-like structures inherent to the RDF data model.

The rest of the paper is structured as follows: Sect. 2 presents related work on access control models for knowledge graphs. In Sect. 3, we describe the SBAC access control model, which is evaluated in Sect. 4. Finally, Sect. 5 offers a conclusion.

2 Related Work

Access control has been a central topic in database and information security research for decades. Classical models such as Mandatory Access Control (MAC) and Role-Based Access Control (RBAC) form the foundation for protecting digital resources. With the emergence of the Semantic Web, many approaches to adapt these traditional models to the RDF data model have been proposed. Kirrane et al. [11] provide a comprehensive survey of access control solutions for the Semantic Web, highlighting both foundational approaches and recent advances.

Role-Based Access Control (RBAC) has been widely studied due to its suitability for organizational structures. Various approaches model roles as OWL classes (e.g., Wu et al. [6] and Finin et al. [8]), enabling reasoning over role hierarchies and inheritance. Ferrini and Bertino [7], for example, integrate RBAC with eXtensible Access Control Markup Language (XACML) and OWL to support constraint reasoning. While semantic reasoning enhances policy expressiveness, many RBAC-based systems require additional mechanisms to handle more dynamic scenarios and context-dependent permissions beyond the rule-level.

Mandatory Access Control (MAC) models enforce centrally defined security labels on subjects and resources. Early adaptations for RDF data often represented security levels using ontologies. For instance, Yagüe del Valle et al. [18] demonstrate how attribute-based approaches can emulate MAC semantics in semantic data environments.

Attribute-Based Access Control (ABAC) determines permissions based on the properties of subjects, resources, and environments. ABAC policies have been modeled in OWL-DL (Cirio et al. [4]) and XACML (Priebe et al. [15]), leveraging ontology reasoning capabilities for fine-grained control. Padia et al. [14] propose a filter-based ABAC approach that uses on-the-fly query rewriting to enforce policies. Although ABAC is considered flexible for Linked Data, it introduces challenges around attribute management and reasoning complexity.

Relationship-Based Access Control (ReBAC) extends ABAC by incorporating relationships between entities. For example, Crampton and Sellwood [5] embed path conditions into queries to capture relationship-based policies, though this impacts query performance due to the additional conditions introduced.

Web Access Control (WAC) [2] applies access control lists (ACLs) to RDF resources in Linked Data systems. In WAC, each resource may be linked to an ACL resource containing authorization rules, typically expressed as RDF triples. This approach provides straightforward, resource-level protection, but can become complex in large or highly interconnected graphs.

Existing work covers a spectrum of protection units, from entire datasets and named graphs to individual triples, triple patterns or views, ontology concepts (such as classes and properties), and specific resources (instances). Notably, the W3C Linked Data Platform Working Group [17] has emphasized the need for fine-grained access control mechanisms that operate at multiple levels of granularity, including triples, triple patterns, named graphs, and individual resources. SBAC operates at the entity-level as defined by shape schemas, thereby providing an intermediate level between resource-level and graph-level protection without the need for triple-level annotations or explicit named graph partitioning of the original dataset.

3 Concept

In the following, we consider the term 'shape' as an abstract concept that describes triple structures and constraints. Concretely, we consider shapes as sets of triples that satisfy a collection of constraints, such as on node kinds (IRI, blank node, literal), permissible value ranges, or datatypes. We refer to a set of triples matching those constraints as a 'shape instance'.

Shapes as a concept have been formalized in multiple ways, such as by the Shape Expressions Language (ShEx) [16] or the Shapes Constraints Language (SHACL) [13]. Our interpretation aligns most closely with that of ShEx, which describes constraints on triples, nodes, and values.

Due to the graph-based nature of RDF, an entity's information may be scattered across the graph via intermediate nodes in nested relations. Defining access control rules that target individual triples can be cumbersome, while rules on entire graphs may be too permissive. Shapes can be used to describe the graph structure of an entity as a set of triples, including path-based patterns. Expressing access policies over shapes, therefore, enables targeting specific subgraphs of the knowledge graph that represent an entity. This approach allows defining rules at the entity level and provides a middle ground between graph-level and triple-level access rules.

Access to specific shapes can be granted to principals, such as users, roles, or groups. It therefore integrates naturally with existing models such as RBAC. An access control policy that grants a principal access to a shape implies access to all triples that match that shape, i.e., its shape instances.

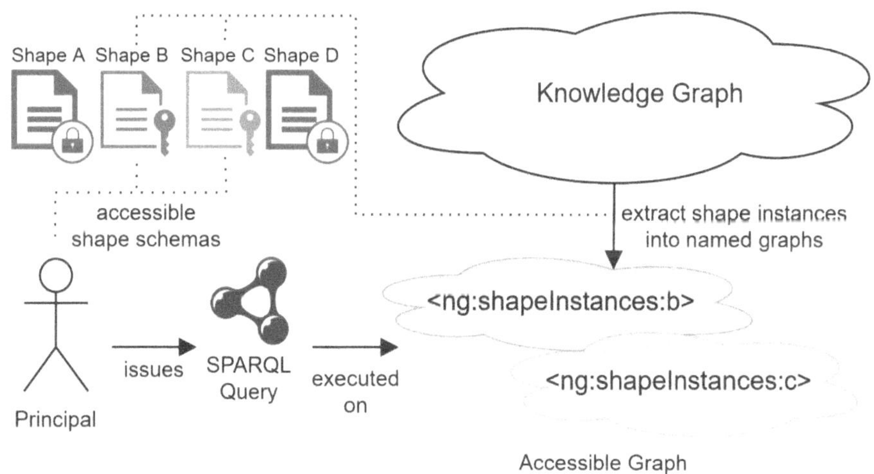

Fig. 1. Abstract illustration of the SBAC approach. A principal is granted access to two shape schemas: Shape B and C. The principal issues a SPARQL query that is evaluated against the accessible graph. The accessible graph consists of the shape graphs derived from the accessible shape schemas.

SBAC enforces access restrictions by materializing the subgraph accessible to the principal. This approach is illustrated in Fig. 1, where a fictitious principal has access to two shapes, *Shape B* and *Shape C*, described in corresponding shape schemas. Each shape schema induces a shape graph, i.e., a subgraph of the knowledge graph that contains triples that satisfy the respective shape. Figure 2 shows the shape graphs *Shape B* and *Shape C*, which correspond to the materialized named graphs *<ng:shapeInstances:b>* and *<ng:shapeInstances:c>* depicted in Fig. 1. The 'accessible graph' is the union of the shape graphs that are accessible by the principal. In the figures, the accessible graph is the union of the shape graphs *Shape B* and *Shape C*. *Shape A* and *D* are not accessible and therefore do not contribute to the accessible graph.

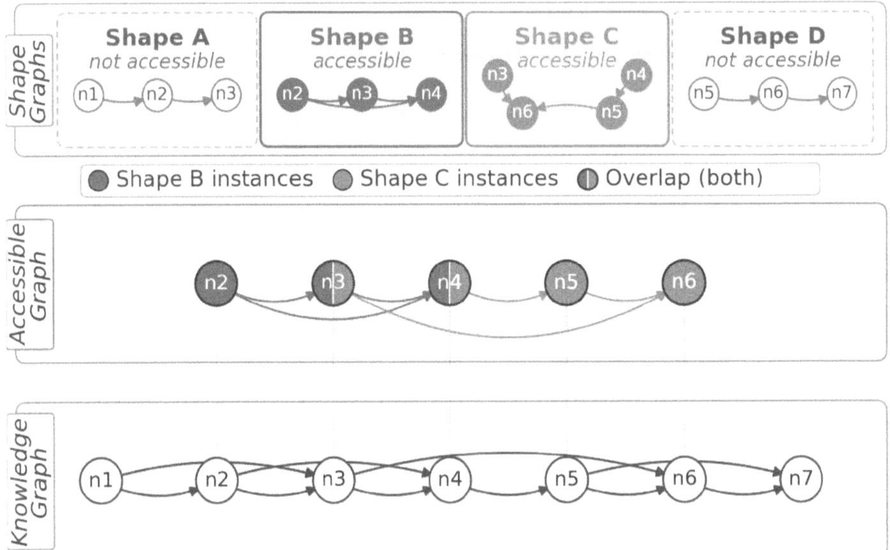

Fig. 2. The figure continues the example from Fig. 1 and shows shape graphs A, B, C, and D, which are derived from the corresponding shape schemas. The accessible graph consists of the shape graphs B and C. The dotted lines indicate the relationship between the nodes of the accessible graph and the knowledge graph.

As can be observed from the figures, it should be noted that the set of shape schemas does not need to cover the entire structure of the knowledge graph: triples that do not satisfy any shape will remain inaccessible to principals. In Fig. 2, for instance, this applies to the relation between *n5* and *n7*. Furthermore, shape graphs may 'overlap', so that a node or relationship occurs across multiple shape graphs, as illustrated by *n3* and *n4* in shape graphs B and C. Such overlaps introduce redundancy and lead to increased memory requirements in the materialized representation. Additionally, a node may be matched by both an accessible and an inaccessible shape. In such a case, the node is part of the accessible graph and, thus, may be accessible to the principal after a positive policy decision.

The policy engine determines whether a SPARQL query is satisfiable with respect to the set of shapes accessible by the principal, which form the accessible graph. Each node of this graph is part of a shape, and each edge represents a triple constraint within that shape. This can be formalized as:

- A **shape node** $s \in S$ corresponds to a shape in a schema.
- A **shape edge** (s, p, c) represents a triple constraint on shape s with predicate p and a constraint c.

A constraint may demand restrictions on the datatype (e.g., xsd:string), node kind (IRI, blank node, literal), value set, or a target shape (i.e., that the object must conform to another shape).

If a principal is allowed to access multiple shapes, the individual shape schemas are merged into a single schema. Each individual shape schema is stored together with the respective start shape. The start shape serves as the root of the shape tree, which is built by traversing all shape edges.

We now turn to the process of determining query satisfiability over the accessible graph. This begins by decomposing a SPARQL query into its constituent Basic Graph Patterns (BGPs) to enable a structural comparison with the accessible shapes.

3.1 Query Decomposition Into BGP Trees

First, the SPARQL query is parsed, and Basic Graph Patterns (BGP) are extracted from the query's WHERE clause. This includes BGPs within UNION constructs, while BGPs within OPTIONAL blocks are skipped, as they are not required to satisfy the query. From the extracted BGPs, a forest of directed trees is constructed, which we refer to as the 'query forest' in the following. A node in this forest represents an RDF term that appears in the query, and an edge represents a triple pattern, which we can formalize as:

- A **query node** $q \in Q$ is a node that may be constrained by a specific node kind, datatype, or value set. These may be implied, for instance, a typed literal implies the corresponding datatype.
- A **query edge** (q_s, p, q_o) represents a triple pattern with subject q_s, predicate p, and object q_o. For cases in which the predicate is a variable, the edge is labeled with a wildcard marker.

3.2 Computation of Initial Variable Bindings

An initial binding is computed that restricts the domains of the query variables. This is done by iterating through each BGP in the query forest and restricting the candidate domains of query variables as follows:

- **Predicate variables** are restricted to the set of predicates from the shape graph whose edge constraints are compatible with the BGP object's node constraints.

- **Object variables** are restricted to nodes reachable via candidate predicates. The resulting domain also records the set of possible datatypes, node kinds, value sets, and target shapes.

If the domain of a variable becomes empty at any point, the query is deemed unsatisfiable, and the policy rejects its execution.

3.3 Constraint Propagation

Once the initial domains have been established, fixpoint iteration is applied to refine variable domains through constraint propagation. This phase only applies to BGPs in which both the predicate and the object are variables. In each iteration, the following two steps are applied:

1. **Predicate domain pruning**: Candidates are removed if they are incompatible with the current object's variable domain. For instance, this occurs when no datatype in the object domain matches any edge reachable via that predicate.
2. **Object domain pruning**: The object variable's domain is intersected with the union of node bindings implied by the remaining predicate candidates.

The iteration terminates when either of the following two cases occurs:

1. A fixpoint is reached, i.e., there are no domain changes after completion of an iteration, or
2. A variable domain becomes empty, which means that the query is unsatisfiable.

It should be noted that this step serves as a pruning step and constitutes a necessary but not sufficient condition for query satisfiability.

3.4 Structural Query Satisfiability

Finally, a recursive satisfiability check is performed over the query forest. For each root of the query forest, the algorithm traverses the tree top-down and attempts to map each query edge to a compatible shape edge in the shape graph. For a query edge (q_s, p, q_o):

1. The set of candidate predicates is determined. If the BGP already specifies a predicate, then this predicate is used. Otherwise, the predicate domain computed in the previous phases is used.
2. For each shape node s in the shape graph, the algorithm checks whether s has an edge with predicate p whose constraints are compatible with q_o. Note that compatibility does not necessarily equal direct matching. For instance, the node kind *IRI* is compatible with the node kind *NONLITERAL*, and certain value sets may be subsets of others.

3. If the matching shape edge references a target shape, the algorithm recurses into the subtree of the query forest rooted at q_o, verifying that that subtree can be satisfied by the target shape's structure.
4. Visited nodes should be marked to prevent infinite recursion, which may occur in the case of circular shape references.

The query is deemed to be satisfiable if every edge in every tree of the query forest can be matched to at least one compatible shape edge.

3.5 Prototype

We implemented a proof-of-concept prototype to demonstrate the feasibility of the proposed SBAC approach. The source code of the prototype is available at https://purl.org/sbac/code. The LinkML modeling language [19] was used to model shape schemas and to translate them to ShEx. We found that constructing the accessible subgraph on demand for each request is not practical due to its computational cost and the resulting impact on query latency. To address this, we introduced a dedicated setup phase in which shape instances are materialized in advance.

In this setup phase, a separate named graph is created for each shape. Each named graph contains all RDF resources that conform to the respective shape definition. Materialization is achieved by translating each shape schema into a SPARQL *CONSTRUCT* query using the ShEx2SPARQL tool [9]. The resulting queries are executed once during setup to populate the corresponding named graphs.

At query time, the accessible graph for a given principal is derived by combining the named graphs associated with the shapes the principal is authorized to access. This way, repeated instance extraction is not needed because it allows us to execute authorized queries over already materialized data.

When dealing with large knowledge graphs that contain substantial numbers of shape instances, the generated *CONSTRUCT* queries may exceed execution time limits in some triplestores. To mitigate this issue, the prototype supports configurable LIMIT and OFFSET parameters for the *CONSTRUCT* queries. In combination with ORDER BY, this enables a pagination-like extraction behavior that processes shape instances in manageable chunks and has proven effective in our prototype.

However, the SPARQL specification explicitly states that LIMIT and OFFSET should not influence the solution set of *CONSTRUCT* queries. Consequently, the pagination strategy depends entirely on implementation-specific behavior and may not be uniformly supported across all triplestores.

4 Evaluation

We evaluated the time to policy decision and query execution in SBAC. For all experiments, we used a machine with 6 CPU cores (3.7 GHz) with 32 GB RAM.

We used the Lehigh University Benchmark (LUBM) [10], which provides a generator to create synthetic RDF datasets based on a realistic university ontology. We used this generator to create three datasets, which consist of approximately 167K, 2.1M, and 22M triples after applying OWL 2 RL reasoning. The LUBM benchmark contains 14 SPARQL queries with varying complexity for performance evaluation. The RDF data is stored in a QLever triplestore [3]. We derived 14 shape schemas in ShEx format from the LUBM ontology, including schemas for professors, lecturers, students, research assistants, publications, courses, and universities. The scripts used for the evaluation, along with the raw measurement data, are provided in the digital appendix at https://purl.org/sbac/data.

4.1 Policy Decision Time

First, we evaluated the performance of policy decisions for varying numbers of shape schemas and varying shape sizes. The policy evaluation does not depend on knowledge graph sizes, because it operates exclusively on schema-level information; knowledge graph data is not used at any point. We considered three experiment scenarios:

1. Increasing number of accessible shapes. For the first scenario, the number of shape schemas is increased from 1 to 1000 in steps of 100. Each of these schemas contains exactly one shape with a single constraint.
2. Increasing number of constraints per shape. For the second scenario, we used a fixed set of 10 shapes. The number of constraints per shape is increased from 1 to 1000 in steps of 100.
3. Combined variation of shape schema count and constraint count. For the third scenario, we experimented with combinations of shape schema counts from 1 to 1000, and constraint counts from 1 to 1000, again with steps of 100.

We ran each configuration of the three scenarios 10 times and calculated the average execution time and standard deviation.

Figure 3 shows the results for the first scenario. It can be observed that the time to make policy decisions increases linearly with the number of shape schemas. Similarly, Fig. 4 shows that the policy decision time also increases linearly with the number of properties, and thereby the number of constraints per shape. The results for the combined variation of the number of shape schemas and the number of constraints per shape are visualized in Fig. 5. All in all, these results reveal that policy decision time is primarily impacted by the number of schemas. The worst performance is observed with large numbers of large schemas. However, the number of schemas has a more severe impact than the number of constraints. This is because each schema must be parsed individually. Consequently, file opening and parsing times add up, significantly increasing the decision time.

4.2 Query Execution Time

Secondly, we evaluated query execution time for principals with access to a different number of shapes. To establish a baseline, each query was first executed

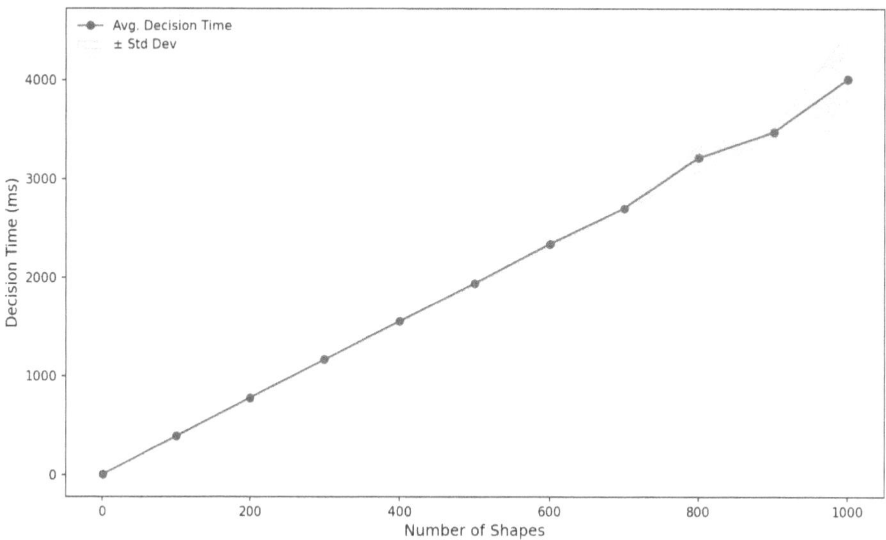

Fig. 3. Policy decision time vs. number of shapes.

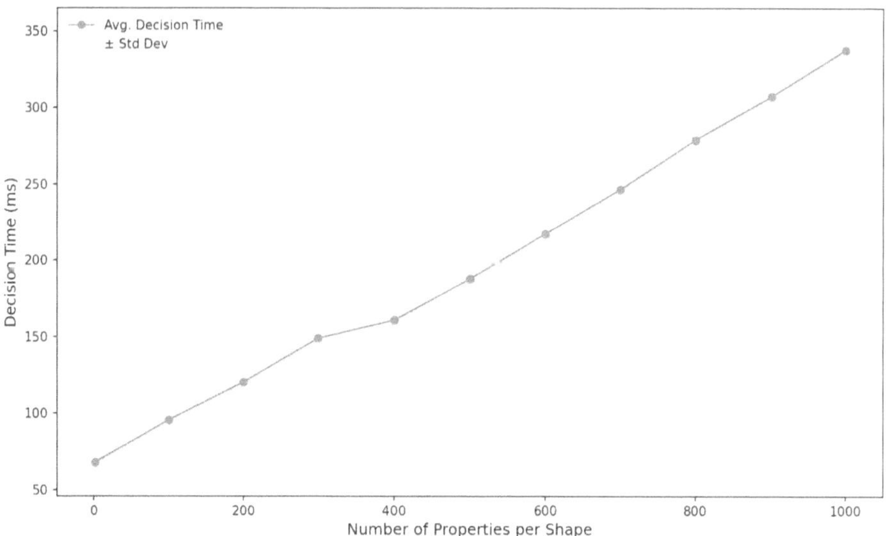

Fig. 4. Policy decision time vs. number of properties per shape.

directly against the SPARQL endpoint. The results are used to determine whether queries executed with SBAC are correct and to assess the overhead introduced by SBAC compared to directly querying an endpoint. For each LUBM query, we evaluated three authorization scenarios:

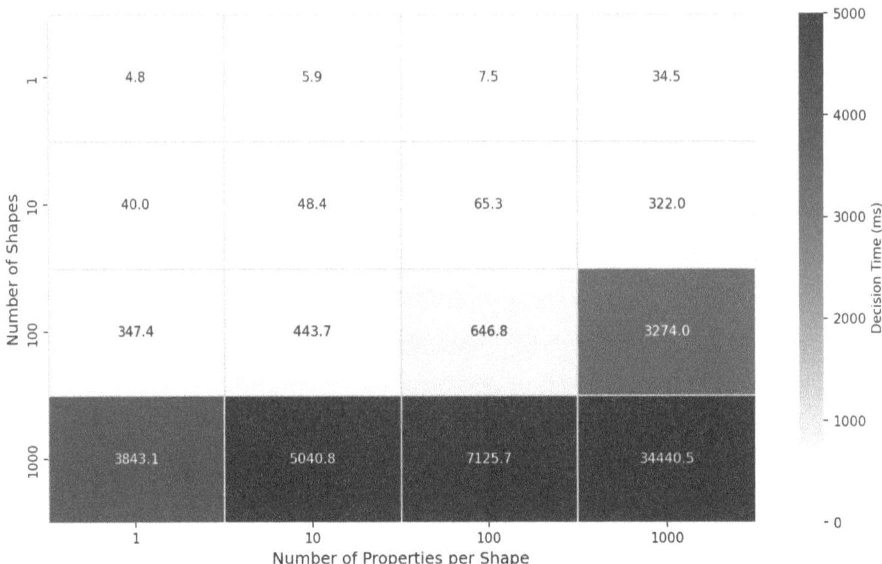

Fig. 5. Policy decision time vs. combination of number of shapes and number of properties per shape.

1. **Admin-level permissions**: The query is executed by a principal with access to all shapes.
2. **Minimal required permissions**: The query is executed by a principal with access only to the shapes required to satisfy the query.
3. **No permissions**: The query is executed by a principal that does not have access to any shapes. Therefore, the query should be rejected.

The results for the LUBM queries are shown in Fig. 6. The execution times for the third scenario (no permissions) are almost identical across all queries and dataset sizes. The size of the knowledge graph does not affect these times because the queries are rejected by the policy.

The query execution times for the admin principal (green) are consistently higher than those for the principal with minimal required permissions (orange). This is not surprising because the accessible graph grows with the number of accessible shapes. Consequently, query complexity increases with the number of accessible shapes.

Notably, all observed query execution times were under 400ms, indicating the practical feasibility of the approach. This result extends to the large knowledge graph with 22 million triples. For this graph, the longest execution times were recorded for queries 6 and 14, at approximately 2500ms and 2000ms, respectively, while all other queries completed well within 1 s.

The query execution times increase with larger knowledge graphs, as expected. However, the relative overhead introduced by SBAC over direct queries (grey) remains consistent. This is because SBAC does not increase query

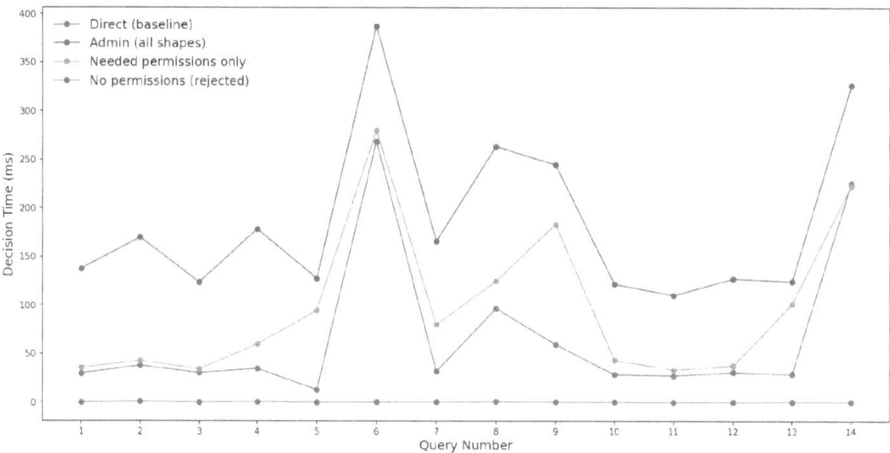

Fig. 6. Query execution times for the medium-sized knowledge graph with 2.1 million triples. Query numbers correspond to the 14 SPARQL queries from the LUBM benchmark.

complexity; rather, it decreases the complexity as the query is executed on the accessible graph instead of the full knowledge graph, thereby reducing the query graph's size.

5 Conclusion

In this paper, we presented a novel access control approach for knowledge graphs, the shape-based access control (SBAC) model. SBAC operates at the schema level. Shape definitions are used to determine whether a query is satisfiable prior to execution. SPARQL queries are executed on a subgraph of the knowledge graph, derived from constraints of shape schemas accessible by a principal.

We demonstrate the feasibility of our approach by implementing a proof-of-concept prototype. We evaluated the prototype and demonstrated that policy decision time scales linearly with both the number of shape schemas and the number of constraints per shape, with the former being more impactful due to schema parsing overhead. Policy decision-making does not depend on the knowledge graph's size because it relies solely on shape schemas. Experiments measuring query execution with increasingly large LUBM datasets demonstrate that SBAC does not introduce substantial overhead. SBAC restricts queries to the subgraph accessible by the principal, thereby reducing query complexity. Across all evaluation scenarios, query execution times remained reasonable. Overall, the results indicate that shape-based access control is both feasible and efficient even for large knowledge graphs.

Acknowledgments. This work is supported by the Deutsche Forschungsgemeinschaft (DFG, German Research Foundation) – Project-ID 514664767 – TRR 386, by the European Union's HORIZON Research and Innovation Programme under grant agreement

No. 101120657, project ENFIELD (European Lighthouse to Manifest Trustworthy and Green AI) and by the European Union's Erasmus+ Programme under grant agreement No. 101177485, project Across (European University for Cross-Border Knowledge Sharing).

Disclosure of Interests. The authors have no competing interests to declare that are relevant to the content of this article.

References

1. The Linked Open Data Cloud. https://lod-cloud.net/
2. Web Access Control. https://solidproject.org/TR/wac
3. Bast, H., Buchhold, B.: QLever: A query engine for efficient SPARQL+Text Search. In: Proceedings of the 2017 ACM on Conference on Information and Knowledge Management, pp. 647–656. CIKM 2017, Association for Computing Machinery, New York, NY, USA (2017). https://doi.org/10.1145/3132847.3132921
4. Cirio, L., Cruz, I.F., Tamassia, R.: A role and attribute based access control system using semantic web technologies. In: Meersman, R., Tari, Z., Herrero, P. (eds.) On the Move to Meaningful Internet Systems 2007: OTM 2007 Workshops. LNCS, vol. 4806, pp. 1256–1266. Springer, Heidelberg (2007). https://doi.org/10.1007/978-3-540-76890-6_53
5. Crampton, J., Sellwood, J.: Path conditions and principal matching: A new approach to access control. In: Proceedings of the 19th ACM Symposium on Access Control Models and Technologies, pp. 187–198. SACMAT 2014, Association for Computing Machinery, New York, NY, USA (2014). https://doi.org/10.1145/2613087.2613094
6. Di, W., Jian, L., Yabo, D., Miaoliang, Z.: Using semantic web technologies to specify constraints of RBAC. In: Proceedings of the Sixth International Conference on Parallel and Distributed Computing Applications and Technologies, pp. 543–545. PDCAT 2005, IEEE Computer Society, USA (2005). https://doi.org/10.1109/PDCAT.2005.247
7. Ferrini, R., Bertino, E.: Supporting RBAC with XACMl+owl. In: Proceedings of the 14th ACM Symposium on Access Control Models and Technologies, pp. 145–154. SACMAT 2009, Association for Computing Machinery, New York, NY, USA (2009). https://doi.org/10.1145/1542207.1542231
8. Finin, T., et al.: RowLBAC: representing role based access control in owl. In: Proceedings of ACM Symposium on Access Control Models and Technologies, SACMAT, pp. 73–82 (2008). https://doi.org/10.1145/1377836.1377849
9. Göpfert, C., Samuel, S., Gaedke, M.: SHEX2SPARQL: Translating shape expressions into SPARQL queries. In: Verma, H., Bozzon, A., Mauri, A., Yang, J. (eds.) Web Engineering, pp. 209–216. Springer Nature Switzerland, Cham (2026). https://doi.org/10.1007/978-3-031-97207-2_16
10. Guo, Y., Pan, Z., Heflin, J.: LUBM: A benchmark for OWL knowledge base systems. J. Web Semant. **3**(2), 158–182 (2005). https://doi.org/10.1016/j.websem.2005.06.005
11. Kirrane, S., Mileo, A., Decker, S.: Access control and the resource description framework: A survey. Semantic Web **8**(2), 311–352 (2016). https://doi.org/10.3233/SW-160236, https://www.medra.org/servlet/aliasResolver?alias=iospress&doi=10.3233/SW-160236

12. Klyne, G., Carroll, J.J., McBride, B.: RDF 1.1 Concepts and Abstract Syntax
13. Knublauch, H., Kontokostas, D.: Shapes Constraint Language (SHACL) (2017). https://www.w3.org/TR/shacl/
14. Padia, A., Finin, T.W., Joshi, A.: Attribute-based fine grained access control for triple stores. In: International Semantic Web Conference (2015). https://api.semanticscholar.org/CorpusID:14559778
15. Priebe, T., Dobmeier, W., Kamprath, N.: Supporting attribute-based access control with ontologies, p. 8 (2006). https://doi.org/10.1109/ARES.2006.127
16. Prud'hommeaux, E., Boneva, I., , Gayo, K.E.L., Kellogg, G.: Shape Expressions Language 2.1. https://shex.io/shex-semantics/
17. The W3C linked data platform working group: access control. https://www.w3.org/2012/ldp/wiki/AccessControl
18. Valle, M., Maña, A., Lopez, J., Troya, J.: Applying the semantic web layers to access control, vol. 2003, pp. 622–626 (2003). https://doi.org/10.1109/DEXA.2003.1232091
19. Vita, R., Overton, J.A., Mungall, C.J., Sette, A., Peters, B.: Fair principles and the IEDB: Short-term improvements and a long-term vision of obo-foundry mediated machine-actionable interoperability. Database **2018**, bax105 (2018)

Automated Estimation of Web Interaction Complexity Based on UI Tests

Sebastian Heil[1(✉)], Julián Grigera[2,3], Ekaterina Pavlova[4], and Martin Gaedke[1]

[1] Technische Universität Chemnitz, Chemnitz 09111, Germany
{sebastian.heil,martin.gaedke}@informatik.tu-chemnitz.de
[2] LIFIA, Fac. de Informatica, Univ. Nac. de La Plata, La Plata, Argentina
julian.grigera@lifia.info.unlp.edu.ar
[3] CONICET, La Plata, Argentina
[4] Siemens Energy Global GmbH and Co. KG, Munich, Germany

Abstract. Evaluating the complexity of user interaction is crucial for engineering usable web applications and to make informed design decisions. Automated approaches are increasingly being investigated due to the time, cost and expertise requirements of conducting empirical user studies. However, these approaches require creating extra artifacts otherwise not useful for software production, focus on static aspects of the user interface, or require specially instrumented running interface versions. Thus, we explore the feasibility of automated interaction complexity estimation through the analysis of existing web UI tests. We propose a novel software architecture for the analysis of UI tests and study the suitability of 11 different candidate UI test metrics from the domains of UI analysis, program understanding, and cognitive modeling. By conducting an experiment with 38 participants, we compared human-delivered assessments to the UI test metrics. From this experiment, we obtained 2 linear and multiple linear regression models that can be used to predict interaction complexity. Additionally, we obtained a second set of multiple linear regression models based on a wider range of metrics, using Principal Component Analysis to narrow the input down to 3 components. These results suggest that automatically extracted UI test metrics can help determine interaction complexity, using existing artifacts. Our method is well-suited for integration into CI/CD pipelines, supporting the incremental and iterative nature of modern agile practices.

Keywords: Web User Interfaces · User Interaction · Complexity · IXD · UI · Automated Testing · UI Testing · Human-centric AI

1 Introduction

Measurement of interaction complexity is an important activity for engineering usable web application frontends and guiding design decisions. It serves as a foundation for a systematic approach of iteratively building, evaluating, and

A. Mauri et al. (Eds.): ICWE 2026, LNCS 16625, pp. 32–46, 2026.
https://doi.org/10.1007/978-3-032-29372-5_3

improving user interfaces to control user cognitive effort [3]. Complexity is usually measured through user studies, but these require a high level of resources and methodological expertise. Therefore, research on automating complexity measurements has received increasing attention in academia [8,20,22,29,32]. Automation, further accelerated by advances in AI, allows for a high measurement frequency that leads to smaller increments being created more often, which is a key factor for integrating with agile software development methods [15].

However, current automation approaches exhibit several limitations. Approaches like KLM, FLM and GOMS are domain-specific languages (DSLs) that require creating artifacts to model the interaction based on which the automatic analysis is performed [9,10,12], but these artifacts have no intrinsic use in the software production. Other approaches only require existing artifacts, e.g. the UI source code [22,23,28,30], screenshots of the UI [8,20,29], or a combination [32]. These approaches, however, only consider static properties of the user interface, mostly ignoring dynamic micro-interactions of users. Such interaction aspects can be automatically analyzed based on log analysis [1,26] but, to create the logs, real users running special versions of the user interface are required. Not only is this semi-automatic approach therefore limited in applicability but also comes with legal privacy-related challenges of user tracking.

Ideally, an automation method for measuring web interaction complexity should not require involvement of users, make use of existing artifacts of web development only, and capture the dynamics of user interaction. Reduced costs spent on user evaluations, increased consistency, and a higher evaluation frequency that facilitates iterative frontend development cycles are the potential outcomes of lowering the barrier of automatic web UI assessments. UI tests are an artifact type that represents "human-like" [13] user interactions and serves its own purpose in professional software development. Additionally, UI tests are maintained alongside the UIs, so evaluations based on them also evolve, enabling the continuous monitoring of complexity within CI/CD cycles. Recent research has even demonstrated their automatic creation [13]. These characteristics make UI tests a valuable resource for iterative assessments of web interaction complexity without the need for additional artifacts.

In this paper we propose a novel automated approach leveraging UI tests to measure the interaction complexity of web user interfaces. We address the challenges of devising a suitable software architecture and the selection of suitable complexity-related UI test metrics. Our contributions are: a novel approach to repurpose UI tests for measuring web UI complexity, an empirical study with a diverse group of participants comparing human and automated measures, and a set of regression models for predicting human assessments of complexity.

2 Approach

Our proposal consists in automating the assessment of interaction complexity to simplify iterative web engineering processes. Thus, we propose a software architecture – UIT-IC– that leverages source code and execution logs of UI tests (UITs) to estimate interaction complexity (IC) of the web UIs they cover.

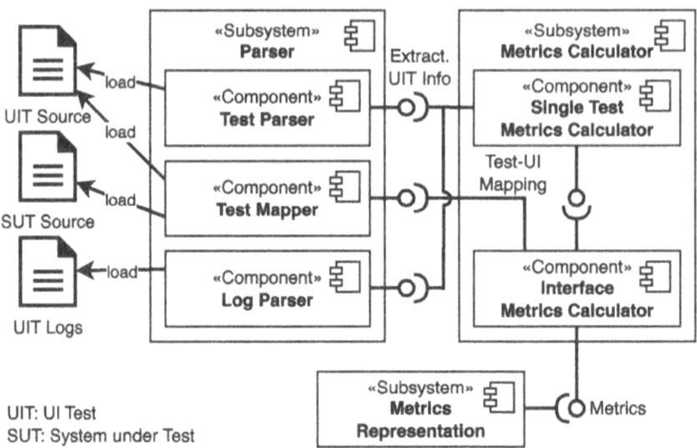

Fig. 1. UIT-IC Architecture.

From a software engineering perspective, our approach applies automatic software measurement techniques on UI tests to produce software metrics related to interaction complexity. From the perspective of HCI, these metrics are instrumentations that operationalize the latent interaction complexity construct.

2.1 Analysis Architecture and Artifacts

Figure 1 provides an overview of the main subsystems and components of the UIT-IC architecture and their interactions with each other: The `Parser` reads information from the UI tests and extracts data, which is then used by the `Metrics Calculator` to produce the output metrics per interface. Lastly, the `Metrics Representation` prepares a suitable representation for the integration of the analysis results into the calling system (e.g. a CI/CD pipeline). The UIT-IC architecture requires three input artifacts:

1. UI Tests source code, which represents the programming language-specific files containing the implementation of the UI tests using a UI testing framework like Selenium, Playwright or Cypress, used for static analysis,
2. System-under-Test (SUT) source code, required to match the information about the UI tests to the user interfaces which they are testing,
3. UI Tests execution logs, which are the textual representations of the framework-specific outputs produced when running the tests on the user interface and allow for dynamic analysis of timings etc.

The `Parser` subsystem extracts relevant information from these three input artifacts. Using the `Test Parser`, it identifies UI Tests, their location and metadata. The `Test mapper` is responsible for determining the corresponding user interface for each UI test analyzed. Execution logs information is extracted by the `Log Parser`, e.g. the time required to run a test.

The UI test information extracted by the `Parser` is the input for the computation of UI test metrics by the `Metrics Calculator`. This computation runs in two stages: first, metrics for individual UITs are computed by the `Single`

`Test Metrics Calculator`. Usually, a user interface has more than one UIT representing various features and corner cases to be tested on it. Thus, in the second stage these results are then aggregated to metrics at the UI level by the `Interface Metrics Calculator`, using the Test-UI mapping previously derived by the `Test Mapper`. We detail the actual metrics computed at test and UI level in Sect. 2.2. The final computation results are then passed to the `Metrics Representation` which transforms them into suitable format for the integration with the initiating system calling the analysis infrastructure. In the case of a CI/CD-pipeline, this is a formatted console output. For research purposes, the final representation uses a CSV-based tabular format.

2.2 Candidate Metrics

The `Metrics Calculator` features a plugin architecture that supports the definition of test and UI level metrics. This approach represents the realisation of a algorithmic/metric-model based method[1], in which stimuli affecting the human perception are mapped onto objectively computable quantities [2]. These *metrics* can be derived automatically through the analysis of software artifacts and need to be empirically assessed to demonstrate their correspondence with the actual subjective constructs – in our case interaction complexity. To the best of our knowledge, the idea to use UI tests for complexity analysis has not been investigated before. Thus, we had to identify potentially suitable metrics based on established theories and studies from three related research areas: UI analysis, program understanding and cognitive modeling.

UI analysis metrics related to complexity focus on measurable characteristics of the UI [2,6,7,25]. As some of these UI characteristics are implicitly reflected in the UI tests, they served as inspiration for the first group of metrics in this study. UI analysis metrics studied comprise of UI elements count [2,7,24], navigation graph complexity [27], scrolls count [9], and user actions count [5,30].

Program understanding metrics are traditional software metrics measured through static analysis of the source code structure or dynamically through code execution and monitoring runtime behavior which measure complexity with regard to readability, maintainability or development effort estimations. As UI tests represent software artifacts themselves, such metrics can be applied to indirectly measure complexity based on the assumption that complex interaction is reflected in increased software complexity of the UI tests. Program understanding metrics studied here are UIT SLOC [4,16,31], the counts of UIT statements, assert statements, wait statements [21,31], and the test execution time [16].

Cognitive modeling metrics are measured using dedicated artifacts (cf. GOMS/ KLM [9]) that represent interactions and consider cognitive characteristics/ differences in the cognitive load caused by different types of actions. UI tests are software artifacts that exhibit similarities to these models as they are also representations of interactions with user interfaces, so that cognitive

[1] cf. Taxonomy proposed by Akca et al. [2].

modeling metrics can be applied in a similar way to UI tests. The two metrics studied are the weighted sum of user actions and the homing actions count [9]

2.3 Proof-of-Concept Implementation

While the UIT-IC architecture presented in Fig. 1 is agnostic to specific technologies, we implemented a proof-of-concept as CLI application for easy integration with CI/CD pipelines using Kotlin and the Spring Boot framework. The implementation supports UI tests written in Selenium[2], due to its high popularity and the availability of more than 225 thousand repositories on GitHub using it. The implementation is part of our replication package[3].

3 Experimentation

To evaluate our approach, we conducted an experiment in which we compared the candidate complexity metrics calculated automatically against real user complexity assessments. We formulated this as a correlation study. The overall procedure consisted of analyzing the complexity of several WUIs using 2 sets of complexity measurements: those calculated by UIT-IC, and user-provided assessments. The overall design of the experiment is outlined in Fig. 2.

3.1 Materials

The study was conducted on 4 different web applications, for a total 16 WUIs. Our selection was based on domain diversity, and UI tests availability. The 4 websites were the following:

- **Alf.IO:** a booking and scheduling application.
- **Lime Survey:** a popular platform for creating polls and events.
- **Zimbra:** a collaborative software suite.
- **OpenOLAT:** an online education platform.

For each of the 16 WUIs a task was defined. The selected tasks were typical interactions, like creating appointments, adjusting settings, or creating a test for a given course.

Since we aimed for a group of WUIs with diverse levels of complexity, we assessed each interface's complexity using a 3-level scale, as other existing studies [14, 17]. This ensured the experiment data has various complexity levels, so the potential differences can be noted in the resulting metrics. However, as this evaluation was made by hand, it can differ from the results of experiment participants and objective metrics. The list of applications and interfaces, along with extra information like the complexity estimation can be found in Table 1.

---

[2] https://www.selenium.dev/.

[3] Replication package available at: https://doi.org/10.5281/zenodo.18481281.

Table 1. Description of interfaces chosen for the experiment

Application	Category	Test Language	Interface	Number of Tests	Complexity
Alf.IO	Booking and scheduling	Java	Ticket purchase	1	low
Lime Survey	Polls and Events	PHP	Survey	2	medium
			Questions group	2	medium
			Labels	3	medium
Zimbra	Groupware	Java	Briefcase	75	low
			Task	97	low
			Email	194	low
			Calendar	371	medium
			Contact	167	low
			Preferences	84	medium
OpenOLAT	Learning and Courses	Java	Group	8	high
			Test	1	high
			Portfolio	7	high
			Resource folder	3	medium
			Course	12	high
			Question bank	3	high

Additionally, we created a survey for collecting the participants' assessments, as well as their demographic information. The survey also collected the time the participants took for answering each question. It was hosted in the LimeSurvey[4] platform (coincidentally, one of the assessed web applications).

3.2 Participants

A total of 38 participants took part of the study: 24 male, 14 female (average age 30.1, 7.8 SD). We applied the convenience sampling method, most of them students or recent graduates - 92.1% completed their Bachelor or higher. The self-denoted countries of residence are Germany (73.7%), Russia (7.9%), Argentina (7.9%), Romania (5.3%), India (2.6%) and Nepal (2.6%). The input devices used along the keyboard were mouse (52.6%) and touchpad (39.4%).

3.3 Experiment Design and Procedure

The study was conducted online, and participants self-moderated their assigned tasks. This design helped us obtain more participants in a shorter time period. Each participant had to provide 40 assessments on two of the four applications available (20 assessments each). This design ensured each interface received multiple independent assessments. The order in which both the applications and the tasks were provided was randomized, to avoid a potential learning effect.

Regarding the procedure, each participant first received some introductory information explaining the overall process and the collected data. At this point,

[4] https://www.limesurvey.org/.

participants were able to contact the researcher to ask any question about the study. This part was important since they were also informed that once started, the study could not be paused. Once the participants were ready, they were provided with the link to start the evaluation, which started with the demographic survey. Then the main part of the study began, and they were presented with the tasks for the first application. After completing each task, they answered the assessment questions. This process was repeated for the second application. Finally, they were allowed to leave feedback on the study and the session was over. The expected completion time was expected to be between 15 and 20 min.

We designed the list of questions to gather the complexity assessments from the existing literature. We based our questionnaire on the 13-topic survey but Ling et al. [19], which showed good reliability and validity and was specifically adapted for the evaluation of interface complexity. Out of the original 13 categories (each with 2/4 statements), we selected 10 categories with 2 statements each. The criteria for this selection were minimizing repetition and simplifying formulations. The final survey includes statements related to locating information (e.g. "1.1 I know where to look to see the information I need"), interpreting visual structure (e.g. "2.2 The website uses too many different sizes, colors, fonts, and icons"), and handling task-related demands (e.g. "10.2 I feel overwhelmed by the amount of interaction required by the website"). Each of the 10 categories addresses a specific dimension of complexity, from visual and informational load to cognitive and action-related challenges.

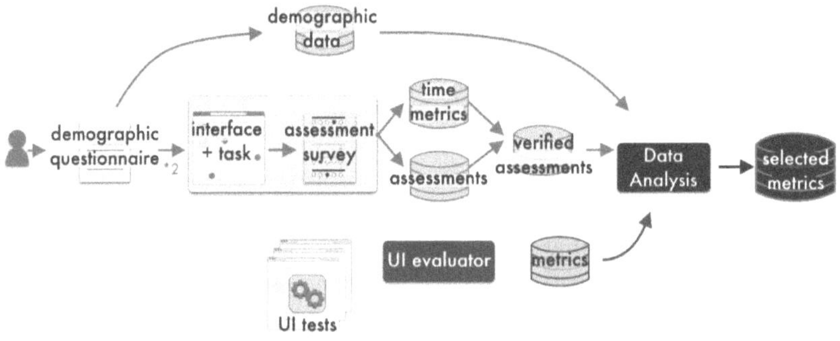

Fig. 2. Experiment design.

3.4 Results

We gathered the results for all 4 applications, both **metrics** (using our tool) and participants' **assessments**. Regarding the metrics, we calculated 1 **visual complexity** metric, 2 **navigation** metrics, and 8 **task complexity** metrics, for a total of 11 candidate metrics.

Regarding the participants' results, we gathered the assessments for the 38 participants. We obtained 55 valid assessments out of 76. We discarded 17 incomplete ones, and 2 for taking too long according to our outlier analysis.

To compare the metrics with the assessments, we used the median across all participants, obtaining one value for each interface. We assessed the inter-rater reliability using the Kripendorff's alpha test, which is well suited for the Likert scale[5]. The results ultimately showed poor levels of agreement (discussed in Sect. 3.6), but we still proceeded with the medians for the analysis. We used the Spearman correlation coefficient to make the comparison, since the data was not normal. We calculated the correlation to examine the degree of the relationship between all measurements, namely 11 automated metrics and 20 user-provided assessments. Out of the 220 pairs of measurement correlations, 7 showed significant, strong negative correlations ($p < 0$, $p > 0.5$). The values for these 7 pairs are shown in Table 2. Others showed weak or no significant correlation ($p < 0.3$ or $p >= 0.05$). Despite the lack of significance in some cases, the limited dataset size ($n = 16$) suggests these metrics may still be valuable.

Table 2. Correlation coefficients (p-values) for user experience factors

	2.2 Many elements	3.1 Busy site	3.2 Adequate spacing	4.2 Too much info	8.2 Hard to find
Nav. graph complexity	**−0.58 (0.02)**	−0.38 (0.15)	−0.33 (0.21)	−0.02 (0.93)	0.05 (0.86)
Homing actions	−0.23 (0.39)	−0.34 (0.20)	0.04 (0.89)	**−0.51 (0.04)**	**−0.52 (0.04)**
Wait statements	**0.53 (0.03)**	**0.52 (0.04)**	**0.52 (0.04)**	0.36 (0.18)	0.23 (0.38)
Weighted actions sum	−0.48 (0.06)	**−0.51 (0.04)**	−0.22 (0.42)	−0.42 (0.10)	−0.46 (0.08)

Following the correlation study, we continued with regression analysis, since we are interested in predicting user-assessed complexity from the automated metrics. To this end, the 7 most correlated pairs presented earlier were analyzed. The two models showed the best results were (1) **"Average number of wait statements"** to **2.2 There are many elements** and (2) **"Average navigation complexity & Average number of wait statements"** to **"2.2 There are many elements"**. Both models are shown in the following equations:

$$y = 2.318 + 0.299 * x \tag{1}$$

$$y = 3.819 + 0.136 * x1 + -0.002 * x2 \tag{2}$$

The first model (Eq. (1)) showed significance $F = 16.473$, p-value $= 0.01$ and predictive power $R^2 = 0.541$; the second model (equation (2)) showed significance $F = 8.606$, p-value $= 0.04$ and $R^2 = 0.570$. The former is plotted on the chart in Fig. 3, to show the difference between real and predicted values (we do not provide a scatterplot for the latter, since it is a multiple linear regression with two input variables).

[5] https://www.statisticshowto.com/krippendorffs-alpha/.

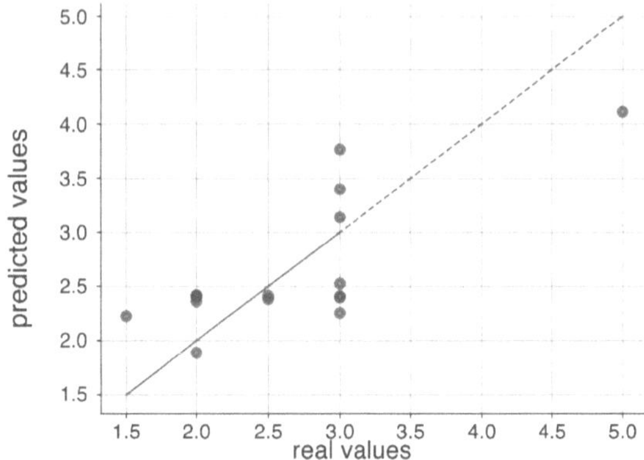

Fig. 3. Scatterplot illustrating the regression model for the metric "Average number of wait statements" and the assessment "2.2 There are many elements".

Since the obtained regressions models are able to predict a limited number of subjective metrics, we intended to create a more comprehensive model using other objective metrics. However, the number of objective metrics is considerably large (11), so we tried to reduce this number by analyzing the relationships between them to select the most relevant ones. Again, we used the Spearman rank correlation to calculate the cross-correlations of the objective metrics. Table 3 shows the significant results of cross-correlation coefficient calculation, where strong correlation is emphasized with bold.

Table 3. Significant Spearman cross-correlation coefficients, p (p-value)

	Average number ofUI elements	Average number of homing	Average number of scrolls	Average number of user actions	Average weighted user action sum
Average number of UI elements	-	0.674 (0.004)	**0.843 (0.000)**	0.729 (0.001)	**0.924 (0.000)**
Average number of homing actions	0.674 (0.004)	-	0.774 (0.000)	**0.968 (0.000)**	0.639 (0.008)
Average number of scrolls	**0.843 (0.000)**	0.774 (0.000)	-	**0.849 (0.000)**	**0.888 (0.000)**
Average number of user actions	0.729 (0.001)	**0.968 (0.000)**	**0.849 (0.000)**	-	0.715 (0.002)
Average weighted user actions sum	**0.924 (0.000)**	0.639 (0.008)	**0.888 (0.000)**	0.715 (0.002)	-

Results allowed removing 3 metrics strongly correlated with others: "Average number of user actions", "Average number of scrolls" and "Average number of UI elements". We removed these instead of their correlated counterparts, since the latter built significant regression models with some of the user assessments.

After this analysis we narrowed the list down to 8 metrics, but we reduced it further using *Principal Component Analysis (PCA)*. To determine the number of components we used the broken stick method, which leverages the amount of variance each components explains, compared to what would be expected by chance. The plot (Fig. 4) showed that three components sufficiently capture the variance in the data.

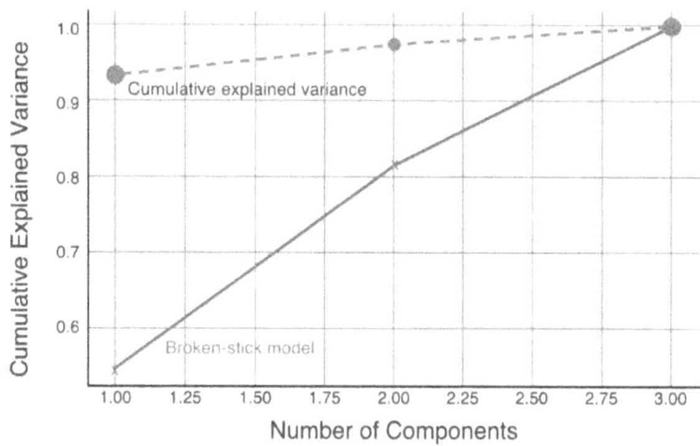

Fig. 4. PCA, finding the number of components with broken-stick method.

The explained variance ratios for the components are 0.935419 for PC1, 0.038880 for PC2, and 0.024404 for PC3. Using these 3 components, we repeated the process of generating regression models with the subjective metrics. Some of the obtained models are displayed in Table 4.

Table 4. A sample of the regression models generated after the Principal Component Analysis results.

Metric	F-statistic	p-value	R^2	Model
2.2 There are many elements	2.500	0.109	0.385	$y = 2.656 + -0.002 * x1 + 0.007 * x2 + -0.021 * x3$
3.1 Website is busy	2.875	0.080	0.418	$y = 3.656 + -0.003 * x1 + 0.002 * x2 + -0.018 * x3$
4.1 Difficult information management	2.679	0.094	0.401	$y = 3.469 + -0.00 * 5x1 + 0.003 * x2 + -0.023 * x3$

3.5 Discussion

The results allowed to draw several insights. In the first place, some of the objective metrics (4) showed significant correlations with other subjective metrics. Two of the metrics, "Average number of wait statements" and "Average number of homing actions" also had more than one correlation to the subjective metrics. Regarding their interpretation, the metric "Average number of wait statements" captures waiting times in the UI tests, which are typically used to wait for elements to appear or react. This could explain correlations with metrics such as "2.2 There are many elements" and "3.1. Website is busy". The metric "Average number of homing actions" negatively correlated with subjective metrics about finding information, which is less expected, considering homing action is an additional effort and would be assumed to cause the interface to appear more confusing for the information-finding process and not vice-versa.

The cross-correlation of the objective metrics, part of which is shown in Table 3, produced some high coefficients. This can be explained by the way the metrics were captured. In the case of the most correlated ones, some similar markers of UI interactions were used e.g. "Average number of scrolls per test" and "Average number of user actions per test".

Overall, the use of UI test analysis to assess interface complexity has demonstrated moderate effectiveness in predicting usersâĂŹ perceived complexity. Since UI tests primarily capture user interactions, the metrics related to interaction complexity showed stronger correlations with subjective user evaluations.

3.6 Threats to Validity

Our experiment was subject to some validity threats. Regarding external validity, demographic data mostly described a consistent group of young well-educated and computer-advanced participants. Therefore, their assessments might differ from those of the more general public, due to the more intensive use of complex websites, higher exposure to the Web in general, and specifically desktop UIs. Even if we could have aimed at more diverse backgrounds, we opted for the convenience method, since at this stage we prioritized the number of volunteers rather than their personal traits.

Additionally, the selected materials, such as web applications with their UI tests and corresponding tasks, may introduce threats to external validity due to under representation, and also a potential bias in the selection process (although that threat is more related to construct validity). To mitigate the first threat, the experiment conditions mirrored real-world scenarios: participants were unsupervised, used existing tools, and were not in a controlled environment. To decrease bias in material selection, applications were chosen from commonly used application categories, and the tasks represented typical interactions.

Regarding construct validity, the inter-rater agreement showed low values, which could be due to the low number of evaluations per interface and to the complexity of the questions. As some questions were more specific and technical in the sphere of interface design, participants may not have interpreted the concepts correctly, leading to more diverse scores. Even if we did not anticipate this effect, given the homogeneous group in terms of demographics, typical mitigation measures involve interacting with participants in additional sessions to improve consistency. This design would have compromised the number of participants in our evaluation, but should be considered for further experiments. Another mitigation measure for follow-up evaluations could consist in increasing the number of assessments *per interface.*

4 Related Work

In this section, we provide a brief overview on related work discussing background and recent research in the analysis of Interaction complexity and its automation.

4.1 Interaction Complexity and Metrics

There are many approaches that analyze UI complexity. Two well-known methods to predict user performance without requiring participants are KLM and

GOMS, even if they measure aspects related to complexity rather than complexity itself. The Keystroke-Level Model (KLM) [9] assigns an estimated time to each interactive component, providing a time estimate for the entire UI. Estimates are based on measured average execution times for the specific target user group and operators using the target application. GOMS (Goals, Operators, Methods, and Selection rules) [10] helps identifying the steps involved in achieving a goal and includes the mental processes, decision-making, and strategies used to perform a task (while KLM is purely focused on physical actions).

Another approach for predicting and comparing interaction complexity is the *Big I* notation [11], which is based on the Big O notation for algorithmic complexity. Big I expresses interaction complexity as a mathematical function, and it was designed for scenarios in which efficiency of use is critical. It is applied to interaction concepts, which can be useful even for early lo-fi prototypes.

4.2 Automated Analysis of Interaction Complexity

Visual clutter is analyzed to reduce the cognitive load of users using metrics such as feature congestion, subband entropy [29], or edge density [20]. Similarly, assessment of visual complexity [22,32] aims at facilitating usersâĂŹ cognition of a WUI. The analysis result can be either a scalar value [32], or 3D representation of spatial complexity distribution similar to a heat map [22]. A comprehensive survey on methods for visual complexity analysis was conducted by Akça and Tanriöver [2]. In their proposed taxonomy [2], UIT-IC would belong to Metric-Model Based methods, however neither in the child group of GUI Component Oriented nor GUI Image Oriented. Instead of using UI components or image features of GUI screenshots, UIT-IC proposes the novel idea of using UI tests as the main input for complexity analysis.

In a work focused on mobile applications, Riegler and Holzmann [28] devised a tool to analyze screenshots and interaction data to quantify UI complexity using metrics of their own. They consider aspects like object separation or color consistency, while the user interaction data used is dwelling time. Even if dwelling time is a simple metric, this is one of the few works in the field to consider user interaction at all in UI complexity measurement.

5 Conclusion and Future Work

In this article, we proposed UIT-IC, a novel procedure for evaluating the complexity of web user interaction in an automated way. Our method uses existing UI tests, providing a key advantage over other methods since there is no need for additional artifacts. Leveraging existing UI tests also enables continuous evaluation of UI complexity as the tests evolve, making UIT-IC a practical addition to CI/CD pipelines. To the best of our knowledge, UI tests were not used before for the purpose of complexity assessment.

To develop a solution, we derived a set of candidate metrics extracted from different components of the UI tests cycle: source code, web application source code and UI test execution logs. This allowed us to extract 11 metrics that can be used to predict complexity in aspects such as visual design, navigation, and interaction. These metrics were gathered and systematized based on existing research in the field of UI complexity assessment.

To explore the feasibility of our proposal, we conducted a study with 38 participants, in which we gathered their complexity assessments in 4 different web applications. These applications were also assessed by an implementation of UIT-IC that captured our automated metrics, and we analyzed correlations between them, in order to propose prediction models. Of all investigated regression models, 2 are shown to successfully predict human-rated complexity in terms of number of visual elements.

Finally, by applying different analysis techniques like cross-correlation and Principal Component Analysis (PCA) on the metrics, we were able to reduce the metrics down to 3 components while still keeping the variability in the data. We used these results to generate another set of simpler regression models still able to predict the human assessments of complexity.

In future work, we plan to investigate the applicability of UIT-IC for predicting task load, e.g. compared to NASA-TLX [18], or cognitive load, e.g. compared to tapping [3]. Another promising research direction is the combination of UIT-IC with methods for automated creation of UI tests [13] to investigate the impact on the reliability of metrics. Our current study was focused on Selenium-based UI tests. Future experiments can replicate the approach for other testing frameworks that are increasingly popular such as Playwright[6] or Cypress[7], which would provide insights on the testing platform-dependence of UIT-IC and also provide a wider basis for experimentation with public repositories. We are also currently experimenting with a variation of our approach that includes an intermediate step of mapping UI tests onto GOMS/KLM models. This direction, if successful, would allow to connect UIT-IC with established and validated cognitive modeling techniques.

Acknowledgements. This work is supported by the EUâĂŹs HORIZON Research and Innovation Programme under grant agreement No 101120657, project ENFIELD.

Disclosure of Interest. The authors have no competing interests to declare that are relevant to the content of this article.

References

1. Abb, L., Rehse, J.R.: Process-related user interaction logs: state of the art, reference model, and object-centric implementation. Inf. Syst. **124**, 102386 (2024). https://doi.org/10.1016/j.is.2024.102386
2. Akça, E., Ömer Özgür Tanriöver: A comprehensive appraisal of perceptual visual complexity analysis methods in GUI design. Displays **69**, 102031 (2021)

[6] https://playwright.dev.
[7] https://www.cypress.io.

3. Albers, M.J.: Tapping as a measure of cognitive load and website usability. In: SIGDOC 2011 - Proceedings of the 29th ACM International Conference on Design of Communication, pp. 25–32 (2011). https://doi.org/10.1145/2038476.2038481
4. Albrecht, A., Gaffney, J.: Software function, source lines of code, and development effort prediction: a software science validation. IEEE Trans. Softw. Eng. **SE-9**(6), 639–648 (1983). https://doi.org/10.1109/TSE.1983.235271
5. Alsmadi, I., Al-Kabi, M.: GUI structural metrics. Int. Arab J. Inf. Technol. **8**, 124–129 (2011)
6. Bakaev, M., Heil, S., Khvorostov, V., Gaedke, M.: In: Web Engineering: 18th International Conference, ICWE. Springer (2018). https://doi.org/10.1007/978-3-319-91662-0_10
7. Bakaev, M., Heil, S., Khvorostov, V., Gaedke, M.: Auto-extraction and integration of metrics for web user interfaces. J. Web Eng. **17**, 561–590 (2019). https://doi.org/10.13052/jwe1540-9589.17676
8. Bakaev, M., Speicher, M., Heil, S., Gaedke, M.: I don't have that much data! reusing user behavior models for websites from different domains. In: Bielikova, M., Mikkonen, T., Pautasso, C. (eds.) Web Engineering, LNCS, vol. 12128, pp. 146–162. Springer International Publishing, Cham (2020). https://doi.org/10.1007/978-3-030-50578-3_11
9. Card, S.K., Moran, T.P., Newell, A.: The keystroke-level model for user performance time with interactive systems. Commun. ACM **23**(7), 396–410 (1980). https://doi.org/10.1145/358886.358895
10. Card, S., Moran, T., Newell, A.: The model human processor- an engineering model of human performance. Handb. Percept. Hum. Perform. **2**(45–1), 1–35 (1986)
11. Degen, H.: Big i notation to estimate the interaction complexity of interaction concepts. Int. J. Hum. Comput. Interact. **38**(16), 1504–1528 (2022)
12. El Batran, K., Dunlop, M.D.: Enhancing KLM (keystroke-level model) to fit touch screen mobile devices. In: Proceedings of the 16th International Conference on Human-computer Interaction with Mobile Devices & Services, pp. 283–286 (2014)
13. Fan, Y., Wang, S., Fei, Z., Qin, Y., Li, H., Liu, Y.: Can cooperative multi-agent reinforcement learning boost automatic web testing? An exploratory study. In: Proceedings of the 39th IEEE/ACM International Conference on Automated Software Engineering, pp. 14–26. ACM, New York, NY, USA (2024). https://doi.org/10.1145/3691620.3694983
14. Georges, V., Courtemanche, F., Sénécal, S., Baccino, T., Léger, P.M., Frédette, M.: Measuring visual complexity using neurophysiological data. In: Information Systems and Neuroscience: Gmunden Retreat on NeuroIS, pp. 207–212. Springer (2015). https://doi.org/10.1007/978-3-319-18702-0_28
15. Grigera, J., Espada, J.P., Rossi, G.: Ai in user interface design and evaluation. IT Professional **25**(2), 20–22 (2023). https://doi.org/10.1109/MITP.2023.3267139
16. Hada, B.: Software testing metrics guide; definition, types & example (2023). https://www.lambdatest.com/learning-hub/software-testing-metrics
17. Harper, S., Michailidou, E., Stevens, R.: Toward a definition of visual complexity as an implicit measure of cognitive load. ACM Trans. Appl. Percept.(TAP) **6**(2), 1–18 (2009)
18. Hart, S.G.: Nasa-Task Load Index (NASA-TLX); 20 years later. In: Proceedings of the Human Factors and Ergonomics Society Annual Meeting, vol. 50, no. 9, pp. 904–908 (2006). https://doi.org/10.1177/154193120605000909
19. Ling, C., Lopez, M., Shehab, R.: Complexity questionnaires of visual displays: a validation study of two information complexity questionnaires of visual displays. Hum. Fact. Ergon. Manuf. Serv. Ind. **23**(5), 391–411 (2013)

20. Mack, M.L., Oliva, A.: Computational estimation of visual complexity. In: The 12th Annual Object, Perception, Attention, and Memory Conference (2004)
21. Magni, S., Ozcan, M.: UI testing best practices (2024). https://github.com/NoriSte/ui-testing-best-practices
22. Michailidou, E., Eraslan, S., Yesilada, Y., Harper, S.: Automated prediction of visual complexity of web pages: tools and evaluations. Int. J. Hum. Comput. Stud. **145**, 102523 (2021). https://doi.org/10.1016/j.ijhcs.2020.102523
23. Miniukovich, A., De Angeli, A.: Computation of interface aesthetics. In: Proceedings of the 33rd Annual ACM Conference on Human Factors in Computing Systems, pp. 1163–1172. ACM, New York, NY, USA (2015). https://doi.org/10.1145/2702123.2702575
24. Miniukovich, A., Sulpizio, S., De Angeli, A.: Visual complexity of graphical user interfaces. In: Proceedings of the 2018 International Conference on Advanced Visual Interfaces, pp. 1–9 (2018)
25. Oulasvirta, A., et al.: Aalto Interface Metrics (AIM)): a service and codebase for computational GUI evaluation. In: The 31st Annual ACM Symposium on User Interface Software and Technology Adjunct Proceedings - UIST 2018 Adjunct, pp. 16–19. ACM Press, New York, New York, USA (2018). https://doi.org/10.1145/3266037.3266087
26. Paganelli, L., Paternò, F.: Intelligent analysis of user interactions with web applications. In: Proceedings of the 7th International Conference on Intelligent User Interfaces, pp. 111–118. ACM, New York, NY, USA (2002). https://doi.org/10.1145/502716.502735
27. Riegler, A., Holzmann, C.: UI-CAT: calculating user interface complexity metrics for mobile applications. In: Proceedings of the 14th International Conference on Mobile and Ubiquitous Multimedia, vol. 30-November-2015, pp. 390–394. ACM (2015). https://doi.org/10.1145/2836041.2841214
28. Riegler, A., Holzmann, C.: Measuring visual user interface complexity of mobile applications with metrics. Interact. Comput. **30**(3), 207–223 (2018). https://doi.org/10.1093/iwc/iwy008
29. Rosenholtz, R., Li, Y., Nakano, L.: Measuring visual clutter. J. Vis. **7**(2), 17 (2007). https://doi.org/10.1167/7.2.17
30. Taba, S.E.S., Keivanloo, I., Zou, Y., Ng, J., Ng, T.: An exploratory study on the relation between user interface complexity and the perceived quality. In: Web Engineering: 14th International Conference, ICWE 2014, vol. 8541, pp. 370–379 (2014). https://doi.org/10.1007/978-3-319-08245-5_22
31. Weyuker, E.: Evaluating software complexity measures. IEEE Trans. Software Eng. **14**(9), 1357–1365 (1988)
32. Wu, O., Hu, W., Shi, L.: Measuring the visual complexities of web pages. ACM Trans. Web **7**(1), 1–34 (2013). https://doi.org/10.1145/2435215.2435216

A Low-Code Approach for the Automatic Personalization of Conversational Agents

Aaron Conrardy[1,2](✉), Alfredo Capozucca[2], and Jordi Cabot[1,2]

[1] Luxembourg Institute of Science and Technology, Esch-sur-Alzette, Luxembourg
{aaron.conrardy,jordi.cabot}@list.lu

[2] University of Luxembourg, Esch-sur-Alzette, Luxembourg
alfredo.capozucca@uni.lu

Abstract. The rise of Large Language Models (LLMs) has increased the demand for Conversational Agents (CAs) capable of understanding human conversations as part of web applications. While traditional CAs consist of deterministic states, LLMs enhance their capabilities to handle open conversations, handling arbitrary requests. Numerous tools exist that allow non-technical users to create such CAs. Yet, the creation of personalized CAs able to adapt to the profile of end-users to offer an optimal user experience remains in the hands of experienced developers implementing ad-hoc personalizations. In this work, we propose a pipeline that follows a low-code/no-code approach to facilitate the modeling and generation of personalized CAs. A pilot user study was performed to get preliminary results on perceived usability and usefulness and the full pipeline has been implemented on top of an open-source low-code platform.

Keywords: Conversational agent · Low-code · Model-driven · Personalization

1 Introduction

Conversational Agents (CAs) are software applications that interact autonomously with end-users in natural language, supporting task completion, conversational web, service delivery, as well as social engagement and entertainment [4,5,21]. Known under other names such as chatbots or digital assistants, they have become a ubiquitous component of modern platforms and services. While their adoption was already increasing before the widespread use of Large Language Models (LLMs), recent advances in LLMs have further established CAs as a common additional interaction modality in web applications and more. CAs may support different types of conversations, ranging from predefined, task-oriented dialogues based on deterministic rules to open-ended interactions enabled by LLMs, or a combination of both.

Personalized CAs (PCAs) aim to further elevate the users' experience by personalizing their interaction with the CA. Personalization refers to adapting

A. Mauri et al. (Eds.): ICWE 2026, LNCS 16625, pp. 47–61, 2026.
https://doi.org/10.1007/978-3-032-29372-5_4

systems to better fit an individual user's needs, preferences, and context [13] offering an optimal user experience.

At a high level, personalization typically consists of two processes: user profiling and system adaptation [13] where the latter takes care of personalizing the interaction to the specific attributes of the user. For instance, for extroverted users, aligning CAs to act extroverted by adapting communication styles has shown to increase engagement and usage intention [3]. While these processes are well-studied [22], their implementation in CAs remains complex and requires deep technical expertise [24].

In this sense, this paper aims to facilitate the personalization of CAs, enabling non-technical people to define the type of users they want to support, the adaptations to be done for each user type and the generation of the corresponding personalized agents. To do so, we propose a new low-code pipeline to model and automatically generate PCAs. A style of model-driven development [8,12], low-code development reduces the need for manual programming by relying on higher-level, graphical models to describe system behavior. Such approaches have already been applied to the development of CAs [5] and, partially, to the personalization of user interfaces [25,26] but, to the best of our knowledge, not to the challenge of creating PCAs.

The rest of this paper is structured as follows. Section 2 presents an overview of the proposed pipeline. Section 3 presents the modeling of PCAs, followed by Sect. 4 that describes how these PCA models are transformed into the actual agents. Tooling support is discussed in Sect. 5. Section 6 discusses a user study to validate our approach. Section 7 presents the related work. The paper is concluded in Sect. 8.

2 Overview of Our Low-Code Pipeline for the Development of PCAs

In this section, we present our low-code pipeline for designing and generating PCAs. Figure 1 illustrates the four main activities:

1. **Modeling the user and agent profiles**: The PCA designer models the user profiles (representing the types of users we target in our CA), the base agent model (with the common functionality) and the agent profiles (representing the different agent adaptations to be mapped to the corresponding user profiles). Separating the agent profile from the base agent model makes the agent profiles agent-agnostic, as they can be applied to any agent. Similarly, separating user profiles from agent profiles also enables the mapping of the same agent profile to different users, fostering reusability.
2. **Design time personalization**: Based on the user and agent profiles, the agent model is enriched via a model-to-model (M2M) transformation that adapts any agent answer hardcoded in the model. At this time, adaptations can include translation [27], complexity variation [20] and integration of cultural values [19]) among others. An LLM is used to automate these adaptations. Note that design-time adaptation is always preferred when possible as

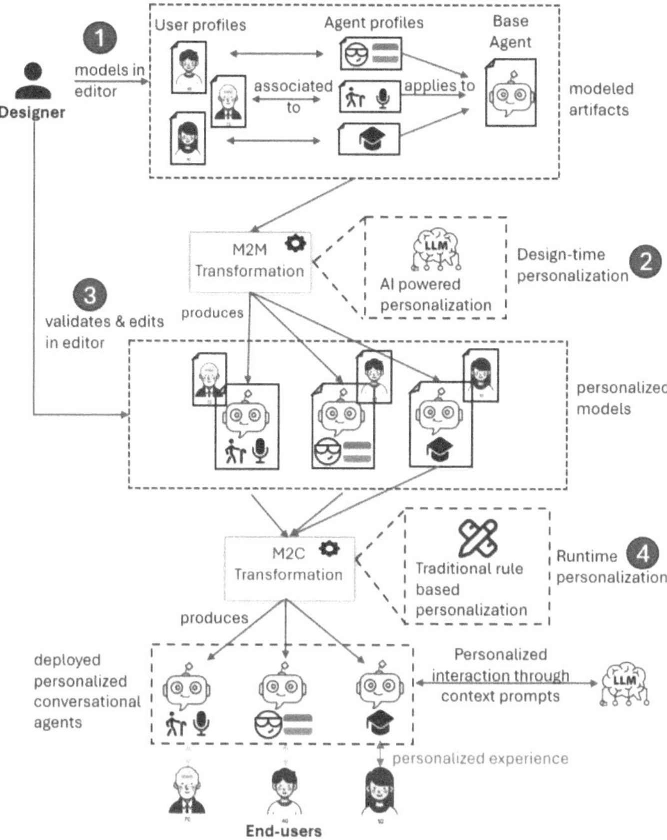

Fig. 1. Overview of steps of low-code personalized agent creation pipeline.

it improves runtime performance (removing the need for additional calls at every agent request) and it enables the agent validation before putting it into production.

3. **Manual model validation and update**: At this stage, designers can validate the personalized texts in each model and apply manual modifications if needed (e.g., improving the adapted text or adding unique states to one of the personalized agent models for a deeper adaptation). At the end of this phase, we have a set of personalized agent models linked to specific user profiles. The next step will complete the adaptation process.
4. **Runtime personalization**: As part of a final model-to-code (M2C) transformation and, based on the specified customization in the agent profile, appropriate code excerpts are included by the deterministic code-generation templates. This code extends the agent behavior with additional adaptations that will be dynamically triggered when the corresponding user interacts with the agent.

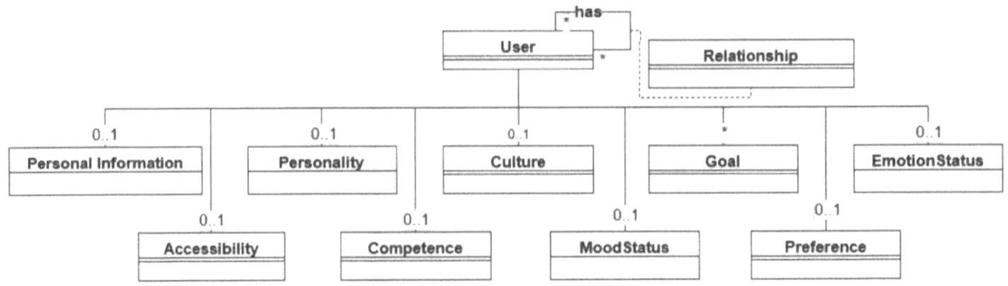

Fig. 2. High-level view of user metamodel from [9].

3 Modeling Users, Agents, and Agent Profiles

To support the modeling of the previously discussed artifacts, we define a set of interrelated domain-specific languages (DSLs). Each DSL is presented by describing both their abstract (using a metamodel expressed as a UML class diagram) and concrete syntax (using a graphical or form-based notation).

To illustrate our approach, we use as a running example a personalized gym assistant designed to provide accessible and adapted advice to different user profiles. The agent's core task is to provide pre-defined gym-related advice on nutrition and exercises, and be able to handle any other query via generative AI as a fallback. Two user profiles are considered to receive a personalized experience: (1) an elderly user that only speaks their native language, and (2) a paraplegic user who cannot use their legs. The former prefers oral interaction, simple and formal text with a conversation in their mother tongue. The latter must not receive exercise recommendations involving the lower body, guaranteeing that adequate advice is given.

3.1 User Modeling

User profile models have the goal to describe the end-user of an application [10]. They can either describe individual users or user categories (e.g., elderly users in our running example) to which then real users are mapped to.

Abstract Syntax. For this metamodel, we reuse the user metamodel we proposed in [9], with Fig. 2 showing a high-level view. The metamodel consolidates results of a Systematic Literature Review (SLR) on user modeling that we performed [10], providing a complete and detailed overview of users via the proposed formalization, allowing the definition of user profiles with various attributes.

Concrete Syntax. Conforming to the rules of the abstract syntax, as part of this work we have developed a graphical notation to model user profiles.

Figure 3 shows a partial user profile model for our running example, representing the paraplegic user profile, containing the information on the disability and what it affects, as it is relevant for the personalization. The full list of icons of our graphical notation is available in our online tool (see Sect. 5).

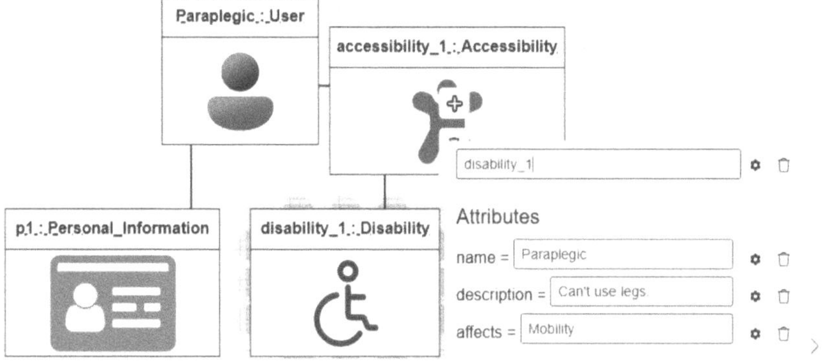

Fig. 3. Paraplegic user profile model in graphical notation.

3.2 Agent Modeling

The base agent model reflects the conversational states of the agent, thus, its core functionality.

Abstract Syntax. The metamodel to describe agents is shown in Fig. 4 (classes in blue). Note that this is a simplified version, omitting attributes and (sub)classes not relevant to showcase the personalization pipeline, as it follows a formal-state-machine-like syntax commonly used when defining CAs [16].

At its core, the metamodel includes the *State*, *Body* of states, executed *Actions* in a given body, *Transitions* that define when to jump from one state to another once specific *Conditions* are fulfilled, and *Intents* that represent the possible messages an end-user might pose when interacting the agent. Note that for the actions, one can choose between sending a pre-defined response, an AI generated response via an LLM, or an AI generated response using retrieval augmented generation (RAG) based on an available database.

Concrete Syntax. We propose a graphical notation that strongly follows the UML state machine formalism[1].

Figure 5 displays our running agent example using this graphical syntax. For simplicity, the agent answers only one question before returning to an idle state. The model consists of four states: an initial greeting state that automatically transitions to an idle state, two predefined response states (*TrainingPlan* and *Nutrition*), and an *OtherQuestions* state handled by an LLM. Three intents (*Muscles_intent*, *Nutrition_intent*, and *Other*) control transitions to the corresponding states. After each response, the agent returns to the idle state.

3.3 Modeling Agent Personalizations

The key element is to model the personalization options we want our PCA to offer to all or some of the user profiles we want to support.

[1] https://www.omg.org/spec/UML/2.5.1/About-UML.

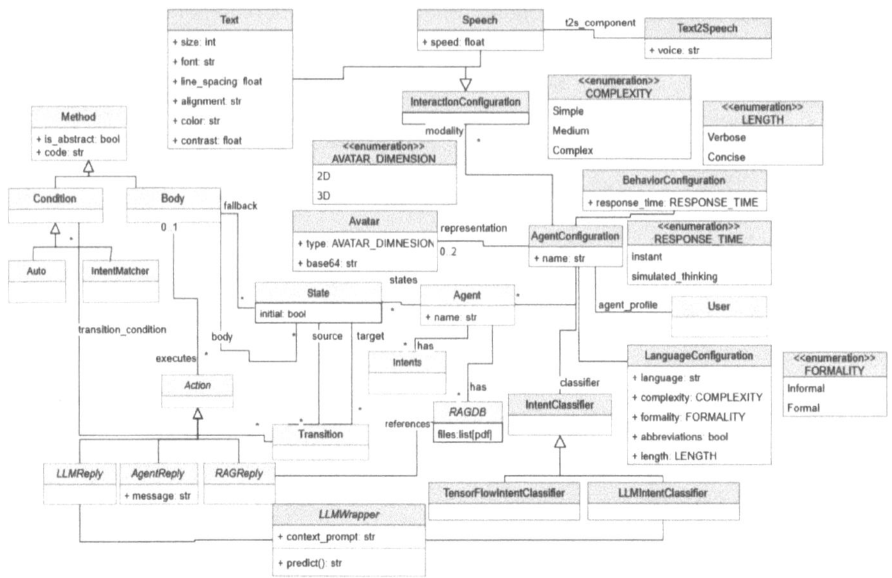

Fig. 4. Agent and agent profile metamodel.

But before deciding which of the adaptations we want to include in our agent, we need to establish the set of possible adaptations available for agents and what benefits each adaptation could potentially bring.

Unfortunately, there is not a general taxonomy of personalizable components suited for CAs. Therefore, and based on the individual personalization ideas published in the literature (e.g., see [1,14,17,22]), we propose in Table 1 a non-exhaustive list of personalizable components in CAs, consolidated into four distinct categories: (1) Content, (2) Presentation, (3) Behavior, and (4) Modality. These four categories are inspired by an assessment scheme that was used in an SLR on PCAs in health care [17], where we renamed *User Interface* to *Presentation*, *Delivery Channel* to *Modality* and *Functionality* to *Behavior*, and broadening their definition in what they capture. A takeaway here is that both the conversation of the agent and the UI it will take place on need to be personalized.

Abstract Syntax. Based on the taxonomy in Table 1, we have defined the metamodel for modeling agent configurations, visible in Fig. 4 (red classes). Related to Modality, *InteractionConfiguration* defines the used modalities. For Presentation, *Text* and *Speech* allow for the specification of stylistic changes related to the chosen channel of communication. *Avatar* defines the visual representation of the CA. *Language Configuration* relates to stylistic changes in the used language. Related to Behavior, *BehaviorConfiguration* lets users change if the agent pretends to type out a message or instantly responds. For Content, it is enough that the information of the user profile is provided, as the semantics will be changed

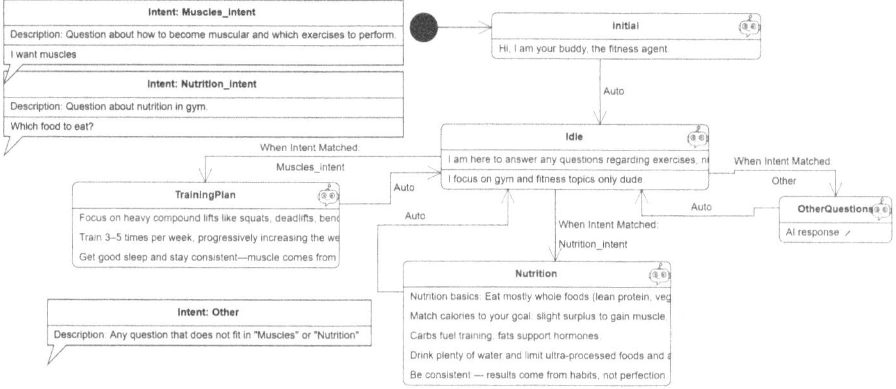

Fig. 5. Graphical agent model representing the gym assistant agent.

based on that information, which is represented by the association between the agent configuration and the user. Additionally, the components *IntentClassifier* (necessary for natural language understanding), *LLMWrapper*, *RagDB*, *Platform* and *Text2Speech* define technological configurations of the agent, focusing on used tools and methods to run the agent.

Concrete Syntax. To specify the agent profile, we decided to implement it via a form-based syntax, given the configurational and feature-like nature of the agent configuration. Figure 6 contains the agent configuration in the form-based syntax created based on the requirements for the Elderly profile, where the four personalization categories are represented. The configurable content in each pillar is straightforward, such as setting Language Complexity to *Simple* in Presentation, selecting *Speech* as modalities for both input and output in Modality, or setting the boolean to adapt content to the user profile to true.

3.4 Linking the Models

In a final step, the personalization model needs to be mapped to the affected base agent model and target user profile, illustrated in Fig. 4 in the metamodel with the association starting from the class *Agent*, respectively *User* to *Agent Configuration*. This straightforward connection is implemented via forms, where the designer defines the mapping that is then stored on top of the defined models.

4 Generating the Personalized Conversational Agents

We will now explain the two-step personalization process of our pipeline, depending on whether the personalization can be completely done at design time or it is part of the runtime execution of the agent.

This process is repeated for every agent profile we want to add to our base agent model, resulting in a family of related agents that share the same core

Table 1. Overview of personalization dimensions with embedded definitions and representative examples.

Category (definition)	Aspect	Example (with reference)
Content (adapts *what* is shown or done, i.e., the semantics of the interaction)	Selection/structure	Adaptive conversation paths [17]; paragraph length adapted to cognitive capabilities [22]
	Enrichment	Response tailored to fit user constraints [17]
Presentation (adapts *how* content is delivered without changing its meaning)	Language and style	Code-switching [22]; simplified text [14]; text formality [1,22]
	Visual/auditory form	Larger text for elderly users [25]; emotional tone of voice [22]; avatar appearance [14]
Behavior (adapts *how the interaction unfolds* over time)	Interaction management	Response timing, turn-taking, and proactiveness [14,22]
	Social and repair strategies	Clarification questions [22]; small talk or humor [14]
Modality (adapts the *input/output channels* used for interaction)	Channels	Text, speech, images/video, gestures, or haptics [17,22]

behavior but present it on different shapes and styles depending on the personalization applied to generate each of them.

4.1 Design Time Personalization

Design time personalization in the model-to-model transformation is only applied to the predefined textual responses in the agent model, and only if the agent profile specifies changes related to nondeterministic personalization aspects. These include changes in *Language*, *Style*, *Sentence Length*, *Abbreviations*, *Language Complexity* and adapting the *Content* to fit the user profile. For each aspect, an external LLM is prompted to adapt all the predefined messages to fit the specific requested adaptation for the task.

Personalization aspects are applied sequentially: after each step, the resulting output replaces the previous version and is used as input to the next aspect. This sequential design constrains each LLM call to a single aspect, reducing prompt complexity and limiting cross-interference between aspects. Listing 1 reflects the used prompt when *Sentence Length* is set to concise, with other prompts following a similar structure, available in the replication package[2]. This process

[2] https://github.com/Aran30/LowCodeConversationalAgentPersonalization_replication.

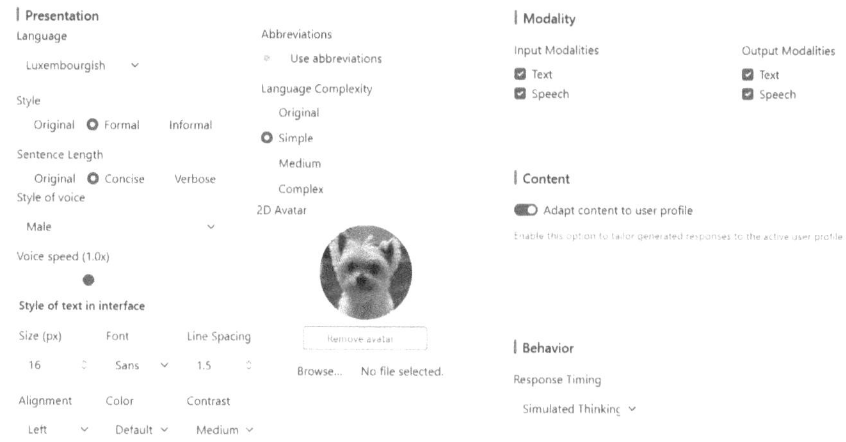

Fig. 6. Form-based configuration specification.

```
You are an editing engine focused on brevity. Rewrite each numbered
text to be concise while preserving the original meaning. Remove
redundancy, trim filler, and keep sentences short. Return the
rewritten texts as a numbered list in the same order.
```

Listing 1: Prompt for concise sentence generation.

outputs the base agent model with the personalized textual responses for a given agent configuration.

4.2 Runtime Personalization

Runtime personalization requires generating code that guarantees a personalized runtime interaction. For each personalization aspect, deterministic rules are applied, adding the necessary bits of code (de)activating or modifying certain agent features or wrapping agent calls to external services to make sure the call response is adapted to the personalization requirement.

Among the former we have *Style of Voice*, *Voice Speed*, *Style of text in interface*, *Avatar*, *Input and output Modality* and *Response Timing*. For the latter, a context prompt will be added describing the expected personalization aspects the LLM should adhere to when preparing the response. If necessary, a call to a second LLM to either confirm the adaptation is correct (e.g. checking the content is suitable for the target age) or forcing a reiteration of the adaptation (e.g. if the second LLM detects the adaptation is insufficient) can be also added.

Figure 7 illustrates some personalization aspects for our running example.

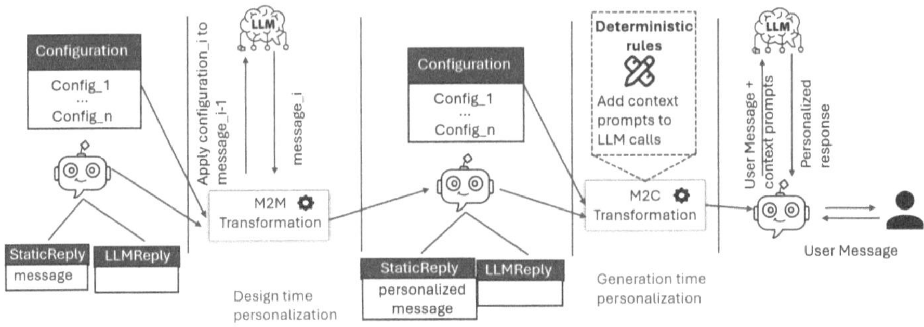

Fig. 7. Process for nondeterministic personalization aspects.

5 Tool Support

The complete pipeline has been implemented by extending the open source BESSER framework [2], which focuses on the low-code/no-code development of smart software. Note that the screenshots shown in Sect. 3 were taken directly from the tool. More precisely, we extended three components of the BESSER suite[3], which are all grouped in the replication repository[4].

First, we extended the BESSER Agentic Framework (BAF). In itself, the framework acts as a Python-based library to create CAs following a state-machine-like formalism. We extended it to be able to, at design time, specify agent variations of state actions and user profile, and at runtime, allow end-users to choose a profile to trigger the corresponding personalized interactions, visible in Fig. 8.

Second, we extended the core low-code BESSER platform. In particular, we added new transformations and generators to implement the personalizations as described in the Sect. 4.

Finally, we added new modeling perspectives to the BESSER Web Modeling editor to enable the graphical modeling of the profiles and the form-based configuration for the personalization.

6 Pilot Study

A pilot user study was conducted to evaluate our CA personalization tool regarding the following two research questions (RQs): perceived usability (RQ1) and perceived usefulness (RQ2). The study further aimed to explore whether users with different technical backgrounds could understand and complete the personalization workflow. The previously shared replication package also contains the study handout and questionnaire data.

[3] https://github.com/BESSER-PEARL.
[4] https://github.com/Aran30/LowCodeConversationalAgentPersonalization_replication.

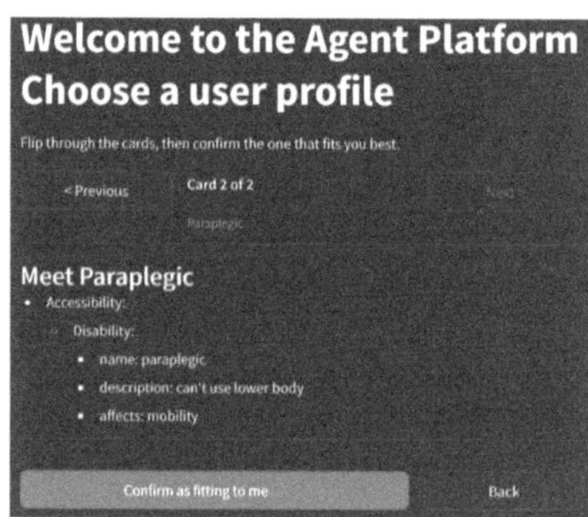

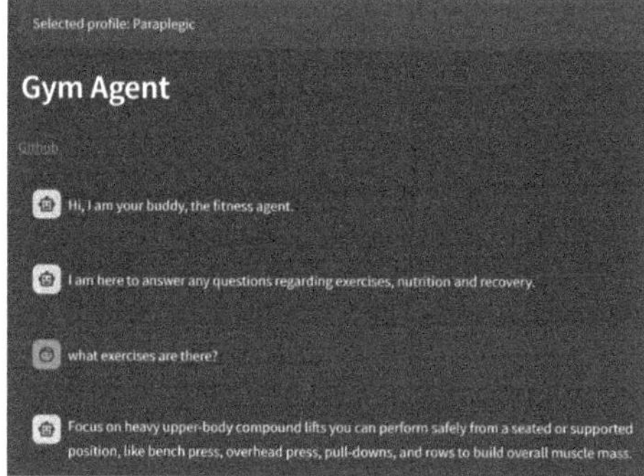

Fig. 8. Profile picker and chat with personalized agent for paraplegic user.

Participants. Eight participants were recruited for the exploratory study through direct contact to obtain the required profiles. Four participants had a technical background with prior experience in software development and modeling, while the other four had no programming experience (with the exception of one who reported limited experience) and no prior exposure to software modeling. This diversity was intentional, as the study aimed to explore early perceptions across the two target user profiles of the tool: expert (technical) and layman (non-technical).

Procedure. After signing a consent form, participants received a document describing the running example and the tasks required to complete one iteration of the CA personalization pipeline. Upon opening the web-based modeling tool, they were presented with a pre-modeled gym agent, which they inspected and explained to the study supervisor to confirm their understanding of the model's syntax and semantics. Next, based on task descriptions, participants created two predefined user profiles (*Elderly* and *Paraplegic*), defined two agent profiles, mapped user profile to agent profile, and triggered the M2M transformation to generate personalized models. Participants also compared the adapted and original models to identify the differences that occurred through the design time adaptations. Finally, they generated and interacted with the personalized agent. The tasks were designed to capture participants' initial understanding and impressions of the personalization process. Afterward, participants completed a questionnaire including the System Usability Scale (SUS) [7] and perceived usefulness and ease-of-use items adapted from the Technology Acceptance Model (TAM) [11], both widely used and validated instruments for measuring usability and technology acceptance. Responses were collected on a five-point Likert scale ranging from 1 ("Strongly Disagree") to 5 ("Strongly Agree").

Results. Table 2 contains the result of the questionnaire, the completion time, and the intervention count as averages based on the participants' profile. The answers from the questionnaires are normalized to 100 to match the standardized SUS score.

Table 2. Comparison of expert and layman evaluation results

Metric	Experts	Laymen
SUS Score	92.50	78.75
Perceived Usefulness (PU)	95.00	85.00
Perceived Ease of Use (PEOU)	96.60	71.60
Average completion time (min)	39.75	43.25
Average number of interventions (number)	2.25	3.75

RQ1 (Usability). The high average scores that reflect usability (SUS and PEOU) for both experts (SUS: 92.50, PEOU: 96.60) and laymen (SUS: 78.75, PEOU: 71.60) indicate good usability overall. Nonetheless, a clear difference in perception between experts and laymen (ΔSUS: 13.75, ΔPEOU: 25.00) is observed. A possible explanation would be the lack of familiarity with modeling tools for the laymen compared to the experts. In contrast, the delta between experts and laymen for completion time (Δ3.50) or interventions (Δ1.50) is very low, showcasing a similar performance. Independent of the participant profile, minor usability concerns have been noted. Most notably, we observed that it was unclear sometimes that elements in the user profile editor needed to be linked with each other, and the agent configuration page was perceived as overloaded, which increased the likelihood of overlooking elements. Addressing these and adding better documentation would increase usability.

RQ2 (Usefulness). Participants of both profiles perceived the pipeline to have a high usefulness, as evident by the high scores in the questionnaire (PU: 95.00 for experts and 85.00 for laymen). A small difference is observable between the profiles (ΔPU: 10), which possibly stems from modeling experts understanding and appreciating the advantages of the approach more than laymen.

Threats to Validity. Several factors may threaten the validity of the claims made in this study. Regarding internal validity, as participants were acquaintances of the study supervisor, there is a risk of response bias towards more positive evaluations, although they were explicitly encouraged to provide honest and critical feedback. Concerning construct validity, the instruction sheet may have provided substantial guidance, potentially reducing the perceived complexity. Yet, we argue this reflects the documentation typically provided in production-ready tools. For external and conclusion validity, the small sample size limits the generalizability of the results and the statistical power, meaning observed trends should be interpreted with caution and confirmed in larger replications.

7 Related Work

We comment on two types of related works: those focusing on a model-driven approach for the generation of CA and those proposing ad-hoc adaptation techniques for CAs. As we discuss, there are no model-driven approaches that target the automatic personalization of CAs that could be embedded in a web application.

Low-Code and Model-Driven Approaches for Developing CAs. Model-driven approaches have been applied in the past to the development of web and mobile UIs, see for instance, tools and languages such as IFML [6], OOWS [15] or UWE [18] among many others. Yet, these do not include a CA perspective, their support for specifying user profiles is limited to key-value pairs and the offered personalization is limited. Newer approaches focus more on personalization [25,26], albeit not targeting either CAs and only providing textual syntaxes, therefore not catered towards non-technical users.

There are also a few approaches targeting low-code development for CAs (see this SLR conducted by Ouaddi et al. [5]), though, similar to the approaches above, they do not cover personalization aspects. As an example, a recent no-code approach was proposed to enable the creation of voice CAs on top of existing web-pages as a plug-in [23]. The approach does not focus on personalization or catering to diverse user profiles.

Personalization in Agents. Personalizing CAs is not a novel topic in itself, as evident by the existence of SLRs covering this topic (e.g., [1,17] to name a few) that provide insights about techniques that exist or types of personalization and their benefits. Yet, tools that facilitate the creation of such personalized agents combining various existing personalization options are lacking. Our pipeline acts as an initial attempt to facilitate the creation of personalized CAs by leveraging technologies that showed positive results in the past in a way that non-technical users could benefit from.

8 Conclusions

This paper presented a pipeline for designing and generating personalized conversational agents using low-code and no-code principles. Our proposal enables the specification of user-specific agent profiles, linking users with customized agents derived from a core agent specification via a combination of deterministic transformations and LLM customizations.

As further work, we plan to increase the types of personalizations available and automatically propose personalization templates for the most common types of users. We also plan to extend the personalization to other types of UIs (e.g., for extended reality scenarios) and add some quality checks to the configuration process to detect potentially wrong or inconsistent personalization options. Finally, larger scale user studies shall be conducted to further validate the pipeline's usability, but also scalability and quality of generated personalization.

Acknowledgments. This work is supported by the Luxembourg National Research Fund (FNR) PEARL program, grant agreement 16544475.

References

1. Ait Baha, T., El Hajji, M., Es-Saady, Y., Fadili, H.: The power of personalization: a systematic review of personality-adaptive chatbots. SN Comput. Sci. **4**(5) (2023). https://doi.org/10.1007/s42979-023-02092-6
2. Alfonso, I., Conrardy, A., Sulejmani, A., Nirumand, A., Ul Haq, F., Gomez-Vazquez, M., et al.: Building Besser: an open-source low-code platform. In: International Conference on Business Process Modeling, Development and Support, pp. 203–212 (2024). https://doi.org/10.1007/978-3-031-61007-3_16
3. Amin Kuhail, M., Bahja, M., Al-Shamaileh, O., Thomas, J., Alkazemi, A., Negreiros, J.: Assessing the impact of chatbot-human personality congruence on user behavior: a chatbot-based advising system case. IEEE Access **12**, 71761–71782 (2024). https://doi.org/10.1109/ACCESS.2024.3402977
4. Baez, M., Cappiello, C., Cutrupi, C.M., Matera, M., Possaghi, I., Pucci, E., et al.: Supporting natural language interaction with the web. In: Web Engineering: 22nd International Conference, ICWE 2022, Bari, Italy, July 5–8, 2022, Proceedings, pp. 383–390 (2022). https://doi.org/10.1007/978-3-031-09917-5_26
5. Benaddi, L., Ouaddi, C., Jakimi, A., Chaibi, H., Chehri, A., Jeon, G., et al.: A survey on model-driven engineering and domain-specific languages for chatbot development: requirements, challenges and solutions. Expert Syst. **42**(10), e70124 (2025). https://doi.org/10.1111/exsy.70124
6. Brambilla, M., Fraternali, P.: Interaction Flow Modeling Language: Model-Driven UI Engineering of Web and Mobile Apps with IFML. Morgan Kaufmann (2014)
7. Brooke, J.: Sus: A "quick and dirty" usability scale. In: Usability Evaluation in Industry, pp. 189–194 (1996)
8. Cabot, J., Clarisó, R.: Low code for smart software development. IEEE Softw. **40**(1), 89–93 (2023). https://doi.org/10.1109/MS.2022.3211352
9. Conrardy, A., Capozucca, A., Cabot, J.: Towards a unified user modeling language for engineering human centered ai systems (2025). https://arxiv.org/abs/2505.24697
10. Conrardy, A., Capozucca, A., Cabot, J.: User modeling in model-driven engineering: a systematic literature review. J. Object Technol. **24**(2), 2:1–14 (2025). https://doi.org/10.5381/jot.2025.24.2.a12
11. Davis, F.D.: Perceived usefulness, perceived ease of use, and user acceptance of information technology. MIS Q. **13**(3), 319–340 (1989). https://doi.org/10.2307/249008
12. Di Ruscio, D., Kolovos, D., de Lara, J., Pierantonio, A., Tisi, M., Wimmer, M.: Low-code development and model-driven engineering: two sides of the same coin? Softw. Syst. Model. **21**(2), 437–446 (2022). https://doi.org/10.1007/s10270-021-00970-2
13. Fan, H., Poole, M.S.: What is personalization? Perspectives on the design and implementation of personalization in information systems. J. Organ. Comput. Electron. Comm. **16**(3–4), 179–202 (2006). https://doi.org/10.1080/10919392.2006.9681199
14. Feine, J., Gnewuch, U., Morana, S., Maedche, A.: A taxonomy of social cues for conversational agents. Int. J. Hum Comput Stud. **132**, 138–161 (2019). https://doi.org/10.1016/j.ijhcs.2019.07.009
15. Fons, J., Pelechano, V., Pastor, O., Valderas, P., Torres, V.: Applying the Oows model-driven approach for developing web applications. In: The Internet Movie Database Case Study, pp. 65–108. Springer, London (2008). https://doi.org/10.1007/978-1-84628-923-1_5

16. Huq, S.M., Maskeliūnas, R., Damaševičius, R.: Dialogue agents for artificial intelligence-based conversational systems for cognitively disabled: a systematic review. Disabil. Rehabil. Assist. Technol. **19**(3), 1059–1078 (2024). https://doi.org/10.1080/17483107.2022.2146768
17. Kocaballi, A.B., Berkovsky, S., Quiroz, J.C., Laranjo, L., Tong, H.L., Rezazadegan, D., et al.: The personalization of conversational agents in health care: Systematic review. J. Med. Internet Res. **21**(11), e15360 (2019). https://doi.org/10.2196/15360
18. Koch, N., Knapp, A., Zhang, G., Baumeister, H.: UML-Based Web Engineering, pp. 157–191. Springer (2008). https://doi.org/10.1007/978-1-84628-923-1_7
19. Li, C., Chen, M., Wang, J., Sitaram, S., Xie, X.: Culturellm: incorporating cultural differences into large language models. In: Advances in Neural Information Processing Systems, vol. 37, pp. 84799–84838 (2024). https://doi.org/10.52202/079017-2693
20. Murgia, E., Pera, M.S., Landoni, M., Huibers, T.: Children on ChatGPT readability in an educational context: myth or opportunity? In: Adjunct Proceedings of the 31st ACM Conference on User Modeling, Adaptation and Personalization, pp. 311–316 (2023). https://doi.org/10.1145/3563359.3596996
21. Nagarhalli, T.P., Vaze, V., Rana, N.K.: A review of current trends in the development of chatbot systems. In: 2020 6th International Conference on Advanced Computing and Communication Systems (ICACCS), pp. 706–710 (2020). https://doi.org/10.1109/ICACCS48705.2020.9074420
22. Namvarpour, M.M., Razi, A.: The art of talking machines: a comprehensive literature review of conversational user interfaces. In: Proceedings of the 7th ACM Conference on Conversational User Interfaces (2025). https://doi.org/10.1145/3719160.3736621
23. Ripa, G., et al.: Generating voice user interfaces from web sites. Behav. Inf. Technol. **43**(13), 3129–3152 (2024). https://doi.org/10.1080/0144929X.2023.2272192
24. Skuridin, A., Wynn, M.: Chatbot design and implementation: towards an operational model for chatbots. Information **15**(4) (2024). https://doi.org/10.3390/info15040226
25. Wickramathilaka, S., Grundy, J., Madampe, K., Haggag, O.: Adaptive and accessible user interfaces for seniors through model-driven engineering. Autom. Softw. Eng. **32**(2), 74 (2025). https://doi.org/10.1007/s10515-025-00547-z
26. Yigitbas, E., Jovanovikj, I., Biermeier, K., Sauer, S., Engels, G.: Integrated model-driven development of self-adaptive user interfaces. Softw. Syst. Model. **19**(5), 1057–1081 (2020). https://doi.org/10.1007/s10270-020-00777-7
27. Zhu, W., Liu, H., Dong, Q., Xu, J., Huang, S., Kong, L.: Multilingual machine translation with large language models: empirical results and analysis. In: Findings of the Association for Computational Linguistics: NAACL 2024, pp. 2765–2781 (2024). https://doi.org/10.18653/v1/2024.findings-naacl.176

LLM-Driven Orchestration of Pervasive Web Interfaces in Extended Reality

Luca Cordioli(✉), Andrea Pesciotti, Francesca Vittoria Rabiti, Federico Rosa, Desara Xhumari, and Maristella Matera

Department of Electronics, Information and Bioengineering, Politecnico di Milano, Milan, Italy
{luca.cordioli,maristella.matera}@polimi.it,
{andrea.pesciotti,francescavittoria.rabiti,federico3.rosa,
desara.xhumari}@mail.polimi.it

Abstract. In spatially complex and hand-busy contexts, traditional menu-based web browsing imposes interaction constraints. This paper extends a framework originally conceived for goal-driven web interfaces to eXtended Reality (XR) and discusses how LLMs can be leveraged to dynamically orchestrate pervasive interfaces for the Web, decomposing natural language intents into executable user interface components. A user study shows that AI-driven orchestration of XR Web interfaces supports effective interaction with low perceived workload, while highlighting open challenges in intent interpretation and context management.

Keywords: Goal-driven Web browsing · LLM-driven orchestration of Web Interfaces · eXtended Reality on the Web

1 Introduction

Large Language Models (LLMs), multimodal technologies, and conversational agents have the potential to change users' experiences on the Web, being able to support interactions that are more natural and flexible than traditional graphical user interfaces [10,12,14]. Yet, despite these advances, most users still interact with *static visual structures*: menus, buttons, and persistent controls that must be navigated, selected, and dismissed manually.

Prior work on adaptive, model-based, and generative interfaces explores how to customize or synthesize UIs in response to user needs [3,4]. However, these approaches assume that an interface exists first and is then adapted. Users remain responsible for navigating and managing interface state. In contrast, many real-world activities would be improved by systems being able to *know what matters in a given moment*. This observation motivates a shift from interface adaptation to *interface orchestration*, to treat user interfaces as ephemeral, task-scoped tools that appear, transform, and disappear as the task unfolds [5].

A. Mauri et al. (Eds.): ICWE 2026, LNCS 16625, pp. 62–77, 2026.
https://doi.org/10.1007/978-3-032-29372-5_5

In line with this trend, this paper proposes an approach for the orchestration of *intent-driven interfaces* for web-based immersive systems. Rather than embedding intelligence into a fixed user interface, we treat the interface itself as a dynamic artifact orchestrated by an AI agent. Importantly, the system operates over a predefined set of interface components and interaction primitives, and does not generate arbitrary interface structures at runtime. The agent interprets high-level user intents and task progression to instantiate, replace, or retire spatial interface components at runtime. Interfaces are shown only when relevant, remain visible only while useful, and are removed once their role is complete.

This design choice raises fundamental questions for human-centered web engineering. While ephemeral interfaces can reduce visual clutter and navigation overhead, they may also affect users' sense of control, predictability, and trust, all concerns particularly salient in AI-mediated interaction [1]. To address these aspects, this paper also discusses the results of a user study exploring how users perceive and experience intent-driven interface orchestration in hands-free immersive tasks. Based on the resulting insights, we distill design implications for this new paradigm. This work extends prior research on goal-driven interfaces [5] to XR environments, providing a concrete architectural instantiation and an exploratory evaluation in a hands-free scenario.

The paper is organized as follows. Section 2 discusses the main related works. Section 3 then describes our proposed architecture for orchestrating spatial UIs in XR environments. Sections 4 and 5 respectively report on the framework technical evaluation and a user study. Both evaluations were conducted on an intent-driven, hands-free XR application developed using the proposed architecture. Finally, Sect. 6 discusses the results and outlines our future work.

2 Background and Related Work

Model-Based and Adaptive UIs. Model-based UI engineering has investigated how abstract representations of interaction and task models can be used to generate concrete user interfaces that adapt across platforms and contexts. However, these approaches still rely on persistent interface structures that users must explicitly navigate. In contrast, intent-driven orchestration shifts attention from adapting persistent interfaces to managing the lifecycle of UI components as a function of task relevance, reducing the need for explicit navigation [5].

Ephemeral and Transient Interaction Techniques. This paradigm reduces visual complexity and interaction overhead by temporarily revealing interface elements, improving performance in visually rich environments [7,8,11]. However, it focuses on individual widgets or UI elements, leaving the UI structure unchanged.

Conversational and Multimodal Interfaces. Conversational interaction has long been studied as a natural modality for controlling interactive systems. Research on conversational web interfaces has identified recurring interaction patterns and design challenges associated with dialogue-based interaction on the Web [12].

More recent systems leverage LLMs to translate natural language commands into executable actions, enabling more expressive and fluid interaction [10,14].

These works demonstrate the potential of language-based interaction. However, they typically operate within predefined interface structures, focusing on command interpretation and execution rather than managing interface presence or lifecycle. Prior work has also emphasized the importance of predictability, transparency, and user control in AI-mediated interfaces [1]. These concerns become particularly salient when interfaces are dynamically modified at runtime, highlighting the need for principled orchestration mechanisms.

Generative and Malleable User Interfaces. Recent research has explored generative and malleable user interfaces, in which AI systems synthesize or reshape interface structures from high-level specifications or natural language input [3,4]. These approaches emphasize flexibility and user agency, allowing users to iteratively explore and customize interface layouts and behaviors.

While generative UI approaches are well suited to exploratory or design-oriented scenarios, they often assume interaction contexts in which users actively engage in interface manipulation. In contrast, hands-free and immersive tasks place a premium on minimizing interaction effort and cognitive overhead rather than enabling interface exploration.

Hands-Free Interaction and Assistive Interfaces in XR. Extended Reality (XR) head-mounted displays have been explored for hands-free task assistance in procedural scenarios. Interaction in XR differs from desktop settings: users operate in hands-busy contexts with limited manual input, requiring continuous attention allocation between physical and virtual content. Persistent virtual panels and overlays risk increasing visual clutter in immersive environments. Transient UI components have been shown to reduce clutter and improve immersion in visually rich contexts [7,11]. To mitigate these issues, existing XR systems for task assistance typically rely on predefined interface layouts or step-based overlays that remain visible throughout task execution [2]. While effective in delivering guidance, such approaches provide limited support for dynamically managing interface presence as task context changes, often requiring users to explicitly control when interfaces appear or disappear.

Recent work has explored automatic adaptation of XR interfaces based on task and contextual factors. Lindlbauer et al. [9] use combinatorial optimization to decide *which level of detail* to display for predefined applications based on cognitive load and viewing context. However, their approach adapts *within* a fixed set of applications determined at design time—optimizing detail levels rather than interface composition. In parallel, LLMs have been integrated into XR systems to enable natural language interaction [6,13]. These systems use LLMs for command interpretation but maintain static interface structures where the LLM executes actions within a predefined UI. In contrast, our work uses LLM-interpreted intent to orchestrate interface *lifecycle*: determining which interface compositions are instantiated, when they replace existing ones, and when they are withdrawn based on task progression—treating interface presence itself as a consequence of conversational context rather than a design-time decision.

Overall, this body of work highlights a gap in current XR interaction models: while natural language and AI increasingly support *what* actions users can perform, less attention has been devoted to systematically managing *when* interfaces should be instantiated, maintained, or withdrawn in hands-free immersive scenarios. Addressing this gap requires treating interface presence and components' lifecycle as first-class design concerns.

3 Intent-as-Boundary Architecture for Interface Orchestration in XR

We propose an intent-as-boundary architecture for orchestrating spatial user interfaces in XR environments, derived from a framework for orchestrating intent-driven interfaces on the Web [5], but specialized for spatial XR UIs. The architecture enforces a separation between probabilistic intent interpretation and deterministic interface execution. It is grounded in three guiding principles that define architectural constraints on how interface components are instantiated, replaced, and dismissed at runtime.

Interface as a Consequence of Intent. Interface components are treated as consequences of user intent rather than prerequisites for action. User intent is interpreted and represented as a typed, declarative signal that does not directly manipulate interface state. Task-relevant operations are executed through deterministic client-side logic, while interface components are instantiated only when they contribute to task understanding or execution.

Layered Interface Lifecycle Management. Spatial interfaces are organized according to a layered lifecycle model that governs their visibility and coexistence semantics. This lifecycle is enforced by deterministic client-side orchestration rules and is based on the following layers:

- **Persistent Layer:** UI components that remain visible across task phases (e.g., active timers) and are not affected by changes in task focus (Fig. 1a).
- **Main Layer:** Mutually exclusive UI components that occupy central focus and reflect the current task state (e.g., a step-by-step guide or a list-based interface) (Fig. 1b).
- **Overlay Layer:** Transient UI components that provide short-lived information (e.g., feedback) and automatically dismiss after a predefined duration (Fig. 1c).

Automatic Context Restoration. To support fluid multi-turn interaction, the system preserves interface context across short conversational interruptions. When a temporary overlay is displayed in response to a tangential query, the previously active main interface is restored after the overlay is dismissed. This restoration mechanism supports single-level context recovery and is designed to handle brief, non-nested interruptions without requiring explicit recovery commands.

3.1 The Request–Response Cycle

Figure 2 illustrates the requestresponse cycle underlying the proposed architecture. The cycle is designed around a strict separation between intent interpretation and interface execution, with responsibilities clearly divided between stateless server-side components and deterministic client-side orchestration.

(a) Persistent layer (b) Main layer (c) Overlay layer

Fig. 1. Interface layers arranged hierarchically (top–down).

Each interaction follows a requestresponse cycle: the client sends the user utterance and a snapshot of the application state to a stateless backend, which returns a structured intent processed by the client to update the interface.

3.2 Client-Side Orchestration

The client is implemented as a WebXR application using a declarative rendering paradigm. Its role is to manage application state, dispatch intents, and translate intent-derived state transitions into spatial interface behavior.

At the entry point of the client, a *State Manager* acts as a context aggregation mechanism. It monitors the applicationvs state (e.g., active tasks, current step, and other interface-relevant data). When an interaction is triggered, the client freezes a consistent state snapshot, packages it with the transcribed user utterance, and sends all these data to the back-end.

Once a structured intent is received back from the server, the client applies deterministic orchestration rules that map the intent to *UI state transitions*. An *Interface Manager* is responsible for mapping the captured context onto concrete spatial UI components. Decisions are derived exclusively from the intent-driven state through declarative, slot-based rules rather than imperative scene manipulation: persistent components are rendered independently of task focus, main-layer components are selected based on the task and context in a mutually exclusive way, and overlay components are transient, time-bounded, and do not alter the underlying interface state. This component then manages intent-driven state transitions by mounting or unmounting spatial components, enforcing rendering constraints.

3.3 Server-Side Intent Interpretation

Intent interpretation is handled by a stateless server-side component, the *Reasoning & Intent Extractor*, exposed as a web API. Each client request creates an ephemeral session and includes a complete snapshot of the application state, including active tasks, interface-relevant data, and the transcribed user utterance.

The reasoning handler uses an LLM with structured function calling to map natural language input to intents represented as typed actions. The system prompt encodes orchestration constraints that regulate interface behavior, e.g., an intent should trigger a data update only versus a full interface transition.

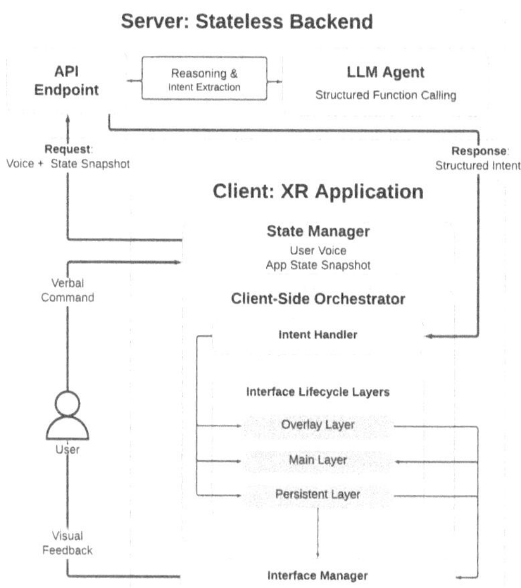

Fig. 2. Overview of the intent-driven orchestration workflow. The client transmits a snapshot of yje application state to a stateless backend, which returns structured intents. The client then translates structured intents into deterministic state transitions that govern spatial interface rendering.

The backend does not execute intents nor mutate application state. It acts solely as an interpreter that maps natural language input to declarative intent representations, which are later processed by the client. Before returning the response, the reasoning handler verifies the structural validity of the LLM output with respect to the expected function schema. Semantic validation and error recovery are intentionally limited and discussed as architectural trade-offs.

LLM Interaction Design. The LLM is used for stateless intent interpretation via structured function calling. It receives the user utterance together with a snapshot of the current application state. A predefined set of callable tools constrains the space of structured actions. When a tool is selected, its arguments are mapped to a normalized intent consumed by deterministic client-side logic. If no tool is invoked, the model returns a textual response handled as a generic query intent.

3.4 Intent-to-Interface Mapping

On the client, the extracted intents are mapped to interface behavior through an explicit set of deterministic orchestration rules that govern interface lifecycle transitions. These rules jointly consider the intent type, its parameters, and the current application state to determine admissible interface configurations. For instance, intents that modify application state result in transient overlays that provide feedback without altering the active main-layer. In contrast, inspection or navigation intents replace the active main-layer interface, while task-progress intents instantiate new main layer interfaces and preserve persistent components.

Crucially, the orchestration function is deterministic: given the same intent and application state snapshot, it always produces the same interface configuration, despite the probabilistic nature of intent interpretation.

Intent Representation and Orchestration. User utterances are mapped by the LLM to structured intents via function calling, encoding an action and its parameters (e.g., {`''intent'':''NAVIGATE'',''direction'':''next''`}). On the client, intents are processed through deterministic rules that map intent types to interface transitions, such as updating the current view (`NAVIGATE`), replacing the main interface (`SUGGEST_RECIPE`), or adding persistent components (`TIMER`).

Example Interaction. For instance, the utterance "Set a timer for 10 min" produces {`''intent'':''TIMER'',''seconds'':600`}, which results in adding a timer to the persistent layer without interrupting the current task, optionally accompanied by a transient overlay notification.

3.5 Implementation Stack

The current framework prototype uses web-native technologies, i.e., Next.js with unified client–server routing, built on React and TypeScript using the App Router architecture. The intent interpretation is based on an LLM with function calling and explicit JSON schemas, implemented using the OpenAI gpt-4o-mini model for intent decomposition and tool invocation. The application state is managed on the client, through a modular state store with isolated feature slices, implemented via a lightweight client-side state management library (Zustand). Persistence is achieved through a relational database accessed via an ORM for synchronized task data, using a PostgreSQL backend managed through Prisma.

The I/O layer is handled through local wake-word detection and browser-based audio capture combined with cloud-based speech-to-text for the voice interactions, relying on the OpenAI whisper-1 model for speech-to-text transcription, and through WebXR with declarative 3D rendering via React-based bindings for the XR interactions, built on top of Three.js and WebXR bindings.

All the UI components execute within the browser runtime of a standalone XR headset: intent-driven UI orchestration can be thus realized using standard web technologies without relying on platform-specific SDKs.

3.6 The Cooking Assistant App

To illustrate the framework in a real-world scenario, we consider the Cooking Assistant application that we employed in our experimental setup (see Sect. 5). The app supports hands-free recipe retrieval and guided cooking within an XR environment through a set of domain-specific callable components:

- `SUGGEST_RECIPE`, `GENERATE_RECIPE`, and `NAVIGATE` are components in the "main" layer enabling the retrieval of recipe suggestions, the display and start of a guided cooking session, and the preparation step progression.
- `SHOPPING_LIST and FRIDGE_INVENTORY` are further "main" components to display the ingredient lists.
- `MANAGE_INGREDIENTS` are "overlay" components for adding or removing ingredients, with pop-ups for confirmation of actions.
- `CLARIFICATION` is an "overlay" asking for clarifications when the user's utterance is not understood.
- `TIMER` is a "persistent" component creating and managing cooking timers.

A prompt such as *"What can I cook with these ingredients?"*, expressed through a voice request combined with visual grounding (i.e., by looking at or selecting the ingredients available in the physical space), is resolved by the LLM through `SUGGEST_RECIPE`, which renders a list of candidate recipes in the main interaction layer. A subsequent command (e.g., *"Open the cheesecake recipe"*) updates the same component to display a structured preview of the selected recipe. When the user issues *"Let's start"*, the LLM returns a `GENERATE_RECIPE` intent, which instantiates the guided cooking interface and activates the first preparation step.

Navigation commands such as *"Next step"* are mapped to `NAVIGATE`, resulting in deterministic updates of the active step within the ongoing session. Timer-related utterances (e.g., *"Set a timer for 10 min"*) invoke the `TIMER` component, creating a concurrent countdown without interrupting the cooking flow. Similarly, inventory-related requests (e.g., *"Scan the fridge"*) activate the `FRIDGE_INVENTORY` component within the same orchestration model.

Ingredient updates (e.g., *"Remove sugar"*) invoke the `MANAGE_INGREDIENTS` overlay component, prompting confirmation pop-ups to ensure safe and explicit state transitions. When the user's utterance is ambiguous or underspecified, the LLM activates the `CLARIFICATION` component, generating a contextual prompt to disambiguate the intent before proceeding with orchestration.

4 Technical Validation

We conducted a quantitative performance analysis aimed to isolate the processing time required by the three main phases of the interaction loop described in Sect. 3: (i) *Intent Extraction*, (ii) *Content Planning*, and (iii) *Component Selection*. The validation was performed in a controlled local environment using the implementation stack described in Sect. 3.5. The application ran on a desktop machine equipped with an Intel i5-13600KF processor, while the XR interaction was deployed on a Meta Quest 3 head-mounted display. Data were collected over $N = 10$ independent execution cycles of the test suite.

Since the backend utilizes a single-shot LLM transaction to perform both intent classification and content generation, we adopted a *differential analysis*:

- **Baseline Measurement:** We measure the latency of simple retrieval tasks (e.g., *"Scan the fridge"*, *"Check inventory"*) that require intent classification but minimal or no generative content. This establishes the physiological baseline for the Intent Extraction phase.
- **Differential Calculation:** We measure the latency of complex generative tasks (e.g., *"Generate cooking steps"*, *"Provide recipe based on those ingredients"*) and subtract the baseline. The resulting difference represents the overhead attributed to the *Content Planning* phase (token generation).
- **Client-Side Measurement:** We instrument the client-side router to measure the exact execution time of the *Component Selection* logic, which maps the structured intent to the specific React component.

Results. Table 1 provides a breakdown of the time elapsed from the initial user prompt to the final execution of the spatial interface transition. Specifically, it reports the average execution time and standard deviation for the **Intent Extraction** (Phase 1), the estimated overhead for **Content Planning** (Phase 2), and the deterministic **Component Selection** on the client-side (Phase 3).

Table 1. Average values (N = 10) for the System Latency by phase.

Phase	Description	Avg Time	Std. Dev
1. Intent Extraction	Baseline latency for intent classification and round-trip networking.	924.37 ms	±393.43 ms
2. Content Planning	Estimated overhead for generating complex structured task data.	$\approx$ 4.04 s	-
3. Component Selection	Client-side deterministic mapping of intent to UI components.	0.0004 ms	$<$ 0.001 ms

The data highlights a clear dichotomy in the system's performance profile. The **Component Selection** phase (Phase 3) exhibits negligible latency (< 0.01 ms), showing that in the proposed *Client-Side Orchestration* architecture, the deterministic logic used to mount, unmount, or switch spatial components introduces zero perceptible overhead, ensuring that the interface remains responsive as soon as the intent is received. Conversely, the **Content Planning** phase (Phase 2) represents the significant bottleneck, adding approximately 5 s to the interaction loop for complex tasks. This shows that the perceived delay is not due to the orchestration logic itself, but is intrinsic to the sequential token generation process of current LLMs. Then, Phase 1 (**Intent Extraction**) sets an interaction floor of approximately 1.8 s, which aligns with typical response times for cloud-based LLM APIs.

5 User Study

A formative user study was conducted to explore how an intent-driven XR app supports hands-free interaction in a realistic task context. For this purpose, a cooking assistant was developed. The study focused on identifying recurring interaction patterns, breakdowns, and user expectations when interacting with the proposed orchestration model in a realistic task context. The evaluation in particular addressed the following dimensions:

- **Task Effectiveness**, based on task completion and observed errors.
- **Perceived Workload**, measured through the NASA-TLX index.
- **Perceived Usability**, measured through the System Usability Scale (SUS).

Experimental Design. The study involved 7 participants with different levels of experience with voice-controlled assistants. The study was conducted in a controlled environment simulating a kitchen workspace. The setup included a headset running the cooking assistant prototype and a table with the required ingredients and utensils.

The task consisted of preparing a no-bake cheesecake served in a glass, chosen to represent a realistic hands-busy cooking scenario while remaining simple and time-bounded. The task required participants to interact exclusively through voice commands while visually following the instructions provided by the system. The task involved identifying available ingredients, requesting a recipe and following the preparation steps using voice commands.

To ensure consistent experimental conditions across sessions, ingredient identification and recipe provisioning were handled using a Wizard-of-Oz approach. Since these functionalities normally rely on AI models for image-based ingredient recognition and content generation, and may produce variable outputs, fixed hardcoded ingredients and recipe steps were used during the study. This ensured that all participants interacted with identical content, allowing the evaluation to focus on the interaction and interface behavior.

Procedure. Each session lasted approximately 30 min. At the outset, participants were informed about the study's purpose and asked to provide informed consent. They then completed a questionnaire that collected demographic information and their familiarity with voice-based technologies and cooking activities.

Participants received an introduction to the system, including an explanation of the voice-based interaction modality and the hand gesture required to activate the assistant. The overall workflow of the application, consisting of ingredient detection, recipe suggestion and guided cooking, was explained without providing examples of command formulations: participants had to rely on their own expectations and natural language strategies during interaction. In a brief practice phase, participants tested the assistant activation and issued a simple, unrelated voice command to become familiar with the interaction and the headset, and ensure the device was correctly positioned and comfortable to wear.

Participants then carried out the cooking task while wearing the HDM. Throughout the task, the experimenters documented interaction-related observations, focusing on encountered problems and interaction errors such as command repetitions and recovery attempts. Video recordings were collected to enable later analysis of interaction behavior. After completing the task, participants filled out the NASA-TLX and SUS questionnaires. The session concluded with an open feedback phase, during which they were invited to share comments about their experience, perceived difficulties, and overall impressions of the system, as well as to reflect on how the interaction compared to their usual methods for consulting recipes (e.g., cookbooks or mobile devices).

Results for Task Effectiveness. All the participants were able to successfully complete the assigned tasks in a limited time (less than 10 min). An intent recognition failure occurred at least once per session when users attempted to navigate recipe steps employing context-dependent statements (e.g., *"I have added the butter"*) instead of explicit commands (e.g., *"Next step"*). In all other cases, the system correctly mapped user utterances to the intended components. The study does not include a formal measurement of intent recognition accuracy; observed errors and recovery behaviors provide indicative evidence of how user utterances were interpreted.

Results for the Perceived Usability and Cognitive Load. The SUS questionnaires suggest a generally positive perceived usability and relatively low perceived workload. The average score was M = 77.86 with variance = 80.06 (SD = 8.95), ranging from 6085. This suggests that participants generally perceived the interface as usable, with moderate variability across individual experiences.

The mean value for the NASA-TLX index was M = 13.93/100 with variance = 207.11 (SD = 14.39). It indicates a low overall workload, but the relatively high variance shows uneven experiences. Across the subscales, *frustration* (M = 1.71/20) and *effort* (M = 2.14/20) were generally low, while *mental and physical demand* were slightly higher but still modest (33.6/20). These results suggest that the hands-free approach can support guided cooking with low perceived effort for most users, while still affecting some users due to factors such as input or commanding difficulties, delays, and XR comfort issues.

Qualitative Analysis. The analysis of post-task feedback and observational notes was conducted through thematic grouping of recurring observations, highlighting the following themes related to the interaction flow.

Hands-Free Guidance and Reduced Interaction Overhead. Participants consistently valued the ability to access instructions without using their hands. The step-by-step guidance was described as intuitive and supportive allowing participants to focus on the physical task rather than on interface management. Some participants noted that having instructions continuously available without requiring manual interaction was advantageous compared to consulting a phone.

Context Enrichment as a Perceived Advantage. Participants highlighted the ingredient identification and recipe suggestion as major benefits compared to traditional recipe lookup methods. They perceived system's ability to tailor the recipe based on available ingredients as reducing the need for explicit input. They felt the assistant was aware of the ongoing task context.

Breakdowns in Implicit Progress and task Understanding. Despite the perceived benefits, participants frequently expected the system to infer task progress from contextual cues or brief utterances. Phrases such as *"I'm done"* were often not interpreted as signals to advance to the next step, requiring users to rely on explicit navigation commands (e.g., *"Next"*). This behavior was perceived as rigid and less natural, indicating that accurate intent recognition alone was insufficient to meet expectations of cooperative task progression.

Activation and Control Friction. Several interaction issues were related to the activation mechanism. While the pinch gesture used to activate voice input became easier with use, participants reported that having to explicitly manage microphone activation disrupted interaction flow. Requests for alternative activations, such as wake words or fully hands-free modes, were frequently reported.

Hardware-Related Constraints and Trust Considerations. Some limitations were attributed to the XR hardware rather than to the interface orchestration itself, including visual discomfort (e.g., grey hands), motion sickness, and perceived delays. Trust and acceptability concerns also emerged: one participant expressed strong reluctance to use a system involving continuous visual sensing, highlighting privacy concerns that may affect adoption independently of usability.

6 Discussion and Conclusion

The work described in this paper is an exploratory contribution towards defining AI-driven interface orchestration in XR. The proposed architecture aims to illustrate how intent-driven orchestration can be operationalized using web-native technologies, and how interface presence and lifecycle can be managed as a function of task relevance, also in hands-free immersive scenarios. The conducted evaluation highlights the technical feasibility of UI component orchestration in XR environments and the general acceptability by the final users of the resulting interaction paradigm. The emerging limitations in particular highlight challenges that can help identify interesting future directions to consolidate the paradigm.

Participants frequently expected the system to infer task progress and intent from contextual cues or short utterances (e.g., indicating completion of a step), but such implicit commands were not consistently recognized. As a result, users often had to rely on explicit navigation commands, which some perceived as rigid and less natural. This highlights a key limitation of intent-driven orchestration when intent is interpreted in isolation from task-level context: accurate command recognition alone is insufficient to support cooperative, step-based activities.

Issues related to command activation and control further affected the interaction. Although the gesture-based activation mechanism became easier with use, participants expressed a preference for more flexible or implicit activation strategies. From an orchestration perspective, these findings suggest that activation and listening strategies should be treated as first-class concerns and explicitly integrated with intent understanding and task state, rather than as low-level interaction mechanisms.

Trust and acceptability also emerged in relation to AI-mediated orchestration. Participants' concerns about continuous sensing and system autonomy indicate that effective command understanding alone is not sufficient: users also need to understand when and why the system listens, interprets, and acts. Clearer feedback about system state and interpretation could help align user expectations with system behavior and increase confidence in AI-driven orchestration.

System latency affected user experience; future work should focus on streaming LLM responses rather than further optimizing client-side rendering.

Overall, the findings suggest that intent-based UIs orchestration can effectively support hands-free, sequential tasks such as cooking. However, its success depends on moving beyond command execution toward orchestration models that integrate task context, implicit progress inference, and transparent control.

6.1 Design Implications

Balance Explicit Commands with Cooperative Task Progression. Designers face a trade-off between predictability and naturalness in sequential task contexts. Explicit commands (e.g., "Next step") improve reliability and reduce ambiguity, but participants frequently expected the system to infer task progress from contextual cues (e.g., "I'm done"), leading to breakdowns when these were not recognized. Systems should anchor intent interpretation to explicit task state while progressively supporting implicit progress signals where recognition confidence is sufficiently high, providing graceful fallbacks when implicit input fails.
Extend Context Recovery Beyond Single-Level Interruptions. Persistent components (e.g., timers) should not disrupt the active interface layer. More broadly, orchestration models should support recovery from nested or parallel interruptions, not only from simple overlay dismissals, to handle realistic task complexity. Participants benefited from being able to continue the task without losing context when additional actions were triggered, but more complex interruption patterns remain an open design challenge.
Provide Transparency and Feedback on System Interpretation. Systems should make explicit when they are listening, interpreting, and acting, and provide immediate feedback on how user input is processed. In XR orchestration contexts, users should understand not only what the system did, but when and why

a given interface layer was instantiated or dismissed. This helps align user expectations with system behavior and increases trust in AI-mediated interaction.

Treat Activation as an Orchestration Concern. Interaction activation mechanisms should be treated as first-class orchestration concerns rather than low-level interaction details. Participants reported that explicit gesture-based activation disrupted task flow, and frequently requested more implicit or wake-word-based alternatives. Activation strategy should be integrated with task state and intent understanding, so that the system listens when appropriate rather than requiring users to manage microphone control manually.

Optimize for Perceived Latency Through Intermediate Feedback. Systems should prioritize perceived responsiveness over raw processing speed. The dominant latency source in the proposed architecture is LLM token generation, not client-side orchestration. Designers should therefore provide immediate intermediate feedback upon activation (e.g., an acknowledgment signal or partial response) to bridge the gap between user input and interface transition, reducing the perceived cost of intent processing delays.

6.2 Scope and Limitations

This work is intentionally scoped as an architectural and exploratory contribution, rather than as a comprehensive empirical validation of AI-driven interface orchestration in XR. The proposed architecture aims to illustrate how intent-driven orchestration can be operationalized using web-native technologies, and how interface presence and lifecycle can be managed as a function of task relevance in hands-free immersive scenarios.

Evaluation Scope. The user study was designed as a formative evaluation to surface recurring interaction patterns, breakdowns, and user expectations. As such, it does not aim to provide statistically generalizable results or comparative performance claims. The limited number of participants also reflects that it is intended to support qualitative analysis of interaction behaviors.

Wizard-of-Oz Components. Some app functionalities, such as ingredient recognition and recipe provisioning, were implemented using a Wizard-of-Oz approach to ensure consistent experimental conditions across participants. This choice was made to isolate and evaluate the proposed orchestration mechanisms, independent of the variability introduced by computer vision or content-generation. The study does not cover the accuracy of vision perception or generation components.

Domain Specificity. The prototype and evaluation focus on a single procedural task domain, namely guided cooking. Cooking was selected as a representative hands-busy scenario that requires sequential guidance, frequent context updates, and minimal manual interaction. While the discussed architectural patterns are not inherently domain-specific, the current evaluation does not claim generalization to other domains characterized by non-sequential tasks, nested interruptions, or long-term conversational memory.

6.3 Outlook

This work contributes an architectural perspective and empirical insights that can inform future research on AI-driven orchestration of UI components on the Web. Promising directions include extending orchestration models to support richer task representations, hierarchical context recovery, and multi-domain scenarios, and exploring more explicit and formal representations of interface lifecycles. Treating interface orchestration as a first-class design concern is not merely an implementation strategy, but a foundational shift toward more adaptive, lightweight, and human-centered immersive interaction models for the Web.

Acknowledgment. This research is partially funded by Google award for the research "Direct Manipulation in Multimodal Intent-Based User Interfaces".

References

1. Amershi, S., et al.: Guidelines for human-ai interaction. In: Proceedings of the CHI 2019 (2019)
2. Bohus, D., Andrist, S., Saw, N., Paradiso, A., Chakraborty, I., Rad, M.: SIGMA: an open-source interactive system for mixed-reality task assistance research – extended abstract. In: 2024 IEEE Conference on Virtual Reality and 3D User Interfaces, Abstracts and Workshops (VRW), pp. 889–890. IEEE, Orlando, FL, USA (2024)
3. Cao, Y., Jiang, P., Xia, H.: Generative and malleable user interfaces with generative and evolving task-driven data model. In: Proceedings of the CHI 2025 (2025)
4. Chen, X.A., Knearem, T., Li, Y.: The GenUI study: exploring the design of generative UI tools to support UX practitioners and beyond. In: Proceedings of the 2025 ACM Designing Interactive Systems Conference, pp. 1179–1196 (2025)
5. Cordioli, L., Matera, M.: From navigation to intention: reframing the web experience through goal-driven interfaces. In: 2026 ACM Conference on the World Wide Web (WebConf 2026) (2026)
6. De La Torre, F., Fang, C.M., Huang, H., Banburski-Fahey, A., Amores Fernandez, J., Lanier, J.: LLMR: real-time prompting of interactive worlds using large language models. In: Proceedings of CHI 2024. ACM (2024)
7. Döring, T., Sylvester, A., Schmidt, A.: Ephemeral user interfaces: valuing the aesthetics of interface components that do not last. Interactions **20**(4), 32–37 (2013)
8. Findlater, L., Moffatt, K., McGrenere, J., Dawson, J.: Ephemeral adaptation: the use of gradual onset to improve menu selection performance. In: Proceedings of CHI 2009, pp. 1655–1664. ACM, Boston MA USA (2009)
9. Lindlbauer, D., Feit, A.M., Hilliges, O.: Context-aware online adaptation of mixed reality interfaces. In: Proceedings of the 32nd ACM Symposium on User Interface Software and Technology, pp. 147–160. ACM, New Orleans LA USA (2019)
10. Masson, D., Malacria, S., Casiez, G., Vogel, D.: DirectGPT: a direct manipulation interface to interact with large language models. In: Proceedings of CHI 2024, ACM (2024)
11. Patterson, D., Costain, S.: The effectiveness of transient user interface components. User Interfaces **162** (2015)

12. Pucci, E., Possaghi, I., Cutrupi, C.M., Báez, M., Cappiello, C., Matera, M.: Defining patterns for a conversational web. In: Proceedings of CHI 2023, pp. 118:1–118:17. ACM (2023)
13. Srinidhi, S., Lu, E., Rowe, A.: XaiR: An XR platform that integrates large language models with the physical world. In: Proceedings of ISMAR 2024, pp. 759–767. IEEE (2024)
14. Yang, J.J., Shi, Y.: ReactGenie: a development framework for complex multimodal interactions using large language models. In: Proceedings of the of CHI 2024, ACM (2024)

Console Clutter: A Cross-Browser Measurement of Console Messages

Thomas Helbrecht[1(✉)] and Jannis Rautenstrauch[2]

[1] Saarland University, Saarbrücken, Germany
research@thomashelbrecht.de
[2] CISPA Helmholtz Center for Information Security, Saarbrücken, Germany
jannis.rautenstrauch@cispa.de

Abstract. Anybody who opened the browser developer tools on a random website was likely shocked by the wall of warnings and errors while the visited website appeared to function correctly. Although the developer tools and the contained *console tab* have existed in modern browsers for more than ten years and are regularly used by web developers and power users, there is limited information on the quantity and nature of messages developers encounter when opening the console, and whether these messages differ between browsers.

We close this research gap by performing the first systematic analysis of the browser console message ecosystem across the three main browser engines (Blink, Gecko, WebKit) on the landing pages of 51,984 websites. In total, we collected 2,088,416 messages, averaging 13.39 messages per website, with a maximum of 10,143 messages on one website in Firefox. While developer-caused messages (e.g., `console.log`) appear similarly across browsers, browser-caused messages (e.g., Cookie warnings or Content Security Policy errors) are strikingly different in both content and amount. With our in-depth analysis, we discover how console messages can reveal common misconfigurations and implementation issues. Lastly, we open-source our measurement framework to enable further research into the browser console message ecosystem.

Keywords: Console messages · Web measurement · Web debugging · Browser developer tools · Cross-browser analysis

1 Introduction

In 2025, 6.04 billion people used the internet [15] to surf more than 1.3 billion websites [22]. To allow web developers to better debug websites, browsers introduced developer tools such as the browser console as far back as 2006 [12].

Anecdotal evidence shows that developers are annoyed by confusing messages and differences between browsers [10,24], however, there is no systematic evaluation of message differences across browsers. To close this research gap, we perform the first systematic analysis of the browser developer tools message

A. Mauri et al. (Eds.): ICWE 2026, LNCS 16625, pp. 78–93, 2026.
https://doi.org/10.1007/978-3-032-29372-5_6

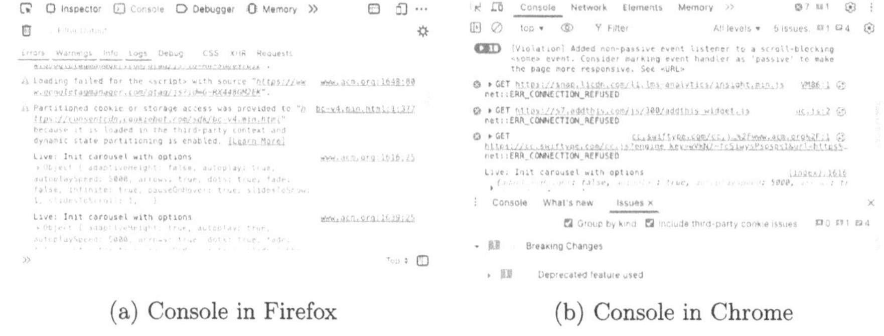

(a) Console in Firefox (b) Console in Chrome

Fig. 1. Browser console excerpts when visiting https://www.acm.org/.

ecosystem. We created a framework to comprehensively collect *console messages* available in the developer tools across all three major browser engines, collecting both messages emitted by websites using the Console API as well as warnings and errors produced by the browser. We then perform a large-scale measurement study across 51,984 landing pages in all three browsers collecting a total of 2,088,416 messages out of which 1,557,329 are browser-caused and 531,087 belong to developer-caused Console API calls. During our in-depth analysis of the collected messages, we discovered significant browser differences with Firefox being more verbose in the total number of messages. We also reveal how console messages can be used as a proxy to discover implementation issues on websites.

To summarize, our paper makes the following contributions:

- We designed and implemented an open-source framework [13] to collect messages from the developer tools, which can differentiate between browser-caused and developer-caused messages (see Sect. 3).
- We performed the first large-scale measurement of the browser console ecosystem on 51,984 landing pages in Chromium, Firefox and Safari (see Sect. 4).
- We extracted insights from our in-depth analysis, discovering vast differences across the browsers in both type and amount of messages (see Sect. 5).

2 Background: The Browser Console

Early browsers included the *view source* functionality to allow users to see the HTML source code of a website as early as 1992. Later, many developers used `alert` calls to debug their applications [14]. However, with the success of the Web 2.0 more advanced debugging capabilities were required and the first browsers included what is now known as the *browser developer tools* in 2006 [12]. Although the feature set differs between browsers, all provide core functionalities such as a web inspector for viewing DOM hierarchy. Crucially, they include the *browser console*, which displays messages created using the Console API (e.g., `console.log`) and other messages about page problems such as JavaScript errors. Figure 1 shows the browser console when visiting the ACM homepage in Firefox and Chrome.

Modern browsers support different types of console messages (see Fig. 1), visualized using different colors, icons, and additional information. The types of supported messages, their visual and internal representation is not standardized. Still, we can distinguish three types of console messages: *developer-caused messages*, *browser-caused messages*, and *page errors*, and describe the structure of these messages using the following three data points:

- **Content:** The content of the message that is displayed in the browser console. Modern browsers have pretty-printing capabilities and e.g., can render clickable URLs or display interactive JavaScript objects.
- **Log Level:** Each message has a log level, which determines the color the message is printed in, e.g., warnings are yellow. Additionally, modern browsers allow to filter messages by log level and prepend various icons for the different levels. The default log level is *log*, which has no color and no icon.
- **Source Location:** Each message has a responsible source location. This allows quick access to the source code emitting the message. Some general console messages have an empty source location.

Developer-Caused Messages. A simple console message can be produced by calling `console.log("Hello World!")` from JavaScript using the Console API [26]. We label all messages from methods of this API *developer-caused* messages as they only occur if a developer invoked them. Aside from website JavaScript, browser extensions and service workers can produce those.

Browser-Caused Messages. Apart from messages explicitly created using JavaScript, browsers also emit messages to inform developers about errors, signal failures in website functionality or announce feature deprecations. We call these messages *browser-caused* messages, as they originate from the browser implementation. Each browser vendor decides which messages to emit, and even messages on shared issues may appear different in terms of content and visualization.

Page Errors. The third type of messages in the console are page errors. This category contains both JavaScript Errors [6] such as TypeError and DOMExceptions [27] such as NotFoundError. Page errors can be explicitly thrown by JavaScript code, e.g. using `throw new Error("err")`, or automatically thrown, e.g., when accessing non-existing variables. These messages are accompanied by a stack trace and can be caught using the `try...catch` construct.

3 Methodology: Measuring the Console Ecosystem

In the following section, we elaborate on our crawling pipeline, capable of extracting all information rendered in the developer tools.

3.1 Automated Message Collection

To automate the collection process of the browser console, we implemented our web crawler using the Playwright browser automation framework [18]. The framework's integration with each browser developer tools protocols' console event enabled access to all console messages including browser-caused messages. However, the captured console events do not distinguish between browser-caused and developer-caused messages. Thus, we retrofitted a mechanism for distinguishing browser-caused and developer-caused messages.

1. *Firefox:* The browser-caused console output follows a fixed message structure [20], which we used to identify browser-caused messages.
2. *Chromium & WebKit:* The console output does not provide clear information on the message originator, we patched the browsers to prefix messages originating from the Console API.

3.2 Template Extraction

Using our patched variants of Chromium and WebKit, along with the message structure for Firefox, allowed us to filter for browser-caused console messages. However, the collected messages contain dynamic data and lack information about the causing browser component. To recover the responsible *templates* (static strings with placeholders for data) and link them with their browser implementation, we developed a two-stage pipeline, first reducing the messages to template candidates by omitting dynamic data and then iteratively linking the candidates with the respective templates in the browser source code.

Dynamic Data. Due to browser-caused messages containing dynamic data inlined into static templates, such as URLs, header values or numbers, we replaced these with placeholders. While we replaced all URLs in console output, we approached replacing header values by capturing all available values during a page visit and replace full header values if they occur in messages. Lastly, since we found that console messages also contained numeric strings signifying misconfigured values such as in WebGL details, we also replaced all numbers.

Recovering Templates. To obtain the source code locations of the collected browser-caused messages, we used subsequences of each unique filtered message and queried the respective source code repository. For instance, by searching for *Loading failed for the <script> with source* in Firefox source code mirror on GitHub we were able to find the exact source code location emitting this message and extracting the full template. We iteratively performed this process until all browser-caused messages were matched to a template.

3.3 Template Categorization

In addition to collecting the source code location of each template responsible for browser-caused console output, we categorized the templates according to the involved feature through manual inspection of the containing source code. Further, we grouped all categories into five high-level concepts: *Security-related (S)*, *Privacy-related (P)*, *Content-related (C)*, *Networking (N)* and *Other (O)*. For example, the *Loading failed for the <script> with source* template was categorized as *request-failures (N)*.

4 Results

In the following, we present the state of the browser console message ecosystem. We start with describing our measurement setup, proceed with an overview of the collected data and compare developer- and browser-caused output. We further expand on page errors, concluding with case studies.

4.1 Measurement Setup

In order to obtain a dataset of console output in the wild, we performed a crawl of sites taken from the Tranco list [16], generated on the 12th November 2024[1], using Playwright as the browser instrumentation framework. We partitioned the top 1 million list in buckets of size 100,000 and picked 10,000 sites uniformly at random for each bucket to select 100,000 sites. We visited each site once, collecting data from the landing page, on which we stayed for 30 seconds after loading. We used Chromium (v130.0.6723.31), Firefox (v131.0) and WebKit (v18.0).

4.2 High-Level Overview

We successfully collected data on 51,984 sites for all three web browsers. The low success rate originates from our use of an unfiltered Tranco list, containing many inaccessible sites such as `a-msedge.net`.

On the sites we visited, we captured a total of 2,088,416 console messages, with more than 78% of sites having at least one message. Table 1 shows the distribution of all messages, browser-caused, developer-caused and string-unique messages across sites and browsers. The total amount of messages in Firefox (1,396,566) is much higher than in Chromium (327,626) and WebKit (364,224), Firefox also recorded about 7,000 more sites with any message. This substantial difference in message counts is due to browser-caused messages, as all browsers produced a similar number of developer-caused messages.

4.3 Developer-Caused Console Messages

Our crawl yielded a total of 531,087 developer-caused console messages. WebKit was the most verbose with 189,528 messages. Notably, all three web browsers produced a similar amount of output of this overarching category, with the total spanning less than 18,000 messages apart on roughly the same amount of sites.

[1] Available at https://tranco-list.eu/list/LJ274/1000000.

Table 1. Distribution of console messages per category

Type	Browser	Messages per Site			Total Messages	Number of Sites with Messages
		Mean	Median	Max		
All	Chromium	6.30	2	2,377	327,626	40,635
	Firefox	26.87	11	10,143	1,396,566	47,720
	WebKit	7.01	2	6,925	364,224	40,725
Browser-Caused	Chromium	3.83	2	2,375	155,729	31,441
	Firefox	25.71	12	10,142	1,226,904	47,012
	WebKit	4.29	2	2,395	174,696	34,961
Developer-Caused	Chromium	4.23	1	2,003	171,897	23,749
	Firefox	3.56	0	2,003	169,662	23,164
	WebKit	4.65	1	6,921	189,528	23,635
String-Unique	Chromium	3.66	1	848	99,419	40,635
	Firefox	13.20	8	1,367	296,238	47,720
	WebKit	3.94	2	518	90,349	40,725

Table 2. Distribution of developer-caused console messages

Message Type	Total Messages			Sites with at least 1 Message		
	Chromium	Firefox	WebKit	Chromium	Firefox	WebKit
log	97,953	94,984	92,616	18,755	17,952	18,593
warning	24,790	24,725	28,093	6,990	7,154	7,287
error	11,970	16,569	21,992	2,764	2,568	2,810
debug	9,105	9,035	15,239	1,638	1,419	1,652
clear	13,349	11,036	3,176	119	58	54
info	6,129	6,566	8,258	2,536	2,561	2,693
endGroup	2,708	1,167	4,536	1,022	217	1,327
startGroupCollapsed	1,631	793	3,873	897	131	1,208
trace	1,075	1,065	3,285	291	283	555
table	1,894	921	2,585	110	97	372
dir	255	273	2,640	86	83	364
dirxml	215	234	2,466	62	59	334
startGroup	345	375	360	89	92	91
timeStamp	0	1,042	0	0	666	0
timeEnd	262	328	407	74	83	81
count	214	234	0	61	59	0
countReset	0	234	0	0	59	0
timeLog	0	79	0	0	2	0
assert	2	2	2	2	2	2

Message Type. Table 2 shows the distribution of types attached to developer-caused console messages, displaying the total amount captured and sites with at least one message. Overall, we collected 19 types of developer-caused console messages. The most common type by far was *log*, followed by *warning*, both occurring roughly the same across browsers. Comparing the other categories, substantial differences become apparent, in particular far less *error*-type messages were observed in Chromium. Likewise, the least amount of messages of type *clear* was collected in WebKit. Four types were never observed in WebKit and three never in Chromium. We verified that these are supported in all browsers, but are incorrectly reported as types *log* or *timeEnd* in Chromium and WebKit.

Message Site. 52.26% of developer-caused messages originate from first-party scripts, and 47.74% from third-party scripts. The third-party messages belong to a total of 2,655 unique sites with the majority of messages belonging to a few key players such as Google and Facebook.

Message Content. Out of the 531,087 collected developer caused messages, only 97,529 were unique (combination of type + message content). Messages related to the **JQMigrate** library appeared most often (20,095 messages logging the same version string). This was followed by developers logging objects from their JavaScript code (e.g. variables or DOM nodes). Some other common messages were error or log messages from libraries or frameworks such as odoo (OwlError), Google Maps API, or LiteSpeed. JavaScript types such as *undefined*, *RegExp*, or *function* were also commonly observed. We discovered that for many of the JavaScript types Firefox reports only the type name in the collected console message event whereas WebKit and Chromium report the stringified version. Note that the collected event and what is displayed in the console can differ, as the browser consoles use pretty printing. The pretty printing functionality differs across browsers, for instance, while Firefox displays a *RegExp* or *function* object interactively, Chromium and WebKit display a static string representation.

4.4 Browser-Caused Console Messages

Message Types. Table 3 shows the distribution of browser-caused console messages types, displaying the mean, median, and maximum per site, and the total amount captured. It reveals several inequalities across browser vendors, with the first being that Firefox produced significantly more messages for the message type *warning* both in total and in the number of affected sites. Second, while Chromium and WebKit emitted a similar amount of console output typed as *error*, WebKit emitted substantially more *info* messages than Chromium. Moreover, although Firefox produced more *info* messages than WebKit in total, the number of sites with at least one *info* message is four times higher in WebKit. Only Chromium uses the *verbose* type. Messages of this type concerned mostly DOM-related hints regarding the creation of forms.

Table 3. Distribution of browser-caused console messages

Type	Browser	Messages per Site			Total Messages	Number of Sites with Messages
		Mean	Median	Max		
warning	Chromium	1.27	0	1,028	66,179	13,125
	Firefox	19.45	9	8,471	1,010,973	46,635
	WebKit	0.75	0	764	39,230	9,481
error	Chromium	1.44	0	2,375	75,056	21,141
	Firefox	2.05	0	2,359	106,812	15,680
	WebKit	1.53	0	2,395	79,643	21,400
info	Chromium	0.17	0	70	8,898	2,703
	Firefox	2.10	0	357	109,119	4,460
	WebKit	1.07	0	855	55,823	18,267
verbose	Chromium	0.11	0	34	5,596	3,676
	Firefox	0.00	0	0	0	0
	WebKit	0.00	0	0	0	0

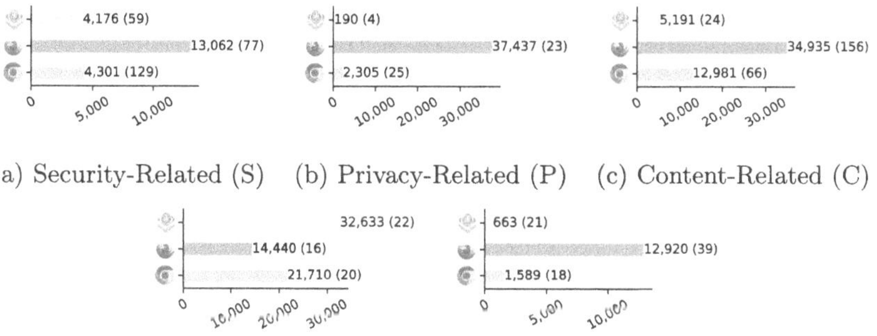

(a) Security-Related (S) (b) Privacy-Related (P) (c) Content-Related (C)

(d) Networking (N) (e) Other (O)

Fig. 2. Number of sites with browser-caused messages per browser across high-level concepts and constituting unique templates in parentheses.

Template Concepts. To understand the involved browser components, we labelled each detected console message template with a category and a high-level concept. Figure 2 shows the number of sites having messages belonging to a concept for all browsers and the number of unique templates in parentheses.

Figure 2a shows that Firefox has messages related to security on most sites. Regarding privacy-related messages (see Fig. 2b), Firefox produces output on most sites. Firefox also produces the most messages related to the content concept (see Fig. 2c) and the catch-all other concept (see Fig. 2e). For the networking concept (see Fig. 2d), messages were produced on most sites by WebKit followed by Chromium.

Table 4. Top ten templates per browser

Id	Template	Category (Concept)	Sites	Total
	Chromium:			
TC1	Failed to load resource: Error	*request-failures (N)*	18,664	43,539
TC2	[GroupMarkerNotSet(crbug.com/242999)!: Number] Automatic fallback to software WebGL has been deprecated. Please use the –enable-unsafe-swiftshader flag to opt in to lower security guarantees for trusted content.	*webgl (C)*	5,995	9,977
TC3	The resource URL was preloaded using link preload but not used within a few seconds from the window's load event. Please make sure it has an appropriate 'as' value and it is preloaded intentionally.	*preload (N)*	4,493	17,720
TC4	[DOM] Input elements should have autocomplete attributes (suggested: " Name "): (More info: Static URL)(%o)?	*autofill (C)*	3,293	4,828
TC5	Slow network is detected. See Static URL for more details. Fallback font will be used while loading: URL	*styles (C)*	2,209	8,334
TC6	A preload for ' URL ' is found, but is not used because the request credentials mode does not match. Consider taking a look at crossorigin attribute.	*preload (N)*	908	1,971
TC7	Mixed Content: The page at ' URL ' was loaded over HTTPS, but requested an insecure element ' URL '. This request was automatically upgraded to HTTPS, For more information see Static URL	*mixed-content (S)*	901	10,830
TC8	Unrecognized feature: ' HeaderVal '.	*permissions-policy (P)*	808	828
TC9	Mixed Content: The page at ' URL ' was loaded over HTTPS, but requested an insecure Data ' URL '. This request has been blocked; the content must be served over HTTPS.	*mixed-content (S)*	770	1,752
TC10	Error with Permissions-Policy header: Unrecognized feature: ' HeaderVal '.	*permissions-policy (P)*	747	1,994
	Firefox:			
TF1	Cookie " Name " does not have a proper "SameSite" attribute value. Soon, cookies without the "SameSite" attribute or with an invalid value will be treated as "Lax". This means that the cookie will no longer be sent in third-party contexts. If your application depends on this cookie being available in such contexts, please add the "SameSite=None" attribute to it. To know more about the "SameSite" attribute, read Static URL	*cookies (P)*	35,147	707,776
TF2	The value of the attribute " Name " for the cookie " Name " has been overwritten.	*cookies (P)*	19,251	33,780
TF3	This page uses the non standard property "zoom". Consider using calc() in the relevant property values, or using "transform" along with "transform-origin: 0 0".	*styles (C)*	17,717	18,291
TF4	downloadable font: Glyph bbox was incorrect (glyph ids Data) (font-family: " Name " style: CSS weight: Number stretch: Number src index: Number) source: URL	*fonts (C)*	11,459	16,554
TF5	Cookie " Name " has been rejected for invalid domain.	*cookies (P)*	10,369	57,913
TF6	" URL " has been classified as a bounce tracker. If it does not receive user activation within the next Number seconds it will have its state purged.	*tracking (P)*	10,207	10,774
TF7	This page is in Quirks Mode. Page layout may be impacted. For Standards Mode use "<!DOCTYPE html>".	*html (C)*	8,321	12,420
TF8	The resource at " URL " preloaded with link preload was not used within a few seconds. Make sure all attributes of the preload tag are set correctly.	*preload (N)*	6,163	16,812
TF9	Layout was forced before the page was fully loaded. If stylesheets are not yet loaded this may cause a flash of unstyled content.	*styles (C)*	6,078	7,874
TF10	A resource is blocked by OpaqueResponseBlocking, please check browser console for details.	*request-failures (N)*	5,629	17,716

(continued)

Table 4. (*continued*)

	WebKit:			
TW1	Failed to load resource: Error	*request-failures (N)*	19,168	44,959
TW2	Successfully preconnected to URL	*preconnect (N)*	18,266	55,822
TW3	The resource URL was preloaded using link preload but not used within a few seconds from the window's load event. Please make sure it wasn't preloaded for nothing.	*preload (N)*	5,497	16,782
TW4	window.styleMedia is a deprecated draft version of window.matchMedia API, and it will be removed in the future.	*styles (C)*	3,331	6,954
TW5	The page at URL requested insecure content from URL . This content was automatically upgraded and should be served over HTTPS.	*mixed-content (S)*	1,014	11,421
TW6	Origin URL is not allowed by Access-Control-Allow-Origin. Status code: Number	*cors (S)*	937	1,892
TW7	Refused to execute URL as script because HeaderVal is not a script MIME type.	*mime-type (C)*	865	1,201
TW8	[blocked] The page at URL requested insecure content from URL . This content was blocked and must be served over HTTPS.	*mixed-content (S)*	703	2,763
TW9	Viewport argument key " Name " not recognized and ignored.	*html (C)*	483	604
TW10	Failed to preconnect to URL . Error: Error	*request-failures (N)*	397	455

Most Common Templates. The 1,557,329 browser-caused messages belong to a total of 703 unique templates. In Table 4 we present the top-ten templates occurring on most sites for each browser (the full list of 703 templates is accessible online [13]). The most common template was the same for Chromium (**TC1**) and WebKit (**TW1**) and concerned the failure to load a resource. The most common template in Firefox (**TF1**) concerned the `SameSite` attribute of cookies. This template that occurred 707,776 times on 35,147 sites is by far the most emitted message overall and is mainly responsible for the huge verbosity of Firefox. However, other messages also occur more often in Firefox with the tenth-most popular template (**TF10**) occurring on 5,629 sites whereas **TC10** only occurs on 747 sites and **TW10** on 397 sites.

Three out of the top ten messages from Firefox (**TF1, TF2, TF5**) concerned cookie issues, while the other vendors top message templates did not concern any cookie related information. A commonality concerns the output of messages regarding preloading, where each vendor reported them among their most occurring templates per domains (**TC3, TF8, TW3**). Both Chromium and WebKit had many warnings about mixed content (**TC7, TC9, TW5, TW8**), while Firefox had no mixed-content related message in its top ten.

4.5 Page Errors

Table 5 shows the distribution of page errors based on their name across all three vendors, showing both their total count and the number of sites they were found on. We collected 92,518 page errors on 12,241 sites across all three browsers.

For both `TypeError` and `ReferenceError`, we detected errors on a similar amount of sites, although the totals differ significantly with Chromium having the most `TypeErrors`. In WebKit, we collected 13,288 messages that are incorrectly reported as page errors by Playwright. Looking at the internal representation of console messages and page errors in WebKit, these messages are emitted with the type *JavaScript* and level *error*, which Playwright interprets as an page error even though they cannot be caught using try/catch [17]. We note that for developers, page errors and console messages of type *error* look identical on the WebKit console and cannot be easily distinguished.

If developers throw errors themselves, they are often using the generic *Error* type of JavaScript, however we also found a large number of developer-defined names, which we labelled as *Custom Error*. They have 63 distinct names, such as `AxiosError`. Another discrepancy is visible in errors named *SyntaxError*, where Firefox has significantly fewer.

Table 5. Count and unique sites per JavaScript Error

Error Name	Chromium		Firefox		WebKit	
	Total	Sites	Total	Sites	Total	Sites
TypeError	17,726	3,514	11,006	3,565	5,614	3,918
ReferenceError	8,760	1,818	9,640	2,071	3,700	2,078
ConsoleMessageLike	0	0	0	0	13,288	4,884
Error (Generic)	4,545	889	6,270	832	1,532	1,082
Error (Custom Name)	1,822	924	1,466	740	1,934	1,142
SyntaxError	1,538	1,062	578	272	1,502	1,198
DOMException	591	351	748	120	147	133
RangeError	37	5	30	1	34	5
EvalError	3	3	2	2	2	2
URIError	1	1	1	1	1	1
Total	35,023	7,190	29,741	6,559	27,754	11,429

4.6 Case Studies

Extending on the numbers, we investigated outlier sites and interesting patterns.

Outliers. The site with the most browser-caused console messages, had a total of 10,143 messages in Firefox. We manually visited the site to ensure this was not a collection error and observed a similar amount of messages. 8,468 of those messages were about improper SameSite attributes of cookies and 1,670 rejections of cookies due to invalid domain. The crawler found the most developer-caused messages on a site in WebKit, where 6,919 out of the 6,925 of messages were produced by printing an OwlError, which can be attributed to the odoo library.

Local File Inclusions. A potential privacy issue are console messages informing about the attempted inclusion of local files, revealing information about the developer's file system. An example console message leaking the file system structure of a developer is: `Not allowed to load local resource: file:///C%7C/Users/sysw7/AppData/.../favicon.ico`. Similarly, we found attempts of probing for browser extensions: `Not allowed to load local resource: chrome://rumola/content/rumola48.png`. Tests for this particular resource were found on various government websites. The requested file belongs to the Rumola chrome extension, used for bypassing CAPTCHAs [1].

Anti-Debugging Techniques. The Console API allows to clear the browser console using the `console.clear` function. Sites with a high number of these calls showed usage of anti-debugging techniques, e.g. through the inclusion of the JavaScript library *disable-devtool* [5]. The usage of such libraries aims to inhibit the use of the developer tools on websites. Notably, it fails to restrict data collection through our data collection pipeline.

5 Discussion

In this section we discuss the main insights gained by our results and how researchers and browser vendors can go forward improving the browser console for developers and using it for research.

5.1 Main Insights

Flood of Messages. The maximum number of console messages on a site we observed was 10,143 and a total of 2,605 sites had more than 100 messages in at least one browser. With such high message quantities, the console ceases to be useful to developers and they might develop notification fatigue. Browser vendors seem to be aware of the issue and for example try to de-duplicate similar or identical messages. Unfortunately, Playwright does not expose details about whether console messages were merged with prior output. Furthermore, we found browser features aware of their verbosity, implementing mechanisms for suppressing excessive output. We found that Chromium suppresses further messages after four WebGL messages have been printed and WebKit stops after 256 such messages. Firefox implements a preference setting that allows the user to define the maximal number of WebGL warnings per context, which defaults to 32. Most importantly, the Chrome team noticed that "the console was full of warnings and error messages" and introduced the Issues tab, an additional developer tool with structured messages, to declutter the console in 2019 [25]. However, we observed that this was only partially successful as there where still more than 332 sites with more than 100 messages in Chromium.

Browser Differences. Our results show that there are significant differences in the amount and types of messages a developer encounters in different browsers. In particular, a developer using Firefox is exposed to more messages on average. Developers are only informed about certain issues in some browsers, and even if all browsers emit a message about an issue, the message itself is usually phrased quite differently. We also found that the implementations of browser console messages differs between browsers with Firefox colocating most of their templates in central files to allow for easy translation. In contrast, WebKit and Chromium opt for string concatenation directly in the code where an issue is detected, e.g., in the CSP parser if a CSP parsing errors is encountered. We also discovered typos and broken console messages in Firefox. For instance, we found that CSP messages were empty in certain conditions. The triaging process further revealed undefined messages for invalid *report-to* directive groups. Another inconsistency we observed was WebKit's direct passing of operating system library errors, such as for failed DNS resolution, into console messages.

Console Messages for Measurement Studies. Our framework and collected console output reveals not only insights about the browser console message ecosystem, but also the state of the web, with console messages exposing implementation mistakes or hinting at general misunderstandings when considering them at scale. Web measurement studies can leverage console messages to pre-filter websites of interest, e.g., all with a certain message of type *error*. For example, studies on CORS [9], Mixed-Content [4], or XFO [3] implemented custom tools to collect data on these topics and often reimplemented browser functionality such as custom header parsers. If the browser-caused console messages emitted on these topics are detailed enough, e.g., for XFO all browsers report a message when an invalid header value is received, some research questions could be answered by using the console messages without the need of custom tooling.

5.2 Going Forward

Our results clearly indicate that there is no consistency and agreement across the browsers in how to implement console messages and for which events messages should be displayed. In addition, on many websites the amount of messages is really high, impeding effective usage of the console without deduplication. We propose further standardization of console messages with a centralized location of message templates to allow translation, user-friendlyness, and to ease studies on console messages. Browsers should provide complete console message data through their APIs to facilitate collection by tools like Playwright. Overall, we see this study as a first glance into the world of browser console messages. We suggest to perform user studies to see what kind of messages (and which presentation) are helpful for developers similar to past work on end-user facing security warnings that improved significantly over the last few years [23].

6 Related Work

Although the browser console was introduced in 2006 [12], there exists almost no research on it and we are not aware of any large-scale measurement on console output. Thus, in this section, we survey related work in the area of the browser console, web developer studies and browser security warnings.

Browser Console. García et al. [8] developed a browser extension to collect browser console messages and evaluated their extension on 50 popular websites in Chrome, Firefox and Edge. Their evaluation shows that in addition to the *traceable* message categories they can collect, such as *console.log*, many other, often browser-specific, *non-traceable* messages such as security header warnings are emitted by browsers that cannot be collected by their browser extension.

We solve the issue of *non-traceable* messages by relying on Playwright's console event that has access to all emitted messages. We then perform the first large-scale measurement showing significant differences across browsers.

Web Developer Studies. In several web developer user studies, the participants mentioned the use of the browser console or were annoyed or confused by inconsistent or difficult to understand messages highlighting the practical relevance of the browser console for web developers and the need for more research. In a survey of 109 JavaScript developers, 88.1% mentioned that they have seen console messages as a deprecation solution and 46% have used console messages to deprecate API [21]. More severely, more than half of the 12 participants of another study complained about inconsistencies in console messages, omitting helpful information depending on the involved browser vendor in a developer study about Content-Security-Policy misconfigurations [24].

Browser Security Warnings. End-user facing browser security warnings have been studied much more than console messages [2,7,11,19]. In 2013, Akhawe and Felt [2] analyzed 25 million warning impressions collected from Mozilla Firefox and Google Chrome's in-browser telemetry data. Their study revealed differences in user behavior depending on the presented warning.

Our results on the inconsistencies of browser console messages across browsers highlight the need for further (user) studies on how browsers should design their developer facing console messages.

7 Conclusion

In this paper, we investigated the browser developer tools message ecosystem, comparing what information is displayed across Chromium, WebKit and Firefox. For this, we developed a framework to comprehensively collect information from the developer tools, capturing console messages and page errors.

Analyzing a total of 2,088,416 console messages and 92,518 page errors across the landing pages of 51,984 sites, not only revealed a high amount of messages on many sites but also substantial browser differences. Moreover, our inspection of browser source code creating console output revealed inconsistent implementation approaches and a lack of coordination between browsers. These inconsistencies are worsened by differences in browser tooling, apparent in Chromium's Issues tab rendering information not necessarily present in the browser console.

As we consider this study a first glance into the world of browser console messages, we outlined research opportunities and open-source our framework [13] (MIT LICENSE, permanently available on Zenodo).

Acknowledgments. This work was conducted in the scope of a dissertation at the Saarbrücken Graduate School of Computer Science.

Disclosure of Interests. The authors have no competing interests to declare that are relevant to the content of this article.

References

1. Rumola - bypass CAPTCHA - Chrome Web Store (2022). https://chromewebstore.google.com/detail/rumola-bypass-captcha/bjjgbdlbgjeoankjijbmheneoekbghcg
2. Akhawe, D., Felt, A.P.: Alice in warningland: a large-scale field study of browser security warning effectiveness. In: USENIX Security Symposium (2013). https://www.usenix.org/conference/usenixsecurity13/technical-sessions/presentation/akhawe
3. Calzavara, S., Roth, S., Rabitti, A., Backes, M., Stock, B.: A tale of two headers: a formal analysis of inconsistent Click-Jacking protection on the web. In: USENIX Security Symposium (2020). https://www.usenix.org/conference/usenixsecurity20/presentation/calzavara
4. Chen, P., Nikiforakis, N., Huygens, C., Desmet, L.: A dangerous mix: large-scale analysis of mixed-content websites. In: Information Security (2015). https://doi.org/10.1007/978-3-319-27659-5_25
5. Chen, T.: Disable-devtool (2025). https://github.com/theajack/disable-devtool
6. Ecma International: ECMAScript 2026 Language Specification (2026). https://tc39.es/ecma262/multipage/
7. Egelman, S., Cranor, L.F., Hong, J.: You've been warned: an empirical study of the effectiveness of web browser phishing warnings. In: ACM CHI Conference on Human Factors in Computing Systems (2008). https://doi.org/10.1145/1357054.1357219
8. García, B., Ricca, F., del Alamo, J.M., Leotta, M.: Enhancing web applications observability through instrumented automated browsers. J. Syst. Softw. (2023). https://doi.org/10.1016/j.jss.2023.111723
9. Golinelli, M., Arshad, E., Kashchuk, D., Crispo, B.: Mind the CORS. In: IEEE International Conference on Trust, Privacy and Security in Intelligent Systems and Applications (2023). https://doi.org/10.1109/TPS-ISA58951.2023.00035
10. Gorski, P.L., Iacono, L.L., Wiefling, S., Möller, S.: Warn if secure or how to deal with security by default in software development?. In: IFIP International Symposium on Human Aspects of Information Security & Assurance (2018). https://pub.h-brs.de/frontdoor/index/index/year/2020/docId/4947

11. Harbach, M., Fahl, S., Yakovleva, P., Smith, M.: Sorry, i don't get it: an analysis of warning message texts. In: Adams, A.A., Brenner, M., Smith, M. (eds.) FC 2013. LNCS, vol. 7862, pp. 94–111. Springer, Heidelberg (2013). https://doi.org/10.1007/978-3-642-41320-9_7
12. Hatcher, T.: 10 years of web inspector (2016). https://webkit.org/blog/5718/10-years-of-web-inspector/
13. Helbrecht, T. Rautenstrauch, J.: Artifacts for Console Clutter: A Cross-Browser Measurement of Console Messages (2026). https://zenodo.org/records/18694496
14. Jay: A history of debugging on the web (2021). https://thehistoryoftheweb.com/checking-under-the-hood-of-code/
15. Kemp, S.: Digital 2026: Global overview report (2025). https://datareportal.com/reports/digital-2026-global-overview-report
16. Le Pochat, V., Van Goethem, T., Tajalizadehkhoob, S., Korczyński, M., Joosen, W.: Tranco: a research-oriented top sites ranking hardened against manipulation. In: Network and Distributed System Security Symposium (2019). https://doi.org/10.14722/ndss.2019.23386
17. Microsoft: wkPage.ts (2024). https://github.com/microsoft/playwright/blob/v1.48.1/packages/playwright-core/src/server/webkit/wkPage.ts#L538-L548
18. Microsoft: Fast and reliable end-to-end testing for modern web apps (2026). https://playwright.dev
19. Molyneaux, H., Kondratova, I., Stobert, E.: Understanding perceptions: User responses to browser warning messages. In: HCI for Cybersecurity, Privacy and Trust. Springer (2019). https://doi.org/10.1007/978-3-030-22351-9_11
20. Mozilla: nsScriptError.cpp (2024). https://github.com/mozilla/gecko-dev/blob/8fddaf56928e193b70c8e38973f6cd3dd5e3bb7d/dom/bindings/nsScriptError.cpp#L334
21. Nascimento, R., Figueiredo, E., Hora, A.: JavaScript API deprecation landscape: a survey and mining study. IEEE Softw. **39**(3) (2021). https://doi.org/10.1109/MS.2021.3103134
22. Netcraft: December web server survey (2025). https://www.netcraft.com/blog/december-2025-web-server-survey
23. Reeder, R.W., Felt, A.P., Consolvo, S., Malkin, N., Thompson, C., Egelman, S.: An experience sampling study of user reactions to browser warnings in the field. In: ACM CHI Conference on Human Factors in Computing Systems (2018). https://doi.org/10.1145/3173574.3174086
24. Roth, S., Gröber, L., Backes, M., Krombholz, K., Stock, B.: 12 angry developers-a qualitative study on developers' struggles with CSP. In: ACM SIGSAC Conference on Computer and Communications Security (2021). https://doi.org/10.1145/3460120.3484780
25. Scheffler, J., Schneider, S.: How we built the chrome DevTools issues tab (2020). https://developer.chrome.com/blog/issues-tab
26. WHATWG: Console: Living standard (2026). https://console.spec.whatwg.org
27. WHATWG: Web IDL Standard (2026). https://webidl.spec.whatwg.org/#idl-DOMException

OASQuali: Automated Quality Analysis of OpenAPI Specifications

Alix Decrop(✉), Mikel Vandeloise, Patrick Heymans, and Gilles Perrouin

NADI/PReCISE, Faculty of Computer Science, University of Namur, Namur, Belgium
{alix.decrop,mikel.vandeloise,patrick.heymans,gilles.perrouin}@unamur.be

Abstract. The rapid adoption of modern web architectures (i.e., REST APIs) relies on clear and accurate documentation. The OpenAPI Specification (OAS) standard is widely adopted for this purpose, as it is machine-readable and provides a range of API-related fields. However, maintaining high-quality documentation is complex, as the frequent omission of important information significantly hinders the effectiveness of testing tools and API understanding. To address this problem, we introduce OASQuali, a tool that quantifies OAS quality across five dimensions: format, version, metadata, servers, and descriptions/examples. We conduct a large-scale empirical evaluation with 2,529 public specifications. Our results reveal a mean documentation quality of 67.11%. While aggregate quality is independent of API size, we identify a systemic "semantic gap" in large-scale implementations: As APIs enlarge, they become more up-to-date with OAS versions (53.10% → 88.00%). However, the quality of their descriptions and examples drastically decreases (42.18% → 24.00%). Notably, the absence of parameter examples in 86.95% of specifications represents a major bottleneck for operational clarity. OASQuali provides a rigorous framework for revealing these deficiencies, paving the way for more thoroughly documented web services.

Keywords: OpenAPI Specification · REST APIs · Automated Analysis · Quality Metrics

1 Introduction

Many modern web architectures rely on REpresentational State Transfer (REST) APIs [9] that communicate via the HTTP protocol [8]. While these interfaces leverage standardized methods and headers, the diversity in implementation patterns, ranging from parameter handling to authentication mechanisms, makes simple protocol knowledge insufficient for integration [11]. Consequently, developers depend on documentation, predominantly using the widely adopted OpenAPI Specification (OAS) standard, to define machine-readable contracts in JSON or YAML formats [19].

A. Mauri et al. (Eds.): ICWE 2026, LNCS 16625, pp. 94–108, 2026.
https://doi.org/10.1007/978-3-032-29372-5_7

However, maintaining high-quality OAS documentation is a complex and error-prone task. Prior research indicates that more than half of published specifications contain inconsistencies relative to their actual implementation [11]. Furthermore, the frequent omission of optional fields, such as human-readable descriptions and response examples, significantly degrades API usability [12]. Ambiguous endpoints, such as `GET /status` lacking descriptive metadata or structural schemas, hinder integration and prevent the effective use of automated testing and mock generation tools [5,10]. Such ambiguities also affect API users, who may not understand operations and/or parameter usage.

Existing research has primarily focused on structural metrics for maintainability [4] or the automated detection of REST design rule violations [3]. Yet, the automated assessment of API documentation usability (e.g., metadata presence, rich descriptions and examples, up-to-date OAS version, etc.) remains largely unaddressed [15]. This paper bridges this gap by investigating the quality thresholds of public REST API documentation through a multidimensional analytical lens.

Overall, this paper provides the following contributions:

- **OASQuali:** A deterministic tool to automate OAS quality assessment. Unlike standard validators, it fully resolves modular specifications (handling reference dependencies) to ensure metrics are calculated on the complete API specifications.
- **Quality Framework:** A formalization of OAS quality as a multidimensional vector that covers format (Structural Integrity), OAS version (Evolutionary Maturity), metadata (Administrative Governance), servers (Operational Readiness), and descriptions/examples (Semantic Communicability).
- **Empirical Evaluation:** A large-scale study of 2,529 public specifications originating from the *APIs.guru* directory [2], revealing that while average quality is tolerable, significant deficiencies persist regardless of API size.
- **Replication Package:** A publicly available repository containing our implementation of OASQuali and the curated dataset to ensure study reproducibility [7].

The remainder of this paper is structured as follows: Sect. 2 provides the background and related work; Sect. 3 details the tool methodology and architecture; Sect. 4 presents our empirical results; Sect. 5 discusses the implications of our findings; Sect. 6 addresses the potential threats to validity; and Sect. 7 concludes the paper with future research directions.

2 Background and Related Work

REST Architecture and HTTP. Modern web services predominantly implement the REpresentational State Transfer (REST) architectural style [9]. REST defines a set of constraints, including statelessness, a uniform interface, and client-server decoupling, to ensure scalability and evolvability. These services leverage the HyperText Transfer Protocol (HTTP) [8] for communication, utilizing standard methods (`GET`, `POST`, `PUT`, `PATCH`, `DELETE`) to perform CRUD (Create, Read, Update, Delete) operations on resources identified by URIs.

OpenAPI Specification (OAS). The OpenAPI Specification [19] (formerly known as Swagger) is the industry-standard for documenting REST APIs. An OAS document provides a machine-readable contract (in JSON or YAML) covering API metadata, available endpoints, parameter constraints, response schemas, and other API-related fields. Designed for automation, such specifications are also frequently rendered via tools such as *Swagger Editor* [17] to serve as a primary documentation for human developers.

Related Work. The automated analysis of REST API documentation has evolved along four primary research axes. While significant progress has been made in structural and architectural validation, the assessment of semantic quality remains underexplored.

- **Documentation Reliability vs. Implementation:** Hosono et al. [11] conducted a validation of consistency between documentation and implementation, revealing that nearly half of the specifications diverge from actual API behaviour. Their work focuses on correctness (fidelity to code) rather than intrinsic quality (content usability). Similarly, studies on API evolution show that breaking changes are often undocumented, emphasizing the accuracy of the specification yet overlooking its communicability. Additionally, Sohan et al. [18] identified usage examples as a critical component for the effectiveness of REST API documentation.
- **Structural Metrics and Maintainability:** A significant body of work focuses on complexity metrics derived from static analysis. Bogner et al. [4] adapted classic software quality metrics (e.g., Weighted Methods per Class) to service interfaces to assess maintainability. Serbout et al. [14,15] introduced *APIstic*, a framework computing over 800 structural metrics (e.g., schema depth, parameter counts) to analyse API ecosystems. While these approaches provide important insight into structural complexity, they are descriptive rather than normative regarding documentation richness: a technically complex API can be valid even if it lacks human-readable descriptions.
- **Design Compliance and Rule Enforcement:** Building on Massé's foundational REST rules [12] (e.g., using noun-based URIs or avoiding file extensions), tools like *RESTRuler* [3] automate the detection of syntactic violations (e.g., URI styles or misuse of HTTP methods). Complementarily, Singjai et al. [16] focus on ensuring conformance between API descriptions and higher-level architectural design decisions. These tools ensure syntactic and architectural compliance but do not evaluate the semantic utility of the content (e.g., the meaningfulness of a parameter example).
- **API Discovery and Recommendation:** Approaches like *API-Miner* by Moon et al. [13] leverage NLP (Sentence-BERT) and graph-based learning to improve API discovery. While they utilize descriptions to compute semantic similarity, they do not treat documentation richness as a standardized quality metric for developers.

Despite these contributions, existing tools focus mainly on architectural compliance or structural complexity. The automated assessment of human-related usability and semantically valid descriptions/examples through OAS remains largely unexplored. OASQUALI addresses this gap by providing a deterministic framework to quantify documentation richness.

Terminology. In the remainder of this paper, an *API* refers to a REST (or RESTful) service, and a *specification* denotes its documentation in the OAS format [19].

3 Methodology

The design of OASQUALI is motivated by the need for a deterministic framework to assess the structural and semantic quality of OpenAPI Specifications. To bridge the gap between raw interface definitions and quantifiable metrics, we propose a multi-stage analysis pipeline that systematically decomposes the specification's layers.

Specification, Acquisition, and Normalization. To ensure programmatic flexibility, OASQUALI implements two acquisition modalities:

- **Local Mode:** Tailored for static analysis, it accepts path descriptors for JSON or YAML files, performing automatic normalization and metadata extraction from file headers.
- **In-Memory Mode:** Designed for integration into Continuous Integration (CI) pipelines, it processes pre-parsed objects.

Referential Resolution and Dereferencing. A critical challenge in OAS analysis is the modularity offered through the `$ref` keyword (i.e., a reference to an element definition for reusability purposes). Performing a naive static analysis on the root document would yield incomplete metrics and underestimate documentation coverage. OASQUALI incorporates a preprocessing layer that traverses the specification to resolve all JSON pointers. This process "flattens" the API's object graph into a canonical, fully expanded representation, ensuring that subsequent quality evaluations are validly executed on OAS files.

Structural Validation and Compliance. Once flattened, the specification undergoes a two-tier validation protocol acting as a fail-fast gatekeeper:

1. **Syntactic Integrity:** A raw syntax verification ensures that the document adheres to JSON/YAML serialization standards.
2. **Schema Conformance:** Formal validation against official OpenAPI schema (v2.0, v3.0.x, v3.1.x). The engine logs specific `OpenAPIValidationError` instances to provide high-granularity feedback.

Multi-dimensional Quality Assessment. We formalize the quality of an OpenAPI Specification $\mathcal{S}$ as a multidimensional vector:

$$\mathcal{Q}(\mathcal{S}) = \langle \mathcal{I}, \mathcal{E}, \mathcal{G}, \mathcal{O}, \mathcal{C} \rangle$$

where each component represents an orthogonal dimension of usability:

- **Structural Integrity ($\mathcal{I}$):** Syntactical validation of JSON and adherence to the OAS metamodel.
  Motivation: While Massé defines rules for URI syntax [12], our metric extends this to the syntactic validity of the entire machine-readable specification, ensuring interoperability with tooling [19].
- **Evolutionary Maturity ($\mathcal{E}$):** Enforcement of Semantic Versioning (SemVer) patterns for OAS via regular expression matching.
  Motivation: Fielding emphasizes evolvability as a key constraint [9]. We operationalize this by verifying standard versioning patterns, a vital practice for client stability in distributed systems.
- **Administrative Governance ($\mathcal{G}$):** Verification of API metadata availability (i.e., API title, licence, contact).
  Motivation: Massé highlights the need for clear metadata to facilitate consumption [12]. Notably, we quantify this by enforcing the presence of legal (licence) and social (contact) metadata, which are often neglected in practice.
- **Operational Readiness ($\mathcal{O}$):** Evaluation of server presence, reachability, and security (HTTPS enforcement and active probes).
  Motivation: Unlike theoretical design guides [12], this dimension empirically verifies the static reachability of the implementation, addressing the reliability gap identified by Hosono et al. [11].
- **Semantic Communicability ($\mathcal{C}$):** Calculation of coverage metrics for description and example fields in OAS files.
  Motivation: While Massé advocates for "self-descriptive messages" [12], he does not provide metrics for documentation richness.

We associate with each dimension a set of *evaluations*. These evaluations correspond to specific checks performed by OASQuali and are listed in Table 1. For example, the evaluation `oas-version` checks a specification's adherence to the last version of the OAS standard, while the evaluation `parameter-examples` measures example coverage relative to the number of API parameters.

Synthesis and Scoring Mechanism. The final phase synthesizes outcomes into a structured report. For each dimension d, a success ratio S_d is calculated as:

$$S_d = \frac{\sum \text{passing evaluations of } d}{\sum \text{total evaluations of } d}$$

The global Composite Quality Index (CQI) is then derived from the weighted sum of these ratios:

$$CQI = \sum_{d \in \{\mathcal{I},\mathcal{E},\mathcal{G},\mathcal{O},\mathcal{C}\}} S_d \times w_d$$

where S_d is the success ratio of the dimension d and w_d is the weight assigned to the dimension d ($\sum w_d = 1$). By default, each dimension is assigned an equal weight (since we have five dimensions: $w_d = 0.2$), facilitating objective benchmarking across heterogeneous datasets.

4 Evaluation

The empirical assessment of OASQuali quantifies documentation quality across a diverse corpus of public OpenAPI Specifications and identifies prevalent structural and semantic deficiencies.

4.1 Research Questions

This study addresses three fundamental research questions (RQs):

- **RQ.1 (Formalization):** How can documentation quality be modelled as a set of quantifiable evaluations, derived from the OpenAPI Specification standard?
- **RQ.2 (State of Practice):** What is the quality distribution among public OpenAPI Specifications, and does API size correlate with documentation maturity?
- **RQ.3 (Critical Pitfalls):** Which specific quality evaluations exhibit the highest failure rates, and what are the implications for API usability?

4.2 Dataset

The evaluation corpus comprises 2,529 OAS files retrieved from the *APIs.guru* directory [2]. This dataset ensures external validity through significant heterogeneity, spanning diverse application domains (e.g., finance, geolocation, aviation, etc.) and varying API sizes.

4.3 Experimental Setup

We evaluated OASQuali on a machine with a 2.4GHz processor and 16GB of RAM. The protocol involved:

1. Local acquisition of specifications and metadata via the APIs.guru REST API.
2. Execution of the OASQuali analysis pipeline across the entire dataset.

As OASQuali is deterministic, results are reproducible and independent of stochastic variance. To ensure the practical utility of our tool, we evaluated its performance on standard consumer-grade hardware. The pipeline processes most specifications in under two seconds, demonstrating its viability for real-time integration into Continuous Integration (CI) environments without introducing significant latency.

4.4 RQ.1 - Formalization: Quality Evaluations

To define and quantify our quality evaluations, we operationalize the multidimensional quality model introduced in Sect. 3. While the quality vector $\mathcal{Q}(\mathcal{S})$ provides the theoretical framework, this step maps the dimensions to 17 deterministic evaluations.

Structural Integrity ($\mathcal{I}$), Evolutionary Maturity ($\mathcal{E}$), and Administrative Governance ($\mathcal{G}$) dimensions are assessed through binary presence and validity checks. The Operational Readiness ($\mathcal{O}$) dimension extends such checks by also assessing server reachability through HTTP requests and response analysis. In contrast, the Semantic Communicability ($\mathcal{C}$) dimension employs more sophisticated heuristics. For `description` fields, the engine executes a sequential validation pipeline comprising three stages. First, it ensures existence and normalization by verifying that the field contains non-whitespace characters, which are then stripped and lowercased for consistent matching. Second, to distinguish meaningful documentation from placeholders (e.g., "TBD", "fix me"), a verbosity threshold is applied where the word count W_d must exceed a configurable limit (default $W_{min} = 3$). The default count filters out trivial/non-informative outputs, which were frequently observed during preliminary experiments and did not convey meaningful content. Finally, for route operations, a keyword context check verifies the description against a dictionary of functional terms (e.g., "retrieve", "list" for `GET` operations) to ensure that the text accurately describes the performed action. For dimensions measuring coverage (`descriptions` and `examples`), a score S is calculated:

$$S = \frac{V}{F} \times 100$$

where V is the count of valid instances and F is the total number of related functions (routes, responses, or parameters). An evaluation is successful if $S \geq 80\%$. This threshold was chosen as a conservative heuristic to ensure significant narrative depth/coverage of the expected content. Table 1 details the mapping between quality dimensions and concrete evaluations.

RQ.1 Summary. We established 17 evaluations to quantify OpenAPI Specification quality, based on the five dimensions defined in the quality vector $\mathcal{Q}(\mathcal{S})$. This realization transitions from binary validation to a nuanced assessment of an API's maturity for both humans and machines.

4.5 RQ.2 - State of Practice: Quality Assessment

To assess documentation maturity, we executed OASQuali across the full dataset of 2,529 public OpenAPI Specifications. For each specification, we operationalize the Composite Quality Index (CQI) introduced in Sect. 3, assigning a default equal weight $w_d = 0.20$ to each of the five dimensions to ensure a balanced assessment.

Table 1. Set of 17 evaluations formalized from the quality vector $\mathcal{Q}(\mathcal{S})$, to assess the quality of an OpenAPI Specification.

Dimension	Evaluation	Description
$\mathcal{I}$	`validate-json`	Validate JSON serialization standards.
	`validate-oas`	Validate adherence to the OAS metamodel.
$\mathcal{E}$	`oas-version`	Verify version $\geq$ 3.0.0 for modern feature support.
$\mathcal{G}$	`api-title`	Verify presence of the API title field.
	`api-description`	Verify presence of the API-level description.
	`api-contact`	Verify presence of contact metadata.
	`api-version`	Verify presence of a Semantic Version identifier.
	`api-licence`	Verify presence of legal licensing terms.
	`api-terms`	Verify presence of terms of service.
$\mathcal{O}$	`server-url`	Verify presence of server endpoint definitions.
	`server-validity`	Verify validity of defined endpoint URLs.
	`scheme`	Verify enforcement of secure protocols (HTTPS).
$\mathcal{C}$	`route-descriptions`	Validate route description verbosity and keywords.
	`response-descriptions`	Validate response description verbosity.
	`parameter-descriptions`	Validate parameter description verbosity.
	`response-examples`	Verify presence of valid response examples.
	`parameter-examples`	Verify presence of valid parameter examples.

The analysis reveals a mean documentation quality of 67.11%, with individual scores ranging from 28.00% to 96.67%. To investigate the impact of API size (in terms of routes/operations) on documentation standards, the APIs of the dataset were categorized into five percentile-based bins: *micro* (bottom 5%), *small*, *medium*, *large*, and *very large* (top 5%). Small, medium, and large sizes are divided evenly into three bins of the remaining 90%. Due to significant outliers in the *very large* category, specifically three APIs containing 2,958, 11,422, and 22,361 routes respectively, a logarithmic scale was applied to the x-axis for distribution analysis.

As illustrated in Fig. 1, quality scores are distributed heterogeneously across all size categories. The results indicate that aggregate documentation quality is independent of API size, within a stable range between $\approx$ 70% for micro APIs and $\approx$ 65% for very large APIs. This suggests that API scale is not directly correlated to overall API documentation quality when considering all five quality dimensions together.

However, a granular dimensional analysis reveals divergent trends as API scale increases:

- **Evolutionary Maturity ($\mathcal{E}$):** OAS versioning quality increases significantly with size (53.10% $\rightarrow$ 88.00%), suggesting that larger APIs are more frequently updated to modern standards.
- **Semantic Communicability ($\mathcal{C}$):** Conversely, semantic quality sharply declines (42.18% $\rightarrow$ 24.00%), highlighting a systematic lack of descriptions

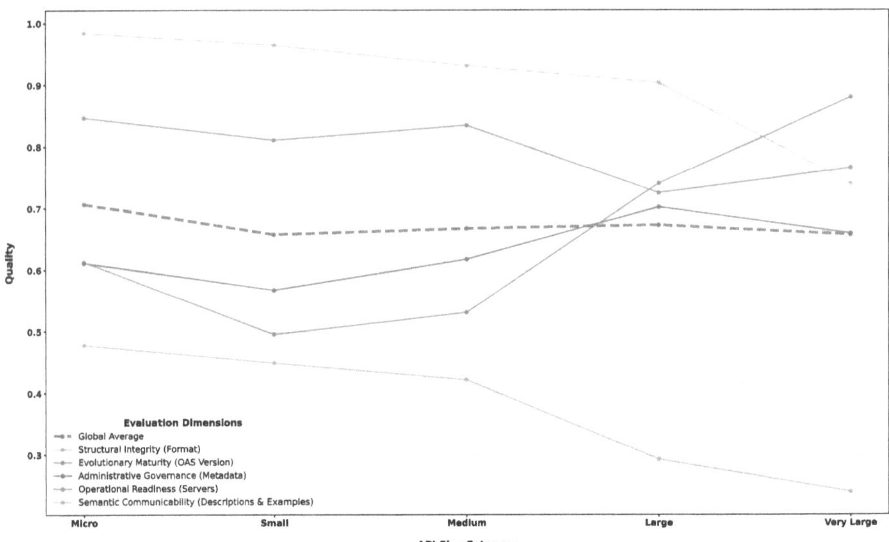

Fig. 1. Distribution of documentation quality across percentile-based API size categories.

and examples in complex APIs. Moreover, the semantic communicability dimension has the lowest score among all dimensions, suggesting an important gap in documented descriptions/examples in REST API documentation.
- **Structural Integrity ($\mathcal{I}$):** Format-related compliance steadily decreases (98.41% $\rightarrow$ 74.00%), likely due to the increased maintenance burden and higher probability of syntax errors in large-scale API specifications.

RQ.2 Summary. Public OpenAPI Specifications exhibit a moderate average quality of 67.11%. While aggregate quality is independent of API size, our results suggest that larger APIs tend to prioritize evolutionary standards over semantic clarity. Furthermore, the decline in format compliance among large-scale API specifications suggests that maintenance complexity remains a significant barrier to structural integrity.

4.6 RQ.3 - Critical Pitfalls: Highest Failure Rates

To identify the primary contributors to documentation deficiency, we analyze the failure rates across the 17 deterministic evaluations. Figure 2 illustrates the frequency of failing evaluations by identifier (introduced in Table 1), pinpointing specific evaluations for which compliance is most frequently violated.

The evaluation `evaluate-parameter-examples` (related to parameter examples) indicates that the most frequent failures occur in 86.95% of the analyzed dataset. This maps to a lack of actionable data samples for API parameters. Similarly, the evaluation of route descriptions (`evaluate-route-descriptions`) constitutes the third most frequent failure, with 63.90% of specifications failing to meet the verbosity and keyword thresholds for route-level documentation. These findings align with the study by Sohan et al. [18], which identified usage examples as a critical component for the effectiveness of REST API documentation.

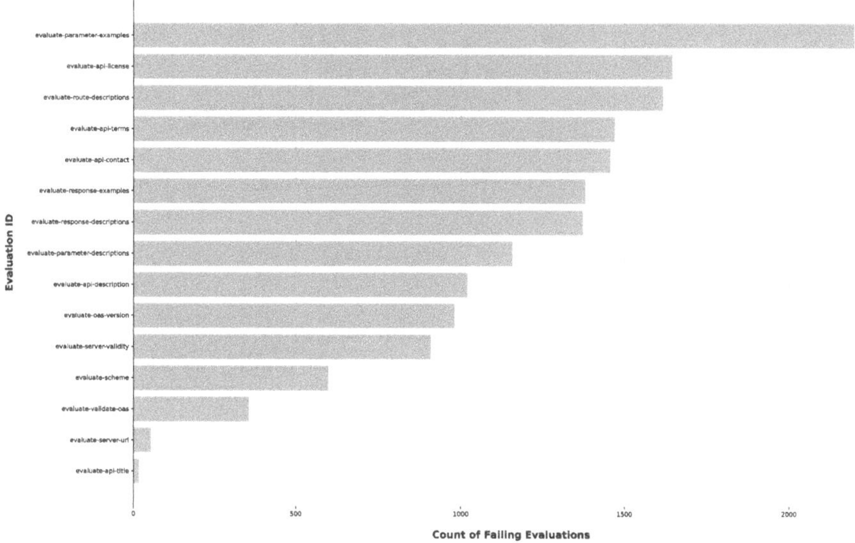

Fig. 2. Frequency of failing evaluations by identifier ($N = 2,529$).

The distribution of failures across the five quality dimensions is summarized in Fig. 3. By aggregating the results, we observe that the Semantic Communicability ($\mathcal{C}$) dimension is the primary source of poor documentation quality, accounting for 37.1% of the aggregate failures. This is followed by Evolutionary Maturity ($\mathcal{E}$) (23.6%) and Administrative Governance ($\mathcal{G}$) (22.5%).

While Structural Integrity ($\mathcal{I}$) is the lowest contributor to overall failures (4.3%), it remains a factor in larger specifications. These results demonstrate a significant disparity between machine-readable structural validity and the presence of descriptive and operational metadata.

RQ.3 Summary. Documentation deficiencies are predominantly related to the Semantic Communicability ($\mathcal{C}$) dimension (37.1% of failures). The most frequent individual failures are the absence of parameter examples (86.95%) and insufficient route descriptions (63.90%). These findings indicate that while structural compliance is largely achieved, specifications systematically lack the semantic depth required for operational clarity.

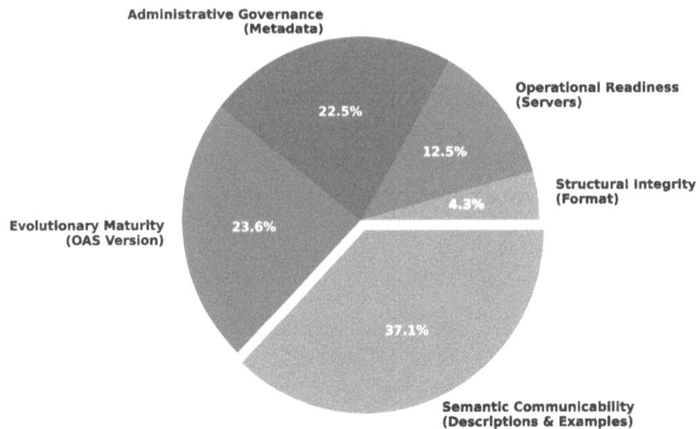

Fig. 3. Breakdown of quality failures categorized by evaluation dimensions.

5 Discussion

The evaluation of 2,529 public OpenAPI Specifications reveals a paradoxical landscape of documentation quality. While aggregate quality metrics appear relatively stable across API size categories, granular dimensional analysis uncovers significant structural shifts that impact the practical utility of these machine-readable specifications.

Evolutionary Standards vs. Semantic Depth. Our analysis demonstrates a distinct prioritization of technical modernization over communicative richness in large-scale APIs. Compliance with Evolutionary Maturity ($\mathcal{E}$) significantly improves with scale, increasing from 53.10% in micro APIs to 88.00% in the very large category. This trend suggests that larger organizations ensure better alignment with modern OAS versions. However, this technical maturity does not imply Semantic Communicability ($\mathcal{C}$), which drops from 42.18% to 24.00% as API size increases. This "semantic gap" indicates that narrative documentation, specifically descriptions and examples, does not proportionally scale with functional complexity. In large ecosystems, documentation appears to be treated as a syntactic requirement rather than a medium for human comprehension or automated consumption.

Maintenance Complexity and Structural Fragility. The observed decline in Structural Integrity ($\mathcal{I}$) among large-scale specifications, dropping from 98.41% to 74.00%, highlights the significant maintenance burden associated with complex specifications. Large APIs are more susceptible to format and schema violations, likely due to the challenges of manual maintenance or the limitations of automated generation tools when dealing with massive object graphs. Given that structural compliance is the primary gatekeeper for most OAS tooling, this decline in integrity for large APIs represents a critical instability in the web engineering pipeline. Adding this to the observation that 86.95% of all analyzed specifications lack parameter examples, the reliability of downstream automated processes such as testing and mock generation is heavily compromised.

Bottleneck of Operational Clarity. The pervasive failure of semantic evaluations, accounting for 37.1% of all documented quality deficiencies, identifies a significant bottleneck for API usability. The systemic absence of parameter examples (86.95%) and route-level descriptions (63.90%) confirms that most public specifications lack the operational clarity necessary for efficient integration. As noted by Sohan et al. [18], the absence of concrete usage examples directly impacts developer effectiveness. In an engineering context increasingly focused on automated integration, neglecting the semantic layer remains a primary obstacle to achieving high-quality web services.

Tool Limitations. OASQUALI focuses on static analysis of OAS files, which may exhibit some limitations. Indeed, the tool does not assess specification and implementation consistency (e.g., verify if all implemented routes are documented, if undocumented endpoints exist, if schemas and HTTP status codes match the actual implementation, etc.). This aspect requires code-level/dynamic analysis, which is not considered in the scope of this work. Moreover, as the tool is mainly static, a successful server availability evaluation does not necessarily mean that the implemented service behaves exactly as documented at runtime. Thus, the tool is better suited as a documentation quality checker than a full API correctness validator.

6 Threats to Validity

The validity of our findings is subject to several threats, which we categorized and mitigated as follows.

Construct Validity. Construct validity concerns the extent to which our 17 evaluations accurately represent the multidimensional quality vector $\mathcal{Q}(\mathcal{S})$. **(1)** To mitigate the risk of arbitrary metric definition, our evaluations are grounded in established architectural principles and an inductive analysis of the OAS standard. **(2)** The application of word-count thresholds and keyword matching in the semantic dimension ($\mathcal{C}$) reduces the risk of treating placeholder text as valid documentation.

Internal Validity. Internal validity refers to the correctness of our analysis pipeline and the accuracy of the resulting metrics. **(1)** A primary threat is the presence of bugs in our tool's implementation. We mitigated this through extensive unit testing and manual cross-validation of results. **(2)** Naive static analysis often fails to resolve complex `$ref` dependencies (cf. Sect. 3), leading to skewed coverage metrics. To solve this issue, we utilized an OAS library capable of dereferencing specifications by replacing references with their actual data.

External Validity. External validity relates to the generalizability of our findings. **(1)** While the APIs.guru directory provides high heterogeneity, it may not fully represent private enterprise APIs or niche domains. We mitigated this by analyzing over 2,529 specifications, ensuring a statistically significant sample size across various scales and industries. **(2)** Our study is restricted to the OpenAPI Specification. While OAS is the de facto industry standard, our findings may not extend to other formats like RAML or Blueprint. **(3)** API specifications are dynamic entities. Since our dataset reflects a static snapshot from February 2026, subsequent updates may have resolved some identified quality deficiencies.

7 Conclusion and Future Work

We introduced OASQuali, a deterministic tool that assesses OpenAPI Specification (OAS) quality, which aims at documentation usability rather than structure. By formalizing quality through a 5-dimensional vector $\mathcal{Q}(\mathcal{S}) = \langle \mathcal{I}, \mathcal{E}, \mathcal{G}, \mathcal{O}, \mathcal{C} \rangle$ and defining a set of 17 quality evaluations related to these dimensions, we conducted a large-scale empirical study on 2,529 public specifications extracted from the APIs.guru directory. Our analysis revealed a mean global quality of 67.11%. Crucially, while aggregate quality remains independent of API size, we identified a significant "semantic gap" in large-scale implementations: as APIs expand, evolutionary compliance increases (53.10% → 88.00%), yet semantic communicability drops (42.18% → 24.00%). The systemic absence of parameter examples (86.95%) and route-level descriptions (63.90%) remains the primary bottleneck for both API user experience and automated integration. Overall, the multi-faceted approach of our tool supports REST API governance processes [1]. Future work will follow three research axes:

1. **LLM Integration:** We aim to leverage Large Language Models (LLMs) to automatically generate missing semantic metadata (i.e., descriptions and examples) identified by OASQuali. We plan to extend our prior work [6] in this direction to bridge the observed semantic gap. Moreover, domain-specific ontologies could be included with the help of LLMs, so that semantic relevance may be checked in a more realistic way.
2. **Quality Over Time:** We plan to track the evolution of quality metrics over time, assessing how documentation matures across successive API versions.
3. **Cross-Format Generalization:** We intend to extend our tool to support alternative Interface Description Languages (IDLs) such as RAML and API Blueprint, enabling a comparative study of quality across documentation standards for REST APIs.

Use of Generative AI. Generative AI was used for limited rephrasing purposes in this paper. The authors have carefully reviewed the final content of the paper and take full responsibility for it.

Acknowledgments. Gilles Perrouin is an FNRS Research associate.

Disclosure of Interests. The authors have no competing interests related to the content of this article.

References

1. Ahmad, M., Geewax, J.J., Macvean, A., Karger, D., Ma, K.L.: API governance at scale. In: Proceedings of the 46th International Conference on Software Engineering: Software Engineering in Practice, ICSE-SEIP '24, pp. 430–440. Association for Computing Machinery, New York, NY, USA (2024). https://doi.org/10.1145/3639477.3639713
2. APIs.guru: APIs.guru - Wikipedia for Web APIs (2026). https://apis.guru
3. Bogner, J., Kotstein, S., Abajirov, D., Ernst, T., Merkel, M.: RESTRuler: towards automatically identifying violations of RESTful design rules in web APIs. In: 2024 IEEE 21st International Conference on Software Architecture (ICSA), pp. 123–134 (2024). https://doi.org/10.1109/ICSA59870.2024.00020
4. Bogner, J., Wagner, S., Zimmermann, A.: Collecting service-based maintainability metrics from RESTful API descriptions: static analysis and threshold derivation. In: Muccini, H., et al. (eds.) ECSA 2020. CCIS, vol. 1269, pp. 215–227. Springer, Cham (2020). https://doi.org/10.1007/978-3-030-59155-7_16
5. Corradini, D., Montolli, Z., Pasqua, M., Ceccato, M.: DeepREST: automated test case generation for REST APIs exploiting deep reinforcement learning. In: Proceedings of the 39th IEEE/ACM International Conference on Automated Software Engineering, ASE '24, pp. 1383–1394. Association for Computing Machinery, New York, NY, USA (2024). https://doi.org/10.1145/3691620.3695511
6. Decrop, A., Devroey, X., Papadakis, M., Schobbens, P.Y., Perrouin, G.: You can rest now: automated rest API documentation and testing via LLM-assisted request mutations (2025). https://arxiv.org/abs/2402.05102
7. Decrop, A., Vandeloise, M.: OAS Quality Tool (2026). https://github.com/alixdecr/oas-quality-tool
8. Fielding, R., Nottingham, M., Reschke, J.: RFC 9110: HTTP Semantics (2022). https://www.rfc-editor.org/rfc/rfc9110.html
9. Fielding, R.T.: Architectural styles and the design of network-based software architectures. University of California, Irvine, Irvine, USA (2000)
10. Hatfield-Dodds, Z., Dygalo, D.: Deriving semantics-aware fuzzers from web API schemas. In: Proceedings of the ACM/IEEE 44th International Conference on Software Engineering: Companion Proceedings, ICSE '22, pp. 345–346. Association for Computing Machinery, New York, NY, USA (2022). https://doi.org/10.1145/3510454.3528637
11. Hosono, M., Washizaki, H., Fukazawa, Y., Honda, K.: An empirical study on the reliability of the web API document. In: 2018 25th Asia-Pacific Software Engineering Conference (APSEC), pp. 715–716 (2018). https://doi.org/10.1109/APSEC.2018.00103
12. Massé, M.: REST API design rulebook: designing consistent RESTful web service interfaces. O'Reilly Media, Inc. (2011)
13. Moon, S.Y., Kerr, G., Silavong, F., Moran, S.: API-miner: an API-to-API specification recommendation engine. In: Proceedings of the 1st IEEE/ACM Workshop on Software Engineering Challenges in Financial Firms, FinanSE '24, pp. 9–16. Association for Computing Machinery, New York, NY, USA (2024). https://doi.org/10.1145/3643665.3648049

14. Serbout, S., Lauro, F.D., Pautasso, C.: Web APIs structures and data models analysis. In: 2022 IEEE 19th International Conference on Software Architecture Companion (ICSA-C), pp. 84–91 (2022). https://doi.org/10.1109/ICSA-C54293.2022.00059
15. Serbout, S., Pautasso, C.: APIstic: a large collection of OpenAPI metrics. In: Proceedings of the 21st International Conference on Mining Software Repositories, MSR '24, pp. 265–277. Association for Computing Machinery, New York, NY, USA (2024). https://doi.org/10.1145/3643991.3644932
16. Singjai, A., Zdun, U.: API description-based conformance assessment of architectural design decision. In: 2022 IEEE International Conference on Service-Oriented System Engineering (SOSE), pp. 59–68 (2022). https://doi.org/10.1109/SOSE55356.2022.00013
17. SmartBear Software: Swagger Editor (2026). https://editor.swagger.io
18. Sohan, S.M., Maurer, F., Anslow, C., Robillard, M.P.: A study of the effectiveness of usage examples in rest API documentation. In: 2017 IEEE Symposium on Visual Languages and Human-Centric Computing (VL/HCC), pp. 53–61 (2017). https://doi.org/10.1109/VLHCC.2017.8103450
19. The Linux Foundation: OpenAPI Initiative (2026). https://www.openapis.org

Toward Reliable LLM-Integrated Web Architectures for Teacher-Aligned Automatic Student Grading

Jonas Gwozdz[1,2](✉) and Andreas Both[1]

[1] Web and Software Engineering (WSE) Research Group, Leipzig University of Applied Sciences (HTWK Leipzig), Leipzig, Germany
[2] Netresearch DTT GmbH, Leipzig, Germany
jonas.gwozdz@htwk-leipzig.de

Abstract. Web-based learning assistants increasingly integrate large language models (LLMs) for adaptive assessment and feedback. However, production deployment still faces engineering challenges in teacher alignment, operational reliability, traceability, and governance. Prior work on LLM-based short-answer grading lacks a repeatable incremental teacher-feedback protocol and a deployment-ready architecture with explicit observability and governance boundaries. This paper contributes a reusable, model-agnostic web architecture for teacher-aligned grading and a fold-wise train-size sweep protocol, evaluated with five LLMs to estimate how much teacher feedback is required to reach target accuracy levels. The highest observed teacher-aligned accuracy was 90.67%, and the results reveal model-dependent trade-offs among alignment quality, error profile, calibration, and token cost—with practical implications for practitioners deploying autonomous LLM grading services in production web environments.

1 Introduction

Large language models (LLMs) enable new forms of adaptive assessment in web-based learning environments. In practice, however, out-of-the-box LLM grading often fails to match a specific teacher's interpretation of correctness [3,7,13]. For classroom deployment, grading quality is not defined by generic benchmark performance but by alignment with teacher expectations, defined course learning outcomes, and the class maturity.

From a web engineering perspective, this gap calls for a service architecture that treats teacher feedback as a first-class component: one that captures grading decisions, adapts model behavior incrementally, and remains auditable across the full deployment lifecycle. The central challenge is that teacher expectations are often implicit and become explicit only through repeated grading decisions. Our design, therefore, treats teacher feedback as the primary adaptation signal and uses learning analytics to monitor whether automatic grading behavior converges toward teacher-aligned decisions. Confidence-based routing—where

A. Mauri et al. (Eds.): ICWE 2026, LNCS 16625, pp. 109–124, 2026.
https://doi.org/10.1007/978-3-032-29372-5_8

high-confidence predictions are auto-accepted and uncertain cases are escalated to teacher review—implements a progressive autonomy model that gradually reduces teacher workload as empirical evidence accumulates [5,12].

Our research follows a long-term agenda dedicated to providing AI-enabled architectures and methods that are both robust and safe. The scope of this paper is teacher-aligned grading adaptation, i.e., the on-the-fly personalization of AI-driven components. Personalization of downstream micro-learning tasks is included in the architecture view but is outside the empirical scope of the current evaluation. Here, we address the following research questions:

RQ1 How can LLM-based grading be adapted to produce decisions that align with teacher judgments for short-answer responses?

RQ2 How much teacher feedback is required before teacher-aligned automatic grading reaches target accuracy levels?

To answer these questions, we contribute a reusable web architecture and a controlled evaluation protocol, and validate both with real classroom assessment data. Figure 1 provides a big-picture overview of the architecture and adaptation loop. A replication package covering prompts, scripts, and analysis artifacts (personal data was removed) accompanies this paper [1].

The paper is structured as follows: Sect. 2 summarizes related work; Sect. 3 introduces the architecture and adaptation process; Sect. 4 defines the evaluation protocol and reports results; Sect. 5 discusses implications and limitations; Sect. 6 concludes the paper.

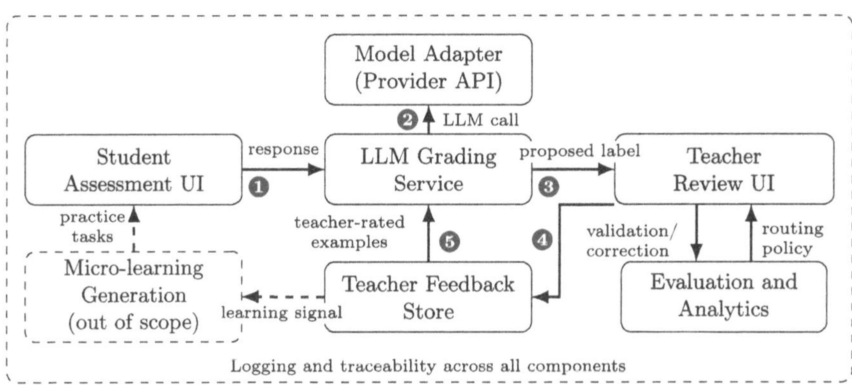

Fig. 1. Reference architecture for teacher-aligned grading. Numbered arrows show the adaptation loop: **1** student response, **2** LLM call, **3** proposed label, **4** teacher validation, **5** feedback for next cycle. The dashed module is outside the empirical scope.

[1] https://github.com/WSE-research/ICWE26-Appendix-Reliable-LLM-IntegratedWeb-Architectures-for-Teacher-Aligned-Grading.

2 Related Work

Research on automated short-answer grading established core validity requirements: alignment with expert raters, transparent scoring criteria, and reproducible evaluation protocols [1,18], with early systems such as C-rater demonstrating feasibility two decades ago [11]. Consistent with this framework, we treat agreement with teacher judgments as the primary quality criterion.

Recent studies show that LLM graders can reach competitive short-answer performance, though quality depends on prompt design, rubric specificity, model family, and domain [7,13,14]. Several approaches leverage teacher-derived supervision: Chu et al. optimize teacher-guideline prompts iteratively to improve scoring agreement [3], Woodrow et al. align generated student feedback via Direct Preference Optimization on teacher preferences [19], and Zhao et al. demonstrate that few-shot in-context examples improve LLM grading [20]. These studies confirm that teacher signals improve alignment, but none quantifies the required feedback volume under a controlled incremental protocol, nor provides a deployment-ready web architecture—the combined contribution of this paper.

Teacher-in-the-loop strategies emphasize selective automation, deferring uncertain cases to teachers to control false-pass and false-fail rates [5,12]. Hori and Yamauchi show that carefully selected teacher labels reduce annotation effort [10], but no prior work quantifies the feedback budget for stable teacher-aligned accuracy under incremental prompting—the focus of RQ2. Related findings on LLM-as-a-judge robustness show that confidence signals can be miscalibrated and sensitive to evaluation setup, motivating explicit error monitoring across feedback stages [4,8,15,17].

When grading systems operate as web services, reliability and traceability become first-class concerns. Microservice studies show that retry and circuit-breaker policies affect robustness and performance [16], and observability research highlights logs, metrics, and traces as central governance mechanisms [6]. LLM provider integrations inherit these concerns and add failure modes from API non-determinism and model drift [2].

In summary, prior grading studies lack a repeatable incremental-feedback protocol and a deployment-ready architecture; reliability research addresses general service robustness but not teacher-in-the-loop educational grading; and no domain-specific architecture guidance exists for autonomous LLM grading services. This paper addresses both gaps: a controlled feedback protocol (Sects. 4–5) answering RQ1 and RQ2, and a reusable reference architecture with explicit observability and governance boundaries (Sect. 3).

3 Approach and System Design

The architecture is designed as a reusable reference for web-based grading systems that integrate external LLM services. The core design goal is to separate stable web-engineering responsibilities (state management, feedback capture, observability, and governance) from replaceable grading-model implementations.

This separation allows deployment teams to change model providers, prompts, or routing policies without redesigning the surrounding web application.

Figure 1 shows the *architecture and interaction boundaries*. Student answers entered through the assessment interface are passed to the grading service. The grading service builds a request from the target answer and current teacher-rated exemplars, then invokes an external LLM provider through a model adapter. The returned decision is presented in the teacher review interface, where the teacher can confirm or correct the label. Confirmed teacher decisions are persisted in the feedback store and become available for the next grading cycle.

The evaluation and analytics module continuously computes alignment metrics from held-out data and generates operational signals for selective automation, such as confidence-threshold routing policies. A cross-cutting logging and traceability layer records request IDs, prompt versions, parse outcomes, retries, confidence values, and final decisions across all modules. These records support auditability, failure diagnosis, and post-hoc reproducibility. A downstream micro-learning generation module is represented as an optional dashed component. This module is included at the architecture level but excluded from the empirical analyses in Sect. 4.

At runtime, the system executes an *iterative adaptation workflow*. First, the grading service retrieves the prompt template and a train-size-specific sample of teacher-rated examples for the target question. Second, the service requests a structured decision from the selected LLM provider. Third, the teacher reviews the prediction and confirms or corrects it. Fourth, the confirmed decision is written to the feedback store and indexed for future in-context sampling. This loop progressively translates implicit grading expectations into explicit prompt-grounded behavior. By design, the workflow supports selective automation. When confidence and parse-quality criteria are satisfied, predictions can be routed directly to automatic acceptance (i.e., the Enterprise Integration Pattern "Message Router" is used here). Cases below the policy threshold are routed to teacher review. This design keeps human oversight explicit while allowing automation coverage to increase only when empirical evidence supports it.

The architecture is reusable because component contracts are defined at interface level. The grading service consumes three inputs (question text, teacher-rated exemplars, and target answer) and produces a typed output (`correct`, `confidence`, and parse metadata). Any model provider that satisfies this interface can be integrated through the adapter without modifying the teacher interfaces or analytics pipeline.

Similarly, the feedback store and analytics module can be replaced independently as long as they preserve the event schema for teacher validation, prompt versioning, and prediction outcomes. This modularity supports portability across courses, institutions, and model ecosystems. The empirical evaluation in Sect. 4 instantiates this architecture with one dataset and one prompt family, but the architectural contracts are not tied to that specific instantiation.

4 Experimental Evaluation

This section specifies the empirical protocol used to evaluate teacher-aligned adaptation. We use real-world short-answer responses from a university computer science course with actual teacher feedback. To address the research questions, we simulate incremental teacher feedback under controlled fold splits. The design quantifies grading quality and required teacher effort as a function of available in-context teacher-rated examples.

4.1 Dataset and Evaluation Design

We evaluate the approach on de-identified responses from a bachelor-level computer science course on Git and version control. The underlying formative assessment contains 25 items (16 multiple-choice and 9 short-answer items). This paper focuses on the short-answer items because multiple-choice scoring is deterministic and does not require LLM-based interpretation. We use manual review data as question-answer-teacher rating triples. Each triple contains the question text, the student's answer, and a binary teacher rating. Rows without a complete triple are excluded. To avoid duplicated observations, we deduplicate responses by question ID, question text, user ID, and answer text.

For the k-fold experiment, a question is eligible if at least 50 teacher-rated responses are available. From each eligible question, we sample exactly 50 rated responses without replacement using a fixed random seed. In the current dataset snapshot, this yields 9 eligible short-answer questions and a pooled evaluation set of 450 question-answer pairs. Of these 450 pairs, 252 (56.0%) were rated correct by the teacher (i.e., they are meeting the teacher's expectations); a majority-class baseline predicting "correct" for every response would achieve 56.0% accuracy, establishing the naive lower bound against which all model results should be compared. The evaluation target is teacher-aligned binary correctness on held-out responses.

4.2 Experimental Setting

We evaluate few-shot adaptation with a fold-wise train-size sweep protocol. For each question-specific pool ($N = 50$), we perform 5-fold cross-validation, producing fold sizes of 10 responses per fold. In each fold, the 10-fold responses are the test set, and the remaining 40 responses are the candidate set for in-context examples. In this protocol, n denotes the number of teacher-rated in-context examples in the prompt, not the total fold subset size. This design keeps the test volume constant across train-size values and isolates the effect of the number of teacher-rated examples in the prompt.

We run the experiment for train-size values n ranging across eleven levels (0, 1, 3, 5, 10, 15, 20, 25, 30, 35, 40). The upper bound $n = 40$ is the natural protocol ceiling: with a per-question pool of 50 responses and 5-fold cross-validation, each fold leaves 40 responses available as training candidates, so no larger prompt size is possible without data leakage. For each fold and each n, we sample n in-context examples from the fold-specific training candidates and evaluate all fold test responses. Consequently, each pooled response is evaluated exactly once per train-size value n (across folds), which yields 50 evaluations per question and train-size value. With 9 questions, 11 train-size values, and one repeat, this corresponds to 4,950 LLM grading calls per model.

All model calls are executed through a unified OpenRouter[2] API interface under a shared prompt schema. The five evaluated models are: Anthropic Claude Haiku 4.5, DeepSeek V3.2, Alibaba Qwen 3.5 397B A17B (no-reasoning mode; reasoning was disabled to maintain comparable output-token counts and inference cost across all five models), Google Gemini 2.5 Flash Lite, and Z.ai GLM 4.7 Flash. Full provider model identifiers, the evaluation run timestamp (2026–02-18), and the complete API call log are included in our artifact package (see footnote 1). We selected this cohort to cover both proprietary (Anthropic, Google) and open-source (DeepSeek, Alibaba, Z.ai) architectures at the early-2026 efficiency frontier. By focusing on "Flash-tier" models, we compare diverse model families under comparable inference-cost constraints.

The system prompt requires JSON output with the keys `correct` (boolean) and `confidence` (decimal number in the range $[0, 1]$). The user prompt includes the question text, the sampled teacher-rated in-context examples, and the target student's answer. The course was conducted in German; all question texts and student responses are in German. The prompt templates are in English and embed the German question texts and student answers as runtime-filled slots. Figure 2 shows the prompt template. Default runtime settings are `temperature` = 0.2, `timeout` = 45 seconds, `max_output_tokens` = 250, and `parse-retry-attempts` = 2 (i.e., if an output is empty or unparseable, the request is retried and logged).

System prompt

```
You are a Git tutor evaluator. Use the provided human-rated examples as grading
guidance. Return ONLY JSON with keys: 'correct' (boolean) and 'confidence' (0..1).
```

User prompt

```
Question: {question_text}
```

Human-rated examples (one block repeated per i)

```
Example {i} answer: {example_i_answer_text}  human_rating: {0|1}
```

(if no examples: "No human-rated examples provided.")

Target student answer

```
{target_answer}
```

Fig. 2. Prompt template used in our evaluation (English; runtime-filled slots contain German course content). Blue = system prompt; green = user prompt; amber = few-shot examples; violet = target answer; red = runtime-filled slots.(Color figure online)

[2] https://openrouter.ai/.

Per train-size value and question, we report accuracy, false-pass and false-fail counts, mean confidence, calibration gap, expected calibration error (ECE; 10 bins), and thresholded selective-automation behavior (selected-set accuracy and coverage). All aggregate rates use the full evaluation volume per model (4,950 tasks). During consolidation, 119 outputs of Claude Haiku 4.5 initially marked as non-parsable were deterministically recovered from valid JSON followed by unsolicited explanatory text, without additional model calls.

4.3 Teacher-Alignment Results

To address RQ1, we ran our experiment with the five chosen models. Each model processed 4,950 grading tasks, corresponding to 9 questions, 11 train-size values ($n \in \{0, 1, 3, 5, 10, 15, 20, 25, 30, 35, 40\}$), 5 folds, and 10 test responses per fold. Table 1 summarizes aggregate alignment and error characteristics. Figure 3 visualizes the train-size adaptation trajectories across the full $n = 0$ to $n = 40$ range.

In this run configuration, Claude Haiku 4.5 showed the highest observed overall teacher-aligned accuracy (88.87%) and the highest observed accuracy at $n = 40$ (90.67%). DeepSeek V3.2 showed strong adaptation from $n = 0$ to $n = 40$, with an increase of 17.11% points, and reached 90% accuracy at both $n = 30$ and $n = 40$. Gemini 2.5 Flash Lite showed the largest gain over the full range (18.44% points) but remained below 90% and retained the highest false-fail rate. GLM 4.7 Flash had the smallest adaptation gain (1.56% points over the full range) and the highest false-pass rate (FPR). Across models, gains over train-size values were model-dependent and not strictly monotonic. To characterize uncertainty at the protocol ceiling, each model at $n = 40$ is evaluated on the available held-out responses. Claude achieved 90.67% with a Wilson 95% confidence interval of [87.62%, 93.02%]. DeepSeek achieved 90.00% with a Wilson 95% confidence interval of [86.88%, 92.44%]. The observed gap is 0.67% points, and the confidence intervals overlap substantially. Paired McNemar tests at $n = 40$ (continuity-corrected, $\alpha = 0.05$, Holm–Bonferroni correction across all 10 pairs) confirm that the differences between Claude and DeepSeek ($p_{\text{raw}} = 0.710$), between Claude and Qwen ($p_{\text{raw}} = 0.377$), and between DeepSeek and Qwen ($p_{\text{raw}} = 0.749$) are not statistically significant. Claude significantly outperforms both Gemini ($p_{\text{holm}} = 0.049$) and GLM ($p_{\text{holm}} < 0.001$); DeepSeek and Qwen each significantly outperform GLM ($p_{\text{holm}} \leq 0.001$). The comparisons DeepSeek vs. Gemini, Qwen vs. Gemini, and Gemini vs. GLM do not reach significance after Holm correction ($p_{\text{holm}} = 0.202$ in all three cases), though their bootstrap 95% confidence intervals for the accuracy difference exclude zero. Bootstrap confidence intervals (10,000 resamples) confirm that the top-three accuracy differences are consistent with zero, while the gaps toward the lower-performing models exclude zero.

Figure 3 shows that model trajectories differ in both slope and saturation point. Claude remains near the top level across most train-size values and reaches the highest observed peak. DeepSeek improves strongly through $n = 15$ and continues an upward trend through $n = 40$, indicating it had not saturated at

$n = 25$. Gemini benefits from additional examples up to $n = 25$ but remains non-monotonic beyond that point. GLM and Qwen show flatter trajectories at larger n, indicating weaker gains from additional in-context teacher feedback in the evaluated range.

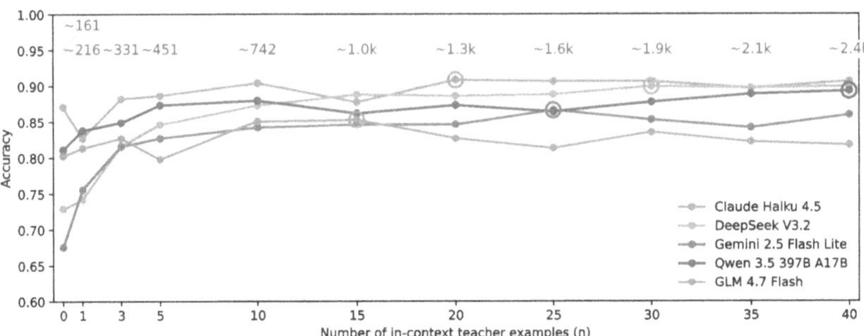

Fig. 3. Teacher-aligned accuracy versus number of in-context teacher examples n across full runs. Hollow rings indicate each model's earliest peak accuracy. Grey values at the top of the chart show the cross-model average prompt token count per request at each n; output tokens remained below 40 across all runs.

Table 1. Teacher-aligned grading results across full runs (percent values). Δ = Accuracy(n=40) − Accuracy(n=0). Qwen 3.5 397B A17B was evaluated in no-reasoning mode. Rows are sorted by accuracy at $n = 40$.

Model	Accuracy	Accuracy ($n = 0$)	Accuracy ($n = 40$)	Δ	False-pass rate	False-fail rate
Claude Haiku 4.5	88.87	87.11	90.67	+3.56	3.49	7.64
DeepSeek V3.2	85.17	72.89	90.00	+17.11	2.89	11.94
Qwen 3.5 397B A17B	86.46	81.11	89.33	+8.22	2.22	11.31
Gemini 2.5 Flash Lite	82.10	67.56	86.00	+18.44	1.52	16.38
GLM 4.7 Flash	82.36	80.22	81.78	+1.56	7.98	9.66

4.4 Confidence and Calibration

Confidence increased from $n = 0$ to $n = 40$ for all models, with Δ mean confidence between +0.0142 and +0.0717. Within each model, confidence and teacher-aligned accuracy trajectories across train-size values were positively correlated ($r = 0.5222$ for GLM to $r = 0.9646$ for DeepSeek). This indicates that larger in-context teacher feedback budgets generally increase both signals in the evaluated dataset and protocol.

Cross-model confidence, however, was not a direct proxy for teacher alignment quality. Claude showed the highest observed overall teacher-aligned accuracy (0.8887) with lower mean confidence (0.8836) than Qwen (0.9549) and Gemini (0.9304). Figure 4 and Table 2 show that calibration quality was model-dependent. Claude was close to calibrated (gap −0.0051, ECE 0.0236), while DeepSeek, Qwen, Gemini, and GLM showed positive calibration gaps, indicating overconfidence to varying degrees. Full reliability diagrams and Brier score breakdowns are provided in the artifact package (see footnote 1).

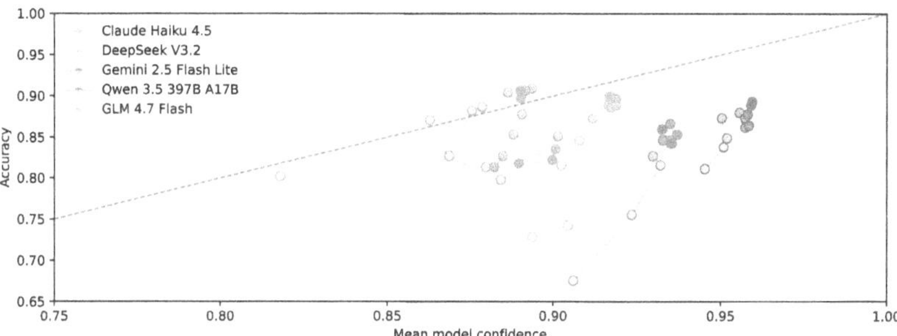

Fig. 4. Mean confidence versus empirical teacher-aligned accuracy across train-size values for each model. The diagonal indicates perfect calibration. Lighter points denote smaller train-size values; darker points denote bigger train-size values.

Table 2 shows that thresholded routing at confidence ≥ 0.95 raises selected-set accuracy for all models; full coverage–accuracy sweep data are in the artifact package (see footnote 1).

Table 2. Calibration summary and selective-automation behavior at confidence threshold 0.95. All values are in the range [0, 1].

Model	Accuracy	Mean confidence	Calibration gap	ECE (10 bins)	if conf. ≥ 0.95	
					Accuracy	Coverage
Claude Haiku 4.5	0.8887	0.8836	−0.0051	0.0236	0.9756	0.3725
DeepSeek V3.2	0.8517	0.9115	+0.0598	0.0601	0.9706	0.3093
Qwen 3.5 397B A17B	0.8646	0.9549	+0.0903	0.0905	0.8868	0.9117
Gemini 2.5 Flash Lite	0.8210	0.9304	+0.1094	0.1101	0.9493	0.3545
GLM 4.7 Flash	0.8236	0.8815	+0.0578	0.1169	0.8996	0.2756

4.5 Feedback-Budget Thresholds

To operationalize RQ2, we report threshold attainment: the minimum number of in-context teacher examples required to reach selected teacher-aligned accuracy targets. Table 3 shows that required feedback volume differs substantially by model. Claude reached 90% accuracy at $n = 10$, while DeepSeek reached 88% at $n = 15$ and 90% at $n = 30$. Gemini and GLM required $n = 25$ and $n = 10$, respectively, to reach 85%. Qwen reached 85% at $n = 5$ and 88% at $n = 10$, but did not reach 90%.

Table 3. Minimum train-size value n required to first reach target teacher-aligned accuracy. †GLM's trajectory is non-monotonic: accuracy peaks around $n = 10$–15 and falls below the 85% threshold by $n = 40$ (81.78%); the threshold attainment is therefore transient.

Model	n for $\geq 85\%$	n for $\geq 88\%$	n for $\geq 90\%$
Claude Haiku 4.5	0	3	10
DeepSeek V3.2	10	15	30
Qwen 3.5 397B A17B	5	10	–
Gemini 2.5 Flash Lite	25	–	–
GLM 4.7 Flash †	10	–	–

4.6 Cost Analysis

Table 4 reports measured token usage and API cost for the full runs, together with per-token pricing obtained from the provider API at the time of evaluation. Claude showed the highest observed alignment quality but also the highest total cost (12.93 USD). Two independent factors explain this premium. First, Claude's per-token pricing is substantially higher: 1.00 USD/M input and 5.00 USD/M output, compared with 0.26 USD/M and 0.38 USD/M for DeepSeek. Normalizing Claude's completion tokens to the DeepSeek level ($\approx$ 86K), its cost would already be 7.02 USD—more than five times DeepSeek's 1.33 USD—purely from the pricing differential. Second, Claude generated 1.27M completion tokens compared with 86–116K for all other models, because it appended unsolicited explanatory text after valid JSON; this verbosity adds a further 5.91 USD, bringing the total to 12.93 USD. Enforcing a structured-output mode for Claude would substantially narrow the cost gap. DeepSeek achieved near-top alignment at substantially lower cost (1.33 USD), providing a strong cost-quality trade-off. GLM had the lowest cost (0.27 USD) and the lowest cost per 1,000 evaluations (0.05 USD), with lower alignment quality than Claude and DeepSeek. The aggregate cost over all five complete runs was 18.47 USD.

Figure 5 visualizes the cost–accuracy trade-off as a Pareto frontier. Four models are Pareto-efficient: GLM (0.05 USD/1k, 81.78%), Gemini (0.11 USD/ 1k, 86.00%), DeepSeek (0.27 USD/1k, 90.00%), and Claude (2.61 USD/1k, 90.67%) each offer the best accuracy attainable at their respective cost tier. Qwen is the only Pareto-dominated model: at 0.68 USD/1k it costs more than DeepSeek while achieving lower accuracy (89.33% vs. 90.00%). Among the Pareto-efficient models, Claude's 0.67%-point accuracy gain over DeepSeek comes at nearly a ten-fold cost premium and is not statistically significant ($p = 0.710$), making DeepSeek the practical optimum for cost-sensitive deployments.

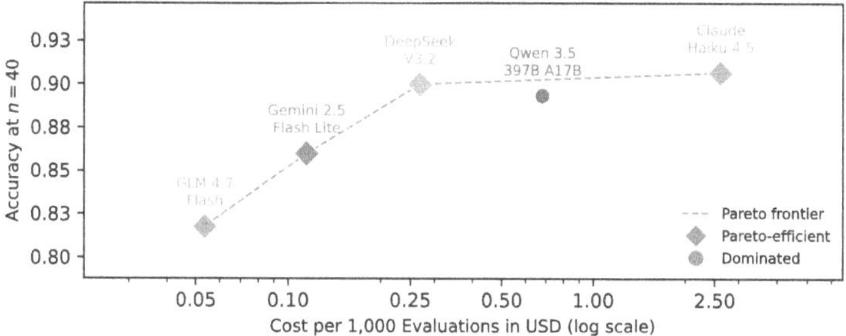

Fig. 5. Cost–accuracy Pareto frontier at $n = 40$. The x-axis shows USD per 1,000 evaluations (log scale); the y-axis shows teacher-aligned accuracy. Diamond markers indicate Pareto-efficient models; the circle indicates the dominated model (Qwen). The dashed line connects the Pareto front.

Table 4. Measured token and cost summary for full runs (4,950 evaluations per model). Input and output prices (USD per million tokens) are from the provider API at the evaluation date (2026–02-18) and may change over time. Cost values are in USD; the last column reports USD per 1,000 evaluations. Qwen 3.5 397B A17B was evaluated in no-reasoning mode.

Model	Prompt tokens	Completion tokens	Input (USD/M)	Output (USD/M)	Cost (USD)	USD/ 1,000
Claude Haiku 4.5	6,589,385	1,268,419	1.00	5.00	12.93	2.61
DeepSeek V3.2	5,493,448	86,219	0.26	0.38	1.33	0.27
Qwen 3.5 397B A17B	5,162,449	98,193	0.46	1.82	3.37	0.68
Gemini 2.5 Flash Lite	5,439,029	90,297	0.10	0.40	0.57	0.11
GLM 4.7 Flash	5,288,162	115,680	0.06	0.40	0.27	0.05

4.7 Per-question Variability

Aggregate accuracy obscures substantial per-question heterogeneity. Figure 6 shows per-question accuracy, false-pass rate, and false-fail rate at $n = 40$ for all five models. Accuracy at $n = 40$ ranged from 64% to 98% across questions and models. Question r1q17 (which required students to describe exactly four git commands for a multi-step repository task, cf. online appendix (see footnote 1)) was consistently the most challenging, with accuracy between 64% and 80%

across all models and a cross-model range of 16% points. Questions r1q10 and r1q15 showed the largest inter-model range (22 and 20% points, respectively), indicating that these questions were less challenging for some model families than others. Question r1q13 was the least challenging, with accuracy between 92% and 98% and a cross-model range of only 6% points.

Error pattern analysis across train-size values reveals that false-fail rate dropped sharply from 17.91% at $n = 0$ to 12.49% at $n = 3$, reaching approximately 9% by $n = 10$ where it largely plateaued. False-pass rate remained low and stable across all n values (2.93%–4.31%). This asymmetry, relevant to RQ2, confirms that incremental in-context teacher feedback primarily reduces false-fail errors and that even a small number of teacher-rated examples substantially closes the false-fail gap.

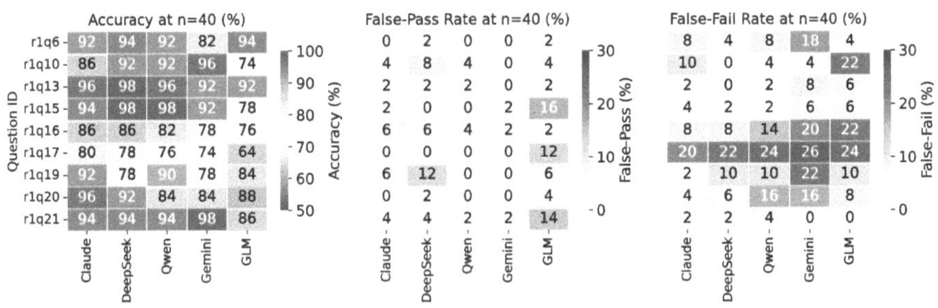

Fig. 6. Per-question teacher-aligned accuracy (left), false-pass rate (center), and false-fail rate (right) at $n = 40$, across all five models. Values are percentages; rows are questions sorted by ID.

5 Discussion

The results provide a direct answer to RQ1. LLM-based grading can be adapted toward teacher-aligned decisions under incremental in-context teacher feedback. Across all evaluated models, accuracy at $n = 40$ exceeded accuracy at $n = 0$, with gains between 1.56 and 18.44% points. Claude (90.67%) and DeepSeek (90.00%) lead the accuracy ranking; their difference is not statistically significant, while both significantly outperform Gemini and GLM after Holm–Bonferroni correction (see Table 1 and Sect. 4.3).

The results also answer RQ2. The required feedback volume to reach target accuracy thresholds is strongly model-dependent. Claude reached 90% at $n = 10$, while DeepSeek reached 90% at $n = 30$, and Gemini required $n = 25$ to reach 85%. These thresholds indicate that deployment planning should treat teacher-feedback budget as a model selection parameter, not as a fixed global constant.

Model trajectories were not strictly monotonic. Claude dropped from 87.11% at $n = 0$ to 82.67% at $n = 1$ before recovering—the largest single-step degradation observed—plausibly due to single-example anchoring; for models with a high zero-shot baseline, waiting until $n = 3$ examples are available may avoid this dip. GLM peaked around $n = 10$ to $n = 15$ and decreased at larger train-size values (81.78% at $n = 40$), confirming that larger feedback budgets are not guaranteed to improve every model. Deployment teams must validate the feedback-volume response empirically per model, as blindly increasing the teacher-rated example pool can degrade accuracy for some model families; full log-curve fit statistics are in the artifact package (see footnote 1).

Error profiles differed systematically across models. Gemini produced the lowest false-pass rate and the highest false-fail rate, indicating conservative grading behavior. GLM produced the highest false-pass rate, indicating a more permissive behavior. These trade-offs have concrete implications for educational risk management. In formative assessment, false-fails carry the higher risk: incorrectly marking a correct answer penalizes students who understood the material, potentially discouraging continued engagement. In summative or high-stakes assessment, false-passes carry a higher risk: granting unearned credit undermines the assessment's validity. This suggests a model-selection heuristic: models with a low false-fail rate (e.g., Claude) align better with formative workflows where protecting correct students is the priority, while models with a low false-pass rate (e.g., Gemini) align better with high-stakes contexts where erring on the side of caution is preferred, despite the higher false-fail burden.

Analysis of in-context label composition revealed a consistent pattern: accuracy was lowest at extreme label ratios (all-correct or all-incorrect context), with GLM uniquely sensitive at low correct-label ratios (false-pass rates 16–31% when fewer than 30% of examples were correct answers). This suggests a concrete deployment strategy: the teacher review interface should guide early feedback collection toward a balanced label mix, operationalized by tracking the running label ratio and surfacing a diversity warning when the in-context pool drifts toward an extreme.

Per-question analysis highlights that not all question types are equally automatable. Question r1q17 (see Sect. 4.7) was the most challenging across all models, with teacher-aligned accuracy at $n = 40$ ranging from 64% (GLM) to 80% (Claude). Critically, four of the five models produced zero false-pass errors on this question, meaning all grading failures were false-fails: the LLMs penalized valid alternative command sequences that the teacher accepted as correct. Excluding r1q17 from the evaluation increases the nine-question average accuracy for every model. This is not proposed as a modification to the main results but as a diagnostic: the low-accuracy pattern for r1q17 reflects a structural mismatch between the LLM's interpretation of the rubric (stricter) and the teacher's implicit acceptance of answer variation (more flexible). The architecture's teacher review interface is designed precisely for this scenario: rather than removing such questions from automation, deployment teams can route low-confidence predictions to teacher review while progressively expanding the teacher-rated example pool to capture the acceptable answer variation. Full automation is not the design goal; graceful human-in-the-loop escalation is.

Operational reliability remained a deployment concern. Structured-output compliance checks and parser robustness should remain first-class deployment criteria alongside alignment accuracy. Dedicated stress tests of fallback policies under provider degradation are left for future work.

Confidence should be treated as a model-specific operational signal; deployment decisions should jointly optimize alignment quality, calibration, parse reliability, and token cost. The FPR-budget analysis reveals a deployment-relevant differentiation that raw accuracy comparisons obscure: under a false-pass budget of $\leq 2\%$, Claude's near-perfect calibration auto-accepts 85% of decisions compared with 43% for DeepSeek—a coverage difference that provides a practical justification for Claude's cost premium where teacher workload reduction is the primary goal; full threshold sweep data are in the online appendix (see footnote 1).

Despite the extensive data analyses, the study has limitations. The evaluation uses one course context, one student cohort and teacher, one response format, and binary correctness labels; extending to partial-credit scoring and multi-scale rubrics is a natural next step, and results have not been validated across different teachers, subjects, or student populations. The protocol uses a fixed train-size grid and a single prompt family; while this ensures fair cross-model comparison, model-specific prompt optimization could yield higher individual performance, and fine-tuning remains an unexplored alternative. Each condition uses a single repetition; multiple repeats would strengthen stability evidence for close model pairs. Because external LLM services evolve rapidly, the specific model rankings reported here are a snapshot tied to the evaluation date, not permanent conclusions. However, the architecture and evaluation protocol are designed to be durable: the model-agnostic adapter allows providers to be replaced, and the fold-wise sweep re-executed, without modifying the surrounding web application—ensuring that the method outlasts any individual model generation.

Web Engineering Implications. The results establish five model-agnostic principles for web architectures integrating LLM grading services. First, teacher-feedback volume is a model selection parameter: required feedback varied from $n = 10$ (Claude, 90%) to $n = 30$ (DeepSeek, 90%) to infeasible within the evaluated range (Gemini and GLM, 90%); deployment teams should calibrate this threshold empirically per model and domain. Second, the learning curve shape is heterogeneous: monotonic rises ($R^2 = 0.93$, DeepSeek) contrast with non-monotonic trajectories ($R^2 = 0.16$, GLM), so increasing the feedback budget does not guarantee improvement for every model. Third, budget models reach a quality ceiling, and their alignment guarantee may be transient. Fourth, the model-agnostic adapter boundary makes these findings reusable: models can be replaced instantly, and the protocol re-executed without redesigning the surrounding web application. Fifth, an LLM-based service cannot be treated as a static function; it requires a circuit-breaking and routing logic that treats model outputs as high-variance signals requiring constant validation.

6 Conclusion

This paper presented two model-agnostic contributions for teacher-aligned automatic grading: a reusable web architecture and a fold-wise train-size sweep protocol for quantifying incremental adaptation requirements. Addressing RQ1, the empirical results show that teacher-aligned automatic grading is feasible, with the highest observed accuracy reaching 90.67%. Holm-corrected McNemar tests establish a statistically supported performance tier at the protocol ceiling: Claude, DeepSeek, and Qwen are mutually indistinguishable ($p_{\text{raw}} \geq 0.377$); Claude significantly outperforms Gemini and GLM ($p_{\text{holm}} \leq 0.049$), and all three top-tier models significantly outperform GLM ($p_{\text{holm}} \leq 0.001$). Addressing RQ2, the results show that required teacher feedback for reaching target accuracy thresholds is model-dependent, with practical thresholds ranging from $n = 0$ to $n = 25$ for 85% alignment and from $n = 10$ to $n = 30$ for 90% alignment. Per-question analysis reveals that accuracy varied from 64% to 98% across questions and models, and that false-fail rate dropped sharply with the first few teacher-rated examples, supporting the case for even a minimal teacher feedback budget. The analysis demonstrates that deployment decisions should jointly consider alignment quality, error profile, calibration, parse reliability, and token cost. Confidence-based routing and architecture-level observability are necessary design primitives for trusted, reliable LLM integration in educational web systems (see [9])—and, more broadly, for any web service that progressively delegates decisions to autonomous AI components.

Generative AI Disclosure Generative AI and AI-assisted technologies were used as objects of study in the evaluated architecture and as engineering tools during experimentation. All study design decisions, analyses, interpretations, and manuscript claims were authored and validated by the human authors.

Disclosure of Interests. The authors have no competing interests to declare that are relevant to the content of this article.

References

1. Burrows, S., Gurevych, I., Stein, B.: The eras and trends of automatic short answer grading. Int. J. Artif. Intell. Educ. **25**(1), 60–117 (2014). https://doi.org/10.1007/s40593-014-0026-8
2. Chen, L., Zaharia, M., Zou, J.: How is ChatGPT's behavior changing over time? Harvard Data Sci. Rev. (2024). https://doi.org/10.1162/99608f92.5317da47
3. Chu, Y., et al.: A LLM-powered automatic grading framework with human-level guidelines optimization. In: Proceedings of EDM 2025, pp. 31–41 (2025). https://doi.org/10.5281/zenodo.15870201
4. Desai, S., Durrett, G.: Calibration of pre-trained transformers. In: Proceedings of EMNLP 2020, pp. 295–302 (2020). https://doi.org/10.18653/v1/2020.emnlp-main.21

5. Funayama, H., Sato, T., Matsubayashi, Y., Mizumoto, T., Suzuki, J., Inui, K.: Balancing cost and quality: an exploration of human-in-the-loop frameworks for automated short answer scoring. In: Proceedings of AIED, pp. 465–476 (2022). https://doi.org/10.1007/978-3-031-11644-5_38
6. Gomes, F., Rego, P., Trinta, F.: A systematic mapping study on observability of microservices-based applications: fundamentals, classifications, and challenges. Computing **107**, 183 (2025). https://doi.org/10.1007/s00607-025-01540-w
7. Grévisse, C.: LLM-based automatic short answer grading in undergraduate medical education. BMC Med. Educ. **24**(1), 1060 (2024). https://doi.org/10.1186/s12909-024-06026-5
8. Gu, J., et al.: A survey on LLM-as-a-judge. The Innovation, art. 101253 (2026). https://doi.org/10.1016/j.xinn.2025.101253
9. Gwozdz, J., Both, A.: Auditing LLM grading for short-answer responses: confidence gating and cross-model agreement. In: Proceedings of IEEE International Conference on Advanced Learning Technologies (ICALT) 2026 (2026)
10. Hori, T., Yamauchi, K.: Low cost active learning framework for short answer scoring. In: Proceedings of PKAW 2024, pp. 176–189 (2025). https://doi.org/10.1007/978-981-96-0026-7_14
11. Leacock, C., Chodorow, M.: C-rater: automated scoring of short-answer questions. Comput. Humanit. **37**(4), 389–405 (2003). https://doi.org/10.1023/A:1025779619903
12. Li, Z., et al.: Learning when to defer to humans for short answer grading. In: Proceedings of AIED 2023, pp. 414–425 (2023). https://doi.org/10.1007/978-3-031-36272-9_34
13. Nawahdah, M., Sawalha, H., Salameh, R., Taha, M.: Evaluating the accuracy and effectiveness of AI-based grading in computer science education. In: Proceedings of IEEE SCME 2025, pp. 1–6 (2025). https://doi.org/10.1109/SCME62582.2025.11104873
14. Poličar, P.G., Špendl, M., Curk, T., Zupan, B.: Automated assignment grading with large language models: insights from a bioinformatics course. Bioinformatics **41**(Suppl. 1), i21–i29 (2025). https://doi.org/10.1093/bioinformatics/btaf196
15. Raina, V., Liusie, A., Gales, M.: Is LLM-as-a-judge robust? investigating universal adversarial attacks on zero-shot LLM assessment. In: Proceedings of EMNLP 2024, pp. 7499–7517 (2024). https://doi.org/10.18653/v1/2024.emnlp-main.427
16. Saleh Sedghpour, M.R., Klein, C., Tordsson, J.: An empirical study of service mesh traffic management policies for microservices. In: Proceedings of ICPE 2022, pp. 17–27 (2022). https://doi.org/10.1145/3489525.3511686
17. Shi, L., Ma, C., Liang, W., Diao, X., Ma, W., Vosoughi, S.: Judging the judges: a systematic study of position bias in LLM-as-a-judge. In: Proceedings of IJCNLP-ACLC 2025, pp. 292–314 (2025)
18. Williamson, D.M., Xi, X., Breyer, F.J.: A framework for evaluation and use of automated scoring. Educ. Measure. Issues Practice **31**(1), 2–13 (2012). https://doi.org/10.1111/j.1745-3992.2011.00223.x
19. Woodrow, J., Piech, C., Koyejo, S.: Improving generative AI student feedback: Direct preference optimization with teachers in the loop. In: Proceedings of EDM 2025, pp. 442–449 (2025). https://doi.org/10.5281/zenodo.15870266
20. Zhao, C., Silva, M., Poulsen, S.: Language models are few-shot graders. In: Proceedings of AIED 2025, pp. 3–16 (2025). https://doi.org/10.1007/978-3-031-98459-4_1

Privacy-Aware Local-First User Modeling from Cross-Device Traces

Alain Simac(✉)

POPS, INRIA Grenoble, Montbonnot-Saint-Martin, France
alain.simac@gmail.com

Abstract. User modeling from cross-device behavioral traces enables personalized interventions and adaptive web experiences, but prevailing approaches depend on centralized data collection that increases privacy risk and reduces user control. We propose a privacy-aware framework for cross-device user modeling that reduces exposure through minimization, on-device processing, bounded retention, and optional local perturbation, operating under a local-first principle: usage events are captured with strict data minimization, stored and processed on-device, and transformed into higher-level behavioral representations for personalization without centralizing raw traces. The framework defines (i) a minimal, content-free event schema for desktop and mobile activity, (ii) on-device feature construction and pattern discovery (sessionization, routine extraction, and sequence clustering) to model habits and contexts, (iii) retention and redaction policies to limit exposure over time, and (iv) transparency and controllability mechanisms that allow users to inspect, exclude, and delete data and derived models. We implement a prototype pipeline and evaluate privacy-utility trade-offs by varying the granularity and retention of collected signals. Utility is measured via routine detection quality, stability of behavioral clusters, and short-horizon behavioral prediction as proxies for personalization readiness. Privacy posture is assessed through data volume reduction, sensitivity aware minimization, and attack-surface analysis under an explicit threat model. Our results show that accurate and stable user models, enabling the creation of a digital phenotype, can be obtained from strictly minimized, locally processed traces, enabling personalization and downstream agentic coaching while substantially reducing exposure compared to cloud-centric baselines. We discuss limitations, deployment considerations, and implications for trustworthy, privacy-aware web engineering in multi-device environments.

Keywords: Privacy-aware user modeling · Local-first computing · Cross-device behavior · Digital phenotype · Differential privacy · Data minimization · On-device machine learning

1 Introduction

User modeling - the construction of persistent representations of individual preferences, habits, and contexts - is a cornerstone of adaptive systems, from recommendation engines and intelligent tutoring to digital wellbeing coaching and proactive assistants. Modern users interact across multiple devices: a desktop during work hours, a smartphone

A. Mauri et al. (Eds.): ICWE 2026, LNCS 16625, pp. 125–140, 2026.
https://doi.org/10.1007/978-3-032-29372-5_9

throughout the day, and a tablet in the evening. Each device captures a partial view of behavioral patterns; cross-device fusion yields a richer, more accurate model. Yet the standard approach to achieving this fusion - transmitting raw behavioral traces to a central cloud service - raises substantial privacy concerns, creates large attack surfaces, and places users in an asymmetric information relationship with service providers [1].

The regulatory landscape increasingly reflects these concerns. GDPR Article 25 mandates data protection by design and default; Article 5 requires purpose limitation and storage minimization; the emerging ePrivacy Regulation extends these requirements to behavioral data collected through browsers and applications. Despite this regulatory pressure, most deployed user modeling systems continue to collect fine-grained, content-rich traces, retain them indefinitely, and perform all inference server-side - a posture that is difficult to audit and costly to redress [2].

We argue that a fundamentally different architecture is both feasible and desirable: one in which cross-device user modeling is performed entirely on-device, using strictly minimized, content-free event traces, with explicit retention limits and user-controlled transparency mechanisms. We term this a local-first user modeling framework, adapting the term from the collaborative software architecture literature [3] to denote a commitment to on-device storage, local inference, and data sovereignty.

The central challenge is demonstrating that useful, stable behavioral representations - sufficient to support personalization and downstream agentic coaching - can be constructed from traces that have been aggressively minimized. This is a non-trivial question: privacy-preserving mechanisms such as epsilon-locally differential privacy (epsilon-LDP) [4] introduce noise that degrades feature quality; short retention windows reduce the historical context available for pattern mining; and content-free schemas discard signals (e.g., page titles, search queries) that are informative but privacy-sensitive. Accordingly, we evaluate the framework as a user-model construction layer rather than as a complete personalization system. Our utility metrics assess whether minimized local traces retain enough behavioral structure to support stable contexts, routines, and short-horizon predictions that a downstream personalization or coaching component could consume.

This paper makes the following contributions:

1. A formal definition of a minimal, content-free cross-device event schema and a four-component local-first user modeling framework (Sect. 3).
2. A concrete on-device processing pipeline implementing sessionization, routine extraction via SPAM-based sequential pattern mining, and behavioral clustering with stability analysis (Sect. 4).
3. A sensitivity-tiered retention and redaction policy mechanism with enforced TTL deletion policy (with documented limitations: key erasure and database compaction are used where secure deletion is not verifiable) and user-controllable redaction (Sect. 4).
4. An empirical evaluation of the privacy-utility trade-off across epsilon values (0.5 to infinity) and retention windows (1 to 90 days), using routine detection F1, cluster ARI stability, and next-event prediction accuracy as utility proxies (Sect. 6).
5. An explicit threat model and attack-surface analysis comparing the local-first architecture to a cloud-centric baseline (Sect. 6).

2 Related Work

Cross-Device User Modeling

Cross-device user modeling has been studied in recommendation systems and web personalization. Gao et al. [5] propose a federated approach using shared embedding spaces, but require server synchronization of model gradients, introducing aggregation attack surfaces. Work on cross-device tracking [6] relies on deterministic identifiers increasingly blocked by privacy-preserving browser policies. Our approach avoids cross-device identity linking entirely: devices synchronize only anonymized behavioral summaries via E2E-encrypted P2P, with no server-side identity graph.

Privacy-Preserving Machine Learning

The differential privacy literature [4, 7] provides the theoretical foundation for our local perturbation mechanism. Local differential privacy (LDP), in which noise is added client-side before any data leaves the device, can offer a stronger per-release disclosure guarantee than central DP under standard assumptions, at a higher utility cost [8]; longitudinal protection depends on composition and release frequency. We apply an ε-LDP-style mechanism with $\varepsilon = 2.0$ as a pragmatic per-release setting in our prototype; we report utility across ε and explicitly discuss composition limits for repeated releases (Sect. 4). Federated learning [10] offers an alternative paradigm in which model gradients rather than raw data are shared; however, federated approaches require server infrastructure, introduce gradient inversion attack surfaces [11], and do not achieve the strict local processing guarantee our framework provides.

Routine detection from smartphone usage logs has been studied using Markov models [12], recurrent neural networks [13], and sequential pattern mining algorithms [14]. The SPAM algorithm [15] that we adapt for our streaming setting is particularly suited to discovering frequent sequential patterns over moderate-length sequences, operating in linear time with respect to the number of sequences. Prior work on on-device behavioral modeling [16] has demonstrated the feasibility of running such algorithms within mobile power and memory constraints; we extend this to a cross-device, privacy-preserving setting.

The HCI and privacy engineering literature has extensively studied user preferences for data transparency and control [17, 18]. Notably, Almuhimedi et al. [19] showed that users who receive periodic reminders about data collected about them become significantly more likely to take privacy-protective actions. Colnago et al. [20] demonstrated that contextual, just-in-time privacy controls are more effective than blanket opt-out mechanisms. Our transparency and controllability component (Sect. 3, component iv) is directly informed by these findings, providing per-feature and per-model deletion granularity rather than all-or-nothing opt-out.

3 Framework Definition

The data minimization principle (GDPR Art. 5(1)(c); Privacy by Design [21]) requires collecting only data strictly necessary for a specified purpose, through schema-level restriction, temporal bounding, and granularity reduction. Despite this imperative, most deployed behavioral modeling systems collect far beyond what is necessary [2]. Our framework enforces minimization structurally at both the schema and pipeline levels (Sect. 3), rather than as a post-hoc compliance measure.

Our framework comprises four components with well-defined interfaces and privacy responsibilities, as illustrated in Fig. 1. Each component is independently testable and replaceable, consistent with the principle of defense in depth for privacy-by-design systems [21].

User Model. The pair (routine template library, cluster assignment function) constituting a persistent, updatable behavioral representation that enables context-sensitive personalization without raw event content. Defining what constitutes a "healthy" pattern and deriving interventions is handled by the companion coaching layer [22]; this paper is scoped to model construction and its privacy properties.

Behavioral Cluster (Context). A partition of the user's weekly activity profiles produced by k-means clustering over session histograms in the 18-dimensional category space. Each cluster represents a stable usage context (e.g., focused morning work; evening leisure) and serves as a coarse context state for downstream personalization without exposing the event log.

Routine Template. A time-anchored sequential pattern of the form (trigger_time_bin, sequence_of_categories, expected_duration), extracted from recurring behavioral traces via SPAM-based pattern mining. Routine templates are used to detect behavioral deviations and surface coaching opportunities; they contain no raw event content or fine-grained timestamps.

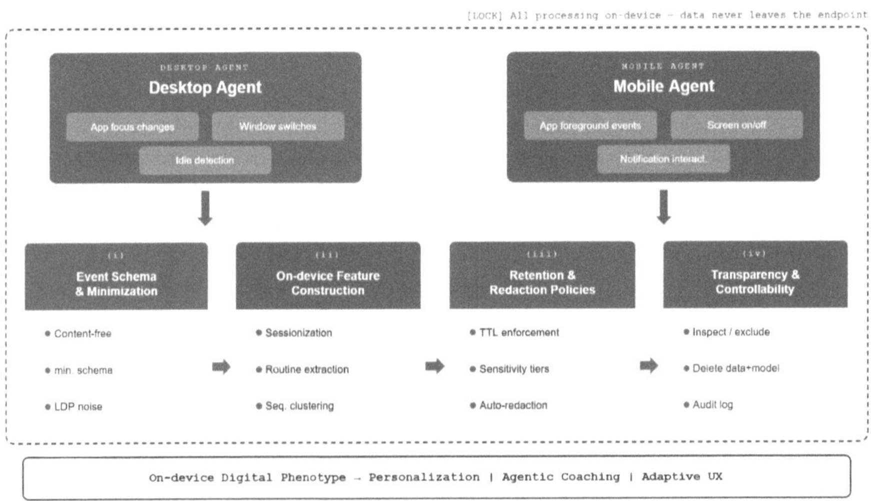

Fig. 1. The four-component local-first cross-device user modeling framework. Desktop and mobile agents feed a shared on-device pipeline. All data remains within the device boundary (red dashed line); only anonymized summaries are exchanged via E2E-encrypted P2P sync.

3.1 Component (i): Minimal Event Schema

The event schema defines the atomic unit of observation. We require it to be: (a) content-free—no URLs, page titles, file names, message content, or contact names; (b) category-level—applications mapped to the 18-category taxonomy; (c) temporally coarsened—timestamps binned to 15-min intervals; and (d) structurally symmetric—the same schema applies to desktop and mobile, enabling cross-device fusion without device-specific feature engineering.

Table 1 lists the 18 application categories used throughout the framework, together with representative applications. The taxonomy was derived from the IAB Content Taxonomy (v3.0) and the iOS App Store category list: overlapping categories were merged and the list was pruned to 18 by removing categories with fewer than 2% representation in a two-week pilot log collected from five participants prior to the main study. The resulting taxonomy covers the behavioral space relevant to cross-device personalization while grouping applications at a granularity that limits sensitive-topic inference.

Formally, an event e is a tuple (t_bin, cat, dur, dev, itype) where t_bin is the 15-min time bin, cat in C is the app category (|C|=18), dur is the session duration in seconds, dev in {desktop, mobile}, and itype in {active, passive, idle} is the interaction modality. Figure 2 contrasts captured and excluded fields and illustrates the LDP noise injection mechanism.

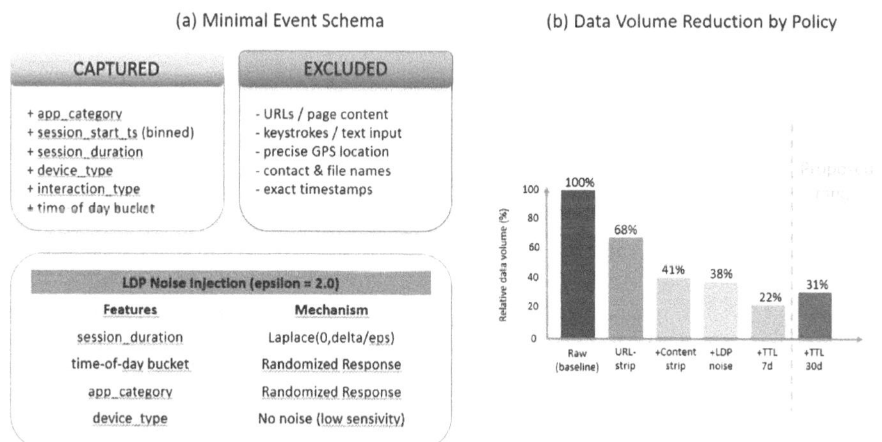

Fig. 2. Event schema design. (a) Fields captured vs. excluded by the minimal schema, and the selective perturbation applied to retained features: app category is kept at coarse 18-category fidelity, session duration is Laplace-perturbed, and interaction type is randomized. (b) Cumulative data volume reduction across successive minimization policies; the proposed configuration (30-day TTL + selective local perturbation) achieves 69% volume reduction relative to unminimized collection.

3.2 Component (ii): On-Device Feature Construction and Pattern Discovery

Given minimized events, the feature construction layer derives three behavioral representations: (a) session-level features, grouping contiguous same-category events within

Table 1. The 18-category application taxonomy: category name, description, and representative applications.

Category	Description	Representative Applications
Productivity	Word processing, spreadsheets, project management	Microsoft Word, Google Docs
Communication	Email, chat, video calls	Microsoft Outlook, Slack
Social	Social networks, forums, community apps	Instagram, Reddit
Entertainment	Video streaming, music, podcasts	Netflix, Spotify
News & Reading	News aggregators, e-books, RSS readers	Apple News,.Pocket
Browser	Web browsing (all content excluded)	Apple Safari, Google Chrome
Finance	Banking, trading, budgeting	PayPal, Mint
Health & Fitness	Exercise, meditation, health tracking	Apple Health, Headspace
Food & Drink	Recipes, food delivery, restaurant apps	UberEats, Yummly
Maps & Navigation	Mapping, transit, ride-hailing	Google Maps, Uber
Shopping	E-commerce, price comparison, deal apps	Amazon, Wish
Education	Online learning, language apps, tutoring	Duolingo,.Coursera
Utilities	System tools, file managers, calculators	Apple Files, SparkEmail
Games	Casual and immersive games	Supercell Clash of Clans, King Candy
Creative	Photo/video editing, design, music creation	Adobe Lightroom,.Figma
Developer Tools	IDEs, terminals, version control clients	GitHub, Jetbrains Toolbox
Calendar & Tasks	Calendar, to-do, reminder apps	Apple Calendar, Todoist
Other / System	Unclassified or OS-level processes	Apple System preferences

a 5-min idle gap; (b) routine templates, recurring time-anchored sequences extracted via SPAM [15] on 7-day sliding windows (s_min = 0.40); and (c) behavioral clusters, obtained by k-means over weekly session histograms (k by silhouette analysis), capturing stable usage contexts such as focused work and leisure browsing.

Routine templates are represented as (trigger_time_bin, sequence_of_cats, expected_duration) triples. They are scored against the current week's behavior to detect deviations and opportunities for coaching interventions. The cluster assignment constitutes the user's context state and is used by downstream personalization and agentic components without exposing the underlying event log.

3.3 Component (iii): Retention and Redaction Policies

Retention follows a three-tier model. Tier 1 (raw events): 30-day rolling TTL, automatic deletion; users may shorten to 7 days. Tier 2 (session aggregates): 90-day TTL; individual sessions may be excluded retroactively. Tier 3 (routine templates and cluster models): retained until explicit deletion, as these abstractions contain no raw content or fine-grained timestamps. TTL enforcement runs nightly; where secure deletion is not verifiable, key erasure and database compaction are used as best-effort mitigations.

The redaction API accepts three operation types: (a) time-range redaction - deletes all events and derived features within a user-specified window; (b) category redaction - excludes all events of a specified category from the model permanently; and (c) full reset - deletes all data and models, returning the system to cold-start state. All redaction operations are logged in an immutable user-readable audit file.

3.4 Component (iv): Transparency and Controllability

The transparency layer surfaces all data held by the system: a chronological event log (minimized schema fields only), the routine template library with per-template behavioral evidence, a cluster summary with estimated context frequencies, and the full audit log of redactions and model updates. Users can toggle individual routine templates, exclude categories from modeling, and export all stored data in JSON format. These controls are rendered through the React Native coaching UI shared with the companion system [22].

To motivate fine-grained controls over a simple on/off toggle: a user may want the system to model work habits for productivity coaching but exclude Health & Fitness app usage for reasons of personal sensitivity. A blanket opt-out disables all modeling; per-category redaction allows selective exclusion. Similarly, users can exclude specific time ranges from routine extraction without a full model reset—a form of contextual, purpose-specific consent shown to be more effective than blanket mechanisms [20].

4 Implementation

4.1 Event Collection Agents

Desktop agents run as background processes using the macOS Accessibility API and Windows UI Automation framework, mapping bundle IDs to the 18-category taxonomy via a local lookup table (updated quarterly). Mobile agents use UsageStatsManager (Android) and DeviceActivityReport (iOS 16+). All agents apply the content-free filter at capture time: raw application names and URLs are never stored, even transiently.

4.2 Privacy Pipeline

Adversary Model. The perturbation mechanism targets an adversary that gains read access to the on-device data store without full OS compromise, covering application-layer breaches, co-resident sandbox escapes, and device loss or theft. We do not claim protection against a compromised operating system or a universal longitudinal DP guarantee, because privacy loss composes over repeated releases.

Perturbation is applied selectively rather than uniformly across all fields. The application category is kept at its already coarsened 18-category representation to preserve sequential structure for routine mining and next-category prediction. Session duration is clipped to [0, 600] s and perturbed with Laplace noise ($\Delta = 600$, budget ε). Interaction type (itype) is perturbed using k-ary randomized response. This design choice reflects a utility-preserving compromise: perturbing the coarse category field itself degraded sequential pattern quality disproportionately in pilot tests, whereas perturbing duration and interaction modality preserved most behavioral utility while still reducing disclosure risk.

At $\varepsilon = 2.0$ with approximately three session-level releases per day, the naïve 30-day sequential budget is $90\varepsilon = 180$. Under RDP composition [7], this corresponds to an approximate equivalent guarantee of $\varepsilon' \approx 19.0$ at $\delta = 10^{-5}$, indicating meaningful cumulative exposure that should be considered in deployment.

4.3 Pattern Mining and Clustering

The SPAM adaptation processes the 7-day sliding window as a sequence database where each transaction is a days sorted session list. We impose a maximum pattern length of 6 and a minimum support of 0.40, yielding between 8 and 34 routine templates per participant in our evaluation. Clustering uses scikit-learns MiniBatchKMeans with k selected from {2,...,8} by silhouette score, retrained weekly. Inference (assigning the current session to a cluster) runs in under 10ms on all tested platforms. All ML models are quantized to 8-bit integers using TensorFlow Lite, keeping model files under 2MB.

4.4 Cross-Device Synchronization

Synchronization exchanges only two types of data: (a) routine template summaries (trigger_time_bin, sequence_of_cats) without durations or raw evidence; and (b) cluster centroids in the shared 18-dimensional category space. Raw events, session logs, and locally noised features are never transmitted. Sync uses a WebRTC data channel with DTLS encryption; a STUN/TURN service is used only for NAT traversal. Network metadata (IP addresses, timing) remains a residual risk that practitioners should mitigate through relay selection and rate-limiting.

4.5 End-To-End Pipeline: Worked Example

To make the pipeline concrete, we trace a single observation through each stage using representative values from our evaluation dataset (participant P07, Tuesday 08:47 local time).

Step 1 - Raw foreground event (captured, never persisted). The desktop agent detects a foreground change to "com.microsoft.VSCode" at 08:47:03. The raw bundle

ID and exact timestamp exist only in volatile memory for the duration of the mapping lookup.

Step 2 - Minimized event tuple (persisted). The bundle ID is mapped to category Developer Tools; the timestamp is coarsened to the 08:45 bin; the session duration (312 s) is clipped to [0, 600] and receives Laplace noise ($\varepsilon = 2.0$, $\Delta = 600$), yielding a persisted value of 287 s. The interaction modality is then passed through the local perturbation step; in this illustrative example, the perturbed output remains active. The persisted tuple is: (t_bin = 08:45, cat = Developer Tools, dur = 287 s, dev = desktop, itype = active).

Step 3 - Session boundary detection. The session layer groups this event with preceding *Developer Tools* and *Browser* events (idle gap < 5 min threshold). A session object is created: (start = 08:30 bin, categories = [Browser, Developer Tools], total_dur = 1′847 s).

Step 4 - SPAM pattern mining (7-day window). After 7 days of similar morning sessions, SPAM identifies the recurring sequential pattern *[Communication $\rightarrow$ Browser $\rightarrow$ Developer Tools]* with support = 0.71 (present on 5 of 7 days). A routine template is created: (trigger_time_bin = 08:30, sequence = [Communication, Browser, Developer Tools], expected_dur = 2′100 s).

Step 5 - Cluster assignment. The weekly session histogram for P07 (high *Developer Tools*, *Communication*, low *Entertainment*) is assigned to Cluster 2 (centroid label: "focused work") by MiniBatchKMeans with silhouette score k = 3. The cluster assignment, not the event log, is passed to the downstream coaching component [22].

5 Experimental Setup

The privacy-utility design trade-offs for each architectural decision (content-free schema, time binning, LDP perturbation, TTL retention, P2P sync, and user redaction) are reflected in the implementation choices summarized in Sect. 4 and evaluated empirically in Sect. 6.

Dataset and Participants

We collected data from N = 32 participants (18 identifying as men, 12 as women, 2 as non-binary; age M = 29.7, SD = 6.4; all knowledge workers using at least two digital devices daily) over a 6-week observation period. Participants installed the collection agent on their primary desktop and smartphone and consented to local data collection under IRB Protocol #2024–0418. No data left participants devices during the study; exit interviews confirmed understanding of the local-first data model. We evaluate across four experimental configurations varying privacy budget (epsilon in {0.5, 1.0, 2.0, 4.0, inf}) and retention window (1, 3, 7, 14, 21, 30, 60, 90 days).

Utility Metrics

We evaluate three personalization-readiness proxies rather than downstream product outcomes. These metrics are intended to assess whether the minimized local representation preserves enough structure to support user-model construction for later personalization or coaching. (1) Routine detection F1: precision and recall of detected routines against ground-truth routines self-reported by participants in exit interviews, thresholded at 0.7 IoU (Intersection over Union) on the time and category dimensions. (2) Cluster ARI stability: Adjusted Rand Index [22] between cluster assignments computed at week k and week k + 1, averaged over weeks 2–6, measuring how consistently the model partitions behavioral contexts. (3) Next-event prediction accuracy: held-out accuracy of a simple multinomial logistic classifier trained on the cluster assignment and time-of-day bin to predict the next app category, evaluated using 5-fold cross-validation within each participant.

Privacy Metrics

Privacy posture is quantified along three dimensions. (1) Data volume reduction: raw byte count of stored features relative to the unminimized baseline (all fields, no noise, no TTL). (2) Sensitivity-aware minimization score: a weighted sum over fields of the product of collection frequency and sensitivity weight (1 = low, 5 = high), normalized to [0,1]. (3) Attack surface score: qualitative assessment against the six threat dimensions in our threat model (Sect. 6), scored on a 1–5 scale per dimension.

6 Results

6.1 Privacy-Utility Trade-Offs

Figure 3 presents the trade-off curves. Panel (a) shows routine detection F1 and cluster stability (ARI) as a function of ε. Both metrics increase monotonically with ε, with diminishing returns beyond ε≈2 in our setup: the marginal F1 gain from ε = 2 to no noise is 0.11, compared to 0.23 from ε = 0.5 to ε = 2. We therefore use ε = 2 as a pragmatic operating point for the prototype, while emphasizing that the effective privacy guarantee depends on release frequency and composition over time.

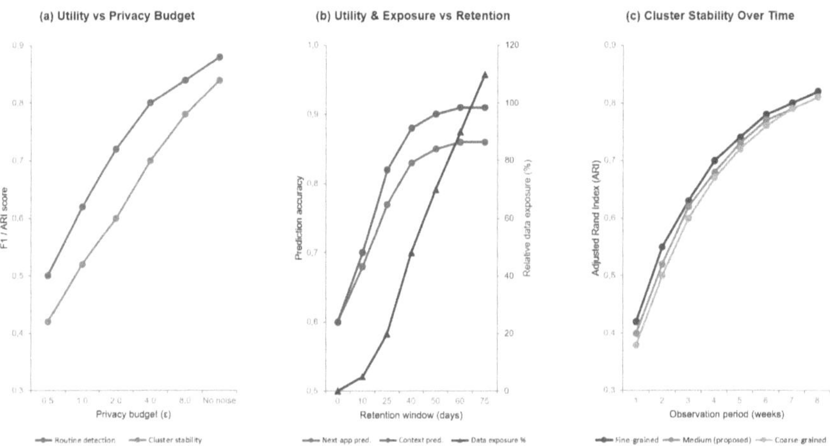

Fig. 3. Privacy-utility trade-off results. (a) Utility metrics vs. LDP epsilon; dotted line marks the selected epsilon = 2.0. (b) Prediction accuracy and data exposure vs. retention window; 30-day TTL offers near-plateau utility at 41% of baseline exposure. (c) Cluster stability (ARI) over observation weeks for three schema granularities; all converge above the stable threshold (ARI = 0.75) by week 5.

Panel (b) shows that both utility metrics plateau around 25–30 days, with negligible improvement beyond 30 days (accuracy gain < 0.02), while data exposure grows linearly with retention. A 30-day TTL captures essentially all utility benefit at 41% of the exposure of an indefinitely retained log; the 7-day configuration achieves 78% of 30-day utility at 22% of its exposure.

Panel (c) shows cluster ARI stability over time for three schema granularities. All three converge above the stability threshold (ARI = 0.75) by week 5. The proposed minimal schema stabilizes slightly later than the unminimized baseline but earlier than the coarse-only schema, confirming that our schema retains sufficient signal for stable clustering.

6.2 Routine Detection Quality

Table 2 reports routine detection (N = 32 participants, see Sect. 5.1) precision, recall, and F1 disaggregated by category class (work, social, wellbeing, entertainment). Work routines - characterized by consistent morning focus sequences - are detected with highest F1 (0.81), reflecting their regularity. Social routines are harder to detect (F1 = 0.68) due to higher session variability. Wellbeing routines (exercise apps, mindfulness) exhibit low recall (0.61) as their temporal anchoring is weaker, though precision is high (0.83), indicating that when detected, they are accurate.

Table 2. Routine detection performance by category class (N = 32, $\varepsilon = 2.0$, 30-day TTL). Values in brackets are 95% bootstrap confidence intervals.

Category	Precision	Recall	F1	Support	Notes
Work / productivity	0.78 [0.73–0.82]	0.85 [0.81–0.89]	0.81 [0.74–0.88]	147	Most regular timing
Social / communication	0.72 [0.65–0.79]	0.65 [0.58–0.73]	0.68 [0.61–0.76]	94	High session variability
Entertainment	0.74 [0.68–0.80]	0.70 [0.64–0.77]	0.72 [0.65–0.78]	118	Evening clustering helps
Wellbeing / health	0.83 [0.74–0.91]	0.61 [0.51–0.72]	0.70 [0.60–0.80]	52	Low temporal anchoring
Micro-learning	0.69 [0.58–0.80]	0.68 [0.57–0.79]	0.69 [0.57–0.80]	38	Short, irregular sessions
Weighted avg	**0.76 [0.73–0.79]**	**0.73 [0.70–0.76]**	**0.74 [0.71–0.77]**	**449**	**All categories, N = 32**

6.3 Threat Model and Attack Surface Analysis

Figure 4 presents the threat model and attack surface comparison. We identify four primary threats: T1 (local malware reading the on-device store), T2 (physical device access), T3 (inference attack reconstructing sensitive attributes from the minimized feature vector), and T4 (linkage attack combining our outputs with external data sources). Figure 4(b) shows that the local-first architecture reduces risk scores across all six attack surface dimensions by an average of 3.2 points (on a 5-point scale) compared to a cloud-centric baseline, with the largest reductions on data-in-transit identifiability (5 to 1) and third-party sharing surface (5 to 1).

Attack surface scores are expert-assigned qualitative ratings on six dimensions (data-in-transit identifiability, third-party sharing surface, retention exposure, local disclosure surface, linkage susceptibility, and transparency/controllability), each scored from 1 (low) to 5 (high) using a fixed internal rubric applied consistently across architectures. Scores are intended as comparative engineering assessments rather than as formal probabilistic risk estimates.

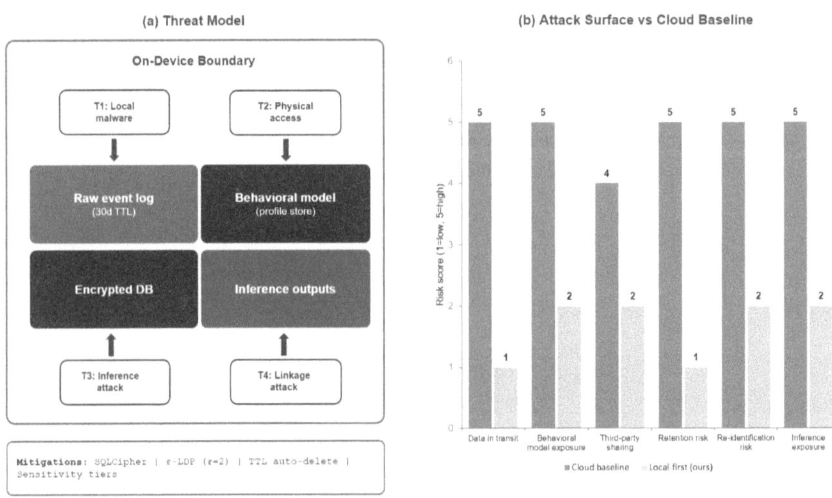

Fig. 4. Threat model and attack surface analysis. (a) Threat model showing on-device assets and the four primary threat categories with mitigations. (b) Risk scores across six attack surface dimensions for the cloud baseline vs. the local-first architecture (1 = low, 5 = high).

The T3 inference attack warrants specific analysis. We evaluate a plurality-estimator adversary who knows the 18-category taxonomy and applies maximum-likelihood reconstruction from the noised feature vector. At $\varepsilon = 2.0$, reconstruction accuracy is substantially degraded relative to the unnoised baseline (97%); residual inference risk increases with release frequency and auxiliary information. For sensitive categories (Health, Finance), an additional content-filtering step further limits reconstructability. Full attacker protocol details and exact accuracy figures are available in the evaluation repository.

6.4 Sensitivity Analysis and Comparison with Related Systems

Table 3 compares our system against three baselines. Versus a cloud-based service: 100% reduction in data-in-transit volume, 59–78% reduction in retention-related exposure (depending on TTL), and elimination of third-party data sharing. Versus federated learning: we additionally eliminate gradient inversion attack surfaces and server infrastructure dependencies, at the cost of cross-device model consistency mitigated by our summary sync protocol. Versus a device-only baseline without minimization: we add 69% data volume reduction and a formally defined per-release perturbation mechanism ($\varepsilon = 2.0$), without claiming a universal longitudinal DP guarantee.

Table 3. Comparison of user modeling approaches across five privacy and utility dimensions. *PRLP: **Per-release local perturbation ($\varepsilon = 2.0$, selected fields)**

Approach	Cross-device	Data off-device	PRLP	User control	F1
Cloud-based service	Yes	All traces	None	Minimal	0.82
Federated learning	Yes	Gradients	Central DP	Limited	0.79
Device-only (no min.)	No	None	None	None	0.85
Our framework	**Yes (P2P)**	**None**	**eps = 2.0**	**Full**	**0.74**

7 Discussion

7.1 Utility-Privacy Frontier and Design Choices

Our results delineate a clear utility-privacy frontier: epsilon = 2.0 and a 30-day retention window represent an operating point at which marginal utility gains from relaxing privacy constraints become small relative to the privacy cost incurred. This finding has practical implications for deployment: system designers can select parameters from this frontier based on their regulatory context and user population, rather than treating privacy as a binary on/off switch.

The 7-day retention configuration - achieving 78% of 30-day utility at 22% of baseline exposure - is particularly attractive for high-sensitivity deployments such as health or financial applications. The primary utility loss is in cluster stability convergence time (reaching the ARI = 0.75 threshold at week 6 rather than week 5), which represents an acceptable two-week delay in model readiness.

7.2 Limitations of Proxy Utility Metrics

A fundamental limitation of our evaluation is reliance on behavioral proxy metrics (routine F1, cluster ARI, prediction accuracy) rather than direct personalization outcomes (e.g., click-through rates, user satisfaction, coaching efficacy). Behavioral prediction accuracy is a necessary but not sufficient condition for personalization quality. Future work should embed the modeling pipeline in a complete personalization system and measure downstream task outcomes in a controlled user study.

A second limitation is the homogeneity of our participant pool (N = 32, knowledge workers, Western demographic). Cross-cultural variation in digital behavior patterns - documented in prior HCI research [23] - may affect the stability and generalizability of the routine templates and cluster structures we extract. A larger, more diverse deployment is needed to characterize this variation.

7.3 The Digital Phenotype as a Privacy-Sensitive Construct

The notion of a digital phenotype - a stable, individualized behavioral signature derived from continuous device usage - is both the value proposition and the privacy risk of user modeling systems. Even a strictly minimized phenotype (18-category, noised, TTL-limited) constitutes sensitive personal data under GDPR Recital 26: it is capable of singling out an individual when combined with auxiliary information. Our framework addresses this through strict local processing and TTL enforcement, but cannot eliminate the risk entirely.

Deployments should implement three additional safeguards: (a) purpose binding—the phenotype used only for user-approved purposes; (b) model opacity—cluster assignments and routine templates consumed internally, not exported in raw form; and (c) periodic re-consent—annual reminders with a frictionless full-reset option.

7.4 Implications for Web Engineering Practice

Our framework has direct implications for web and application engineers building cross-device personalization features. First, content-free event schemas are more tractable than commonly assumed: the 18-category taxonomy covers the vast majority of behavioral variation relevant to personalization and can be extended without breaking privacy properties. Second, on-device inference with quantized models is practical on 2022-and-later mobile hardware, with inference latency under 10 ms. Third, transparency and controllability mechanisms are a prerequisite for user trust, not merely a compliance feature [17]. Fourth, engineers adopting a local-first posture must explicitly opt out of platform backup channels (NSURLIsExcludedFromBackupKey on iOS; android:allowBackup ="false" on Android), exclude sensitive fields from crash reporters and diagnostic payloads, and treat sync metadata as a residual privacy surface—even with encrypted WebRTC payloads, TURN relay timing and IP metadata can support cross-session correlation.

Regarding deployment, the framework supports three integration scenarios: a native OS daemon exposing a local REST API consumed by browser extensions or Electron apps; a Manifest V3 browser extension running the pipeline in a service worker; and a mobile SDK wrapping UsageStatsManager (Android) or DeviceActivityReport (iOS 16 +). A standardized browser API for coarse-grained usage events does not yet exist but would simplify integration significantly.

8 Conclusion

We have presented a privacy-aware framework for cross-device user modeling that achieves stable behavioral representations from strictly minimized, locally processed traces. In our prototype evaluation, routine detection (F1), cluster stability (ARI), and next-event prediction accuracy remain usable under privacy mechanisms and bounded retention, while reducing data exposure relative to an unminimized cloud baseline. The results should be interpreted as evidence that useful personalization signals can be extracted without centralizing raw traces; they do not imply zero risk in transit or a universal DP guarantee for indefinite, high-frequency event streams. We discuss limitations, deployment constraints, and how future work can strengthen formal privacy accounting and longitudinal evaluation.

The local-first approach resolves a false dichotomy that has long constrained the privacy-personalization design space: the assumption that useful user models require centralized raw data collection. Our results show that this assumption does not hold for behavioral pattern-level modeling, at the cost of modest utility reductions that diminish as observation time grows. We release the event schema specification, the LDP pipeline, the retention policy engine, the exact parameter grid (ε values, retention windows, SPAM thresholds), random seeds, and evaluation scripts as open-source components to support reproducibility and adoption by the web engineering community.

Future work will pursue integration with the companion coaching system [22], longitudinal study of phenotype stability beyond 6 weeks, and theoretical analysis of composition across multiple applications sharing the same local phenotype store.

References

1. Luger, E., Moran, S., Rodden, T.: Consent for all: revealing the hidden complexity of terms and conditions. In: CHI 2013, pp. 2687–2696. ACM (2013)
2. Binns, R., Lyngs, U., Van Kleek, M., Zhao, J., Libert, T., Shadbolt, N.: Third party tracking in the mobile ecosystem. In: WebSci 2018, pp. 23–31. ACM (2018)
3. Kleppmann, M., Wiggins, A., van Hardenberg, P., McGranaghan, M.: Local-first software: you own your data, in spite of the cloud. In: Onward! 2019, pp. 154–178 (2019)
4. Duchi, J.C., Jordan, M.I., Wainwright, M.J.: Local privacy and statistical minimax rates. In: FOCS 2013, pp. 429–438. IEEE (2013)
5. Gao, C., et al.: Cross-device user modeling for recommendation: a federated approach. In: WWW 2022, pp. 1612–1622. ACM (2022)
6. Brookman, J., Rouge, P., Alva, A., Yeung, C.: Cross-device tracking: measurement and disclosures. In: Proceedings on Privacy Enhancing Technologies 2017(2), pp. 133–148 (2017)
7. Warner, S.L.: Randomized response: a survey technique for eliminating evasive answer bias. J. Am. Stat. Assoc. **60**(309), 63–69 (1965)
8. Kairouz, P., Bonawitz, K., Ramage, D.: Discrete distribution estimation under local privacy. In: ICML 2016, pp. 2436–2444 (2016)
9. Erlingsson, U., Pihur, V., Korolova, A.: RAPPOR: randomized aggregatable privacy-preserving ordinal response. In: CCS 2014, pp. 1054–1067. ACM (2014)
10. McMahan, H.B., Moore, E., Ramage, D., Hampson, S., y Arcas, B.A.: Communication-efficient learning of deep networks from decentralized data. In: AISTATS 2017, pp. 1273–1282 (2017)

11. Geiping, J., Bauermeister, H., Drautzburg, H., Goldwasser, T., Moeller, M.: Inverting gradients - how easy is it to break privacy in federated learning? In: NeurIPS 2020 (2020)
12. Do, T.M.T., Gatica-Perez, D.: Contextual conditional models for smartphone-based human mobility prediction. In: UbiComp 2012, pp. 163–172 (2012)
13. Zhu, Y., et al.: What to do next: modeling user behaviors by time-LSTM. In: IJCAI 2017, pp. 3602–3608 (2017)
14. Banovic, N., Buzali, T., Chevalier, F., Mankoff, J., Dey, A.K.: Modeling and understanding human routine behavior. In: CHI 2016, pp. 248–260 (2016)
15. Ayres, J., Flannick, J., Gehrke, J., Yiu, T.: Sequential PAttern Mining using a bitmap representation. In: KDD 2002, pp. 429–435 (2002)
16. Ferreira, D., et al.: AWARE: mobile context instrumentation framework. Front. ICT **2**, 6 (2015)
17. Knijnenburg, B.P., Kobsa, A.: Making decisions about privacy: information disclosure in context-aware recommender systems. ACM Trans. Interact. Intell. Syst. **3**(3), 1–23 (2013)
18. Felt, A.P., Ha, E., Egelman, S., Haney, A., Chin, E., Wagner, D.: Android permissions: user attention, comprehension, and behavior. In: SOUPS 2012 (2012)
19. Almuhimedi, H., et al.: Your location has been shared 5,398 times! A field study on mobile app privacy nudging. In: CHI 2015, pp. 787–796 (2015)
20. Colnago, J., et al.: Informing the design of a personalized privacy assistant for the Internet of Things. In: CHI 2020, pp. 1–13 (2020)
21. Cavoukian, A.: Privacy by design: the 7 foundational principles. Information & Privacy Commissioner of Ontario (2009)
22. Hubert, L., Arabie, P.: Comparing partitions. J. Classif. **2**(1), 193–218 (1985)
23. Montag, C., et al.: Smartphone usage in the 21st century: who is active on WhatsApp? BMC. Res. Notes **8**(1), 331 (2015)

Leave No One Behind: Shared-Dictionary Compression in a Legacy-Compatible Global Web-Caching Infrastructure

Benjamin Wollmer[1,4](✉), Florian Bücklers[4], Felix Gessert[4], Fabian Panse[3], Felix Kiehn[1], Maria Fernanda Davila Restrepo[2], and Wolfram Wingerath[2,4]

[1] University of Hamburg, Hamburg, Germany
dbis-research@uni-hamburg.de
[2] University of Oldenburg, Oldenburg, Germany
data-science@uni-oldenburg.de
[3] University of Augsburg, Augsburg, Germany
fabian.panse@uni-a.de
[4] Baqend, Hamburg, Germany
https://research@baqend.com

Abstract. Shared-dictionary compression offers a substantial data reduction when compared to the current de facto standard of stateless compression with Gzip or Brotli. We see some adoption for updates on static files, however we still see no real adoption of shared-dictionary compression on HTML files. In contrast to stateless compression formats, shared-dictionary compression is stateful as it depends on a state defined by a dictionary that may not be available for every request, and not every client supports it. Providing users with different compression formats drastically increases infrastructure traffic and increases cache fragmentation, which results in a reduced cache hit rate. In this paper, we present an end-to-end architecture to automatically apply shared-dictionary compression to all infrastructure traffic and for supported clients. Unsupported clients are gracefully degraded to Gzip or stateless Brotli, while still benefiting from the same underlying shared-dictionary cache to maintain a high cache hit rate. We demonstrate the feasibility of our approach by adapting Speed Kit, an existing multi-tenant web acceleration infrastructure. By analyzing real traffic on more than 400 million page impressions in an A/B test, we show that our approach reduces 82% of our CDN ingress traffic, as well as 39% of the egress traffic, without negatively impacting the performance. Finally, we show how the savings in data transfer directly translate to cost reductions and enable advanced performance optimizations such as predictive preloading.

Keywords: Shared-Dictionary Compression · CDN · Architecture · Cost Optimization · Performance Benchmarking · Edge Computing

A. Mauri et al. (Eds.): ICWE 2026, LNCS 16625, pp. 141–156, 2026.
https://doi.org/10.1007/978-3-032-29372-5_10

1 Introduction

Optimizing the size of transferred files through smarter compression has been an ongoing effort since the beginning of the World Wide Web. Reducing the page weight has the potential to improve the time needed to download and render a web page. Multiple studies indicate that user satisfaction increases with faster page load times, making this an important objective [3]. Still, the advancements in compression primarily focused on image optimization, since images account for a significant share of the page weight for an average page load [5]. Text compression has only recently seen significant developments, with the implementation of shared-dictionary compression across all Chromium-based browsers [1]. Although the implementation as specified in RFC 9842 [11] outlines the tools necessary for implementing shared-dictionary compression on the Web, it does not address strategies for efficient usage. And while they claim significant reductions in file size, we have yet to see real-world examples of its application to HTML files. To the best of our knowledge, shared-dictionary compression is primarily used for updating static assets such as CSS or JavaScript from a previous version, as described in Sect. 1.1 of the specification [10,11].

To address these challenges, we pose the following research question: *How can substantial infrastructure cost savings be achieved through shared-dictionary compression for HTML files without performance impact while maintaining backward compatibility with legacy clients?* This paper presents an end-to-end architecture that automatically generates and applies shared-dictionary compression to all HTML infrastructure traffic and for supported clients, aiming to reduce traffic costs while still maintaining backward compatibility with legacy requests.

Section 2 provides an overview of related work, focusing specifically on text and shared-dictionary compression. Section 3 examines the impact of HTML caching, identifying it as a primary contributor to content delivery network traffic. Additionally, this section discusses challenges introduced by shared-dictionary compression. Section 4 explains how the specification of the compression dictionary transport can be adapted to solve previously discussed problems by designing a legacy-compatible architecture. Section 5 discusses the application of the proposed architecture to Speed Kit, an existing multi-tenant web acceleration infrastructure. Section 6 presents an evaluation of the application on Speed Kit, focusing on its effects on data savings, user performance, and infrastructure costs based on usage by millions of users. Section 7 presents the conclusions.

2 Related Work

Compression Formats. In the three decades following the introduction of Gzip, only two additional compression algorithms have been widely adopted. The first, **Brotli**, received initial browser support in 2016 [4]. Brotli utilizes an internal dictionary integrated into its compression and decompression libraries, which contains common strings frequently found in web and natural language. This dictionary acts as a reference during compression, thereby eliminating the need to store these common strings in the compressed file [4]. Later, the Brotli development team added support for custom dictionaries as alternatives to the internal dictionary. Although this feature was implemented in the library, browser support for custom dictionaries was introduced only recently. **Zstandard**, developed by Facebook, received browser support in 2024. While it generally achieves slightly lower compression ratios than Brotli, it offers faster compression and decompression speeds. Zstandard also supports shared-dictionary compression and provides an internal tool for dictionary training [7].

Shared-Dictionary Compression. The shared-dictionary approach utilized by Brotli and Zstandard was formalized in 2024 through RFC 9842 (Compression Dictionary Transport) [11]. This standard defines two primary use cases. First, any resource can be designated as a dictionary, enabling it to be used to compress other files, typically to facilitate updates between versions or to retrieve related files. Second, a dedicated dictionary file, which may be any raw file, can be used to compress other files. This file functions similarly to Brotli's internal dictionary but is specifically tailored to compress dedicated files. Although the standard specifies methods for integrating shared dictionaries into the web context, there is currently no data regarding its impact on web infrastructure.

Web Corpora Compression. Research on web corpora compression has mainly focused on optimizing storage density and bulk scanning, rather than transmission efficiency for single files via HTTP. As shown in [8], large-scale collections can be compressed to less than 3% of their original size through URL-based reordering and dictionary-based algorithms. However, these approaches are designed for archival storage or analysis. Our architecture is designed to achieve high compression ratios per request while supporting legacy clients

Delta Encoding. Another method for data reduction in compression is pure delta encoding between files [12]. Chan and Woo evaluated this approach by selecting the delta source from the cache by comparing the current request's URL against cached entries. Due to the complexity of maintaining possible deltas in a stateless caching infrastructure, this method has not been adopted to date [6].

In our previous work, we also examined how delta encoding can be used in today's Web. Although potential savings were identified, these are constrained by increased complexity and a reduction in cache hit rates resulting from the introduction of multiple versions of the same file. However, the classification of page types, as commonly defined for modern websites, offers a promising approach for identifying effective delta sources [15].

3 The Price of Data Transfer

According to the Web Almanac data for 2025, the average mobile home page loads 911 KB of image data and only 33 KB of HTML data [5]. This disparity renders the HTML payload comparatively insignificant. Recent advances in caching dynamic files have enabled effective caching of HTML at content delivery networks (CDNs) or clients, thereby altering this imbalance [13]. Unlike images, which are predominantly static, HTML files are typically highly dynamic. Even minor deployments can invalidate all HTML files of a website, potentially affecting hundreds of thousands of files that must then be retransferred to the CDN. Our data indicate that nearly daily deployments account for at least 90% of CDN ingress for HTML traffic, making them the primary driver of CDN costs.

Furthermore, the egress constitutes an additional factor to consider. In general, reducing the HTML file size should result in a proportional reduction in egress data. However, shared-dictionary compression introduces an additional cost: the dictionary itself must be fetched by the client. If users do not continue their sessions after fetching the dictionary, this process generates overhead rather than data savings. Server-side decisions regarding dictionary selection may also lead to clients possessing outdated dictionaries, which are subsequently rejected and not utilized. Since RFC9842 permits the use of multiple dictionaries, it is possible for more than one dictionary to be transferred, further increasing egress. And even when a user continues the session, the initial dictionary download must first be compensated for by requesting enough files to achieve an overall saving.

Even with full support, a dictionary may not be available for initial page impressions (PI), or requests with an outdated dictionary must be delivered in a compatible, dictionary-less format. With dictionary-less compression, recompression to another format can potentially happen directly in the CDN. Content delivered as defined by RFC9842 is compressed using information from the requesting header, but it is not decompressible in the cache because there is no information about the dictionary attached. As a result, for every dictionary-compressed file, at least one generally compatible compression format, such as Gzip, must be transferred. This would increase ingress rather than the intended decrease. And finally, there may also exist multiple dictionaries to be used to compress the same file. As a result, the caching layer becomes fragmented, with multiple versions of the same file served to different users in varying contexts.

3.1 From Speculative Loading to Predictive Preloading

Recent advancements in speculative loading rules in browsers [2] have enabled instant page loads by allowing content to be requested prior to explicit user actions, thereby eliminating download delays. For instance, Speed Kit [13] utilizes predictions based on mouse movements and potential clicks, as well as heatmaps to identify link areas for mobile users. More sophisticated approaches employ statistical models of potential navigation paths, which are executed directly on the client. Whether or not this prediction is used, it still triggers CDN egress that can increase by a factor of 10 to 20, depending on how aggressively the mechanism is implemented. Websites using Speed Kit allocate approximately 90% of their HTML traffic to preloading HTML (cf. Sect. 6). Based on our internal data, this results in about 85% to 95% of navigations using preloaded HTML. Because links on a page are typically related to the currently displayed content, such as recommended products or articles, there is significant potential to achieve high compression ratios in these scenarios. This makes shared-dictionary compression a strong synergy for this approach, as it can reduce or maintain the same byte overhead while increasing the hit rate by preloading additional content.

4 Architecture Design

The previous section outlined the potential of shared-dictionary compression to reduce data transfer, but also highlighted several implementation challenges, including transfer overhead, dictionary management, and cache fragmentation. To address these issues and realize the benefits of this approach, we propose the following architecture, with the main goal of handling the whole CDN ingress as dictionary-compressed content while still being fully compliant with RFC9842.

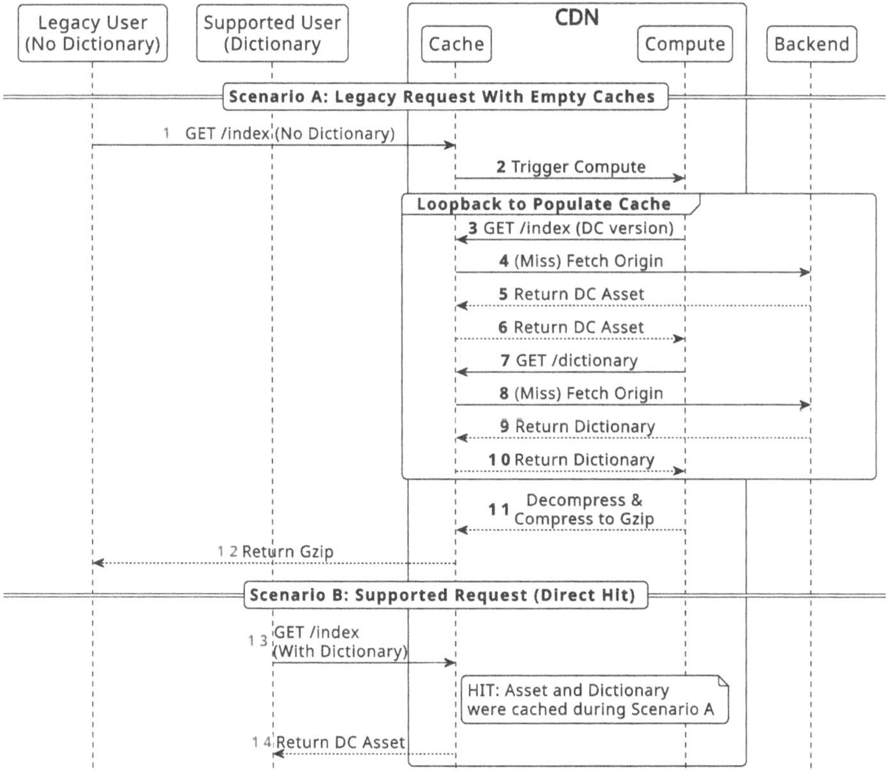

Fig. 1. Regardless of the requested compression, the CDN ingress will always happen with dictionary-compressed content. The recompression ensures that all requests share this underlying format, ensuring at least partial cache hits for follow-up requests.

4.1 Compression Negotiation

Figure 1 illustrates the compression negotiation process, providing an example of an initial state without any cached files. For unsupported clients, either due to the browser lacking RFC 9842 implementation or the absence of a dictionary, the process proceeds as follows: Upon receiving a request **(1)** without a dictionary or cached version available, it will forward this request to the compute module to create a compatible (e.g. Gzip) version **(2)**. The compute module rewrites the request to ensure compatibility with shared-dictionary compression, then returns it to the CDN, thereby creating a processing loop **(3)**. This request does not comply with RFC 9842 because the *Available-Dictionary* header is removed. However, this modification is not visible to the client. But since the response contains a *vary:Available-Dictionary* header, the CDN cannot cache multiple versions of the dictionary-compressed file, which will be relevant later. An additional header is included to inform the CDN that this behavior is intentional and that the server may select the dictionary, which contrasts with the original specification. The CDN forwards the request to the backend to retrieve the file **(4)**. The backend compresses the file using its current dictionary **(5)** and includes a custom header specifying the dictionary ID in the response. The CDN then returns the request to the compute module **(6)** while simultaneously caching the asset. The compute module reads the *Dictionary-Used* header and uses the ID to request the actual dictionary via a loopback to the CDN **(7)**. The dictionary is fetched from the backend **(8–9)**, cached in the CDN, and returned to the compute module **(10)**. Both files are then used to decompress the shared-dictionary-compressed file, which is then recompressed to the desired format (e.g., Gzip) and returned to the CDN **(11)**. The recompressed file is cached before being delivered to the client **(12)**. This process remains transparent to the client. Both processing loops are designed to establish a shared cache between the compute module and clients. After step 12, the Gzip file is delivered, and the cache is populated with the current dictionary, the dictionary-compressed file, and the Gzip variant. Clients requesting either the dictionary or the dictionary-compressed file are now served directly from the cache **(13–14)**.

Removing the *vary* and *Available-Dictionary* headers from the request ensures that any HTTP cache stores only a single dictionary-compressed version of a file. Otherwise, clients using outdated dictionaries would cause the cache to maintain multiple versions. The dictionary-id header is also removed before the HTTP cache lookup to ensure consistency and to assume that clients possess the correct dictionary. After a response from the HTTP cache, the custom dictionary-used header is compared with the original request's dictionary-id header to verify a match. If they match, the *Available-Dictionary* header is appended back to the vary header of the response before returning it. This approach restores compatibility with RFC 9842 and any HTTP cache between the client and the CDN. In the event of a mismatch, the request is rewritten to remove the dictionary-id header and the accept-encoding header is modified to exclude the shared-dictionary format. Standard HTTP caches will then select the next compatible compression format and proceed as described in Fig. 1 step

(1). This can also be reversed: If a supported client makes a request first and an unsupported client follows, the second client will achieve a partial cache hit. In this scenario, all content except the correct format is already cached in the CDN and only needs to be recomputed, rather than fetched from the backend.

The concept of reversing the dictionary selection to let the server decide makes the compute module stateless. At no point does it need to know which dictionary is the current one, as it can always read that information from the header and request the exact dictionary from the backend. This also makes this approach compatible with a server that serves multiple dictionaries simultaneously. If a new dictionary is deployed, the cached version will eventually be overwritten, and the compute module will read the new dictionary.

4.2 Creating a Dictionary

Dictionary generation and updates rely on classifying each HTML document by page type and the frequency of requests for each document. This information can be obtained from access logs or a comprehensive real-user monitoring system. Page types usually already exist on a website because they help segment data for analysis tools such as Google Analytics, and thus, they are generally desired. As we showed in our previous work, any HTML document within the same page type can serve as an effective source file for delta encoding to another HTML document of the same type [15]. For instance, in an online book shop, navigating from one book to another results in HTML files with many overlapping elements. Based on these findings, it is assumed that selecting only a few samples per page type to generate a compression dictionary yields a favorable compression ratio across all pages. From our experience, a standard web shop contains only a few page types, such as home, search, listing, or product, and is generally limited to approximately ten types. To generate a new dictionary, access logs or real-user monitoring (RUM) data are queried to identify the most frequently requested HTML documents for each page type. These documents are then provided to an algorithm that identifies common strings across the samples. The implementation is agnostic to the specific algorithm used; examples include the built-in Zstandard dictionary trainer, the Brotli dictionary generation tool, or Femtozip. The initially generated dictionary is used directly to compress new content. In infrastructures with multiple application servers, which is common in webshops, consensus on the dictionary selection should be achieved through a shared storage service, such as S3, and a message bus or commit protocol. If an outdated dictionary is used for compression, the CDN layer will gracefully handle it, as we discuss in the next paragraph. The dictionary can also be cached on each server until it is replaced by a new version.

The process of generating a new dictionary is initiated by any event that indicates a significant change, such as a new website deployment. In such cases, a new dictionary is always generated according to the established procedure. The decision to adopt the new dictionary is based on a benchmark: a sample of HTML files, representing the most frequently requested files of each page type, is compressed once with the previous dictionary and once with the new version. The average compression ratios of both sets are compared, and if the difference exceeds a predefined threshold, the new dictionary replaces the old one. Otherwise, the newly generated dictionary is discarded. This approach is again supported by the previous findings that files of the same type are sufficiently similar, making the sample representative of the entire set of HTML files. Because only a small number of HTML files are required, the benchmark can typically be completed in a few seconds, depending on hardware and file size.

4.3 Dictionary Delivery

RFC 9842 introduced a new HTML link relation type, which enables browsers to fetch a dedicated dictionary on demand. This tag may be injected on the server side prior to file compression. Alternatively, the dictionary update event can be integrated with existing mechanisms, such as periodic backend requests. In this method, a new dictionary event is appended to the response header and processed by a script, which then initiates a fetch call for the updated dictionary.

According to the specification, supporting browsers first determine which dictionary pattern most closely matches the requesting URL. In the case of a tie, the most recent dictionary is selected. Consequently, the browser can only utilize the newest dictionary, rendering previous versions obsolete.

4.4 Discussion

The architecture itself is compatible with any CDN integration, as long as the delivered HTMLs are cacheable. In Fig. 1, we separated the computation module from the caching layer itself to highlight compatibility with servers like Varnish, which are designed to modify headers and handle caching but not to transform content. Most CDNs offer some kind of computation/edge module within their infrastructure, like Fastly's compute[1] or Cloudflare Workers[2]. But if a more complex logic exists anyway, this can all be integrated into existing edge code without the need for new services.

5 Adapting Speed Kit for Shared-Dictionary Compression

To evaluate the proposed architecture, we adapted Speed Kit. Speed Kit provides HTML caching [13] and RUM through Beaconnect [14]. Currently, Speed Kit uses Fastly as its default CDN, which operates on a modified version of Varnish (VCL)[3]. Given Speed Kit's reliance on Varnish, we offloaded recompression tasks to a dedicated compute module to preserve the existing logic intact. AWS is used for server hosting and storage via S3, with Athena as the query engine. Although Speed Kit supplies most of the essential underlying technology, the following modifications were necessary:

[1] https://www.fastly.com/documentation/reference/compute/.
[2] https://workers.cloudflare.com/.
[3] https://www.fastly.com/documentation/reference/vcl/.

The dictionary generation happens exactly as described in the previous section. We set a raw dictionary target size of 1 MiB. The dictionary itself will also be compressed for delivery, which results in a median size of 119 KiB. While this is still above the average compressed HTML size, we think it is a reasonable overhead for clients. Finding an optimal dictionary size is not covered by our evaluation and is subject to future work. Speed Kit includes a deployment detection mechanism that triggers a revalidation of cached content, which we use to trigger the dictionary generation. After such an event is triggered, Speed Kit has a 5-min grace period before it starts the revalidation process. We hook into this event to query the RUM data as described in the previous section and limit the result to 25 HTMLs, which will be directly revalidated and fed into the dictionary generator. If the dictionary is an improvement over the previous one, it will be used directly to compress the content during revalidation.

The dictionary transfer happens with the piggyback approach. One of Speed Kit's core client-side caching mechanisms is tied to a bloom filter that is periodically requested by the client (c.f. [9]). We append the dictionary id as a response header to this request. The Speed Kit service worker was modified to check for this header to trigger a dictionary fetch.

Prewarming. Speed Kit ensures prewarmed caches in the CDN by loading updated files directly into the CDN before a user requests them. This ensures a high cache hit rate for users. For our approach, we decided to prewarm by requesting content without a dictionary. By doing this, the caches are prewarmed with both a dictionary-less Brotli file and a dictionary-compressed Brotli file.

Predictive Preloading. As described in Sect. 3.1, this feature is also used on most websites of our integration. While this has no effect on how we integrate our design, it is worth mentioning that the preload adds overhead, which is further reduced by our integration.

6 Evaluation

This section presents an evaluation of our shared-dictionary compression approach. We assess data savings for CDN ingress and egress traffic. We also examine overall cost implications and potential impacts on user performance.

6.1 Test Setup

The feature was gradually deployed across 18 websites selected based on contractual agreements and deployment status, rather than targeted sampling. Websites 16 to 18 functioned as examples without preloading. The evaluation period spanned from November 2025 to January 2026, with one month of data collected per website. This timeframe encompasses Black Friday, Christmas, and New Year's, which typically increase page impressions. To ensure comparability

Table 1. The HTML metrics for each website, mapped to a number, show that most websites have a high share of preloaded HTMLs. It shows that PI and HTML size does not indicate the actual CDN traffic, as this is highly influenced by the preloads.

#	Delivered PI (Million)	Ingress (TiB)	Egress (TiB)	Median Raw (KiB)	Median Gzip (KiB)	Median Dcb (KiB)	Preload Share %
1	28.70	0.43	1.28	207.2	47.3	6.9	94.4
2	33.65	1.62	2.65	711.7	70.2	13.7	95.0
3	4.83	0.12	0.31	236.8	50.1	16.3	94.3
4	3.11	0.31	0.60	1687.7	203.3	30.3	89.7
5	3.09	0.58	0.21	778.6	67.1	14.2	84.6
6	9.54	1.44	0.52	250.6	52.9	9.9	91.7
7	6.91	1.12	0.31	222.2	46.2	3.5	94.9
8	20.13	0.93	0.88	207.6	45.5	3.7	95.6
9	41.55	2.61	1.75	192.1	44.3	3.3	96.4
10	16.87	1.23	0.71	215.3	45.0	3.1	92.6
11	33.97	1.86	3.36	1343.5	107.0	21.3	93.6
12	18.44	0.28	1.73	656.5	102.9	13.0	91.4
13	11.96	1.55	1.98	1066.2	187.7	34.0	94.8
14	83.50	1.90	5.79	540.2	72.6	11.8	94.6
15	33.49	1.33	2.24	331.9	56.2	6.9	94.5
16	1.12	1.81	0.11	194.2	48.1	5.5	0.2
17	0.41	0.30	0.04	494.9	118.0	8.5	0.2
18	55.12	2.10	3.68	554.8	65.9	22.4	0.0

despite traffic fluctuations, an A/B test was conducted as described in [13]. The websites were divided into two groups: one utilized the default Speed Kit infrastructure, while the other additionally implemented shared-dictionary compression. Both groups experienced comparable traffic spikes during the evaluation, enabling measurement of relative savings under consistent seasonal influences. As a result, both groups comprised users with and without support for shared-dictionary compression. Table 1 presents an overview of all anonymized websites. Despite notable differences in page impressions across the websites, all evaluation data are reported relative to the control group on the same website. Brotli was selected because it is already dictionaryless supported by the CDN. However, the approach remains agnostic to other compression.

6.2 Data Savings

The initial analysis aimed to quantify the potential reduction in traffic achieved by applying the dictionaries. As shown in Fig. 2, ingress traffic from AWS to the CDN (dark blue) is reduced by a median of 82%. As anticipated, the dictionary itself does not impact ingress data, since it does not update often and is unlikely to be evicted from the cache. The data further demonstrate that websites without preloading (Website 16–18) are less likely to achieve significant gains, as more than 90% of the traffic is generated by preloading.

The red bar illustrates the total CDN egress traffic requested by users. In contrast to ingress traffic from AWS, egress traffic is significantly affected by the dictionary, which must be transferred to each supported user. A saving is

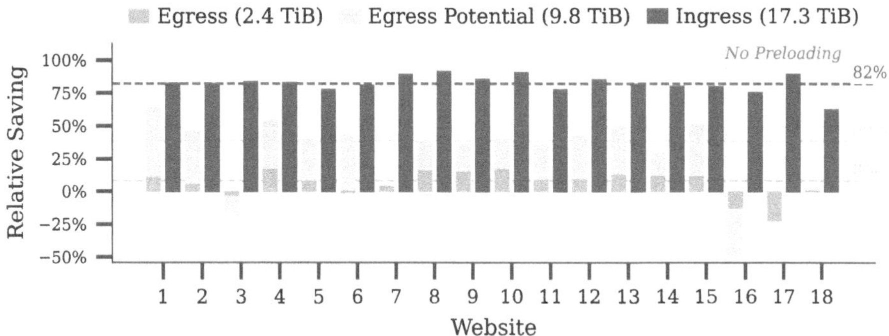

Fig. 2. The outgoing traffic from AWS to the CDN (blue) aligns with anticipated savings, with a median of 82%. Although the compression ratio for individual files remains consistent with egress, the requirement for a dictionary download for each supported user (red) reduces overall savings to a median of 8%. A full rollout with universal browser support (pink) could achieve potential median savings of 39%. (Color figure online)

only realized when the compression benefit exceeds the dictionary's transfer cost. Websites with short session lengths, such as two or three page impressions, often struggle to achieve this threshold, as the dictionary typically benefits users with longer sessions or more preloads.

The issue is even worse for websites with predominantly single-visit users or bot traffic. Conversely, predictive preloading, as previously described, benefits from the presence of the dictionary. The pink bar represents the projected data if this feature were enabled for all users, assuming full browser support. Ingress data serves as an upper bound, as user traffic cannot exceed this compression due to the dictionary transfer limitation. Because both ingress and egress share the underlying dictionary-compressed AWS traffic, the ingress component is not expected to change with a full rollout. The dictionary would not require more frequent transfers to the CDN, and all HTML ingress is already dictionary-compressed.

6.3 Costs

Data savings should generally translate directly into cost savings, as actual network traffic is the primary driver of costs. CDN pricing is generally based on egress traffic rather than on ingress traffic. However, ingress traffic is produced by external egress sources, such as S3, which also incur costs. Since we used Fastly Compute to handle the recompression, we calculated a potential saving based on the limited 500 million requests, at a price of $500 for our AWS egress. Assuming all resources require recompression within the CDN and a median HTML file size of 61.1 KiB, Fastly Compute can process 28.42 TiB of recompression traffic. This results in a 23.31 TiB (82%) reduction in AWS egress traffic. Based on AWS standard pricing[4], for every $500 spent on compute, approximately $2,100 in S3 egress costs can be saved. The potential CDN egress savings are largely determined by usage patterns and the overhead from techniques such as predictive preloading, as shown in Sect. 6.2. Yet, the savings should directly translate.

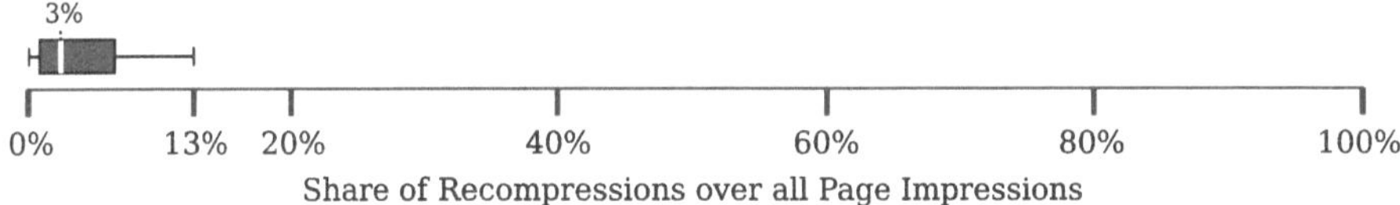

Fig. 3. Given that user-triggered recompressions occur at a median rate of 3%, the resulting overhead can be considered negligible.

6.4 Computation Overhead

There are two points at which new delays are introduced due to computations. The first delay occurs during backend file compression using a dictionary. Previously, outgoing HTML traffic was consistently compressed with Gzip; this has been replaced by dictionary-compressed Brotli. Compression results are streamed directly, preventing precise measurement of actual compression time, as client download behavior may influence timings. Although Brotli typically operates more slowly than Gzip, the Speed Kit architecture's extensive asset caching ensures that this compression step is performed only once per asset.

The second computation happens while recompressing for unsupported clients at the edge. As described earlier, we are currently using VCL for the caching and Fastly Compute for the decompression. The content is then compressed by Fastly's internal compression service. To measure these hops and computations, we looked at those requests which were not dictionary compressed and a cache miss but had a dcb response from the VCL cache. This makes them a "partial" cache miss, since only the recompressed version was missing. This eliminated any outgoing network traffic to our backend, since all needed files are present in the CDN. As Fig. 4 shows, we see an overhead of 32.5 ms for every MiB of uncompressed content ($R^2 = 0.71$), with a median of 37 ms across all websites.

6.5 User Performance Impact

Our primary objective in this optimization was to reduce overall traffic, while also ensuring that user performance remained unaffected. As shown, we identified a computational overhead that could impact users experiencing either a partial cache hit or a full cache miss. However, as depicted in Fig. 3, only 3% of users are

[4] https://aws.amazon.com/de/s3/pricing/.

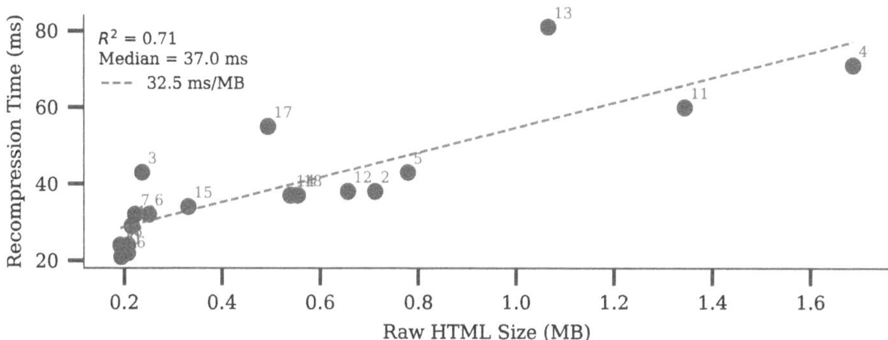

Fig. 4. Isolating the recompression indicates a median overhead of 37 ms.

affected by triggers, making it unlikely that the median user would experience any negative effects. To confirm this, we analyzed key performance metrics that would be expected to change if a significant impact occurred: largest contentful paint (the point at which the browser renders the largest object on the page), first contentful paint (the first time the browser renders any content), and time to first byte (the moment the browser receives the first bytes for this navigation). The download time is measured using a custom performance mark inserted at the end of the HTML, which detects when the HTML is fully available to Speed Kit in the browser. This approach also accounts for any decompression overhead.

We filtered the data to include only users with browsers that could potentially support the feature, regardless of group assignment. This approach was chosen to prevent bias, since dcb is supported only by newer versions of Chromium-based browsers. Including unsupported browsers would have introduced bias toward older devices in the comparison group. Additionally, page load performance is influenced by factors such as whether the user is returning and may have cached resources, or whether the user is newly assigned to a group. To minimize noise, we excluded candidates exhibiting these characteristics from both groups.

Figure 5 shows that the median user is largely unaffected by the architectural change, exhibiting only minor improvements. In contrast, users in higher percentiles generally experience positive effects from the reduced size. The red boxplot further filters the data to include only PI that were full cache hits at the CDN, meaning no recompression was triggered, and no resources were fetched from AWS. This approach isolates the effect of pure size reduction, independent of computational overhead. The data suggest that the median user experiences a modest improvement in these requests, while users with slower performance benefit most. Although direct evidence is lacking, it is likely that clients with unstable or slow internet connections are the primary source of this effect.

6.6 Dictionary Creation

The duration required to generate a new dictionary was evaluated by analyzing the relationship between input size and runtime in the live system. For

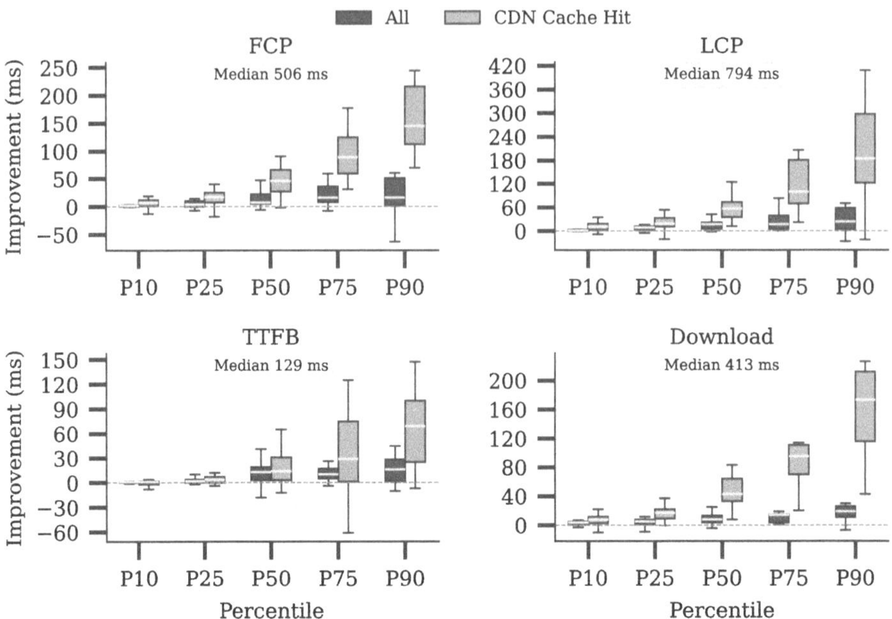

Fig. 5. The median user was not affected by the changes (blue), while users who received cached content had a slight benefit in the higher percentiles (red). (Color figure online)

compatibility, the Durchschlag algorithm from the Brotli repository[5] was translated into Kotlin, which introduces a performance drawback due to JVM overhead. Only a weak correlation ($R^2 = 0.19$) was observed between input size and dictionary generation time. This outcome aligns with expectations, as during a detected deployment, the CDN cache is purged immediately and requests are forwarded, even though they are subsequently cached. During this interval, the server experiences significant load. This is normal behavior of Speed Kit and is not related to the proposed architecture. Nevertheless, because the generation process remains well within Speed Kit's 5-min grace period, it does not pose a challenge for the current configuration.

6.7 Discussion

Our architecture consistently reduces CDN ingress and egress traffic, even with dictionary overhead. We achieved an 82% reduction in ingress transferred bytes, regardless of client support. Although egress improved by only 8% in a 50/50 split, there is potential to increase this improvement to 39% as additional browsers implement the feature. By employing a single dictionary rather than multiple, we maintained a high cache hit rate. The observed performance shows

[5] https://github.com/google/brotli/blob/master/research/durchschlag.cc.

a slight, negligible positive trend. We acknowledge that egress traffic results in a net saving due to the high volume of preloads, though this may not generalize. Egress can be further optimized by adjusting the dictionary size or transferring it only to clients likely to navigate further. Ingress performance remains robust regardless of egress handling. There is also the option to disable dictionary delivery to clients, which would treat all clients as unsupported and may be a viable strategy to target only ingress traffic.

The use of Brotli was driven by Fastly's current support for standard compression to keep our stack consistent. Nevertheless, our architecture is agnostic to other compression approaches, as long as they are supported by the browser. With zstd, the only currently available alternative, similar results are expected.

7 Conclusion

Shared-dictionary compression reduces infrastructure overhead while enabling performance improvements through predictive preloading. Always choosing a one-fits-all dictionary reduced the CDN ingress by 82% and egress by 39%, while reducing the complexity of multiple dictionaries. Expanding browser support could further enhance these benefits by reducing egress traffic. However, several challenges remain. We used a static 1 MiB dictionary, which may hinder optimal egress reduction without predictive preloading. Future work should explore adaptive dictionary sizing and improved strategies for short sessions.

References

1. Compression Dictionary Transport | Can I use... Support tables for HTML5, CSS3, etc. https://caniuse.com/wf-compression-dictionary-transport
2. HTML Standard: Speculative Loading. https://html.spec.whatwg.org/multipage/speculative-loading.html
3. SpeedHub: The ROI of Page Speed. https://www.speedhub.org
4. Alakuijala, J., et al.: Brotli: a general-purpose data compressor. ACM TOI **37**(1) (2018)
5. Barret, R., Indigo, J., Smart, D., Cano, M.: Page Weight, chap. 14. HTTP Archive (2025). https://doi.org/10.5281/zenodo.18246723
6. Chan, M.C., Woo, T.: Cache-based compaction: a new technique for optimizing web transfer. In: IEEE Conference on Computer Communications, INFOCOM '99 (1999)
7. Collet, Y., Kucherawy, M. (eds.): Zstandard Compression and the 'application/zstd' Media Type. RFC 8878, February 2021
8. Ferragina, P., Manzini, G.: On compressing the textual web. In: Proceedings of WSDM '10, pp. 391–400. ACM (2010)
9. Gessert, F., Schaarschmidt, M., Wingerath, W., Friedrich, S., Ritter, N.: The cache sketch: revisiting expiration-based caching in the age of cloud data management. In: Proceedings of BTW 2015, Bonn, GI (2015)
10. Marx, R.: Compression Dictionaries: Early Findings performance.sync() (2025)

11. Meenan, P., Weiss, Y.: Compression Dictionary Transport. RFC 9842, September 2025. https://doi.org/10.17487/RFC9842, https://www.rfc-editor.org/info/rfc9842
12. Mogul, J.C., Douglis, F., Feldmann, A., Krishnamurthy, B.: Potential benefits of delta encoding and data compression for HTTP. SIGCOMM CCR (1997)
13. Wingerath, W., et al.: Speed Kit: a polyglot & GDPR-compliant approach for caching personalized content. In: 2020 36th International Conference on Data Engineering (ICDE). pp. 1603–1608. IEEE. https://doi.org/10.1109/ICDE48307.2020.00142
14. Wingerath, W., et al.: Beaconnect: continuous web performance A/B testing at scale **15**(12), 3425–343 (2022). https://doi.org/10.14778/3554821.3554833
15. Wollmer, B., Wingerath, W., Ferrlein, S., Panse, F., Gessert, F., Ritter, N.: The case for cross-entity delta encoding in web compression (extended) (2023). https://doi.org/10.13052/jwe1540-9589.2217

An End-to-End AI-Powered Big Data Platform for Real-Time Financial News Analysis and Strategic Insights Generation in the Vietnamese Stock Market

Nguyen Viet Chung[1,2] and Phan Duy Hung[1](✉)

[1] FPT University, Hanoi, Vietnam
chung24mse13163@fsb.edu.vn, chungnv@vietplatform.com, hungpd2@fe.edu.vn

[2] Vietnam Technology Platform Joint Stock Company, Hanoi, Vietnam

Abstract. The Vietnamese stock market, as an emerging market, exhibits high sensitivity to information dynamics, which directly influence investor behavior. Manual analysis of financial news is not only time-intensive but also prone to subjectivity and cognitive bias, thereby increasing investment risk. To address these challenges, this study proposes and develops a big data–driven platform that integrates artificial intelligence (AI) within a comprehensive end-to-end architecture. The proposed system automates the entire workflow - from real-time, multi-source news acquisition and preprocessing to deep analysis and strategic insight generation. Leveraging big data technologies such as Apache Kafka and Apache Spark, the platform establishes a high-throughput, scalable data pipeline. At its core, advanced natural language processing (NLP) models execute essential tasks including news categorization, named entity recognition (NER), event extraction, and automatic linkage to relevant stock symbols. The overarching objective is to deliver a transformative technological solution that enhances the efficiency, speed, and objectivity of information processing in the Vietnamese stock market. System-level evaluations demonstrate that the proposed architecture achieves high accuracy (>94% F1-Score in NLP tasks) while strictly satisfying real-time constraints, sustaining a throughput of over 100 messages per minute with an average end-to-end latency of just 11.8 s. By converting unstructured financial news into actionable insights, the platform successfully supports data-driven investment decision-making.

Keywords: AI · NLP · Big Data · Financial News · Stock Market

1 Introduction

1.1 Problem and Motivation

In the context of increasingly volatile financial markets, information disseminated through websites, newspapers, social networks, and other online sources has emerged as a critical factor directly influencing investment decisions [1]. Numerous studies have

A. Mauri et al. (Eds.): ICWE 2026, LNCS 16625, pp. 157–169, 2026.
https://doi.org/10.1007/978-3-032-29372-5_11

demonstrated that news can instantaneously affect investor sentiment, consequently driving fluctuations in stock prices and market liquidity [2]. Nevertheless, the enormous and continuously growing volume of financial news-diverse in both format and language-renders manual processing infeasible [3].

Investors and financial institutions continuously encounter the challenge of efficiently filtering, classifying, and synthesizing information to support timely decision-making [4]. In particular, within the Vietnamese context, most financial news written in Vietnamese remains underutilized, as existing natural language processing (NLP) tools are predominantly optimized for English. This limitation reveals a significant research gap and underscores the urgent need for a system capable of automatically processing Vietnamese financial news in real time [5]. Such a system must handle a complex sequence of tasks, including relevance detection, company and stock symbol identification, topic classification, and content summarization [6]. The motivation behind this research is to develop an intelligent, lightweight, and scalable platform that empowers investors, analysts, and financial institutions to access information more rapidly and accurately. By leveraging advanced techniques in NLP and Machine Learning (ML), the proposed system aims to enhance the quality of financial news analysis in Vietnam and to open new directions for the application of Artificial Intelligence (AI) in the financial domain.

1.2 Related Works

In recent years, the application of Machine Learning (ML) and Natural Language Processing (NLP) in financial news analysis has garnered significant attention from the global research community [7]. Existing studies have primarily concentrated on key directions such as sentiment analysis, stock price movement prediction, financial entity extraction, and domain-specific text summarization [8]. Internationally, many works have leveraged large-scale English-language financial news datasets, including the Reuters Corpus and Financial PhraseBank [9]. Deep learning models, particularly Transformer-based architectures such as FinBERT, have demonstrated outstanding performance in sentiment classification and named entity recognition (NER) for financial texts [10].

In the Vietnamese context, however, research remains limited in both scale and depth. While several studies have explored the use of language models such as PhoBERT for general NLP tasks like text classification or entity recognition, most have focused on non-financial domains. Few in-depth investigations address specific challenges in the Vietnamese stock market, such as automatically linking financial news with stock codes or categorizing market events. This research gap highlights the pressing need to design a comprehensive system tailored to the linguistic and market characteristics of Vietnam. By building upon international advancements and adapting them to local datasets and practical requirements, this study aims to propose an effective solution for the real-time processing of Vietnamese financial news [11].

Unlike conventional NLP pipelines that often string together generic, computationally heavy models resulting in high latency, our proposed architecture introduces a decoupled, hybrid processing paradigm. By deliberately isolating lightweight discriminative tasks (e.g., TF-IDF with XGBoost for filtering) from resource-intensive generative tasks (e.g., localized MoE LLM for summarization), the system entirely mitigates the latency bottlenecks typical of monolithic AI architectures. Furthermore, we differentiate our work from existing English-centric financial tools by engineering a custom linguistic disambiguation layer. This specific design resolves the severe ticker ambiguities and tonal complexities native to the Vietnamese market, which standard off-the-shelf models fail to address.

1.3 Research Objectives and Contributions

The main objective of this research is to build a comprehensive system capable of analyzing and processing Vietnamese financial news in real time, to support the decision-making process in the stock market. To achieve this goal, the following key tasks are set: (i) applying and refining natural language processing techniques, especially Transformer architecture-based models, to Vietnamese financial context [11], and (ii) design a real-time big data processing architecture that can automatically collect, classify, extract information, and summarize news.

The main scientific contributions of this study include:

- Propose a hybrid system architecture: Design and implement a comprehensive (end-to-end) architecture integrating a high-performance big data pipeline (using Apache Kafka and Apache Spark) and a set of specialized AI models for Vietnamese language analysis in the financial sector.
- Design a specialized language processing pipeline: Develop a processing pipeline optimized for the specifics of Vietnamese financial documents, from pre-processing to applying deep learning models for complex tasks such as entity linking and event classification.
- Experimental evaluation and comparison: Provide quantitative evaluation results, comparing the performance between traditional machine learning methods and state-of-the-art language models, thereby demonstrating the superior performance of the proposed architecture in practical contexts.

2 Methodology

2.1 System Architecture

The overall architecture of the "AI for Stock News" system is designed according to a big data processing pipeline model, consisting of many separate layers, each layer is responsible for a specific stage in the processing flow. This separation makes the system highly modular, flexible and easily expandable.

The architecture is built on five main layers (Fig. 1): **(1) Data Collection Layer:** Includes real-time and batch crawlers to fetch raw news data. **(2) Data Streaming Layer:** Uses Apache Kafka as a central message queue to ingest streams and deliver results. **(3) Processing Layer:** The system core, using Apache Spark Streaming to execute the NLP pipeline in parallel. **(4) Storage & Publishing Layer:** Employs PostgreSQL, MinIO, and HDFS for storage, and Kafka for real-time publishing. **(5) Downstream Layer:** End-user applications (Telegram Bot, Dashboards) consume the Kafka channel to display insights. Data flows sequentially through these layers, transforming from raw text into strategic insights.

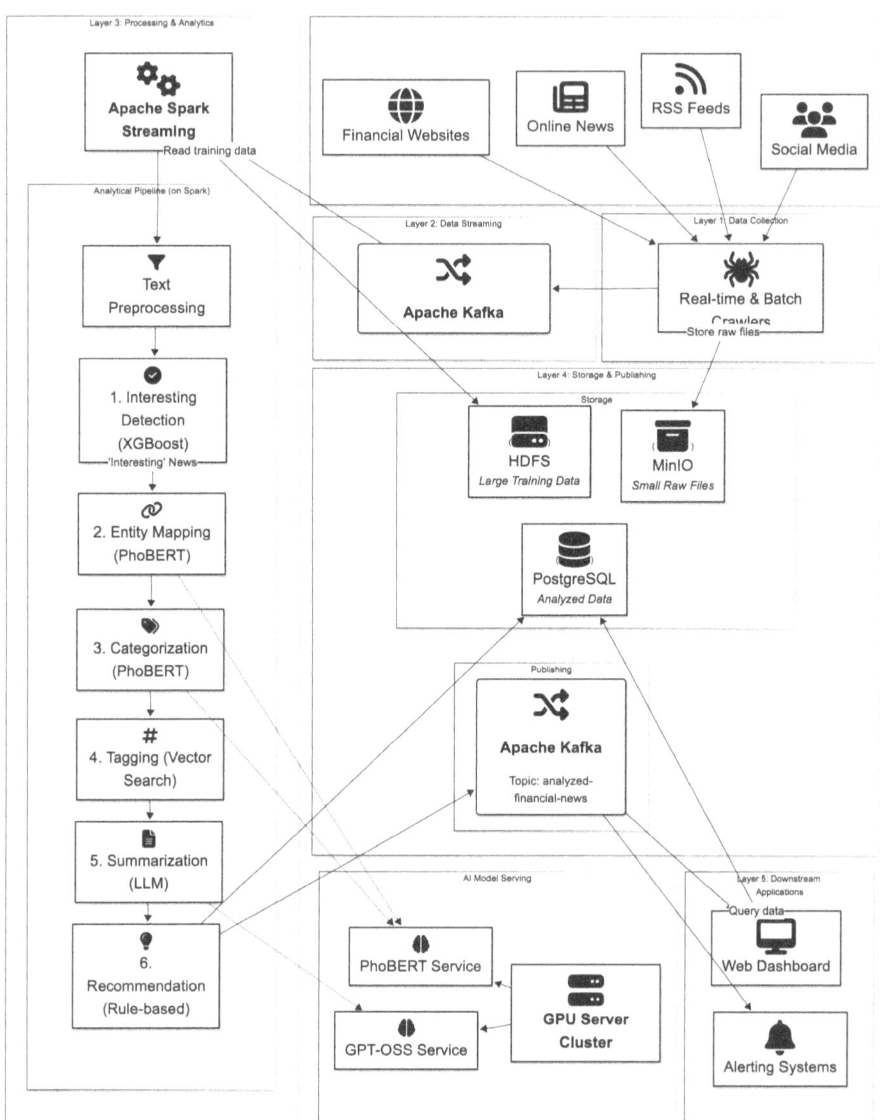

Fig. 1. High-level architecture diagram of the "AI for Stock News" system

2.2 Real-Time Data Processing Pipeline

The backbone of the system is a real-time data processing pipeline built from the combination of two leading big data technologies [12].

Apache Kafka for Stream Ingestion: Apache Kafka was chosen as the underlying technology for the data ingestion layer. It acts as a distributed message queuing system, acting as a "data highway," a reliable central buffer between producers and consumers. Using Kafka brings strategic benefits: decoupling of components, allowing them to operate independently; extremely high throughput and low latency to meet real-time requirements; and high durability and fault tolerance, ensuring no news is lost.

Apache Spark for Stream Processing: If Kafka is the "highway", Apache Spark is the central "processing engine". Spark is a distributed computing framework, designed to process big data quickly thanks to in-memory processing capabilities. The system uses the Spark Structured Streaming module, which views data streams coming from Kafka as an "unbounded data table" and processes them in micro-batches. The entire NLP analysis pipeline is applied in parallel on a computer cluster, allowing the system to process a huge amount of news with high performance.

2.3 Core NLP Analytical Modules

In the Spark environment, clean data streams pass through a series of in-depth analytics modules.

Interesting Detection Module

To solve this problem, a hybrid approach is used. First, the text is converted into numerical vectors through the TF-IDF (Term Frequency-Inverse Document Frequency) feature extraction technique [13]. This technique evaluates the importance of a term t in a document d belonging to a corpus D. The process involves three computational steps:

Term Frequency (TF): Measures the frequency of a word in a text.

$$tf(t, d) = \frac{f_{t,d}}{\sum_{t' \subset d} f_{t',d}}$$

where $f_{(t,d)}$ is the number of times the word t appears in the text d.

Inverse Document Frequency (IDF): Reduce the weight of words that appear frequently in the entire corpus and increase the weight of rare words.

$$idf(t, D) = log \frac{|D|}{|\{d \in D : t \in d\}|}$$

where $|D|$ is the total number of documents in the database, and $|\{d \in D : t \in d\}|$ is the number of documents containing the word t.

TF-IDF Score: Is the product of TF and IDF, representing the final weight of the word.

$$tfidf(t, d, D) = tf(t, d) \times idf(t, D)$$

Then, a second feature vector is generated based on the presence of manually constructed specialized keywords. This aggregated feature vector is used as input to an XGBoost (Extreme Gradient Boosting) model, which is chosen for its superior speed and accuracy [14].

Entity Mapping Module

This module solves the challenging problem of recognizing company names in text and mapping them to their corresponding stock codes. A robust three-step hybrid approach is implemented: (i) Candidate Generation: A PhoBERT model fine-tuned for the Named Entity Recognition (NER) task scans text to identify character strings that are likely to be an organization name (ORGANIZATION). (ii) Dictionary Matching: Candidates are matched against a custom-built knowledge base containing different names and aliases for each listed company. This is the step for highest accuracy and fastest speed. This hybrid approach is specifically engineered to handle unique linguistic challenges in Vietnamese financial texts that standard English-centric NER models fail to address. Unlike English, Vietnamese is a tonal language where semantic meaning relies heavily on diacritics (e.g., "Cổ phiếu" vs. "Cổ phiếu" - though context disambiguates, abbreviations often strip tones). More critically, the Vietnamese stock market features high ambiguity in ticker symbols that overlap with common words (e.g., ticker "CEO" vs. position "CEO", ticker "GAS" vs. commodity "gas"). Our dictionary matching layer incorporates a context-aware filter tailored to Vietnam's HOSE and HNX exchange naming conventions, strictly distinguishing between capitalization in ticker symbols and general vocabulary, a nuance often missed by standard PhoBERT tokenization. (iii) Embedding-based Disambiguation: For ambiguous cases, the system calculates the embedding vector of the sentence context and compares their similarity using the Cosine Similarity measure. The formula is defined as follows:

$$\text{similarity}(A, B) = cos(\theta) = \frac{A \cdot B}{|A||B|} = \frac{\sum_{i=1}^{n} A_i B_i}{\sqrt{\sum_{i=1}^{n} A_i^2}\sqrt{\sum_{i=1}^{n} B_i^2}}$$

where A and B are the embedding vectors representing the context of the sentence and the potential entity, respectively. The entity with the highest similarity score is selected.

Categorization Module:

This module performs a multi-class text classification task to automatically assign each news item to a unique financial event category (e.g., Financial Report, Dividend Payment, Personnel Change). To achieve high accuracy, the chosen method is to fine-tune the PhoBERT language model on a large, manually labeled dataset [15]. The model architecture includes the PhoBERT foundation layer to extract semantic features from tokens [CLS], then passed through a linear layer with an activation function Softmax to transform the output score vector (logits) z into a probability distribution over C classes (categories):

$$\text{Softmax}(z_i) = \frac{e^{z_i}}{\sum_{j=1}^{C} e^{z_j}} \quad \text{for } i = 1,2, \ldots, C$$

The model is trained by minimizing the loss function Cross $-$ Entropy Loss, a standard metric for multiclass classification problems:

$$L = -\sum_{i=1}^{C} y_i log(p_i)$$

where y_i is the true label (1 for the correct class, 0 for the other classes) and p_i is the predicted probability from function Softmax for the i class.

Summarization Module
To generate concise and natural summaries, the system applies the abstractive summarization method. Instead of using commercial API services, a strategic decision was made to implement the gpt-oss-120b model, an open-weight large language model developed by OpenAI. This model features a sparse Mixture-of-Experts (MoE) architecture, designed specifically for complex reasoning and agentic tasks. By leveraging this architecture, the system achieves high-fidelity generation and robust logical deduction tailored for financial strategic insights. This approach offers three distinct benefits: (i) Maximum data security: All sensitive financial information is processed internally and not sent outside. (ii) Customization: Owning the model allows for deeper refinement on specialized data to improve quality over time. (iii) Predictable performance and cost: Eliminate network latency and overhead incurred on each API request, ensuring consistent performance for high-traffic applications.

2.4 Running Example

To illustrate the operational pipeline, consider a raw news snippet just acquired by the crawling layer: "Lợi nhuận quý 3 của FPT tăng đột biến, hoàn thành kế hoạch năm" (FPT's Q3 profit surged, fulfilling the annual target). First, after the preprocessing step cleans the text, the interesting detection module flags the snippet as financially relevant. Next, the entity mapping module identifies "FPT" and accurately links it to the specific "FPT" stock ticker on the HOSE exchange. Subsequently, the categorizing module classifies this event under the "Financial Report" class, while the tagging module assigns relevant contextual keywords via Vector Search. Finally, the LLM-powered summarization (paraphrasing) module generates a concise strategic bulletin. This bulletin is combined with rules from the recommending module to form an actionable signal, which is immediately broadcasted by the publishing layer as a real-time alert for investors.

3 Experiments and Results

3.1 Experimental Setup

Datasets
The system training and evaluation process is based on two large datasets built specifically for the research:

- VnFinNews-10M: This is the core dataset, including 10 million articles collected from reputable financial and economic news sites in Vietnam. Data fields such as categories and tags are manually assigned by editors, providing a high-quality source of "ground truth" for training and evaluating supervised modules.
- VnSocial-20M: Consisting of 20 million posts from social networks, containing diverse content on many topics. This dataset is mainly used to generate negative samples for training and stress testing of the "Interesting Detection" filtering module. For each supervised machine learning task, the data is divided in the standard ratio: 80% for training, 10% for validation, and 10% for testing.

- Implementation Details: To ensure reproducibility, all Transformer-based models (e.g., PhoBERT) were fine-tuned using the AdamW optimizer [16] with a learning rate of 2e-5 and a batch size of 32 over 5 epochs. We employed a linear scheduler with a warmup ratio of 0.1 to stabilize convergence. The fine-tuning of PhoBERT models was performed on standard NVIDIA Tesla A100 GPUs. To optimize deployment efficiency and latency, the inference pipeline was executed on a single NVIDIA H100 Tensor Core GPU (80GB VRAM). We selected the *gpt-oss-120b* model specifically for its architectural efficiency: despite having 117 billion total parameters, it utilizes a sparse activation mechanism with only 5.1 billion active parameters per token. This unique design allows the massive model to fit entirely within the 80GB memory constraint of a single H100 GPU while delivering the high-speed, low-latency reasoning capabilities required for real-time financial data streams. Data availability and sourcing: The VnFinNews-10M dataset was constructed by crawling public financial news from leading Vietnamese economic portals (e.g., CafeF, Vietstock, FireAnt) between 2000 and 2025. Due to strict copyright restrictions, licensing agreements with the news providers, and the proprietary nature of the financial intelligence system, the raw datasets cannot be made publicly available. However, detailed data schemas, crawling methodologies, and aggregated statistical summaries are available from the corresponding author upon reasonable request to support research reproducibility.

Evaluation Metrics

The system performance is evaluated using standard metrics: For classification problems (Categorization, Interesting Detection, NER), the metrics used include Accuracy, Precision, Recall, and F1-Score. For text summarization problems (Summarization), the quality is evaluated using the ROUGE metrics (ROUGE-1, ROUGE-2, ROUGE-L) [17].

3.2 NLP Module Performance

The performance of the core NLP modules is evaluated on the test set. The proposed models based on deep learning are compared with baseline models of traditional machine learning algorithms (SVM, CRF). While newer multilingual models like mBERT or XLM-R exist, prior studies have demonstrated that PhoBERT, being pre-trained specifically on a massive Vietnamese corpus, consistently outperforms multilingual counterparts in monolingual tasks. Therefore, we focus our comparison on establishing the superiority of PhoBERT over established statistical methods in the financial domain. The results are summarized in Table 1, and the detailed predictions of the proposed Categorization model are visualized in the confusion matrix (Fig. 2).

For the Summarization module, the *gpt-oss-120b* model achieves good F1-Score results on ROUGE measures: ROUGE-1 is 0.482, ROUGE-2 is 0.391, and ROUGE-L is 0.455.

Experimental results show that the proposed models significantly outperform baseline methods, confirming the power of deep learning architectures such as Transformer and XGBoost in processing Vietnamese financial documents.

Table 1. Performance Evaluation Results of NLP Modules

Module	Proposed Model	F1-Score (Proposed)	Baseline Model	F1-Score (Baseline)
Interesting Detection	XGBoost + TF-IDF + Keywords	99.2%	Logistic Regression + TF-IDF	96.4%
Entity Mapping (NER)	Fine-tuned PhoBERT	94.6%	Conditional Random Fields (CRF)	87.6%
Categorization	Fine-tuned PhoBERT	94.5%	SVM + TF-IDF	86.9%

Predicted Class

Actual Class	Financial Report	Dividend/Stock	Personnel Change	Major Transaction	AGM/Plan	Macro News
Financial Report	1250	20	10	12	15	4
Dividend/Stock	15	980	12	10	18	5
Personnel Change	10	8	755	8	10	4
Major Transaction	25	12	8	1120	6	10
AGM/Plan	14	20	8	4	890	8
Macro News	6	12	6	15	14	650

Note: Rows represent the actual classes, and columns represent the predicted classes. Diagonal cells (gray) indicate correct predictions.

Fig. 2. Confusion Matrix of the PhoBERT Categorization Model

Deeper Experimental Context on Entity Mapping: While the baseline Conditional Random Fields (CRF) model achieves a respectable F1-Score of 87.6%, our proposed fine-tuned PhoBERT architecture elevates this to 94.6%. This 7% performance margin is not merely a result of switching to a Transformer architecture, but heavily relies on our three-step hybrid pipeline. Deeper error analysis of the baseline reveals that standard sequence labeling struggles significantly with the profound ticker ambiguity in the Vietnamese market-often misclassifying common nouns as tickers (e.g., confusing the ticker 'GAS' with the commodity 'gas', or the ticker 'CEO' with the corporate title). By integrating a custom context-aware dictionary and embedding-based disambiguation (using Cosine Similarity), our system successfully resolves these edge cases, quantitatively validating the necessity of this domain-specific engineering over off-the-shelf NER baseline implementations.

3.3 System Performance Evaluation

The performance of the entire data pipeline is evaluated based on two metrics: Throughput and Latency.

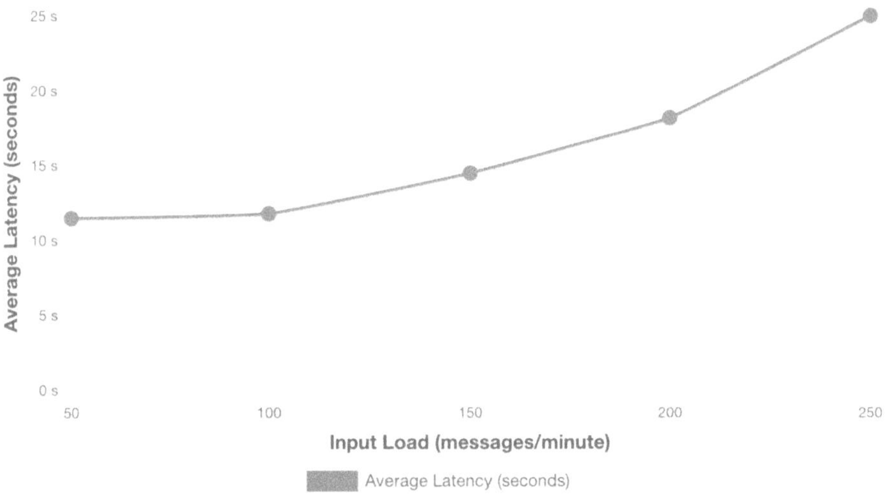

Fig. 3. Relationship between Input Load and Average Latency

Table 2. System throughput evaluation results

Input (messages/minute)	Output (messages/minute)	Success Rate (%)
50	50	100
100	100	100
150	148	98.7
200	185	92.5

Table 3. End-to-end latency evaluation results of the system

Latency Index	Value (seconds)
Average	11.8
Min	8.2
Max	16.5
95th Percentile	14.7

Throughput (Table 2): The system is designed to process at least 100 news/minute. This requirement was empirically derived from observing peak news publication rates across major Vietnamese financial portals during active trading hours. Test results show that the system operates stably and meets 100% of the input load at this level, demonstrating the ability to withstand sudden load peaks in practice.

Latency (Table 3) and Scalability (Fig. 3): The design constraint required the average latency to be less than 15 s, aligning with the real-world operational needs of algorithmic trading where insights must be delivered before market pricing absorbs the news. Measurements on 1,000 messages showed an average latency of 11.8 s, fully meeting the requirement. Furthermore, as illustrated in Fig. 3, the latency grows almost linearly with respect to the input load up to 250 messages/minute. In a Big Data streaming context, this linear scaling is a highly desirable property, demonstrating that the Spark-based horizontal processing pipeline effectively prevents exponential latency bottlenecks during sudden data bursts.

3.4 Discussion

Experimental results have demonstrated that the system not only achieves high analytical accuracy but also meets the strict performance requirements of a real-time system. The architecture combining specialized models such as PhoBERT and XGBoost instead of relying on a single LLM has proven to be optimal in terms of balancing accuracy, performance and cost.

Comparison with Agent-based Approaches: While recent AI Agents demonstrate superior reasoning and enable highly complex workflows, they currently suffer from high latency due to iterative Chain-of-Thought processes (taking seconds to minutes per query) [18]. By decoupling lightweight extraction from heavy generative tasks, our architecture prioritizes deterministic low latency (<15s). Although our system does not explore the multi-step reasoning that agentic frameworks excel at, it effectively fills the gap for real-time, high-throughput alert systems where agentic latency would be prohibitive.

Error Analysis shows that the system sometimes struggles with cases where semantic boundaries are unclear (e.g., confusing the categories "Dividends" and "Shareholders' Meeting" due to overlapping content) or sentences using complex, sarcastic expressions. However, overall, the system has demonstrated great practical significance in automating the analysis process, helping to reduce emotional decisions and move towards data-driven investing.

4 Conclusion and Future Works

This study proposes, designs, and successfully implements an end-to-end, AI-powered big data platform tailored for the real-time analysis of Vietnamese financial news. Rather than focusing on algorithmic innovation, the primary contribution of this research lies in robust system engineering and effective domain adaptation for a low-resource scenario. By applying and adapting existing AI technologies to the specific linguistic nuances of the Vietnamese market, the system successfully resolves language-specific challenges such as profound ticker ambiguity. Furthermore, by integrating a streaming pipeline (Kafka, Spark) with a decoupled hybrid NLP architecture—combining lightweight discriminative models (XGBoost, PhoBERT) with a localized generative LLM—the platform mitigates the latency bottlenecks typical of monolithic AI systems. System-level evaluations rigorously validate this architectural design: the platform not only achieves high NLP task F1-Scores exceeding 94%, but critically satisfies stringent real-time constraints, sustaining a throughput of over 100 messages per minute with an 11.8s average latency. Ultimately, this work provides a scalable, production-ready blueprint for emerging markets.

Building upon this study, future directions include: (i) **Comprehensive Backtesting**: Develop a simulation framework to evaluate trading strategies derived from news-based analytical signals. By executing simulations on historical market data, this approach enables a quantitative assessment of whether adherence to the system's signals can yield superior investment returns. (ii) **Expansion to Multimedia Information Processing**: Enhance the platform's capability to extract insights from non-textual data sources such as images and charts embedded in financial news articles (e.g., extracting financial indicators from business performance graphs) through the integration of advanced Computer Vision techniques. (iii) **Exploration of Complex Forecasting Models**: Design and train machine learning models capable of capturing correlations between sequences of news events and historical price movements, thereby facilitating more accurate forecasting and data-driven trading recommendations.

References

1. Fama, E.F.: Efficient capital markets: a review of theory and empirical work. J. Finance **25**(2), 383 (1970)
2. Ke, Z.T., Kelly, B.T., Xiu, D.: Predicting returns with text data (No. w26186). National Bureau of Economic Research (2019)
3. Loughran, T., McDonald, B.: Textual analysis in finance. Annu. Rev. Fin. Econ. **12**(1), 357–375 (2020)
4. Du, K., et al.: Financial sentiment analysis: techniques and applications. ACM Comput. Surv. **56**(9), 1–42 (2024)
5. Man, X., Luo, T., Lin, J.: Financial sentiment analysis (FSA): a survey. In: Proceedings of IEEE ICPS, pp. 617–622 (2019)
6. Zhang, W., et al.: A survey on aspect-based sentiment analysis. IEEE Trans. Knowl. Data Eng. **35**(11), 11019–11038 (2023)
7. Xing, F.Z., Cambria, E., Welsch, R.E.: Natural language based financial forecasting: a survey. Artif. Intell. Rev. **50**(1), 49–73 (2018)
8. Sohangir, S., Wang, D., Pomeranets, A., Khoshgoftaar, T.M.: Big data: deep learning for financial sentiment analysis. J. Big Data **5**(1) (2018)
9. Malo, P., et al.: Good debt or bad debt: detecting semantic orientations in economic texts. J. Assoc. Inf. Sci. Technol. **65**(4), 782–796 (2014)
10. Araci, D.: FinBERT: Financial sentiment analysis with pre-trained language models. arXiv [cs.CL] (2019)
11. Fatemi, S., Hu, Y.: A comparative analysis of fine-tuned LLMs and few-shot learning of LLMs for financial sentiment analysis. arXiv [cs.LG] (2023)
12. Kreps, J., Narkhede, N., Rao, J.: Kafka: a distributed messaging system for log processing. Proc. NetDB **11**, 1–7 (2011)

13. Qaiser, S., Ali, R.: Text mining: use of TF-IDF to examine the relevance of words. Int. J. Comput. Appl. **181**(1), 25–29 (2018)
14. Chen, T., Guestrin, C.: XGBoost: a scalable tree boosting system. In: Proceedings of 22nd ACM SIGKDD (2016)
15. Nguyen, D.Q., Nguyen, A.T.: PhoBERT: Pre-trained language models for Vietnamese. arXiv [cs.CL] (2020)
16. Loshchilov, I., Hutter, F.: Decoupled weight decay regularization. arXiv [cs.LG] (2017)
17. Lin, C.Y.: ROUGE: a package for automatic evaluation of summaries. In: Proceedings of ACL Workshop (2004)
18. Wei, J., et al.: Chain-of-thought prompting elicits reasoning in large language models. arXiv [cs.CL] (2022)

New Ideas and Emerging Results (NIER)

Reaktor: Go as a First-Class Citizen for Client-Side Web Development Using WebAssembly

Arne Vogel(✉), Moritz Constantin Tietze, and Rüdiger Kapitza

FAU Erlangen-Nürnberg, Erlangen, Germany
arne.vogel@fau.de , ruediger.kapitza@fau.de

Abstract. JavaScript (JS) has been the de facto standard for developing interactive web applications for nearly 30 years. Although it was initially a significant step forward in enabling interactive web pages, JS reaches its limit for complex web applications. Today, games, maps, spreadsheets, and image manipulation require more performance than JS can offer. This is where developers already use WebAssembly, an efficient binary format and compilation target for high-level languages. However, WebAssembly is typically used only to *extend* JS-based applications.

With REAKTOR we promote WebAssembly, exemplified through Go, from its supporting role to a first-class citizen of the web. REAKTOR is a Go framework that adds templating to Go, enables compiling it into efficient WebAssembly and automatically generates the necessary JS code to interact with the APIs provided by the browser. Through the evaluation of REAKTOR, we identified inhibitors of the adoption of WebAssembly-aware high-level languages for full-fledged web development.

1 Introduction

JavaScript (JS) was originally designed as a simple scripting language for browsers, but has since evolved into a general-purpose programming language used for both client- and server-side code [9]. However, with applications growing ever more complex, the language has not kept pace with the performance requirements of modern applications and the ergonomic properties that developers have come to expect from their programming languages [5,10].

While multiple languages have been used in the browser alongside JS, none have reached widespread adoption and were either phased out due to security concerns or because the language was not widely utilized [1,5,13,15,21]. That is, until WebAssembly was introduced [10]. WebAssembly, standardised under the W3C, is a new bytecode that can be compiled from any language, such as C, C++, Rust, and Go [10]. Supported by all major browsers, WebAssembly has made the browser a polyglot programming environment [10,12]. Still, the adoption of WebAssembly has been slow, with adoption slowly rising to 2%, mostly in performance-critical applications [19].

A. Mauri et al. (Eds.): ICWE 2026, LNCS 16625, pp. 173–181, 2026.
https://doi.org/10.1007/978-3-032-29372-5_12

We argue that this is largely due to WebAssembly being limited to a supporting role alongside JS. Without access to the Document Object Model (DOM), it is impossible to create applications using only WebAssembly. JS needs to mediate access to all web APIs and the DOM. This was a deliberate decision to enable cross browser support [6,10], but hinders the full-fledged use of WebAssembly.

We introduce REAKTOR, a Go framework that uses WebAssembly to make Go a first-class citizen on the web. We enable holistic development of web applications using Go, and only Go: that is, developers using REAKTOR can write web applications without writing a single line of JS. The required JS glue code is generated by REAKTOR itself. Go, designed with developer productivity in mind, is particularly well-suited for web development due to its inherent capabilities for concurrency, with coroutines as language constructs, which allow for simpler programming patterns compared to other languages. Additionally, the type system of Go excludes whole categories of bugs that would only be found at runtime in weakly-typed JS. REAKTOR uses a virtual representation of the DOM that is synchronized with the real DOM, called virtual Document Object Model (vDOM), compiled to WebAssembly. This approach keeps all logic and state in WebAssembly for efficient processing. Additionally, we have implemented an HTML-based scripting language, *gox*, which enables developer-friendly HTML-like scripting.

In addition to presenting REAKTOR, we want to promote WebAssembly as a fully-fledged environment for web applications, resulting in three contributions:

- We present REAKTOR, turning Go into a first-class citizen on the web,
- we evaluate REAKTOR, and
- we identify problems with WebAssembly that hinder the adoption of high-level languages for the web.

To encourage exchange, we made the REAKTOR benchmark open source[1]. The rest of the paper is structured as follows: In Sect. 2 we introduce WebAssembly and related work. This is followed by a description of REAKTOR in Sect. 3, before we evaluate our prototype in Sect. 4.

2 Background and Related Work

Next, we will describe WebAssembly, placing it in context by comparing it to preceding languages that have been superseded. Furthermore, we will discuss related projects that use WebAssembly for web development.

Other Languages on the Web: WebAssembly is not the first language introduced next to JS. Flash was used for animations and games, but also for general applications using ActionScript, which was compiled and distributed as bytecode [1]. The proprietary Flash was discontinued when HTML5 standardized many of the APIs needed to replicate Flash's use cases. Another bytecode on the web

[1] REAKTOR software artifact: https://doi.org/10.5281/zenodo.19567322.

was Java applets [13]. Using a sandbox accessed through plugins, it allowed for similar functionality as Flash. For security reasons, Java Applets were blocked around 2010 [13]. Native Client (NaCL) and Portable Native Client (PNaCL) represent another effort primarily from Google to run high-performance code next to JS [5,21]. They allowed the execution of a subset of x86, ARM, or MIPS code in the case of NaCL, or LLVM intermediate representation bytecode in the case of PNaCL, in a sandbox in the browser. PNaCL was deprecated in favor of WebAssembly for its cross-browser standardization and open governance model in a collaboration between all major browser developers [10].

WebAssembly: We will introduce WebAssembly by comparing it to JS. WebAssembly is a bytecode format that can be compiled from a wide range of source languages, such as C, C++, Rust, and Go [10]. WebAssembly has its own memory region, called linear memory (see Fig. 1), in which it can store values of the four data types supported: `i32, i64, f32, f64`. Each source language for WebAssembly uses this memory in its own way, e.g., differing in how they store strings (null-terminated versus size-denominated). Currently, DOM access and event handling require JS glue code, which in turn converts these values for use in browser APIs, as shown in Fig. 1. We will identify the performance overhead of this and propose solutions in Sect. 4.

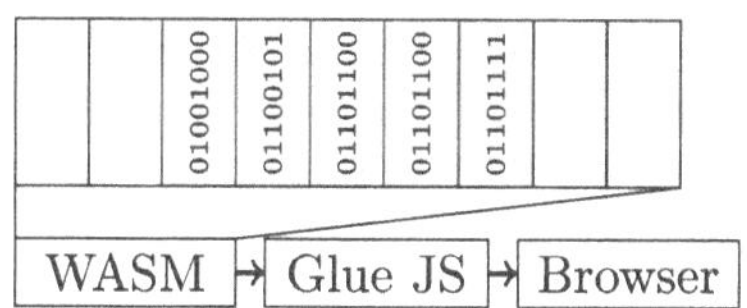

Fig. 1. Any change from WebAssembly has to go through the JS glue code before it can be rendered in the browser.

WebAssembly First Application Development: To the best of our knowledge, this is the first academic paper focussing on enabling web applications in high-level languages using WebAssembly. Next, we will present unpublished projects in various experimental, abandoned, and unevaluated states, for which there is primarily only source code available. Dodrio by Fitzgerald [8] implemented a vDOM library in Rust, which was compiled to WebAssembly. Dodrio is the closest work related to REAKTOR in terms of optimizations implemented, but was not thoroughly evaluated and deprecated 5 years ago. Yew [22], Dioxus [4], and Leptos [14] are other Rust libraries for WebAssembly applications. All three are community projects on GitHub that have not undergone a thorough evaluation. Both Dioxus and Yew use a vDOM and JS glue code that interprets a stream of edits from the vDOM and converts them to mutations in the actual

DOM [4,22]. Leptos does not use a vDOM; instead, it specifies for any nodes on what data it depends and how it would change [14]. This allows Leptos to eliminate diffing and update the entire DOM directly. In REAKTOR, we also use the vDOM abstraction because it does not limit developers in terms of the applications they can create. We have also thoroughly evaluated the concept and identified performance bottlenecks. Works in Go such as Vecty [11], Vugu [20] and DomUI [16] have also used vDOM for optimizations. Although these related works have shown that web development with other high-level languages outside of JS is possible, they are either experimental or abandoned and lack thorough evaluations. We improve on the status quo: with our evaluation of REAKTOR, we highlight the limitations of current WebAssembly-based applications, in the hope of initiating a discussion about a holistic WebAssembly integration.

3 Design and Implementation

In this section, we describe the design of REAKTOR before presenting details about its implementation.

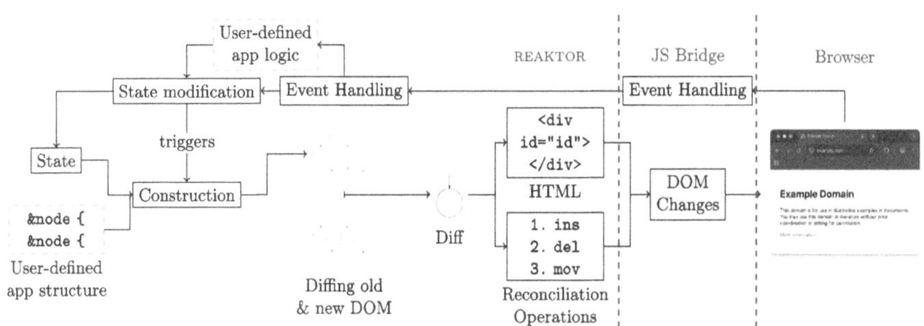

Fig. 2. REAKTOR: user logic and event handling implemented in WebAssembly with JS glue code for browser interactions.

The goal of REAKTOR is to enable the implementation of all user-defined logic and calculation purely in Go. The general design of REAKTOR can be seen in Fig. 2. We use WebAssembly to enable Go-based web applications: the Go code is compiled to WebAssembly and together with JS glue code can execute the application. JS is only used for propagating DOM changes, forwarding events such as button clicks, and initializing the WebAssembly module of REAKTOR. This is necessary as WebAssembly code cannot interact with the DOM directly.

When a website uses REAKTOR, the JS glue code first initializes the compiled Go code as a WebAssembly module. The module itself initializes the global state, which is used to construct the initial vDOM. As shown in Fig. 2, the app logic, as well as the app's structure and state, are part of the WebAssembly module. The engine only runs if there is a state change triggered by an event sent from the JS bridge, such as button clicks or network events. The engine calculates the difference between the old DOM and the new DOM after applying changes and propagates it through the JS bridge to the browser to display. The difference is a set of reconciliation operations, specifically insertions, deletions, or reordering of DOM elements.

REAKTOR uses components, small self-contained functions with associated state to implement interactive elements, e.g., a counter with an initial value that can be incremented. These components can be nested, e.g., a list component can contain multiple counter components. The state of these components is managed with simple setter callbacks or reducer patterns that use a separate reducer function to manage state modifications based on dispatched actions.

To simplify development, we have developed a templating language: *gox*. *gox* is transpiled into Go code, as shown in Fig. 3, enabling syntax similar to standard HTML with templating functionality. The generated code is then compiled to WebAssembly.

Implementation Details: REAKTOR can rerender parts of the DOM that the user has previously focused on, which can result in the user losing focus on the element (e.g., a user typing in a form field). To prevent this, the JS bridge can store focus before a repaint to restore it after the repaint is done. For accessing a core set of browser APIs, such as the Fetch API, we implemented generic functions that forward the request to JS and return the result as events to REAKTOR. Supporting further APIs requires Go code wrappers and the corresponding JS glue code, which could be automatically generated. To identify elements, REAKTOR associates identifiers with vDOM elements, e.g., `root-0:div-1:label` to specify the label of specific elements. These identifiers function as a shared structure between the engine and the JS code to identify elements in the DOM. They are also used as stable, unique keys, which enables reordering and deeper comparison to avoid unnecessary rerendering of elements. An optimisation we implemented for REAKTOR is batch calling. Here, reconciliation operations are written into linear memory instead of being directly applied per bridge call. This way, multiple reconciliation actions can be combined into a single bridge call, for which only one redraw is necessary.

```
<label For={ButtonId}>Clicked {clickNr} times</label>
Children: [] * types.Node { & types.Node {
Content: `Clicked ` + util.ToString(clickNr) + ` times`
```

Fig. 3. HTML scripting with *gox*, *gox* (above) and the generated Go code (excerpt).

4 Evaluation and Discussion

In the following section, we present our evaluation of REAKTOR and draw conclusions about whether it can be considered a fully fledged replacement for JS as an implementation language for web applications. In particular, we aim to answer the following questions: How does REAKTOR perform in established performance benchmarks? What is the overhead of having to go through JS for any changes and can we reduce the overhead with batching? How do bundle sizes compare to frameworks and plain JS?

To accurately compare bundle size and performance, a reference application is necessary for comparison, which we use in this study: TodoMVC [18] and DBMON [3]. The first TodoMVC is a standard web application proposed by TasteJS [7,18]. It describes basic task management functionality and has reference implementations of different JS frontend frameworks and libraries. It automatically performs a long series of user inputs, waiting for the page to update each time before moving on to the next one. The total time it takes for the benchmark to run is measured and compared. Secondly, we use the *DBMON Repaint Rate Challenge* [3]. It features a simple UI that is continually updated. Each time the assessed framework finishes rerendering the page after an update, the next one is randomly generated – with varying degrees of actual UI impact – and the repaint rate is measured. For both benchmarks, we have implemented the framework using REAKTOR in Go for evaluation.

All performance benchmarks are executed on a 2023 MacBook Pro with an Apple M2 processor and 32GB of memory running macOS Sequoia 15.6.1. The utilized browser is Google Chrome 140.0.7339.208. For the TodoMVC-based performance benchmark, Chrome is started with the flag `-disable-web-security`, to use local files embedded in iframes, which this benchmark requires but does not affect the measurements.

Framework	Execution time TodoMVC	Repaint rate DBMON
React	**2116.5** ms	**142** 1/s
Ember	**2093.4** ms	**121** 1/s
AngularJS	**1964.5** ms	**98** 1/s
REAKTOR	**4031.4** ms	**12** 1/s
REAKTOR (batchcalling)	**3967.5** ms	**28** 1/s

Fig. 4. Performance of frameworks with TodoMVC and DBMON.

Implementing the benchmarks using REAKTOR in Go was straightforward, highlighting the comfort of using a type-safe, modern language. The absence of a web-centered ecosystem for libraries (compared to JS) was noticeable, but not detrimental, as relevant features were either part of the Go standard library, available in existing third-party libraries, or easily implementable. We imagine this might change if web development with WebAssembly (in Go or otherwise) gains traction due to the inherent sharing capabilities of WebAssembly. The bundle size (on disk) of this implementation is compared to reference implementations using the same programming paradigms shown in Fig. 5. The increased size for REAKTOR is explained by the need for REAKTOR to ship the entire Go runtime and parts of its standard library: for JS, these are already bundled with the browser. For reference, in a hello world WebAssembly module (≈2.55 MB) the Go Runtime (≈1.76 MB) makes up the biggest chunk, followed by libraries syscall/js (≈124 KB) and fmt package (≈677 KB), the actual hello world code is only roughly ≈1 KB. Note that the streaming compilation of WebAssembly mitigates this. Whereas JS has to be downloaded entirely before it can be executed, WebAssembly can be compiled and interpreted as it is being downloaded [10].

No framework	**0.064** MB
jQuery 3.6.3	**0.224** MB
Angular 17.0.5	**0.324** MB
React 17.0.2	**0.776** MB
REAKTOR	**4.7** MB

Fig. 5. TodoMVC implementations file sizes.

For performance evaluations, we used reference implementations of TodoMVC by TasteJS (React 15.3.1, Angular 2, Ember 2.6.3) [18], and *DBMON* by Mathieu Ancelin (React 15.1.0, Angular 1.3.13, Ember 2.10) [2]. To preserve the original results, all reference implementations were kept as written including framework version. The results are summarized in Fig. 4, showing the average of 10 runs. For TodoMVC 100 tasks with different titles are created, marked as complete, and then deleted. After each of these 300 actions, the benchmark waits for the rendering of the vDOM to finish before processing. The result is the accumulated time of actions, as proposed by Czaplicki et al., as this reflects real-world usage [7]. In Fig. 4, execution time for REAKTOR is higher than for conventional JS frameworks but still within reason with only ≈13.4 ms between interactions. Interestingly, the batching optimization has little effect in this benchmark, as waiting for each action to complete means that only a few reconciliation actions can be batched for each action.

In the *DBMON* benchmark, the repaint rate is measured. In this benchmark, a table of numbers is continuously updated without synchronization points, as in TodoMVC. As a result, the batching optimization shows significant improvements for REAKTOR. Without batch calling, there are ≈2500 calls/s, whereas with batch calling, there are only ≈45 calls/s to the JS glue code. The resulting repaint rate of 28/s is significantly lower than that of established frameworks, while still being sufficient for everyday usage. It should be mentioned that both TodoMVC and *DBMON* are worst-case use cases for REAKTOR with little to no computations (in which WebAssembly shines) as the benchmarks focus on website representation with heavy DOM manipulation and event handling.

To highlight this effect we have measured the time it takes a WebAssembly module to write and transfer DOM changes in a microbenchmark. In the benchmark the module writes bytes to linear memory (the DOM changes) before calling a JS function which reads these values. As shown in Fig. 6, the time a single call takes quickly adds up if it is called 2500 times per second.

Size (KB)	per Call (μs)
1	0.8
2	1.7
4	3.1
8	6.2
16	12.4
32	24.6
64	48.9
128	98

Fig. 6. Timing results for transfer of specific sizes between WebAssembly and JS

Discussion: In line with other research [17], we observe considerable overhead for DOM access due to the required JS glue code. As can be seen in Fig. 4, reducing the number of JS calls more than doubles REAKTOR's performance, which is corroborated by the results in Fig. 6. However, there is still considerable overhead, even with optimisations such as batch calling. Accordingly, from our point of view, state synchronisation for the DOM between JS and WebAssembly modules requires dedicated browser support in the future. In the meantime, without major browser changes, the reuse of runtime and standard library components could decrease the file size overhead of REAKTOR. As with popular JS libraries, such as React or Angular, which are hosted by CDNs that can be cached and reused between different sites, the Go Runtime (≈1.76 MB) and standard library (≈801 KB) could be cached and reused between sites thereby significantly reducing the size of shipped application code.

5 Conclusion

We have introduced REAKTOR, making Go a first-class citizen on the web. With REAKTOR, developers can implement web applications in Go without writing a single line of JS. REAKTOR was also implemented, evaluated, and used to identify issues hindering the adoption of WebAssembly-based web applications. The primary issue among these problems is the absence of direct access to the DOM, which currently requires the use of JS glue code. The latter is detrimental to performance due to the large number of cross-runtime calls required. Although the prevailing sentiment is that the status quo should be maintained for compatibility reasons [6], we argue that deeper integration between WebAssembly and the browser would lead to greater adoption of WebAssembly and enable web applications to be implemented in a variety of modern programming languages. We have demonstrated that web development using Go and WebAssembly is not only generally technologically feasible, but also advantageous under improved circumstances.

References

1. Adobe: Adobe flash player EOL (2020). web.archive.org/web/20211121070427/www.adobe.com/products/flashplayer/enterprise-end-of-life.html

2. Ancelin, M.: DbMon. http://mathieuancelin.github.io/js-repaint-perfs/
3. Lawrence, C., M.: Benchmarking JavaScript frameworks. https://doi.org/10.21427/d72890
4. DioxusLabs: Dioxus: Fullstack app framework for web, desktop, and mobile. https://github.com/dioxuslabs/dioxus
5. Donovan, A., Muth, R., Chen, B., Sehr, D.: PNaCL: Portable native client executables. Google White Paper (2010). http://css.csail.mit.edu/6.858/2015/readings/pnacl.pdf
6. Ehrenberg, D.: When is webassembly going to get DOM support?. https://queue.acm.org/detail.cfm?id=3746174
7. Evan, C.: Blazing fast html. https://elm-lang.org/news/blazing-fast-html-round-two
8. Fitzgerald, N.: Fast, bump-allocated virtual DOMs with rust and Wasm. https://hacks.mozilla.org/2019/03/fast-bump-allocated-virtual-doms-with-rust-and-wasm/
9. Gup, S.y., Ficarra, M., Gibbons, K.: Ecmascript 2026. https://tc39.es/ecma262/
10. Haas, A., et al.: Bringing the web up to speed with WebAssembly. SIGPLAN Not. **52**(6), 185–200 (2017). https://doi.org/10.1145/3140587.3062363
11. hexops: Vecty. https://github.com/hexops/vecty
12. Jangda, A., Powers, B., Berger, E.D., Guha, A.: Not so fast: Analyzing the performance of WebAssembly vs. native code (2019). www.usenix.org/conference/atc19/presentation/jangda
13. Justin Schuh: Saying goodbye to our old friend NPAPI. https://blog.chromium.org/2013/09/saying-goodbye-to-our-old-friend-npapi.html
14. Leptos: Build fast web applications with rust. https://github.com/leptos-rs/leptos
15. Microsoft: What is VBScript?. https://learn.microsoft.com/en-us/previous-versions/1kw29xwf(v=vs.85)
16. reusee: Domui - web frontend framework in pure go. https://github.com/reusee/domui
17. Seweryn, K.J.: The efficiency of rust and WebAssembly compared to plain JavaScript. In: Verma, H., Bozzon, A., Mauri, A., Yang, J. (eds.) Web Engineering, pp. 361–365. Springer Nature Switzerland, Cham (2026)
18. TasteJS: TodoMVC. https://todomvc.com/
19. Vadgama, N.: Webassembly 2025 - the web almanac by http archive. https://almanac.httparchive.org/en/2025/webassembly
20. Vugu: Vugu: A modern UI library for Go+Webassembly. www.vugu.org/
21. Yee, B., et al.: Native client: A sandbox for portable, untrusted x86 native code (2010). https://doi.org/10.1145/1629175.1629203
22. YewStack: Yew: Rust/Wasm client web app framework. https://github.com/yewstack/yew

From Threat Intelligence to Firewall Rules: Semantic Relations in Hybrid AI Agent and Expert System Architectures

Chiara Bonfanti(✉), Davide Colaiacomo, Luca Cagliero(✉), and Cataldo Basile

Department of Control and Computer Engineering, Politecnico di Torino, Turin, Italy
{chiara.bonfanti,davide.colaiacomo,luca.cagliero, cataldo.basile}@polito.it

Abstract. Web security demands rapid response capabilities to evolving cyber threats. Agentic Artificial Intelligence (AI) promises automation, but the need for trustworthy security responses is of the utmost importance. This work investigates the role of semantic relations in extracting information for sensitive operational tasks, such as configuring security controls for mitigating threats. To this end, it proposes to leverage hypernym-hyponym textual relations to extract relevant information from Cyber Threat Intelligence (CTI) reports. By leveraging a neuro-symbolic approach, the multi-agent system automatically generates CLIPS code for an expert system creating firewall rules to block malicious network traffic. Experimental results show the superior performance of the hypernym-hyponym retrieval strategy compared to various baselines and the higher effectiveness of the agentic approach in mitigating threats.

Keywords: Artificial Intelligence for CyberSecurity · Incident response

1 Introduction

Web applications, being publicly accessible, are common targets of cyberattacks. Defenders must secure them with complex and costly measures. At the same time, attackers are increasingly relying on AI-assisted tools for automated exploitation of vulnerabilities [19]. This creates a structural asymmetry in Cybersecurity [2]: attackers only need to target a few weaknesses, while defenders must protect the entire system. As a result, threats are countered with high delays [11].

Defending systems is challenging, as one must select and configure the most appropriate security controls. This process relies on incident reports and technical data on attacker behaviour; this gap has proven challenging to address with LLMs, given their known reliability limitations in sensitive domains [15]. To translate such data into practical defensive actions, the research community has

A. Mauri et al. (Eds.): ICWE 2026, LNCS 16625, pp. 182–190, 2026.
https://doi.org/10.1007/978-3-032-29372-5_13

been considering applying AI to understand the threat described in the report and its consequences for the protected system [16]. However, existing AI-based approaches struggle with the inherent complexity of automatically categorizing sensitive data, which is often exacerbated by severe data imbalance across different threats.

This paper aims to bridge this gap with the capabilities of Agentic AI and responsible use of LLMs to capture the semantics of security events and align them with defensive strategies and secure code generation. While scalability and real-time applicability to production IPS environments are beyond the scope of this work, such research effort is relevant in practice and sets the basis for dedicated integration studies in future extensions.

The main contributions are threefold:

- First, it proposes a **methodology for extracting semantically rich information from CTI reports based on established taxonomic relationships**, i.e., hypernyms and hyponyms. Inspired by their use in semantic search across multiple natural language processing tasks, e.g., automated machine translation [20], we leverage these relationships to enhance the semantic understanding of security events and facilitate mapping to defensive strategies and secure code generation.
- Secondly, it presents an **agentic system** that (*i*) maps extracted info to existing defensive measures and (*ii*) generates CLIPS code artifacts that can be used to configure security controls. The system analyses the threats described in input CTI reports, identifies security controls that can mitigate them, and generates appropriate filtering rules.
- Finally, we perform an **empirical evaluation** of each step of the agentic system.

2 Related Work

Semantic extraction is at the core of the present work [8]. Despite it having recently re-gained interest in the natural language processing community [14], its relevance to the cybersecurity applications related to intrusion prevention is still limited. Recent work in NLP has re-emphasized the role of semantics [14]. Our approach utilizes an iterative prompting strategy [21] to retrieve semantically meaningful features. This strategy employs pre-existing relationships in the input text to form the agent's knowledge base. Taxonomic relationships, such as hyponymy (specific-to-general) and hyperonymy (general-to-specific), are well known in the literature [1] and are a pillar of our LLM's usage [20]. Unlike existing solutions that require additional training data to incorporate ontological structure [22], ours is inference-based.

Our contribution (*i*) leverages this information to solve the aforementioned task. Rather than directly mapping raw text to classifications or code generation, we prompt LLMs in three stages: first, extracting specific domain entities; then, abstracting them into semantic categories; and finally, performing specific operations based on these enriched representations. Unlike methods that perform extraction in a single pass, our method uses semantic information at each stage, enabling the model to leverage explicit structural knowledge to guide categorization and classification toward a progressively enriched understanding of the domain. This is beneficial in Cybersecurity, as CTI reports are often noisy and verbose, while defenders benefit from structured information.

The present strategy (*ii*) extends the CoALA framework [18] with theories drawn from cognitive psychology. Whilst psychology-based AI contributions are well established [12,17,23], our focus is on the practical integration of Ebbinghaus's memory decay and Collins and Quillian's semantic network within a code-generation agent. The Cybersecurity domain remains one of the most productive grounds for symbolic AI, as deterministic reasoning over structured knowledge is preferred to probabilistic methods. CLIPS has a long history in this domain [13,24], providing a rule-based forward-chaining inference engine. Graph-based knowledge representation is well established in agent architectures [10] and offers fertile ground for optimization [5]. Our agent extends the standard implementation with a graph-based knowledge base that tracks concepts and is beneficial to code generation; unlike the decision-tree approach in [6], graphs support incremental updates more naturally.

3 Data

CTI reports are analyst-written documents that gather empirical observations about cyber threats. They describe attackers' targets and *modus operandi* through narrative and concrete evidence, such as malicious IP addresses or compromised URLs. They are often mapped to MITRE ATT&CK (Adversarial Tactics, Techniques, and Common Knowledge), an open-source catalog of attack tactics and techniques. It provides a well-established vocabulary for mapping Cybersecurity prose to structured descriptions of attacker behaviours, thus enabling consistent comparisons across reports. Publicly available CTI-annotated datasets are highly skewed. This well-known characteristic of the Cybersecurity domain [9] creates a low-resource setting in which conventional AI methodologies can underperform [4]. **Dataset A.** CTI Human-Annotated Labels (CTI-HAL) is a human-annotated CTI dataset built from 81 real reports, which contain statements manually mapped to MITRE ATT&CK techniques (116 distinct in total); annotation reliability is assessed through inter-annotator agreement [7].
Dataset B. This corpus is made of CTIs gathered from the Center for Internet Security. It contains 66 malware entries, each including an analyst synopsis and network artifacts. The target labels are entities known as *security capabilities* [3].

4 Methodology

Our pipeline integrates neural and symbolic AI components, as shown in Fig. 1. It implements a Semantic Information Flow (SIF) that transforms CTI reports into filtering rules for security controls (iptables rules in Fig. 1). The SIF comprises neural components (green) and symbolic AI components (red).

An Enhanced CoALA agent executes the initial steps of the SIF. It extracts semantic information from input reports by first retrieving hyponyms and then hypernyms of the security concepts expressed in the prose via an iterative call to an LLM. The last step uses the extracted hypernyms to build valid CLIPS templates that formally represent them.

The Expert System A role is of a syntactic verification layer against potential LLM hallucinations, already thinned out by guardrails and post-inference output controls, while the sequential instantiation of templates, facts, and production rules enables systematic detection of error propagation.

The present study employs best practices to achieve deterministic LLM inference, thereby enabling the use of deterministic algorithms in PyTorch. The random seeds are fixed, CuDNN benchmarking is disabled, and eager attention is forced to avoid nondeterministic fused CUDA kernels. Greedy decoding and explicit device placement further reduced variability across runs. While perfect determinism remains an open challenge in LLM-based systems, these measures provide a solid approximation for reproducible experimentation. CoALA architecture provides a sound foundation that has been extended to address known limitations in knowledge base manipulation, particularly given the constraints of CLIPS programming language `deftemplate` structures.

The Refinement Engine recognises the available security controls to counter threats described in CTI reports. Within this engine, Expert System B uses semantic information about the required security capabilities, leveraging the CLIPS rules generated by the agent. With this information, the engine produces the corresponding filtering rules. This final verification step ensures syntactical correctness, as inaccuracies would prevent acceptance by the security control.

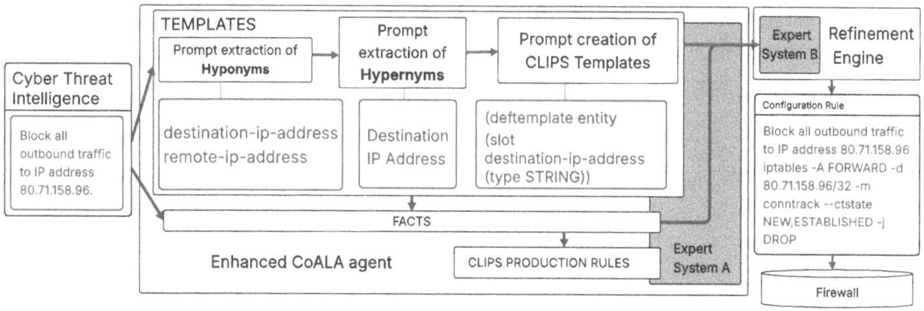

Fig. 1. The architecture of our agentic solution.

5 Results

The experimental evaluation was conducted using dedicated GPU hardware comprising NVIDIA RTX 4090 (44GB VRAM) and RTX 5090 (32GB VRAM) plat-

```
{"cti_name":"RPT1","context":"The malware encodes the data with a
    simple
substitution cipher and single-byte XOR using the 0xAA key.",
"attack_mapping":{"tactic":{"name":"Defense Evasion","id":"TA0005"},
"technique":{"name":"Obfuscated Files or Information","id":"T1027"},
"sub_technique":{"name":"UNKNOWN","id":null},
"motivation":"Encoding with substitution cipher and XOR is
    obfuscation.
The hypernym 'encryption key' with '0xAA' supports this mapping."}}
```

Listing 1.1. Example of our method prompting classification output.

forms, which provided sufficient computational resources to instantiate and compare multiple LLM architectures under controlled conditions.

Task A A multilabel classification experiment was conducted using Dataset A. Three different approaches were investigated: A-1, which employed static (Word2Vec, GloVe) and contextualized embeddings (SecureBERT); A-2, which leveraged prompt-based methods (Chain-of-Thought and ours); A-3, which served as a non-LLM baseline by applying traditional machine learning methods (Naive-Bayes, Support Vector Machine, Random Forest) to the target classification task, as previously used in this domain [9]. Qwen2.5-Coder-14B-Instruct was employed for A-2. LLM usage is tailored to Task A, as, to the best of our knowledge, this work is the first attempt to address semantic-enhanced prompting for CLIPS rule extraction. Evaluation metrics suited for imbalanced multilabel classification (e.g., Hamming loss) were used to ensure a fair assessment of model performance. Table 1 summarizes the results, with $k = 10$ for the top-k accuracy scores. Our semantic extraction excels in weighted F1 score and Top K Accuracy, demonstrating greater ability to shortlist relevant text snippets. BERTScore and ROUGE-L similarities confirm the pertinence of the selection, achieving maximal similarity in the longest common subsequence and competitive results at the embedding level. LLMs with Chain-of-Thought show comparable accuracy scores but significantly worse weighted F1 scores, mainly due to weaker performance on minority classes. To deepen the analysis, we also explored Chain-of-Thought, Zero-Shot, and Few-Shot prompting augmented with semantic information. Each prompt included a confidence threshold, which guided the model's decisions. The results are reported in Table 3. Hyponyms have been shown to be consistently more effective than hypernyms. Notably, enforcing weaker selectivity constraints (e.g., threshold=50%) enhances performance.

Task BThe full pipeline described in Sect. 4 was employed on Dataset B. Qwen2.5-Coder-14B-Instruct and Foundation-Sec-14B-Instruct were both considered; however, the latter's generative restrictions and limited CLIPS support made the former preferable. The evaluation, conducted by four Cybersecurity experts, focused on qualitative judgment of our system's output. It involved multiple criteria, and the results in Table 2 show that all statistical scores used to evaluate annotators imply forms of alignment. Technical Correctness achieved the highest Krippendorff's alpha, indicating strong agreement on syntactic correctness. Scope Calibration, with the highest Spearman correlation, supports consistency in the relative ranking of rule scope. Fidelity to CTI remained high across all scores, indicating satisfactory agreement among annotators.

Table 1. Task A results comparing our hypernym-based prompting approach. Best-performer per metrics is written in boldface.

Task	Method	Task-based Eval.			Semantic Metrics	
		F1 w	Acc. w	Top-k Acc.	BERT Score F1	ROUGE L
A-1	Word2Vec	0.070	0.990	0.250	–	–
A-1	GloVe	0.118	**0.991**	0.382	–	–
A-1	SecureBERT	0.043	0.990	0.210	0.831	–
A-2	CoT	0.308	0.932	0.935	0.862	0.402
A-2	*Ours*	***0.329***	*0.934*	***0.968***	*0.858*	***0.444***
A-3	NB + OneVsRest	0.122	0.911	0.947	0.900	0.337
A-3	SVM + OneVsRest	0.062	0.910	0.947	0.845	0.261
A-3	SecureBERT + RF	0.143	0.914	0.947	0.883	0.308
A-3	Binary Relevance RF	0.183	0.916	0.842	0.885	0.290
A-3	Label Powerset SVM	0.263	0.881	0.895	**0.921**	0.369

Table 2. Task B Inter-rater reliability metrics by dimension.

Dimension	Krippendorff's α	Cohen's κ			Spearman's ρ
		Unweighted	Linear	Quadratic	
Technical Correctness	+0.5768	+0.5371	+0.5625	+0.5817	+0.6942
Fidelity to CTI	+0.5215	+0.3445	+0.4595	+0.5599	+0.5515
Scope Calibration	+0.5030	+0.5827	+0.6540	+0.7251	+0.7143

Table 3. Task A-2 prompting focused analysis.

Method	F1	ACC	TOP-10	BERTScore	ROUGE-L F1
Our Method (3-Stage 50%)	**0.329**	0.934	0.968	0.858	**0.444**
Few-Shot + Hyponyms	0.311	0.935	0.952	0.860	0.411
CoT + Hypernyms	0.308	0.933	0.984	0.865	0.407
CoT Baseline	0.308	0.932	0.935	0.862	0.402
Few-Shot + Hypernyms	0.287	0.929	0.984	0.856	0.400
CoT + Hyponyms	0.294	0.931	0.984	**0.871**	0.391
60% Threshold	0.288	0.934	**1.000**	0.875	0.401
Zero-Shot + Hyponyms	0.238	0.933	0.919	0.848	0.344
Zero-Shot + Hypernyms	0.233	0.931	0.871	0.841	0.327
Baseline (only semantic information)	0.173	**0.937**	0.774	0.843	0.270

6 Conclusions and Future Work

This paper addresses the use of AI in Intrusion Prevention Systems. It explored the adoption of semantic extractors from CTI reports, where CLIPS code is generated for an expert system that creates firewall rules to block malicious network traffic. This underscores the need for ad hoc semantic retrieval modules rather than classical classification approaches used for IDS.

Although the current agent system is intended for research purposes, the findings from Task B show promising results for future usability and deployability, as human annotators achieved satisfactory inter-annotator agreement. This leaves room for further development for downstream usage of filtering rules. Future work should also address determinism in LLM inference, which remains an open challenge; further investigation in this direction would strengthen the reliability of such systems in sensitive cybersecurity domains.

This work represents an initial step toward trustworthy LLM adoption in cybersecurity practice.

References

1. Alharbi, R., Al-Muhtaseb, H., Helmy, T.: Hypernymy relation in NLP: tasks, approaches, resources, and future directions - a systematic literature review. IEEE Access 1–1 (2025)
2. Anderson, R.: Why information security is hard – an economic perspective. In: Proceedings of the 17th Annual Computer Security Applications Conference (2001)
3. Basile, C., Gatti, G., Settanni, F.: A formal model of security controls' capabilities and its applications to policy refinement and incident management. IEEE Trans. Netw. **34**, 1659–1673 (2026)
4. Bonfanti, C., Colombino, M., Coucourde, G., Memari, F., Pinardi, S., Meo, R.: A comparison of pipelines for the translation of a low resource language based on transformers (2025). https://arxiv.org/abs/2509.12514

5. Bonfanti, C., Druetto, A., Basile, C., Ranasinghe, T., Zampieri, M.: A neuro-symbolic multi-agent approach to legal-cybersecurity knowledge integration (2025)
6. Chen, Z.: Knowledge acquisition assisted by clips programming. Eng. Appl. Artif. Intell. **12**(3), 379–387 (1999)
7. Della Penna, S., Natella, R., Orbinato, V., Parracino, L., Pianese, L.: CTI-HAL: a human-annotated dataset for cyber threat intelligence analysis. In: 2025 IEEE European Symposium on Security and Privacy Workshops (EuroS&PW), pp. 69–78 (2025)
8. Gábor, K., Buscaldi, D., Schumann, A.K., QasemiZadeh, B., Zargayouna, H., Charnois, T.: SemEval-2018 task 7: semantic relation extraction and classification in scientific papers. In: Apidianaki, M., Mohammad, S.M., May, J., Shutova, E., Bethard, S., Carpuat, M. (eds.) Proceedings of the 12th International Workshop on Semantic Evaluation, pp. 679–688. Association for Computational Linguistics, New Orleans, Louisiana (2018)
9. Grigorescu, O., Nica, A., Dascalu, M., Rughinis, R.: CVE2ATT&CK: BERT-based mapping of CVEs to MITRE ATT&CK techniques. Algorithms **15**(9) (2022)
10. Jiang, J., et al.: KG-agent: an efficient autonomous agent framework for complex reasoning over knowledge graph. In: Che, W., Nabende, J., Shutova, E., Pilehvar, M.T. (eds.) Proceedings of the 63rd Annual Meeting of the Association for Computational Linguistics (Volume 1: Long Papers), pp. 9505–9523. Association for Computational Linguistics, Vienna, Austria (2025)
11. Lazer, S.J., Aryal, K., Gupta, M., Bertino, E.: A survey of agentic AI and cybersecurity: Challenges, opportunities and use-case prototypes (2026). https://arxiv.org/abs/2601.05293
12. Liang, X., et al.: Self-evolving agents with reflective and memory-augmented abilities (2025)
13. Lunt, T.F.: A real-time intrusion detection expert system (IDES)-final report (1992)
14. Meconi, D., Stirpe, S., Martelli, F., Lavalle, L., Navigli, R.: Do large language models understand word senses? In: Christodoulopoulos, C., Chakraborty, T., Rose, C., Peng, V. (eds.) Proceedings of the 2025 Conference on Empirical Methods in Natural Language Processing, pp. 33897–33916. Association for Computational Linguistics, Suzhou, China (2025)
15. Mezzi, E., Massacci, F., Tuma, K.: Large language models are unreliable for cyber threat intelligence. In: Dalla Preda, M., Schrittwieser, S., Naessens, V., De Sutter, B. (eds.) Availability, Reliability and Security, pp. 343–364. Springer Nature Switzerland, Cham (2025)
16. Sarumathy, P., Rajasree, S., Chandrasekar, A.: An AI-based intrusion prevention system to enhance cloud security. In: 2025 4th International Conference on Sentiment Analysis and Deep Learning (ICSADL), pp. 313–320 (2025). https://doi.org/10.1109/ICSADL65848.2025.10933485
17. Sarangi, S., Talele, C., Salam, H.: Agentic-ToM: cognition-inspired agentic processing for enhancing theory of mind reasoning. In: Christodoulopoulos, C., Chakraborty, T., Rose, C., Peng, V. (eds.) Findings of the Association for Computational Linguistics: EMNLP 2025, pp. 25645–25661. Association for Computational Linguistics, Suzhou, China (Nov (2025)
18. Sumers, T.R., Yao, S., Narasimhan, K., Griffiths, T.L.: Cognitive architectures for language agents (2024)
19. team, T.I.: Disrupting the first reported ai-orchestrated cyber espionage campaign. Tech. rep., Anthropic (2025)

20. Tikhomirov, M., Loukachevitch, N.: Exploring prompt-based methods for zero-shot hypernym prediction with large language models (2024)
21. Wei, J., et al.: Chain-of-thought prompting elicits reasoning in large language models. In: Proceedings of the 36th International Conference on Neural Information Processing Systems. NIPS '22, Curran Associates Inc, Red Hook, NY, USA (2022)
22. Wu, C., Ke, W., Wang, P., Luo, Z., Li, G., Chen, W.: ConsistNER: towards instructive NER demonstrations for LLMs with the consistency of ontology and context. In: Proceedings of the Thirty-Eighth AAAI Conference on Artificial Intelligence. AAAI'24, AAAI Press (2024)
23. Zhong, W., Guo, L., Gao, Q., Ye, H., Wang, Y.: MemoryBank: enhancing large language models with long-term memory. In: Proceedings of the Thirty-Eighth AAAI Conference on Artificial Intelligence. AAAI'24, AAAI Press (2024)
24. Zhou, R., Pan, J., Tan, X., Xi, H.: Application of clips expert system to malware detection system. Int. Conf. Comput. Intell. Secur. **1**, 309–314 (2008)

Visual-Aware Representation of Web Pages for Machine Learning Applications

Radek Burget(✉) and Radek Hranický

Faculty of Information Technology, Brno University of Technology, Bozetechova 2, Brno 612 00, Czechia
{burgetr,hranicky}@fit.vut.cz

Abstract. Applying machine learning to web pages is challenging due to the need to interpret HTML together with associated resources and perform rendering to obtain a meaningful visual and layout-aware representation. As a result, machine learning over web content remains comparatively underexplored. In this paper, we present a platform for visual-aware representation and machine learning over web pages based on the open-source rendering tool FitLayout. The platform provides a server capable of rendering web pages, explicitly capturing their visual and structural properties in an RDF-based representation, and persisting the rendered documents in an integrated storage. The processing pipeline is controlled via a REST API, while SPARQL queries are used to retrieve structured data suitable as input for machine learning algorithms. By explicitly modeling rendered web pages, including fine-grained layout details, the platform enables dataset sharing and supports the reproducibility of experimental results. The architecture supports the complete dataset preparation workflow, from web page collection and rendering through preprocessing and annotation of content elements to downstream learning tasks. We further provide a Python client library that integrates the platform with standard machine learning workflows. As a demonstration, we show how rendered web pages can be transformed into graph-based representations and used to train graph neural networks for recognizing key content elements, illustrating both the applicability of the approach and the reproducibility of the results.

Keywords: Rendered web pages · Visual-aware document representation · Machine learning for web content · Graph neural networks · Reproducible web data analysis

1 Introduction

Machine learning for document understanding has progressed rapidly, particularly for visually rich inputs, such as scanned pages and PDFs. Many successful methods are layout-aware and represent documents as structured objects, often as graphs processed by graph neural networks (GNNs). Comparable approaches for web pages are still less explored.

A. Mauri et al. (Eds.): ICWE 2026, LNCS 16625, pp. 191–198, 2026.
https://doi.org/10.1007/978-3-032-29372-5_14

Web pages are difficult because their layout is produced dynamically by a browser from HTML and external resources, and the rendering output has no standard, persistent representation. Consequently, most existing methods either analyze the Document Object Model (DOM) only (ignoring layout) or treat pages as images (losing content structure), which limits the use of layout-aware models.

Building on our previous work [3], we use RDF descriptions of rendered pages as a machine-learning-ready representation and introduce a software platform based on our FitLayout open-source framework. The platform exposes an API and SPARQL access to the rendered representation, supports the sharing of rendered datasets, and provides a Python client for integration into common machine learning workflows.

We illustrate our approach using a case study on recognizing key content elements. We describe how to construct an annotated dataset of rendered web pages, and how to employ SPARQL queries to transform these pages into graph representations suitable for subsequent processing with GNNs. Finally, we explain how the resulting dataset can be shared to facilitate reproducibility of the results and to enable the application of alternative machine learning methods to the same underlying data.

2 Related Work

Machine learning techniques have been effectively applied to identify key content elements in PDF documents, including table localization and structural parsing with neural methods designed for complex document layouts [5,11] or complex layout analysis [4,13].

In contrast, web information extraction and web document understanding face additional challenges due to the dynamic, browser-rendered nature of web pages and the frequent mismatch between the DOM tree and the visual layout. Consequently, existing approaches often focus either on DOM or template-based extraction [1,10,12], or incorporate visual cues by learning from screenshots/visual contexts [6,8], or from browser-derived render trees [9].

This paper extends our earlier work: In [2], we introduced an RDF-based model of rendered web pages to enable visually aware web scraping (in contrast to the more common DOM-based scrapers); in [3], we presented a general method for creating snapshots of rendered web pages using this representation. In this study, we present an entirely new Python workflow and infrastructure that brings this solution into the Python-based machine learning ecosystem, enabling the use of frameworks such as PyTorch on web page data.

3 Visual-Aware Representation of Web Pages

To exploit the visual properties and layout of web page content in machine learning applications, the input web pages must be rendered, and the rendering results must be explicitly described. We implemented both tasks using the FitLayout framework [3].

FitLayout allows the representation of a single rendered page at different levels of abstraction and provides an ontology suitable for this purpose. The ontology[1] defines the concept of an *Artifact* that describes a single page on some level of abstraction. For machine learning tasks, the following two artifact types (subclasses of *Artifact*) are relevant:

- The *Page* artifact describes a rendered page at the lowest level of abstraction as a set of *Boxes* (thus also called a box tree).
- The *AreaTree* represents an abstraction over the rendered page on the level of visible *visual areas* that are not directly connected to the source HTML code.

In the *BoxTree*, every box is directly linked to a source HTML element, as specified by the CSS formatting model. Each box has visual attributes such as `fontSize`, `color`, `positionX`, and `positionY`. The root box corresponds to the entire page area, and hierarchical relationships are captured via the `isChildOf` property. The *AreaTree* eliminates the rigid reliance on HTML markup by concentrating on visual areas, which can be identified using different techniques (such as page segmentation methods) provided by FitLayout. Finally, each area can be associated with one or more *Tags* via the *hasTag* property, which can be used to label areas during dataset preparation.

As a result, each rendered page is represented by two artifacts (a *Page* and an *AreaTree*), which correspond to RDF subgraphs stored in the FitLayout RDF repository.

4 System Architecture and Processing Pipeline

The proposed system architecture is based on the observation that machine learning workloads are frequently spread across multiple computing nodes with distinct roles: storage nodes equipped with large-capacity storage for persisting data and compute nodes that provide sufficient processing power to carry out neural network training and evaluation.

An overview of the entire architecture is shown in Fig. 1. It is composed of the FitLayout server, which acts as a data storage node with a central RDF repository for persisting page artifacts, and client-side Python applications that control dataset preparation and implement the machine learning methods.

To support the web page processing workflow, the server provides built-in services for creating different *artifacts*:

- *Page rendering* – it renders a web page in a headless Chromium web browser, which is controlled remotely via the Puppeteer library[2]. Then, the visual attributes of every rendered box are determined using JavaScript, and the *Page* RDF graph is created and stored in the repository.

[1] https://fitlayout.github.io/ontology/.

[2] https://pptr.dev/.

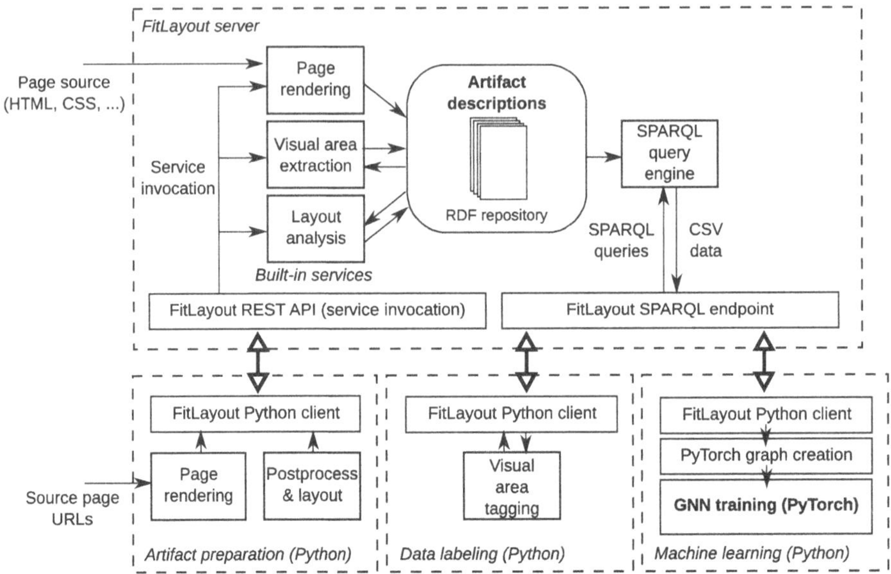

Fig. 1. The complete architectural layout, featuring the FitLayout server as the central data storage node and Python-based compute nodes responsible for dataset preparation as well as GNN training and evaluation.

- *Visual area extraction* – for our task, we use a simple method that directly maps each visually distinct box in a *Page* to a visual area in the resulting *AreaTree* while discarding boxes that do not have any visual effect.
- *Layout analysis* – examines the relative positions of sibling areas in the area tree and adds RDF statements indicating that one area is `above`, `below`, to the `leftOf`, or to the `rightOf` another area. FitLayout offers several implementations of this analysis; we employed an adapted version of the *visibility* method introduced by Gemelli et al. [5], originally designed for PDF documents.

Client applications can call these services through a REST API to generate and store RDF datasets of the rendered pages. Additionally, the server provides a SPARQL endpoint for querying the stored RDF data and inserting new statements. By default, FitLayout also includes an interactive client application with a web-based GUI[3], which makes it possible to view and inspect the stored artifacts.

As Python has effectively become the standard environment for implementing machine learning methods, FitLayout offers a Python client library[4] for its REST API, enabling seamless integration of rendered page data into machine learning workflows.

[3] https://github.com/FitLayout/PageView.

[4] https://github.com/FitLayout/fitlayout-python-client.

5 Python-Based ML Integration

The Python client layer, as shown in Fig. 1, covers two basic tasks: dataset preparation (which includes the preparation of the rendered page artifacts and their labeling) and the implementation of the machine learning applications themselves.

Artifact preparation involves sequentially calling the Page Rendering, Visual Area Extraction, and Layout Analysis services for each input page URL, with the goal of creating an *AreaTree* artifact for every source page. Each of these services is configurable; for instance, the client can set the viewport size used for rendering or use a specific method for spatial relationship discovery.

The optional data labeling step can be used to assign labels (*Tags*) to selected visual regions, which can later serve, for example, for training visual area classifiers. In a typical scenario, the target visual areas are first retrieved with a SELECT query, and subsequently, the *hasTag* statements are inserted into the RDF graph. The query can use both visual characteristics (e.g., color, size, or position) and properties of the underlying HTML, such as element attributes. For instance, in the Klarna web page dataset [7], specific element attributes are employed to indicate the target elements; these attributes can then be straightforwardly converted into labels using this approach.

Finally, to implement the machine learning algorithms, the data on the visual areas used for training or testing can be efficiently retrieved from the repository via SPARQL SELECT queries. These queries make it possible to specify the target visual areas in the same way as in the previous step and select the relevant property values. For instance, when applying GNNs for visual area classification, the source graphs can be efficiently generated using one query to obtain node properties and another to obtain edge properties, as we illustrate in detail in the following section.

6 Case Study: GNN-Based Content Element Recognition

To demonstrate the practical usefulness of the proposed architecture for machine learning on visual-aware web page models, we focus on a sample task: training a GNN-based classifier of visual areas to recognize book titles and prices in a fictional online bookstore[5], a commonly used example target for web scraping. The entire project repository is available at GitHub[6]. The sample project covers the entire workflow from dataset preparation through the application of ML methods to exporting the dataset in a shareable format to support the reproducibility of the entire process.

6.1 Environment Setup

The project contains client Python scripts that implement dataset preparation, data labeling, and machine learning, as described in the following subsections.

[5] https://books.toscrape.com/.

[6] https://github.com/FitLayout/graphlearn.

The FitLayout server is set up by simply running the corresponding Docker image provided by the FitLayout project. For our experiments, we used a two-node configuration, where the server runs on a separate computing node with sufficient storage space. However, the client and server can share a single node when required.

6.2 Dataset Preparation

The entire web page processing workflow starts by rendering the source pages based on a list of URLs. Collecting the input URLs is not covered here; we used a simple script to extract the URLs of pages corresponding to individual books in the bookstore. We collected 1,000 URLs in total and made them available in a text file within the project. The individual subtasks were implemented as short Python scripts that control the dataset preparation by simply calling the corresponding FitLayout services using the FitLayout Python client library:

Page rendering script (`render.py`) invokes the Puppeteer-based rendering service for every input URL using the default viewport width of 1200 px. As a result, the corresponding *Page* artifacts are stored in the built-in RDF repository.

The *Postprocessing & layout* script (`segment.py`) applies the Visual area extraction service on each page, generating an *AreaTree* artifact. It then calls the layout analysis service to infer the spatial relationships between the visual areas, as detailed in Sect. 4.

Finally, the *data labeling* script (`tagging.py`) detects the visual areas corresponding to *book titles* and their *prices* in the repository and inserts the respective `hasTag` statements into the RDF repository, which are subsequently used to train the GNN. In our basic use case, all source pages follow a shared template, enabling the identification of target regions through a single SPARQL query that combines visual features and source HTML element properties. For more heterogeneous input sources, multiple taggers would be required, or in the worst-case scenario, manual labeling would need to be carried out via the FitLayout GUI.

6.3 GNN Training

We implemented the GNN training using the widely adopted PyTorch Geometric (PyG) framework. For each AreaTree, we first build a corresponding PyG graph in which nodes represent visual areas, while edges capture both the parent-child relations in the tree and the spatial relations between sibling areas. Node features are retrieved via a SPARQL query and include text color, background color (RGB), X and Y pixel coordinates on the page, font size and weight, text length, and proportions of letters, digits, and punctuation in the contained text. The target class is encoded as a simple class index (1 for title, 2 for price, and 0 for all other areas). A separate SPARQL query is used to detect nodes that share either a parent-child or spatial relationship; these relationships are then encoded as edges in the PyG graph. In this manner, we create a PyTorch *dataset* that can serve as input for training the GNN.

As a representative GNN architecture, we employ the GCNConv operator from PyG and build a neural network with three convolutional layers to generate graph embeddings. The network consists of an input layer, a hidden layer with 128 channels, and an output layer with 10 channels, followed by a linear classifier. To train the network, we employed a straightforward training loop using the AdamW optimizer, cross-entropy as the loss function, and early stopping.

Our sample dataset, as outlined above, consists of 1,000 area trees containing a total of 37,768 visual areas. Although the primary aim of this sample project is to demonstrate how the proposed architecture can integrate rendered web pages into a Python-based ML workflow—and the underlying model is comparatively simple—the experiments resulted in only 0 to 4 misclassified visual areas across the entire set (depending on how the training and testing data were split). These results indicate that the proposed approach is indeed viable.

6.4 Dataset Sharing

The FitLayout Python client also includes the capability to export and import the complete RDF repository in common RDF serialization formats, such as Turtle or N-Quads. The exported dataset captures all information about the rendered web pages and the generated artifacts (area trees), including their labels and even a screenshot of each page. This makes it possible to publish the dataset and/or reproduce the results even if the original web pages are altered or become unavailable. The dataset created as part of this case study is available at Zenodo[7].

7 Conclusions and Future Work

The implemented platform demonstrates a comprehensive approach to integrating visual-aware representations of rendered web pages into machine learning workflows. By leveraging the FitLayout framework and RDF-based modeling, the system explicitly captures the visual and structural properties of web pages, enabling flexible data extraction and reproducible experiments. The provided Python client library facilitates seamless dataset preparation, labeling, and application of machine learning methods, such as graph neural networks for content element recognition, as illustrated in the case study. This architecture not only bridges the gap between web content and document understanding methods but also supports dataset sharing and reproducibility, addressing the key challenges in web page analysis using machine learning. The RDF-based method of web page representation also paves the way for the use of large language models to analyze them. This is another area of future research.

Acknowledgements. This work was supported by the project Application of advanced techniques for cybersecurity and efficient processing of heterogeneous data, FIT-S-26-9019, funded by Brno University of Technology.

[7] https://zenodo.org/records/18674233.

References

1. Bevendorff, J., Gupta, R., Kiesel, J., Stein, B.: An empirical comparison of web content extraction algorithms. In: Proceedings of the 46th International ACM SIGIR Conference on Research and Development in Information Retrieval, pp. 2594–2603 (2023)
2. Burget, R.: Scraping data from web pages using SPARQL queries. In: Garrigós, I., Murillo Rodríguez, J.M., Wimmer, M. (eds.) Web Engineering, pp. 293–300. Springer Nature Switzerland, Cham (2023)
3. Burget, R., Salem, H.: Creating searchable web page snapshots using semantic technologies. In: Garrigós, I., Murillo Rodríguez, J.M., Wimmer, M. (eds.) Web Engineering, pp. 355–358. Springer Nature Switzerland, Cham (2023)
4. Gemelli, A., Biswas, S., Civitelli, E., Lladós, J., Marinai, S.: Doc2Graph: a task agnostic document understanding framework based on graph neural networks. In: Karlinsky, L., Michaeli, T., Nishino, K. (eds.) Computer Vision - ECCV 2022 Workshops, pp. 329–344. Springer Nature Switzerland, Cham (2023)
5. Gemelli, A., Vivoli, E., Marinai, S.: Graph neural networks and representation embedding for table extraction in pdf documents. In: 2022 26th International Conference on Pattern Recognition (ICPR), pp. 1719–1726 (2022)
6. Gogar, T., Hubacek, O., Sedivy, J.: Deep neural networks for web page information extraction. In: 12th IFIP International Conference on Artificial Intelligence Applications and Innovations (AIAI). vol. AICT-475, pp. 154–163. Thessaloniki, Greece (2016). https://doi.org/10.1007/978-3-319-44944-9_14
7. Hotti, A., Risuleo, R.S., Magureanu, S., Moradi, A., Lagergren, J.: The Klarna product page dataset: Web element nomination with graph neural networks and large language models. Transactions on Machine Learning Research 2024 (2024)
8. Kumar, A., Morabia, K., Wang, W., Chang, K., Schwing, A.: CoVA: context-aware visual attention for webpage information extraction. In: Malmasi, S., Rokhlenko, O., Ueffing, N., Guy, I., Agichtein, E., Kallumadi, S. (eds.) Proceedings of the Fifth Workshop on e-Commerce and NLP (ECNLP 5), pp. 80–90. Association for Computational Linguistics, Dublin, Ireland (2022). https://doi.org/10.18653/v1/2022.ecnlp-1.11
9. Li, Z., Shao, B., Shou, L., Gong, M., Li, G., Jiang, D.: WIERT: web information extraction via render tree. Proc. AAAI Conf. Artif. Intell. **37**(11), 13166–13173 (2023). https://doi.org/10.1609/aaai.v37i11.26546
10. Lin, B.Y., Sheng, Y., Vo, N., Tata, S.: FreeDOM: a transferable neural architecture for structured information extraction on web documents. In: Proceedings of the 26th ACM SIGKDD International Conference on Knowledge Discovery & Data Mining, pp. 1092–1102. KDD '20, Association for Computing Machinery, New York, NY, USA (2020). https://doi.org/10.1145/3394486.3403153
11. Riba, P., Dutta, A., Goldmann, L., Fornés, A., Ramos, O., Lladós, J.: Table detection in invoice documents by graph neural networks. In: 2019 International Conference on Document Analysis and Recognition (ICDAR), pp. 122–127 (2019). https://doi.org/10.1109/ICDAR.2019.00028
12. Truong, B.V., Pham, P., Nguyen, L.T., Nguyen, N.T., Vo, B.: Web data analysis using a hybrid approach of DOM processing and deep learning models. Appl. Soft Comput. **191**, 114651 (2026)
13. Wang, J., et al.: A graphical approach to document layout analysis. In: Fink, G.A., Jain, R., Kise, K., Zanibbi, R. (eds.) Document Analysis and Recognition - ICDAR 2023, pp. 53–69. Springer Nature Switzerland, Cham (2023)

VOIX: A Web-Native Interface for Agents

Sven Schultze(✉), Meike Verena Kietzmann, Nils Lucas Schönfeld, and Ruth Stock-Homburg

Technical University Darmstadt, Darmstadt, Germany
sven.schultze@tu-darmstadt.de

Abstract. The increasing deployment of autonomous AI agents on the web is hampered by a fundamental architectural misalignment: current web applications are designed primarily for human interaction, forcing agents to infer affordances from user interfaces through brittle, inefficient, and insecure interactions. To address this, we introduce VOIX, a web-native framework that enables websites to expose reliable, auditable, and privacy-preserving capabilities for AI agents through simple, declarative HTML elements. VOIX introduces <tool> and <context> tags, allowing developers to explicitly define available actions and relevant state, thereby creating a clear, machine-readable contract for agent behavior. This approach shifts control to the website developer while preserving user privacy by disconnecting the conversational interactions from the website. Ultimately, this work provides a foundational web engineering mechanism for realizing the Agentic Web, enabling a future of seamless and secure human-AI collaboration on the web.

Keywords: Agentic Web · AI Agents · Web Agents · Large Language Models · Human-Computer Interaction · Developer Experience · Web Standards

1 Introduction

The past years have seen rapid progress in large language models (LLMs) and their integration into interactive systems. Increasingly, these models are being deployed as autonomous or semi-autonomous agents capable of acting on behalf of users in complex environments such as the web. Yet, the integration of conversational agents into the existing web ecosystem remains fundamentally misaligned with the current architecture of the web. Today's web is designed for human consumption. Agents must infer available actions by scraping HTML, heuristically parsing Document Object Models (DOMs) or even analyzing screenshots. With these ad hoc practices, even minor state changes can disrupt an agents workflow. Agents are inefficient, as they have to repeatedly rediscover affordances. In addition, they are insecure, since unintended operations or unauthorized data access cannot be ruled out: Sensitive or proprietary information embedded in the web page, such as private messages, financial data, or user details, could be shared without the user's explicit consent.

A. Mauri et al. (Eds.): ICWE 2026, LNCS 16625, pp. 199–208, 2026.
https://doi.org/10.1007/978-3-032-29372-5_15

Further, the current paradigm strips website developers of control over the user experience on their own pages. When an external agent scrapes a site, it bypasses the carefully crafted workflows and interaction patterns designed by the developer. The agent provider, not the site owner, unilaterally decides how to interpret and interact with the page's functionality. This lack of an explicit, machine-readable contract leaves developers unable to communicate their site's capabilities, define safe actions, or protect sensitive data, creating an unpredictable and unstable environment for both agents and the websites they navigate. Recent position papers [5,16] converge on the need for an Agentic Web. In this Agentic Web, machine-readable, standardized affordances are first-class citizens and agents can operate without reverse engineering user interfaces (UI) built for humans.

To this end, we introduce VOIX[1], a web-native framework that embodies this principle through a simple, declarative substrate for robust, privacy-preserving agent–web interaction. VOIX enables websites to explicitly declare actions and relevant state in a way that is equally accessible to autonomous agents, reducing the need for brittle inference from human-oriented user interfaces and lowering the development barrier for rich, multimodal experiences. This shifts agent–web interaction from a model where external providers unilaterally interpret a site's DOM, to one where the site developer defines an explicit, auditable contract for agent behavior.

2 Related Work

The design of VOIX is informed by prior work in web engineering, human-computer interaction, and agent systems. To position our contribution within this landscape, we review related work along three dimensions: (1) machine-readable and actionable web interfaces, (2) conversational and multimodal interfaces, and (3) privacy, safety, and control mechanisms. We conclude with a synthesis of limitations in existing approaches that motivate the design of VOIX.

Machine-Readable and Actionable Web Interfaces. A long-standing goal in web engineering has been to make web content and functionality accessible to machines. Early approaches like the Semantic Web succeeded enabled machine-readable content but lacked standardized mechanisms for invoking actions or modifying application state, limiting their applicability to interactive scenarios.

More recent work shifts toward actionable interfaces for agents. Position papers on the Agentic Web [5,16] advocate replacing human-centric interfaces with machine-native affordances that allow agents to operate more reliably and efficiently. Environments such as WebArena [19] and WebVoyager [4] highlight the limitations of UI-based interaction, where agents must infer functionality from DOM structures or visual representations. Hybrid approaches [13]

[1] VOIX Chrome extension and documentation: https://github.com/svenschultze/VOIX.

that combine browsing with API access improve performance, underscoring the importance of structured, machine-readable interfaces. Emerging standards such as WebMCP formalize tool invocation through typed interfaces, improving reliability compared to UI inference. Related work on the Conversational Web explores alternative interaction paradigms. Pucci et al. [10] propose the Conversation-Oriented Navigation Tree, which abstracts the DOM for conversational access. While improving navigation and summarization, it focuses on interpreting existing interfaces rather than enabling declarative, machine-readable affordances.

Conversational and Multimodal Interaction. Research in human–computer interaction shows that combining multiple interaction modalities improve robustness and usability, particularly in complex tasks. Multimodal systems integrate natural language with direct manipulation, reducing ambiguity and enabling more flexible interaction patterns [8]. Recent LLM-based systems extend these ideas to modern interfaces by augmenting graphical user interfaces with conversational capabilities. Frameworks such as DirectGPT [6] and ReactGenie [15] enable users to combine natural language with traditional UI interactions, while tools like Geno [12] support developers in retrofitting multimodal capabilities onto existing applications. Other work, such as Zhao et al. [18], demonstrates that combining textual and visual inputs improves task efficiency and disambiguation.

Privacy, Safety, and Control Mechanisms. The deployment of autonomous agents raises concerns regarding unintended actions, data exposure, and lack of transparency [1]. Prior work addresses these challenges through mechanisms such as human-in-the-loop interaction, action approval workflows, and verification steps [7]. Within the web ecosystem, earlier efforts such as the Platform for Privacy Preferences (P3P) and Do Not Track focused on declarative privacy preferences but did not address how application functionality is exposed to agents. More recent work emphasizes the importance of explicit contracts and structured interfaces to ensure safe interaction [5]. Systems like Magentic-UI [7] demonstrate that incorporating user oversight can improve both safety and performance.

3 VOIX: A Web-Native Interface for Agents

The literature review revealed the need for a standardized, machine-native protocol for the web that leverages powerful multimodal patterns, yet it also highlights the critical challenges of agent brittleness, implementation complexity, and the need for developer-defined safety and control. To address these challenges, we propose VOIX, a web-native framework for agentic interaction that makes site capabilities and state discoverable and invokable by agents through declarative, typed semantics. VOIX aims to: (1) improve agent reliability and efficiency by eliminating affordance inference; (2) preserve the web's decentralization and backward compatibility; (3) provide human control, privacy, and transparency by design; and (4) remain model- and provider-agnostic so multiple agent stacks can interoperate.

3.1 Design Principles

The design of VOIX is guided by a set of core principles derived from prior work on Agentic Web [5] and multimodal interaction [9]:

R1 Privacy and Safety: Control over privacy and safety must be placed in the hands of developers and users. Developers must be able to define what data is exposed and which tools are safety-critical, as autonomous agents require strict, policy-driven execution boundaries to prevent full-chain failures [3]. Furthermore, users must retain control over their conversational data and choice of LLM provider. This layered approach counters the significant privacy risks of transmitting full page content and sensitive user prompts to third-party cloud services, allowing for localized or heavily constrained data processing [14].

R2 Optimal Representation: The framework must provide an efficient, machine-readable representation of a website's affordances [2]. This representation must be dynamically scoped, containing only the necessary information for the agent to optimally solve its tasks, excluding all other data [17].

R3 Efficient to Host: The architecture must not place the computational and financial burden of LLM inference on the website owner. By operating on the client-side, the framework respects the decentralized nature of the web [16] and removes a major barrier of widespread adoption.

R4 Standardized and Developer-Friendly: The framework must be built on a universal standard using familiar web patterns. By abstracting complex UI logic into unified, declarative tool primitives [11], the architecture avoids the fragility of traditional DOM scraping. This addresses the critical need for easy developer adoption and aligns with the broader industry push, evidenced by the proposal of MCP, toward standardized protocols that are natively compatible across various agents and websites.

R5 Expressive: The framework must also be expressive enough to model the key patterns of effective multimodal interaction as identified by Oviatt [9]. This is a critical requirement for moving beyond simple feature substitution towards truly synergistic and flexible interfaces. Specifically, the framework should handle both simultaneous and sequential integration of inputs, abstract and high-level user inputs, and the ability to implement both complementary and redundant actions.

3.2 Specification

To this end, VOIX defines a clear architectural model that decouples the website's functional capabilities from the agent's reasoning and execution, creating a standardized interface that prioritizes security, privacy, and decentralization. The VOIX architecture distributes responsibilities among three distinct stakeholders:

The Website. acts as the authoritative source of its own capabilities. Its responsibility is to declare a set of invokable tools and expose relevant application context using two new HTML elements: `<tool>` exposes actions with names, parameter types, and natural language descriptions; `<context>` exposes task-relevant state. The website is also responsible for implementing the business logic that executes a tool call and, if necessary, returns a result. Thereby, the websites declares the contract in which an LLM is allowed to interact with it. This happens alongside the development of the user interface, allowing developers integrate their existing application logic seamlessly and to benefit from the entire ecosystem of modern frameworks like React and Vue or server-side like Laravel without the need to install new packages.

The Browser Agent. serves as the intermediary, decoupling the website from the Inference Provider. Its primary functions are to: (a) scan the website to discover and catalog all declared `<tool>` and `<context>` elements; (b) present this catalog to the agent for reasoning; and (c) dispatch events to trigger tool execution on the web page when instructed by the agent. This architectural role is designed to be implementation-agnostic and can be realized through various means, including open-source extensions that support multiple inference providers, enterprise-specific modules with enhanced security and integration, or native browser integrations. Our reference implementation, for instance, is a Chrome extension that demonstrates this open, provider-agnostic model.

The Inference Provider. (e.g., an LLM, which can be cloud-based or a local model hosted by the user) is the decision-making component. It receives the catalog of tools and context from the browser agent and, based on the user's natural language objective, selects the appropriate tool and parameters for execution. Its interaction is with the structured declarations, not the visual UI.

This decoupled architecture supports diverse deployment models: fully private local LLMs, powerful cloud-based models, secure enterprise integrations via SSO, or seamless native browser implementations.

Conceptually, VOIX adapts the backend-focused Model Context Protocol (MCP) for the client-side web, mapping MCP Tools to <tool> and MCP Resources to <context>. A DOM-native approach is essential because Single Page Applications (SPAs) manage dynamic state and security contexts (e.g., cookies, local storage) locally in the browser. Relying on backend MCP servers would bypass these critical client-side security measures and force redundant state synchronization.

3.3 Trust Boundaries

VOIX creates trust boundaries by keeping the user's conversation private while giving the website and the user strict control over data sharing. When a user gives a command, their words are sent directly to their chosen Inference Provider, ensuring the website never sees the original request. Furthermore, the agent does not see the entire state of the webpage; it only has access to the specific information and actions the website explicitly shares. This allows the website to protect potentially sensitive user data that has been entered on the page but is not meant to be shared with a third-party Inference Provider. As a final layer of control, the user can configure the Browser Agent to disable specific contexts they do not want the agent to see. This multi-level system of permissions ensures that interactions are both powerful and privacy-preserving.

This decoupled architecture establishes the necessary control points for securing multi-website interactions. Because the Browser Agent serves as the intermediary, it is uniquely positioned to enforce origin-based isolation, potentially preventing an agent that aggregates data across domains from inadvertently leaking sensitive context from one session to another potentially malicious attacker website. Furthermore, declarative tool definitions can facilitate granular approval workflows. Typed actions provide the semantic context required for the browser to identify high-stakes operations and mandate user confirmation before execution. This architectural alignment supports a "human-in-the-loop" safeguard where the user remains the ultimate arbiter of consequential actions.

Our approach stands in contrast with two prevailing models of web-agent integration, each of which centralizes control at the expense of a key stakeholder. In one model, the website implements its own bespoke LLM support, forcing the user into a position where they must trust the site operator with their conversational data, which may be used in ways that are not transparent or aligned with the user's interests. In the opposing model (e.g., Claude for Chrome[2], Perplexity Comet[3]), an inference provider deploys a universal agent that attempts to infer actions and state from a website's raw HTML and screenshots. This disempowers the website developer, who loses control over both the user experience and data privacy, as the agent may perform unintended actions or access data not meant for exposure. Conceptually, VOIX acts as a modern evolution of legacy machine-readable directives, such as `robots.txt` for crawlers or the Platform for Privacy Preferences (P3P). However, rather than merely asking agents not to scrape, VOIX provides an executable, component-level contract. VOIX, by design, uses this standardized, explicit contract to avoid the pitfalls of centralization and balance the needs of both the user and the website developer.

3.4 Reference Implementation

We contribute a reference implementation of VOIX with a Chrome extension that enables chat and voice interaction with websites. Its operation begins

[2] https://www.anthropic.com/news/claude-for-chrome, accessed May 11, 2026.

[3] https://www.perplexity.ai/comet/, accessed May 11, 2026.

with a script, injected into the website, which discovers all declared `<tool>` and `<context>` elements. This script also actively monitors the DOM for any changes, allowing it to maintain a dynamic and up-to-date model of the available tool and context space.

The primary user interface is a side panel supporting text chat and advanced voice inputs. It utilizes on-device voice activity detection for continuous conversation and offers a transcription mode for editing spoken words. To enhance discoverability, the panel visualizes declared tools and contexts and generates example prompts. Users can also configure any OpenAI-compatible Inference Provider, ensuring full control over data, models, and costs. The agentic LLM interaction in the extension maintains a conversation history. When the user makes a request, the contexts are prepended to the message, and a request is sent to the configured Inference Provider, including the currently available tools. When a tool call is generated, an event is triggered through the injected script to invoke the website's tool handler. If the tool returns something, this is reported back to the LLM Agent, which finally writes a message explaining what happened.

Integrating VOIX into a web application involves two primary steps: first, declaratively exposing the application's state and capabilities through HTML, and second, connecting these declarations to the application's existing logic.

To enable effective action, the `<context>` element exposes application state (e.g., a dynamic task list) as plain text. Actions are defined via `<tool>` elements, where a standard `call` event listener triggers the corresponding JavaScript logic using parameters from the event's detail property. To support data retrieval and error handling, developers can add a `return` attribute; this signals the agent to await a `return` event containing the result payload before proceeding.

4 Discussion

VOIX was architected to specifically address its core design requirements. By embedding machine-readable affordances directly into the DOM, VOIX offers a practical path toward a more robust, decentralized, and privacy-preserving Agentic Web.

The framework's architecture directly satisfies the requirement for Privacy and Safety (R1). By design, VOIX creates a clear trust boundary that separates the user's conversational data from the website's domain. The Browser Agent sends user prompts directly to the user's chosen LLM provider, ensuring the website operator never sees the content of the conversation. Conversely, the website only exposes explicitly declared information via the context tag, protecting sensitive or proprietary user data from being indiscriminately scraped by a third-party agent.

As per the need for an Optimal Representation (R2) of a site's capabilities, the tool and context primitives provide a concise, structured summary of affordances, eliminating the inefficiency and brittleness of parsing entire DOMs. This means that developers could naturally leverage component-based frameworks like React and Vue to dynamically scope these affordances. This pattern ensures that tools are only discoverable when relevant, inherently linking the agent's capabilities to the real-time state of the user interface.

Furthermore, VOIX is architecturally designed to be Efficient to Host (R3). The framework is fundamentally client-side, placing the computational and financial burden of LLM inference on the user's agent and chosen provider, not the website owner. This decentralization removes a significant barrier to entry and aligns with the web's ethos, making the widespread adoption of the standard feasible for developers and organizations of all sizes.

VOIX is built upon familiar web patterns: simple, declarative HTML tags and standard JavaScript event listeners. This makes it inherently familiar to use, with parallels from standard html elements like buttons and forms. This underlines VOIX's adherence to being Standardized and Developer-Friendly (R4). The VOIX architecture is inherently Expressive (R5), supporting the key patterns of effective multimodal interaction by design. The framework allows for the simultaneous or sequential integration of diverse inputs, and facilitates complementary deictic interactions, such as pairing a GUI click with a voice command, and redundant modalities, ensuring users can perform tasks through either the traditional interface or the agentic contract.

4.1 Limitations and Future Work

VOIX introduces a shift from a visual UI paradigm to an affordance-centric design, requiring developers to explicitly model application capabilities. This creates a design trade-off: low-level tools that mirror GUI actions are easy to maintain but offer limited advantages over traditional agents. While high-level, intent-aligned tools improve performance, they require more careful design and may generalize imperfectly. Finding an effective balance remains an open challenge for developers. Further, VOIX introduces ongoing maintenance considerations, particularly in large or evolving codebases. Declarative tool definitions must remain aligned with the underlying interface; otherwise, inconsistencies between GUI functionality and exposed affordances may arise. Tooling and best practices for maintaining this alignment represent an important direction for future work.

5 Conclusion

This work introduced VOIX, a web-native framework designed to resolve the fundamental misalignment between AI agents and the human-first web. By enabling websites to expose reliable, auditable, and privacy-preserving affordances through simple declarative HTML, VOIX offers a concrete solution to the brittleness, inefficiency, and security risks inherent in current screen-scraping and DOM-parsing approaches. By shifting the responsibility of defining agent capabilities from the agent provider to the website developer, VOIX creates a balanced, decentralized architecture that respects user privacy and developer control. It represents a critical and deployable step toward an Agentic Web built for seamless and secure collaboration between humans and AI.

References

1. Chan, A., et al.: Harms from increasingly agentic algorithmic systems. In: 2023 ACM Conference on Fairness Accountability and Transparency, pp. 651–666, ACM, Chicago IL USA (2023). ISBN 9798400701924, https://doi.org/10.1145/3593013.3594033
2. Enomoto, M., Obara, R., Zhang, H., Oyamada, M.: Read more, think more: revisiting observation reduction for web agents (2026). https://doi.org/10.48550/arXiv.2604.01535, http://arxiv.org/abs/2604.01535
3. Gao, Y., Wu, S.: A four-layer security governance framework for LLM-based AI agents **8**(4), 49–55 (2025). https://doi.org/10.23977/jaip.2025.080406, publisher: Clausius Scientific Press
4. He, H., et al.: WebVoyager: building an end-to-end web agent with large multimodal models (2024). https://doi.org/10.48550/arXiv.2401.13919, arXiv:2401.13919
5. Lù, X.H., Kamath, G., Mosbach, M., Reddy, S.: Build the web for agents, not agents for the web (2025). https://doi.org/10.48550/arXiv.2506.10953, arXiv:2506.10953
6. Masson, D., Malacria, S., Casiez, G., Vogel, D.: DirectGPT: a direct manipulation interface to interact with large language models. In: Proceedings of the CHI Conference on Human Factors in Computing Systems, pp. 1–16, ACM, Honolulu HI USA (2024). ISBN 9798400703300, https://doi.org/10.1145/3613904.3642462
7. Mozannar, H., et al.: Magentic-UI: towards human-in-the-loop agentic systems (2025). https://doi.org/10.48550/arXiv.2507.22358, arXiv:2507.22358
8. Oviatt, S.: Ten myths of multimodal interaction. Commun. ACM **42**(11), 74–81 (1999). ISSN 0001-0782, 1557-7317, https://doi.org/10.1145/319382.319398
9. Oviatt, S.: The Paradigm Shift to Multimodality in Contemporary Computer Interfaces. Morgan & Claypool Publishers, San Rafael, Synthesis Lectures on Human Centered Informatics Ser (2015). 781627057516 9781627057523
10. Pucci, E., Possaghi, I., Cutrupi, C.M., Baez, M., Cappiello, C., Matera, M.: Defining patterns for a conversational web. In: Proceedings of the 2023 CHI Conference on Human Factors in Computing Systems, CHI 2023, Association for Computing Machinery, New York, NY, USA (2023). ISBN 9781450394215, https://doi.org/10.1145/3544548.3581145
11. Qiu, Z., Sun, J., Xia, C., Zheng, J., Peng, X.: CI4A: semantic component interfaces for agents empowering web automation (2026). https://doi.org/10.48550/arXiv.2601.14790
12. Sarmah, R.J., Ding, Y., Wang, D., Lee, C.Y.P., Li, T.J.J., Chen, X.A.: Geno: a developer tool for authoring multimodal interaction on existing web applications. In: Proceedings of the 33rd Annual ACM Symposium on User Interface Software and Technology, pp. 1169–1181, ACM, Virtual Event USA (2020). ISBN 9781450375146, https://doi.org/10.1145/3379337.3415848
13. Song, Y., Xu, F., Zhou, S., Neubig, G.: Beyond browsing: API-based web agents (2025). https://doi.org/10.48550/arXiv.2410.16464, arXiv:2410.16464
14. Yan, B., et al.: On protecting the data privacy of Large Language Models (LLMs) and LLM agents: a literature review **5**(2), 100300 (2025). ISSN 2667-2952, https://doi.org/10.1016/j.hcc.2025.100300

15. Yang, J.J., et al.: ReactGenie: a development framework for complex multimodal interactions using large language models. In: Proceedings of the CHI Conference on Human Factors in Computing Systems, pp. 1–23, ACM, Honolulu HI USA (2024). ISBN 9798400703300, https://doi.org/10.1145/3613904.3642517
16. Yang, Y., et al.: Agentic web: weaving the next web with AI agents (2025). https://doi.org/10.48550/arXiv.2507.21206, arXiv:2507.21206
17. Zhang, J., Chen, K., Lu, Z., Zhou, E., Yu, Q., Zhang, J.: Prune4web: DOM tree pruning programming for web agent (2025). https://doi.org/10.48550/arXiv.2511.21398
18. Zhao, M., et al.: Tap&say: touch location-informed large language model for multimodal text correction on smartphones. In: Proceedings of the 2025 CHI Conference on Human Factors in Computing Systems, pp. 1–17, ACM, Yokohama Japan (2025). ISBN 9798400713941, https://doi.org/10.1145/3706598.3713376
19. Zhou, S., et al.: WebArena: a realistic web environment for building autonomous agents. In: The Twelfth International Conference on Learning Representations (2024). https://openreview.net/forum?id=oKn9c6ytLx

ShExpose: Automatic REST API Generation from Shape Expressions for RDF Data Access

Christoph Göpfert(✉) and Martin Gaedke

Technische Universität Chemnitz, 09111 Chemnitz, Germany
{christoph.goepfert,martin.gaedke}@informatik.tu-chemnitz.de

Abstract. The increasing adoption of knowledge graphs in data-intensive applications contrasts with the limited availability of developer-friendly interfaces for managing RDF data. This paper presents an approach for automatically generating RESTful API endpoints from Shape Expressions (ShEx) schemas. Given only a set of ShEx schemas and the endpoint of a triplestore, our approach derives endpoints for creating, reading, updating, and deleting shape instances, as well as attribute-level endpoints for more fine-grained access. The generated REST API is implemented as a layer on top of the SPARQL endpoint, thereby abstracting query formulation from clients while maintaining direct access to the underlying triplestore. To facilitate documentation, client generation, and integration with existing tooling, OpenAPI specifications are automatically generated for all derived endpoints. In contrast to prior approaches, which typically rely on additional configuration, such as hand-crafted query templates or manual mappings of endpoints to SPARQL queries, the proposed approach does not require additional configuration. By exposing RDF data through conventional REST-style endpoints, our approach aims to lower the entry barrier for web developers unfamiliar with Semantic Web technologies.

Keywords: REST API · Sparql Endpoint · Knowledge Graph · Triplestore · Shape Expressions · Data Access · ShExpose

1 Introduction

Knowledge graphs (KGs) have become a foundational infrastructure in the Semantic Web, enabling integration and linkage across domains such as life sciences, linguistics, and open government data [1]. Built on the Resource Description Framework (RDF) [9], KGs express information as machine-readable triples, supporting rich semantics and flexible data integration. However, querying KGs using SPARQL [8] requires a precise understanding of the graph's structure, particularly the underlying ontologies [15], making query formulation time-consuming and error-prone. Meanwhile, mainstream web developers are typically accustomed to RESTful APIs that serve JSON data and may be unfamiliar with

A. Mauri et al. (Eds.): ICWE 2026, LNCS 16625, pp. 209–216, 2026.
https://doi.org/10.1007/978-3-032-29372-5_16

Semantic Web technologies, thereby facing barriers to accessing and reusing KG data. While a software mapping layer or middleware library could serve as an alternative, a REST API offers distinct advantages: (i) it operates on HTTP, supported on virtually all platforms, (ii) combined with OpenAPI, it can be consumed by both humans and machines, and (iii) it decouples client applications from the data layer. A mediation layer that exposes KG content through familiar RESTful endpoints is therefore needed.

Existing approaches address this need in different ways. Some web services offer access via REST APIs alongside their SPARQL endpoints. Notable examples include UniProt [2] and Wikidata[1]. However, their approach is not generalizable, as their REST APIs have been tailored to the respective application. Other tools partially automate the generation of API endpoints, but either rely on an initial configuration phase that involves hand-crafting SPARQL query templates [3,4,10,13], do not provide full support for CRUD (*Create*, *Read*, *Update*, *Delete*) operations [3–5,10], or require the querying party to be familiar with Semantic Web standards [6].

A promising direction to overcome these limitations is the use of shape descriptions as an abstraction layer. Shapes provide a declarative way to describe the expected structure of RDF data, analogous to classes in object-oriented systems. Shapes have already been discussed as interface contracts for web services; notably, the W3C Resource Shapes submission suggested that *"[a] REST service may describe aspects of its interface contract using shapes"* [12]. This is especially relevant because API resources often do not directly correspond to resources in the underlying KG [3].

To address the aforementioned gaps, we present a novel approach that (i) automatically generates RESTful, documented API endpoints on top of a SPARQL endpoint by leveraging shape declarations for SPARQL query generation; (ii) translates REST API requests into SPARQL queries at runtime; and (iii) does not require RDF or SPARQL familiarity from the requesting party.

2 Concept

We introduce ShExpose, an approach for automatically generating REST APIs from Shape Expressions (ShEx) schemas that describe entity structures in KGs. With this system, we intend to bridge the gap between semantic web technologies and conventional web service architectures by deriving REST endpoints with CRUD functionality directly from schemas. Specifically, ShExpose is designed to be domain-independent, to support full CRUD operations mapped to standard HTTP verbs, to use JSON as interchange format, to provide machine-readable OpenAPI documentation, and to minimize configuration overhead.

As discussed in the Introduction, shapes serve as structural descriptions of RDF entities, analogous to classes in object-oriented systems. While traditionally used for validation (e.g., in ShEx and SHACL), our approach treats shapes

[1] https://www.wikidata.org/wiki/Wikidata:REST_API.

as executable specifications for generating API endpoints, building on the idea proposed in the W3C Resource Shape 2.0 submission [12].

2.1 Schema Preparation and Processing

We leverage ShEx as a modeling language for entity descriptions. While ShEx supports expressive validation features, our approach requires only a subset of the ShEx language, which is sufficient to describe entities, their properties, and property ranges. Specifically, ShExpose requires each schema to specify a start shape and does not support cyclic references between shapes, as the system relies on acyclic traversal to derive attribute paths and to generate queries. The modeler is therefore only required to define relevant classes and properties that constitute an entity. To simplify this process, we use the YAML-based LinkML modeling language [14] for schema creation. A LinkML schema defines classes, slots, and types, which correspond to entities, properties, and property ranges.

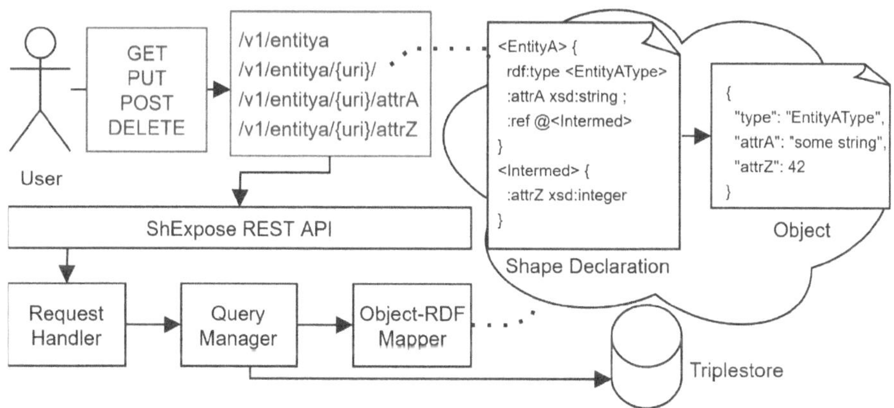

Fig. 1. Conceptual overview of the ShExpose approach.

An entity may be associated with multiple shapes, which we refer to as 'shape fragments'. Shape fragments can be used to split entity definitions into modular components, facilitating schema maintenance. During setup, the LinkML schemas, including fragments, are merged into a unified schema per entity and translated into a single ShEx schema using the LinkML generator toolchain. This merging step assumes that all fragments are consistent with respect to property constraints. If multiple fragments define constraints on the same predicate, they are expected to agree on cardinalities and value ranges. The resulting ShEx files serve as specifications of entity structure to the *Object-RDF Mapper*.

Further, we traverse each shape and create a mapping from the attribute paths to the originating schema fragment. An attribute path consists of the predicates that need to be traversed until the literal value for the entity's attribute is reached. This mapping is used at a later stage by the Query Manager to retrieve only the data required for a specific attribute.

In the object representation, the attribute paths are flattened: for instance, considering *EntityA* in 1, the path *["ref", "attrZ"]* becomes *"attrZ"*, which also maps to the endpoint pattern. When flattening leads to name collisions, the flattened attribute name can be overwritten (aliased) for specific paths. The resulting ShEx schemas are then processed by the *Object-RDF Mapper*. Internally, parts of this functionality are realized using the Linked Data Objects (LDO) framework [11], which provides object-oriented representations of shape-conformant RDF resources and maintains mappings between object properties and RDF predicates.

2.2 Endpoint Generation

At startup, ShExpose processes the available ShEx schemas and derives REST endpoints for each entity description. For every shape, the system generates both entity-level and attribute-level endpoints. Attribute paths are discovered through recursive traversal of the shape definitions, including nested property chains that reference related shapes. For nested structures, ShExpose follows these relations until node constraints are reached. The schema must not include cyclic references, as the traversal would not terminate otherwise.

Each endpoint is bound to the *Request Handler*, which performs runtime validation and forwards valid requests to the *Query Manager*. ShExpose automatically derives an OpenAPI specification that describes all generated endpoints.

The URL structure reflects the logical organization of entities and their attributes. Entity-level creation is exposed using the pattern `/v1/<entity>`, while entity-level read, update, and delete operations follow the pattern `/v1/<entity>/uri/`. Attribute-level CRUD operations are available via `/v1/<entity>/uri/<attribute>`.

2.3 Query Execution

The *Request Handler* validates incoming requests against constraints derived from the ShEx schemas (including datatype, language tag, and structural constraints) and forwards valid requests to the *Query Manager*. The *Query Manager* is responsible for constructing and executing all SPARQL queries. It interacts with both the *Object-RDF Mapper* and the triplestore. For read operations, the *Query Manager* uses the ShEx2SPARQL tool [7] to translate ShEx schemas into SPARQL `CONSTRUCT` queries. Given a shape and a subject URI, the generated query retrieves the triples needed for the current entity, i.e., triples that satisfy the shape's structural constraints as defined in the schema.

For attribute-level requests, the predicate-to-fragment mapping is used to identify the relevant shape fragment, and the *Query Manager* generates a `CONSTRUCT` query from it. Using the fragment rather than the full schema reduces query complexity. For full entity retrieval, all fragments are queried and their results merged. Entity instances are managed by the *Object-RDF Mapper*, which provides an object-oriented view over RDF resources based on the shape declaration. The mapper also tracks modifications made to objects: after a modification, the *Query Manager* computes the difference between the original and updated object state and serializes it into SPARQL `DELETE DATA`/`INSERT DATA` updates, which are then executed against the triplestore. For *Create* operations, new subject URIs are generated by combining the default namespace specified in the configuration file with a generated UUID. Parts of both the *Query Manager* and the *Object-RDF Mapper* are implemented using the Linked Data Objects library.

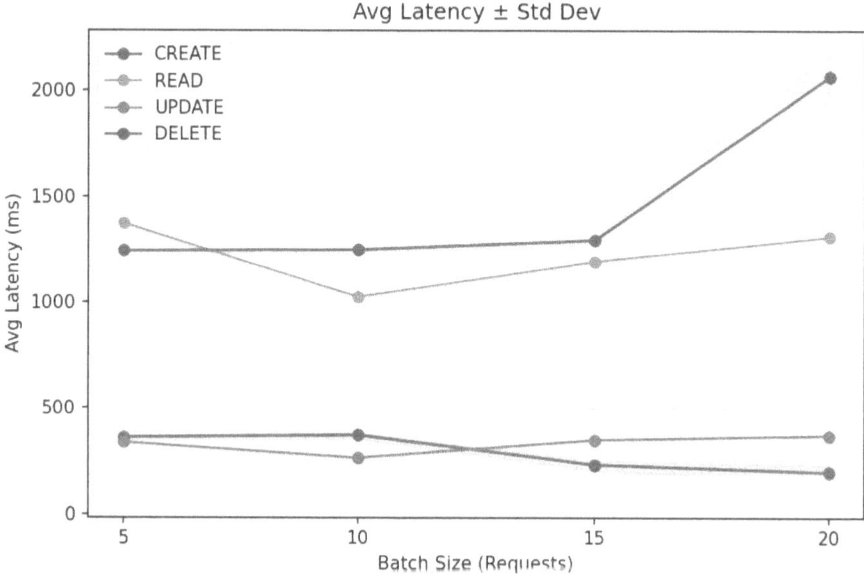

Fig. 2. Avg. latency for CRUD batch reqs. of size 5/10/15/20 on *person* endpoints.

3 Evaluation

We implemented a prototype of ShExpose (source code: https://purl.org/shexpose/code) and evaluated it in a realistic university setting, focusing on end-to-end CRUD request latency. All experiments were conducted on a machine with 6 CPU cores (3.7 GHz) and 32 GB RAM, using the KG TUCgraph maintained at Chemnitz University of Technology, which contains approximately 1.2 million triples. For this experiment, we modeled schemas for the four entity types: person, research project, lab device, and event, each with a slightly different number of attributes (10/7/4/6). The LinkML and ShEx schemas are provided in the source code repository. The raw measurement data and additional figures can be found in the digital appendix at https://purl.org/shexpose/data. These

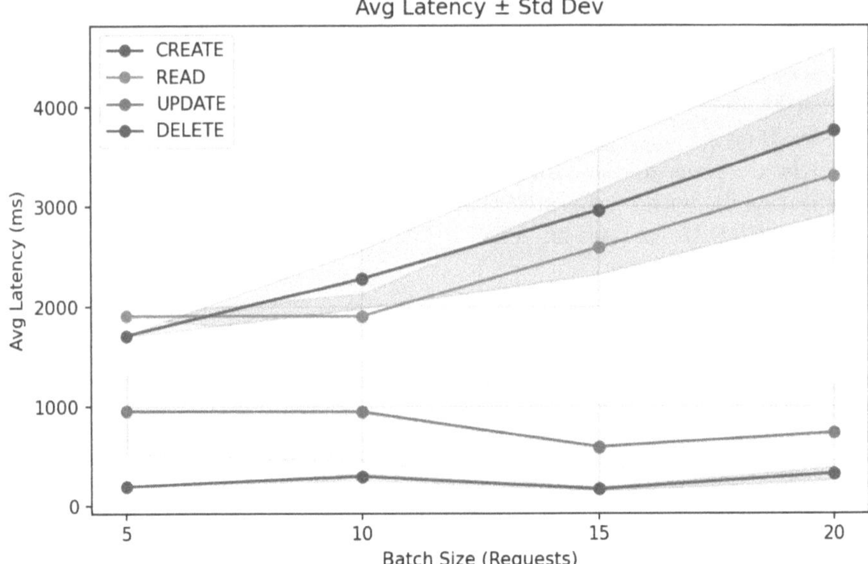

Fig. 3. Avg. latency for CRUD batch reqs. of size 5/10/15/20 on *project* endpoints.

entities represent typical resources in a university's web infrastructure, where low latency is important for a responsive user experience.

We measured latency for batched CRUD requests in batch sizes of 5, 10, 15, and 20. Entity URIs were randomly selected from existing TUCgraph entities. *Create*, *Read*, and *Delete* operations were performed at entity-level, while *Update* modified exactly one random attribute. For each batch size and operation, we recorded average latency and standard deviation.

Figures 2 and 3 visualize the average request latency per batch for the person and research project entities. Additional results are provided in the digital appendix. Across all entity types, *Delete* and *Read* operations exhibit the highest latencies (peaking at 5032ms and 4652ms, respectively), while *Update* (max 1365ms) and *Create* (max 438ms) are more efficient. These differences reflect ShExpose's internal workflow: *Read*, *Delete*, and *Update* require prior retrieval of the entity's RDF data, introducing overhead compared to *Create*. The low *Update* latency results from fetching only the relevant attribute fragment rather than the full entity description.

Overall, the results indicate that the approach scales predictably across entity types, efficiently processing *Create* and *Update* operations while maintaining acceptable latency (<5 s) for entity-level *Read* and *Delete* operations at batch sizes up to 20. For use cases requiring sub-second response times, additional optimizations such as caching may be necessary.

4 Related Work

Several approaches have been proposed to facilitate access to RDF data through web APIs. Table 1 compares them along key dimensions. All compared systems are domain-independent but rely on predefined SPARQL query templates mapped to HTTP endpoints [3–5, 10, 13]. Among them, only CRAFTS [13] supports full CRUD operations; the others focus on read access. While JSON support and machine-readable documentation (typically OpenAPI) are broadly available, all query-template-based systems operate at the query level, meaning endpoints correspond to predefined queries. ShExpose differs in two key ways: it derives entity-level and attribute-level endpoints from shape declarations rather than query templates, and it supports full CRUD operations without requiring manually defined queries.

Table 1. Feature-based comparison of approaches.

Feature	BASIL	CRAFTS	grlc	R4R	RAMOSE	**ShExpose**
CRUD support	✗	✓	✗	✗	✗	✓
Documentation	✓	✓	✓	✓	(✓)	✓
Resource Granularity	query-level	query-level	query-level	query-level	query-level	single, nested
Setup Config	query templates	query templates	query templates	query templates	query templates	shape declarations

5 Conclusion

In this paper, we presented a novel approach to automatically generate RESTful API endpoints from declarative Shape Expressions (ShEx) schemas to enable access to RDF data at the entity-level. Our method derives CRUD endpoints and a corresponding OpenAPI specification from the shape declarations. The approach does not rely on manual query templates or manual endpoint mappings, thereby lowering the entry barrier for web developers who are not familiar with Semantic Web technologies to access KGs.

We evaluated the approach using a real-world university KG, TUCgraph, maintained at Chemnitz University of Technology. Using this graph, we demonstrated that the generated API operates efficiently across multiple entities and varying workloads. The results revealed particularly strong performance for *Create* and attribute-level *Update* operations, while entity-level *Read* and *Delete* operations led to higher latency, likely caused by the required prior data retrieval step. Overall, the results indicate that the approach is suitable for practical web integration scenarios involving commonly used institutional data. For future work, we plan to explore optimization strategies to reduce latency, especially for entity-level *Read* and *Delete* operations.

Acknowledgments. This work is supported by the Deutsche Forschungsgemeinschaft (DFG, German Research Foundation) âĂŞ Project-ID 514664767 âĂŞ TRR 386, by the European Union's HORIZON Research and Innovation Programme under grant agreement No 101120657, project ENFIELD (European Lighthouse to Manifest Trustworthy and Green AI) and by the European Union's Erasmus+ Programme under grant agreement No 101177485, project Across (European University for Cross-Border Knowledge Sharing).

Disclosure of Interests. The authors have no competing interests to declare that are relevant to the content of this article.

References

1. The Linked Open Data Cloud. https://lod-cloud.net/
2. Ahmad, S., et al.: UniProt consortium: the UniProt website API: Facilitating programmatic access to protein knowledge. Nucleic Acids Res. **53**(W1), W547–W553 (2025)
3. Badenes-Olmedo, C., Corcho, O.: R4R: Template-based REST API framework for RDF knowledge graphs
4. Daga, E., Panziera, L., Pedrinaci, C.: A BASILar approach for building web APIs on top of SPARQL endpoints
5. Daquino, M., Heibi, I., Peroni, S., Shotton, D.: Creating RESTful APIs over SPARQL Endpoints using RAMOSE. Semant. Web **13**(2), 195–213 (2022)
6. Garijo, D., Osorio, M.: OBA: an ontology-based framework for creating REST APIs for knowledge graphs. In: The Semantic Web – ISWC 2020, pp. 48–64. Springer-Verlag, Berlin, Heidelberg (2020)
7. Göpfert, C., Samuel, S., Gaedke, M.: ShEx2SPARQL: Translating Shape Expressions into SPARQL Queries. In: Verma, H., Bozzon, A., Mauri, A., Yang, J. (eds.) Web Engineering, pp. 209–216. Springer Nature Switzerland, Cham (2025). https://doi.org/10.1007/978-3-031-97207-2_16
8. Harris, S., Seaborne, A.: SPARQL 1.1 Query Language. https://www.w3.org/TR/sparql11-query/
9. Klyne, G., Carroll, J.J., McBride, B.: RDF 1.1 Concepts and Abstract Syntax
10. Meroño-Peñuela, A., Hoekstra, R.: GRLC makes GitHub taste like linked data APIs. In: Sack, H., Rizzo, G., Steinmetz, N., Mladenić, D., Auer, S., Lange, C. (eds.) The Semantic Web, vol. 9989, pp. 342–353. Springer International Publishing, Cham (2016). series Title: Lecture Notes in Computer Science
11. Morgan, J.: Linked Data Objects (LDO): A typescript-enabled RDF Devtool. In: The Semantic Web – ISWC 2023, p. 230–246. Springer-Verlag, Berlin, Heidelberg (2023). https://doi.org/10.1007/978-3-031-47243-5_13
12. Ryman, A.: Resource Shape 2.0. https://www.w3.org/submissions/shapes/
13. Vega-Gorgojo, G.: CRAFTS: Configurable REST APIs for triple stores. IEEE Access **10**, 32426–32441 (2022). https://doi.org/10.1109/ACCESS.2022.3160610
14. Vita, R., Overton, J.A., Mungall, C.J., Sette, A., Peters, B.: FAIR Principles and the IEDB: Short-term improvements and a long-term vision of obo-foundry mediated machine-actionable interoperability. Database (2018)
15. W3C OWL Working Group: OWL 2 Web Ontology Language Document Overview (2nd edn.). https://www.w3.org/TR/owl2-overview/

A Unified Approach for Sexism Detection in Social Media Memes Under Hard and Soft Evaluation Settings

Lorenzo Calogiuri[1,2](✉), Elöd Egyed-Zsigmond[1], Nathan Nowakowski[1], and Luca Cagliero[2]

[1] INSA Lyon, LIRIS UMR5205 CNRS, 69621 Villeurbanne, France
{elod.egyed-zsigmond,nathan.nowakowski}@insa-lyon.fr
[2] Politecnico di Torino, Turin, Italy
lorenzo.calogiuri@insa-lyon.fr, lorenzo.calogiuri@studenti.polito.it, luca.cagliero@polito.it

Abstract. Sexism detection in social media memes remains challenging due to the inherent complexity of multimodal sources and the possible disagreement among different annotators. Results from the EXIST 2025 Challenge show that current systems often perform unevenly across hard and soft evaluations, where hard settings involve binary sexism prediction whereas soft ones entail probabilistic estimation of the judgment of multiple annotators. We propose a unified approach that jointly models both label types by combining soft label learning under an ensemble strategy, in which two models are trained on distinct, class-unbalanced dataset partitions, with supervised learning of hard labels on borderline cases. Experiments on the EXIST Meme Dataset demonstrate that our approach achieves an enhancement of +7.73% in comparison to the official soft evaluation metric of the competition and +26.47% with respect to the hard evaluation against state-of-the-art methods addressing both evaluation metrics, underscoring the importance of integrating deterministic and probabilistic predictions in sexist-content detection on multimodal data.

Content Warning: This paper includes examples of hateful, explicit and sexist language presented for illustrative purposes.

Keywords: Sexism Identification · Text Classification · Image Classification · Natural Language Processing

1 Introduction

The widespread use of social media has amplified the circulation of harmful content, including sexist memes that combine textual and visual elements. Detecting such content is particularly challenging due to its multimodal nature and the reliance on implicit, contextual, or ironic cues.

The EXIST challenge [9] addresses this task by introducing a dual annotation

A. Mauri et al. (Eds.): ICWE 2026, LNCS 16625, pp. 217–224, 2026.
https://doi.org/10.1007/978-3-032-29372-5_17

framework. Each instance is labeled both with a hard label, obtained via majority voting, and a soft label, representing the full distribution of annotator judgments. This setting highlights the subjective nature of the task and the importance of modeling disagreement. To the best of our knowledge, EXIST is the first benchmark to address sexism detection in both hard and soft evaluation settings. Recent advances in multimodal learning have improved performance in sexism detection. However, existing approaches typically optimize for either hard or soft labels [9], leading to a mismatch between training objectives and evaluation criteria. In particular, methods focusing on hard labels tend to overlook uncertainty, while soft-label approaches may produce more undecided predictions. This work explores how to bridge this gap by combining soft-label modeling with targeted hard-label supervision, proposing a training strategy based on class-unbalanced data partitions and a selective mechanism to refine uncertain predictions using external multimodal knowledge.

2 Related work

Prior work on sexism detection in memes can be grouped into three main directions. First, multimodal approaches combine textual and visual features using early or late fusion strategies [4,7,8]. Second, soft-label prediction methods explicitly model annotator disagreement, often using multi-stage pipelines or specialized training strategies [10]. Third, recent approaches leverage VisionâĂŞLanguage Models (VLMs) and external knowledge to improve contextual understanding [5].

Despite strong performance, these methods often exhibit a degradation in performance between hard and soft evaluation settings, as well as a performance gap between English and Spanish instances [2,10]. Recent work highlights the importance of handling ambiguity explicitly, for instance through ensemble strategies on imbalanced data [11]. In this work, we build on these insights by combining class-unbalanced training with selective integration of hard predictions, enabling consistent performance across both evaluation paradigms.

3 Task and Dataset Overview

We address Task 2.1 of the EXIST Challenge [9], which focuses on sexism detection in memes, in which each meme is annotated by six annotators. Hard labels are obtained via majority voting, while soft labels represent the full distribution of annotator responses. The dataset includes English and Spanish memes, as summarized in Table 1, while Table 2 presents the distribution of hard labels and soft labels among the considered data. The Unlabelled class corresponds to the records where annotator consensus was not reached.

Table 1. EXIST 2025 memes dataset language distribution and splitting (number of memes)

Language	Training	Test
English	2010	513
Spanish	2034	540
All	4044	1053

Table 2. Annotator answer distribution in the EXIST 2025 Memes Training Dataset, English and Spanish combined. For each sub-class, the first value is given by the number of YES answers, while the second value corresponds to the number of NO answers.

Class	Proportion (%)	Sub-class	Proportion (%)
		[6, 0]	14.34
Sexist	50.39	[5, 1]	19.24
		[4, 2]	16.82
		[0, 6]	9.32
Not Sexist	34.17	[1, 5]	11.44
		[2, 4]	13.40
Unlabelled	15.44	[3, 3]	15.44

4 Evaluation metrics

The official metric for this challenge is the Information Contrast Measure (ICM) [1], a hierarchy-aware metric comparing predicted and gold hard labels while accounting for semantic distances between classes, making it suitable for fine-grained classification. We also use ICM-Soft, which evaluates predicted probability distributions against annotator distributions and rewards models capturing uncertainty and disagreement [6]. Additionally, we report their normalized variants, ICM Norm and ICM-Soft Norm, ranging in [0, 1] for more interpretable performance. For binary results, we use F1, and cross-entropy [3] evaluates probability predictions.

5 Dataset split

As shown in Figure 1, the training data is divided into two class-unbalanced partitions, used to train two distinct models which share the same architecture. One partition is biased toward sexist instances (75% sexist, 25% non-sexist), while the other favors non-sexist instances (75% non-sexist, 25% sexist). Predictions are later combined in an ensemble setting. The validation set is used for hyperparameter tuning, while the test set is reserved for final evaluation.

The reason behind this training strategy is straightforward: the class distribution of the training data directly influences model predictions. A model trained predominantly on safe samples will tend to classify ambiguous inputs as safe, whereas a model trained on a majority of unsafe samples will exhibit the opposite bias. However, when both models converge on the same prediction, this likely indicates that the input content is strongly polarized toward either safety or unsafety, allowing us to identify highly polarized memes.

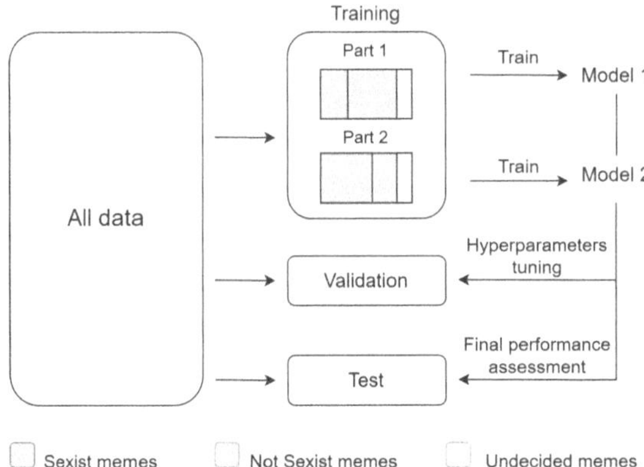

Fig. 1. Data splitting strategy in which two models are trained on distinct, class-unbalanced partitions. Model 1 and Model 2 share the same architecture, shown in Fig. 2.

6 Soft-label learning

We model sexism detection as a soft-label prediction task, where each instance is associated with a probability distribution over classes reflecting annotator disagreement. As illustrated in Fig. 2, text and image modalities are first encoded into a shared latent space. Let $T \in \mathbb{R}^{n \times d}$ and $I \in \mathbb{R}^{m \times d}$ denote the textual and visual representations, respectively. We fuse these representations using bidirectional cross-attention:

$$Z_{TI} = \text{Attention}(T, I, I), \quad Z_{IT} = \text{Attention}(I, T, T) \tag{1}$$

with the integration of residual connections to avoid losing the original information. The resulting enriched representations T^* and I^* are combined into a unified multimodal representation H, which is then passed to a classifier to predict the annotator agreement distribution $\hat{y}$ over the two classes. The model is trained by minimizing the KullbackâĂŞLeibler divergence between the predicted distribution $\hat{y}$ and the target soft labels y:

$$\mathcal{L}_{KL} = \sum_{c} y_c \log \frac{y_c}{\hat{y}_c} \tag{2}$$

This formulation enables the model to capture uncertainty in annotations and learn more nuanced decision boundaries compared to hard-label training. Consequently, to generate soft-label predictions on validation and test data, each meme is processed independently by Model 1 and Model 2, producing two output vectors. These are combined via element-wise multiplication and L1 normalization, which downweights weak predictions, amplifies joint evidence, and reduces entropy when the models agree (e.g., high annotator consensus for Sexist/Not Sexist).

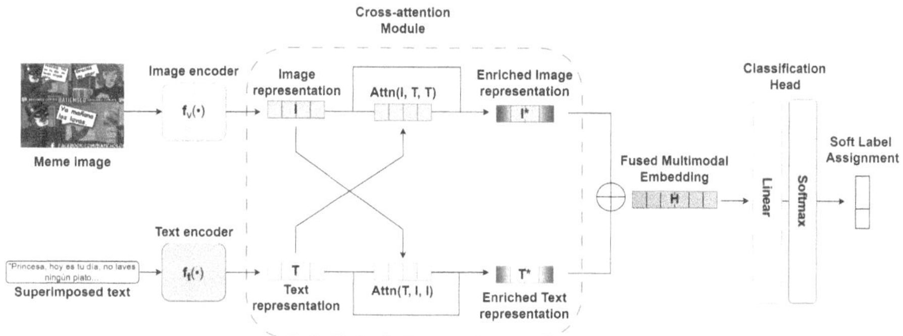

Fig. 2. Architecture of Model 1 and Model 2 for soft-label prediction in the sexism identification task. Although the two models are based on the same pipeline, they are trained using different and class-unbalanced data splits.

7 Hard-labels supervision

To improve predictions in ambiguous cases, we introduce a selective hard-label supervision mechanism based on a VisionâĂŞLanguage Model (VLM). Instead of applying hard supervision globally, the VLM is used only for low-polarized instances identified from the soft-label model. Given a predicted distribution $\hat{y}$, we define its polarization as the maximum class probability. Instances with polarization below a threshold α are considered uncertain. For these cases, the VLM produces a binary prediction $y^{(v)} \in \{0, 1\}$. The VLM output is converted into a probabilistic vector:

$$\tilde{y}^{(v)} = \begin{cases} (\pi,\ 1-\pi) & \text{if } y^{(v)} = 1 \\ \\ (1-\pi,\ \pi) & \text{if } y^{(v)} = 0 \end{cases} \tag{3}$$

being π a value in [0, 1]. Subsequently, the VLM predictions are combined with the probabilistic outputs of the first ensemble model using the same element-wise product followed by normalization strategy described in Sect. 6.

This allows the final prediction to retain the first ensemble model prediction while benefiting from the VLM's richer contextual understanding on borderline or ambiguous memes.

8 Results

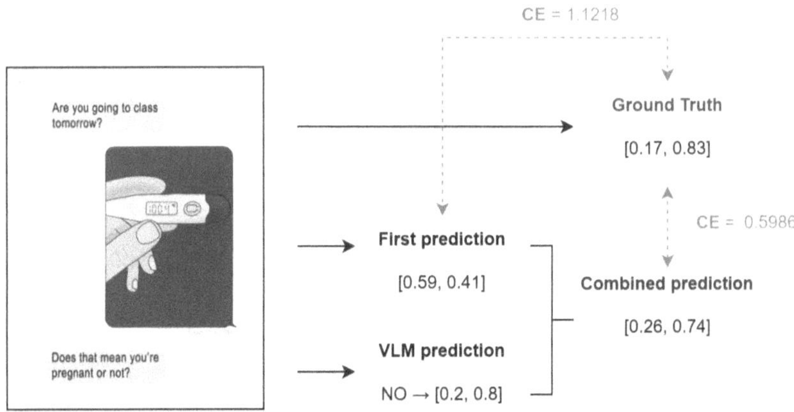

Fig. 3. Example of the VLM-based revision system with hard labels on a borderline meme, characterized by a small difference between the predicted probabilities of YES and NO (adopting $\alpha = 0.70$ and $\pi = 0.8$). In the Figure, CE refers to Cross-entropy computed between the prediction and the ground truth.

Table 3 reports the performance of the proposed approach under both soft and hard evaluation settings. Overall, our method consistently outperforms the sate-of-the-art methods addressing this challenge across all metrics. The ensemble strategy improves soft-label predictions by better capturing annotator uncertainty, while the selective integration of VLM outputs significantly enhances hard-label performance.

Additionally, as showed in Table 4, the gap of the performance between English and Spanish instances is almost negligible, accounting only for an average $\Delta = 2.08$ % on normalized metrics, proving the consistency of the proposed approach also on non-English memes. We observe that the best results are obtained with $\alpha = 0.70$ and $\pi = 0.8$, balancing the contribution of soft predictions and hard supervision. Performance gains are particularly evident in weakly polarized cases cases, for which an example is provided in Fig. 3, where the VLM provides complementary information that refines ambiguous predictions. In contrast, high-confidence predictions remain stable, confirming that the selective mechanism avoids degrading reliable outputs. These results demonstrate that combining soft-label learning with targeted hard-label supervision enables robust performance across both evaluation paradigms.

Table 3. Final results on the test set after applying VLM supervision to borderline memes (mean performance over 3 seeds)

	Soft evaluation			Hard evaluation		
Run	ICM_{Soft}	$ICM_{\text{Soft Norm}}$	Cross Entropy	ICM	ICM Norm	F1
I2C-Huelva_3 [2]	−0.3263	0.4476	1.5189	−0.2772	0.4036	0.4714
VictorUNED_1 [10]	−0.2925	0.4530	1.1028	0.0641	0.5326	0.7051
TrankilTwice_3 [5]	−0.2198	0.4652	1.0394	0.0562	0.5303	0.6942
Ensemble model	−0.1832	0.4711	**0.9615**	0.2331	0.6193	0.7492
+ VLM supervision	**−0.0583**	**0.4908**	0.9858	**0.3216**	**0.6668**	**0.7850**

Table 4. Final results on the test set, grouped by language (mean performance over 3 seeds)

	Soft evaluation			Hard evaluation		
Language	ICM_{Soft}	ICM_{Soft} Norm	Cross Entropy	ICM	ICM Norm	F1(YES)
English	**−0.0416**	**0.4934**	0.9906	**0.3279**	**0.6664**	0.8024
Spanish	−0.1231	0.4808	**0.9815**	0.2907	0.6556	**0.8473**

9 Conclusions and future work

We presented a unified framework for sexism detection in social media memes that combines soft-label learning with selective hard-label supervision. By leveraging class-unbalanced ensemble training and integrating a VisionâĂŞLanguage Model (VLM) only for borderline cases, the proposed approach improves performance across both soft and hard evaluation settings.

Future work will explore adaptive strategies for polarization thresholding, tighter integration of hard supervision with an explainability module, and the extension of the approach to other multimodal classification tasks involving subjective annotations.

Acknowledgments. Experiments presented in this paper were carried out using the Grid'5000 testbed, supported by a scientific interest group hosted by Inria and including CNRS, RENATER and several Universities as well as other organisations. See https://www.grid5000.fr.

Declaration on Generative AI. During the preparation of this work, the authors used GPT-4 and DeepL Write in order to: grammar and spelling corrections, rewriting of unnatural phrases, tone improving. After using these tools/services, the authors reviewed and edited the content as needed and take full responsibility for the publication's content.

References

1. Amigo, E., Delgado, A.: Evaluating extreme hierarchical multi-label classification. In: Muresan, S., Nakov, P., Villavicencio, A. (eds.) Proceedings of the 60th Annual Meeting of the Association for Computational Linguistics (Volume 1: Long Papers), pp. 5809–5819. Association for Computational Linguistics, Dublin, Ireland (2022). https://doi.org/10.18653/v1/2022.acl-long.399
2. Carrillo-Casado, ., Román-Pásaro, J., Mata-Vázquez, J., Pachón-Álvarez, V.: I2C-UHU at exist 2024: Transformer-based detection of sexism and source intention in memes using a learning with disagreement approach. In: Faggioli, G., Ferro, N., Galuščáková, P., de Herrera, A.G.S. (eds.) Working Notes of CLEF 2024 – Conference and Labs of the Evaluation Forum, pp. 978–992. CEUR-WS.org, CEUR Workshop Proceedings (2024). cLEF 2024, Grenoble, France
3. Goodfellow, I., Bengio, Y., Courville, A.: Deep Learning. MIT Press (2016). chapter 5 discusses cross-entropy loss
4. Hakimov, S., Cheema, G.S., Ewerth, R.: Tib-VA at SEMEVAL-2022 task 5: a multimodal architecture for the detection and classification of misogynous memes. In: Proceedings of the 16th International Workshop on Semantic Evaluation (SemEval-2022), pp. 756–760 (2022)
5. Italiani, P., Maqbool, F., Gimeno-Gómez, D., Fersini, E., Martínez-Hinarejos, C.D.: Trankiltwice at exist2025: detecting sexism in memes under multi-lingual settings. In: Faggioli, G., Ferro, N., Galuščáková, P., de Herrera, A.G.S. (eds.) Working Notes of CLEF 2025 – Conference and Labs of the Evaluation Forum, pp. 2012–2022. CEUR-WS.org, CEUR Workshop Proceedings (2025). notebook for the EXIST Lab at CLEF 2025, Madrid, Spain
6. Mostafazadeh Davani, A., Díaz, M., Prabhakaran, V.: Dealing with disagreements: Looking beyond the majority vote in subjective annotations. Trans. Assoc. Comput. Linguist. **10**, 92–110 (2022). https://doi.org/10.1162/tacl_a_00449, https://aclanthology.org/2022.tacl-1.6/
7. Naebzadeh, A., Nobakhtian, M., Eetemadi, S.: Nica at exist clef tasks 2024. In: Conference and Labs of the Evaluation Forum (2024). https://api.semanticscholar.org/CorpusID:271866202
8. Pan, R., Bernal Beltrán, T., García Díaz, J.A., Valencia-García, R.: Umuteam at exist 2025: multimodal transformer architectures and soft-label learning for sexism detection. Working Notes of CLEF (2025)
9. Plaza, L., et al.: Overview of exist 2025: learning with disagreement for sexism identification in tweets, memes, and Tiktok videos. In: Experimental IR Meets Multilinguality, Multimodality, and Interaction: 16th International Conference of the CLEF Association (CLEF 2025), Madrid, Spain, September 9–12, 2025, Proceedings. pp. 266–289. Springer-Verlag, Berlin, Heidelberg (2025). https://doi.org/10.1007/978-3-032-04354-2_16
10. Ruiz, V., de Albornoz, J.C., Plaza, L.: Concatenated transformer models based on levels of agreements for sexism detection. In: Faggioli, G., Ferro, N., Galuščáková, P., de Herrera, A.G.S. (eds.) Working Notes of CLEF 2024 – Conference and Labs of the Evaluation Forum, pp. 1187–1197. CEUR-WS.org, CEUR Workshop Proceedings (2024). notebook for the EXIST Lab at CLEF 2024, Grenoble, France
11. Zhao, H., Yuan, C., Huang, F., et al.: Qwen3guard technical report (2025). https://arxiv.org/abs/2510.14276

Analyzing Status Code Misuses in REST API Specifications

Alix Decrop[1(✉)], Mike Papadakis[2], and Gilles Perrouin[1]

[1] NADI, University of Namur, Namur, Belgium
{alix.decrop,gilles.perrouin}@unamur.be
[2] SnT, University of Luxembourg, Luxembourg, Luxembourg
michail.papadakis@uni.lu

Abstract. Many web APIs rely on the REST architectural style, exploiting HTTP for client-server interactions. Clients typically interpret server responses using status codes, such as `200 OK` (success) or `404 Not Found` (unavailable resource). As REST does not enforce HTTP standards, servers may misuse status codes (e.g., using `500` for a client error instead of `4xx`). Such misuses cause false positives during testing and confuse clients. In this paper, we explore the prevalence of status code misuses in REST APIs. We introduce SCOAS, a tool that detects status code misuses in OpenAPI specifications using 24 rules derived from HTTP standards. We demonstrate that status code misuses are systematic in REST APIs, with 17,767 rule violations detected across 60 specifications. We further discuss their implications and provide recommendations for testers and clients.

Keywords: REST API · OpenAPI · Status Code · Misuse

1 Introduction

Web APIs widely rely on the REpresentational State Transfer (REST) architectural style [8], which uses HTTP for stateless client-server communications. In this context, HTTP status codes are used to indicate the outcome of requests. Typical status codes indicate successes (`2xx`), client errors (`4xx`), and server errors (`5xx`). The OpenAPI Specification (OAS) [13] standard is widely used to document these behaviors, allowing clients and testers to understand API responses correctly. However, this paper finds that REST APIs deviate from status code semantics. We term such deviations *status codes misuses*, which are not benign. For instance, using `2xx` or `5xx` status codes to represent client errors misleads clients, undermines interoperability, and reduces the accuracy of testing tools. Moreover, the use of non-standard or overly generic status codes (e.g., `400` for advanced client errors) hinders debugging due to imprecise/misleading feedback.

REST API design conformance is an active field; Di Meglio et al. [6] analyzed RESTful design rule violations in web apps. Bogner et al. [2] implemented RESTRuler, a tool aimed at detecting design rule violations in OpenAPI descriptions, based on Massé's book on REST API design [10]. Rodriguez

A. Mauri et al. (Eds.): ICWE 2026, LNCS 16625, pp. 225–233, 2026.
https://doi.org/10.1007/978-3-032-29372-5_18

et al. [12] analyzed the compliance of HTTP traffic with REST API principles and best practices. Existing tools [1,3,14] can analyze OpenAPI specification-implementation conformance by checking mismatches and/or undeclared data. Yet, such approaches require source code, do not cover fine-grained misuses, and/or do not focus specifically on HTTP status code semantics.

Therefore, our work investigates HTTP status code misuses in REST APIs at the specification-level, whose prevalence has not been explored so far. We offer the following novel contributions: **(1)** SCOAS, a tool for Status Code Analysis in OpenAPI Specifications. **(2)** A set of 24 status code usage rules, derived from HTTP standards and REST API design/usage. **(3)** A study of status code misuses in 60 REST API specifications. A total of 17,767 misuses were identified, occurring in various APIs (GitHub, Spotify, Stripe, etc.). **(4)** A replication package containing our implementation and evaluation data [4].

2 Approach

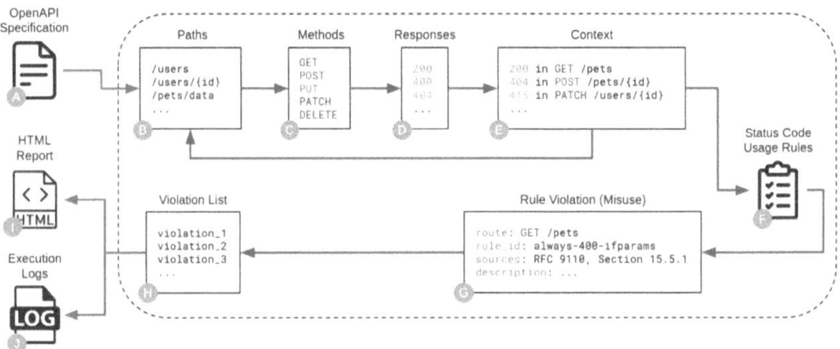

Fig. 1. Overview of our tool SCOAS.

To detect status code misuses, we developed SCOAS (Status Code Analysis in OpenAPI Specifications). Figure 1 illustrates our tool, with orange circles (X) representing each phase. First, an OAS file (JSON format) of a REST API is provided (A). Then, we iterate over all paths specified in the file (B). For each path, we iterate over all described methods (C). For each method in each path, we iterate over all described responses (D). Doing so allows us to generate a status code context (E), composed of a path, method, and response. This is required, as status code usage rules may rely on path data (e.g., path parameters such as `/{id}` for `404 Not Found` responses) and/or method data (e.g., `GET` methods require `200 OK` responses). When a status code context is found, we iterate over all defined status code usage rules (F) (defined in Sect. 3). We verify if rules are violated by performing a static analysis of the context against the rules. If it is the case, we generate a rule violation (misuse) containing the triggering context and related information G. We append it to a list of violations H. The process continues until all status code contexts have been analyzed. SCOAS stops when the iterations are completed (B–E). Upon ending, SCOAS issues an HTML report I and execution logs J.

3 Evaluation

We formulate the following research question: *What is the prevalence of status code misuses in REST API specifications?* By answering it, we aim to analyze and discuss the prevalence of status code misuses in real-world REST API specifications using SCOAS.

Setup. We formed a comprehensive dataset of 60 unique specifications (in the OAS format) from various REST APIs. These specifications were extracted from the Public REST API Benchmark (PRAB) [5], containing diverse APIs (GitHub, Language Tool, Petclinic, etc.). The complete list of APIs along with their structural data can be found in the PRAB repository. Our evaluation was conducted using a laptop with a 2.4GHz processor and 16GB of RAM. SCOAS is deterministic, operates offline, and processes a specification within seconds.

Status Code Distribution. First, we identified which HTTP status codes are commonly used in REST API responses, and defined a set of relevant usage rules. We analyzed the specifications included in our benchmark dataset, and extracted all occurrences of status codes. Figure 2 illustrates the distribution of status codes per REST API. In total, we identified 35 distinct status codes, accounting for 12,028 occurrences. `2xx` and `4xx` are the most frequent ranges (`200 OK` and `404 Not Found` being the most frequent status codes), followed by `5xx` which occurs marginally. We observed a lack of `1xx` and `3xx` codes, less suitable for typical REST interactions [8]. We also identified non-standard status codes (e.g., `0`, `420`, `555`), suggesting API-dependent behaviors.

Status Code Usage Rules. Based on our findings, we defined 24 unique status code usage rules for REST APIs. We selected occurring status codes from the `2xx` range (`200`, `201`, `204`) and the `4xx` range (`400`, `401`, `403`, `404`, `406`, `413`, `415`, `422`), as they are sufficient for typical client-server interactions [4,8,10]. We excluded the `5xx` range, as it describes errors unrelated to an "expected" interaction (e.g., server maintenance or bad gateway). We defined our rules based on a structured manual analysis of official HTTP standards [7], REST API principles [8], and best practices [10]. Notably, we identified statement verbs (e.g., "shall", "must not", etc.) and mapped them to adequate rules for REST API responses. Table 1 presents a subset of the rules (the full list can be found in our replication package [4]).

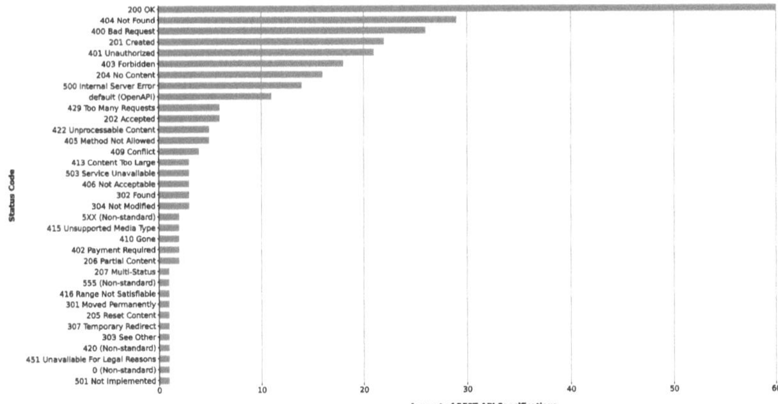

Fig. 2. Distribution of HTTP status codes across REST API specifications.

Table 1. Subset of status code usage rules. **I** = Implement, **NI** = Never Implement.

Identifier	Description
`200-if-get`	**I** `200 OK` in a `GET` method.
`204-if-no-content`	**I** `204 No Content` for a response that does not have content.
`400-if-params`	**I** `400 Bad Request` if there are parameters (syntax).
`404-if-path`	**I** `404 Not Found` if there are path parameters.
`406-if-accept`	**I** `406 Not Acceptable` for unsupported `Accept` header.
`422-if-payload`	**I** `422 Unprocessable Content` if there is a payload (semantics).
`no-201-if-get`	**NI** `201 Created` in a `GET` method.
`no-204-if-content`	**NI** `204 No Content` for a response that has content.
`no-401-if-no-auth`	**NI** `401 Unauthorized` if there is no authentication mechanism.
`no-413-if-no-payload`	**NI** `413 Content Too Large` if there is no payload.
`no-non-standard-codes`	**NI** non-standard status codes.

Status Code Misuses. We implemented the rules and executed our tool to check for rule violations (misuses) in REST API specifications. SCOAS analyzed a total of 12,028 status codes across 4,016 routes, and found 17,767 status code misuses (occurring in all specifications, highlighting their omnipresence). Figure 3 illustrates the number of specifications with at least one rule violation, per rule identifier. Our results indicate that the incorrect and inconsistent use of status codes is systematic in REST API specifications.

We observe that frequent rule violations are related to missing client errors for invalid request syntax/semantics. Indeed, violations of the rule `422-if-params` occurred in 53 specifications; A lack of implemented client errors complicates request debugging. Moreover, violations of rules related to client errors for invalid request headers occurred in up to 39 specifications. This suggests that header-based responses are less documented in REST APIs, perhaps as they

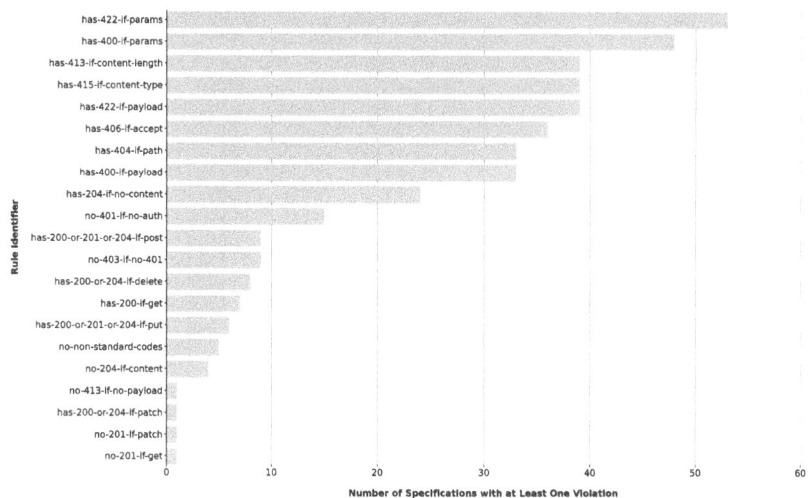

Fig. 3. Distribution of rule violation occurrence across REST API specifications.

are less used compared to parameters and payloads. Nonetheless, documenting such errors remains important as headers are used in REST APIs [11]. In 24 specifications, violations of the rule `204-if-no-content` were reported, as empty and successful responses did not use the `204 No Content` status code (intended for such purpose). This indicates that developers either forget to document response content, or forget to use the `204 No Content` status code for successful and empty responses. Conversely, 4 specifications used `204 No Content` in non-empty responses (violations of `no-204-if-content`), revealing more problematic misuses of the status code. In 15 specifications, `401 Unauthorized` responses were implemented without documented authentication (violations of `no-401-if-no-auth`). Moreover, `403 Forbidden` responses were implemented without `401 Unauthorized` in 9 specifications (violations of `no-403-if-no-401`), suggesting that security mechanisms are often incorrectly documented in REST API specifications. Yet, the OAS standard supports security descriptions through the `security`/`securitySchemes` fields [13]. More severe violations were found, such as the use of non-standard status codes (in 5 specifications), missing `200 OK` responses in `GET` methods (in 7 specifications), and the use of `201 Created` in HTTP methods which cannot create data (in 2 specifications). In consequence, these violations suggest insufficient knowledge of HTTP standards and non-conformance to REST API design rules [10].

We also report the mean number of violations per route (vpr) for all APIs. Figure 4 illustrates this result, with bar colors indicating API size measured by the number of routes. The size is categorized into 5 percentile-based bins: the bottom 10% (p10), the top 10% (p90), and the middle 80% divided evenly into 3 bins. These bins correspond to the following categories: micro, small, medium, large, and very large APIs. As shown, very large APIs always have over 3.5vpr,

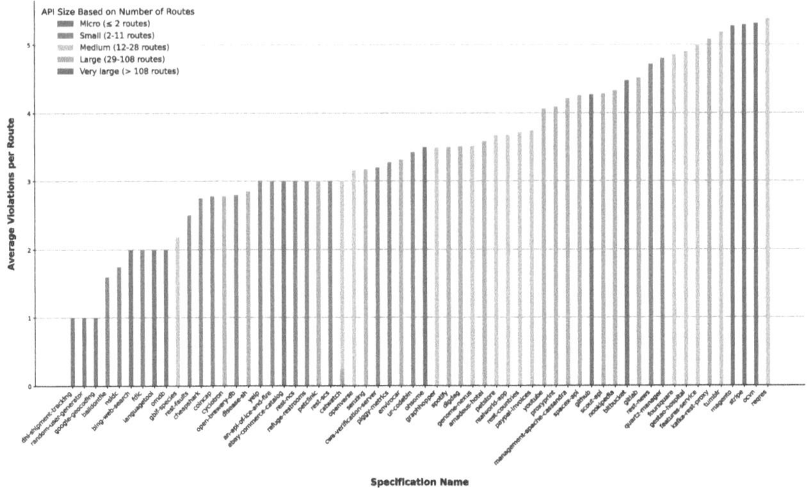

Fig. 4. Mean violations per route for REST API specifications, colored by size.

while micro APIs never exceed the 3vpr threshold. This result suggests that status codes are used more accurately in smaller APIs, potentially due to a lower implementation complexity. However, some small and medium APIs display a higher vpr ratio compared to some large and very large APIs, suggesting that API size alone does not fully determine the prevalence of status code misuses.

Summary: Status code misuses are frequent in REST APIs, with 17,767 rule violations detected across 60 specifications. Common issues include missing client error responses and using security-related status codes without security definitions. Violations per route tend to increase with API size, yet exceptions in smaller APIs indicate that size alone does not determine misuse prevalence. Violations occurred in widely used APIs (e.g., GitHub, PayPal, Spotify, Stripe), indicating that misuses are not limited to smaller or less mature projects.

4 Discussion

Implications for Testing Tools. REST API testing tools rely on status code ranges for test outcomes and to find server errors: `2xx` for valid requests, `4xx` for client errors, and `5xx` for server errors. Golmohammadi et al. [9] highlight that `5xx` status codes are used to identify faults in over 30 different works on REST API testing. Thus, misusing status codes can lead to false positives/negatives in such tools. For instance, if a server responds with `5xx` status codes for client errors, this leads to false positives (inaccurate bug report). This misleads the tester, as this false server error is unlikely to exhibit an interesting behavior.

Similarly, if an API uses `2xx` or `4xx` status codes to represent server errors, this leads to false negatives. This can also happen with client errors if the API always responds with `2xx` status codes. For instance, when sending a request with an invalid path to the Deezer API, a `404 Not Found` client error is expected. However, the API replies with `200 OK`. While this status code indicates a success, an error message is found in the response body with an API-defined `600` code. This deviates from REST API design (non-standard status codes), and confuses tools if no additional response parsing is performed. Similarly, false positives can be observed in popular API frameworks such as Spring. For instance, the Spring Petclinic REST API returns `500 Internal Server Error` status codes when a path does not exist (i.e., `NoResourceFoundException`), instead of `404 Not Found`. While it is possible to specify status code mappings in Spring, they can be omitted and thus the `500` code is used as a fallback.

Recommendations for Testers: REST API testing tools should always analyze responses in depth to avoid false positives/negatives from status codes. Response messages should be parsed to check for errors, and status code mappings should be set up when APIs implement their own codes.

Implications for Clients. Another implication of misusing status codes is that API clients are prone to receiving ambiguous responses from servers. For instance, in a microservice architecture with loosely coupled REST APIs, the services would rely on HTTP standards to understand responses. However, if a service always responds with `200 OK` status codes, other services following HTTP standards would interpret all requests as valid. Doing so could cause various problems, such as rendering errors on pages, propagating invalid responses to downstream services, or logging misleading success messages. Status code misuses also introduce other client-related problems. Without precise client errors codes from the server, debugging invalid requests becomes a difficult task. For instance, a server could respond with overly generic `400 Bad Request` status codes, instead of more specific codes such as `401 Unauthorized` (for a lack of authentication) or `413 Content Too Large` (for unsupported content size). Moreover, front-end applications often use status codes to display messages (e.g., "Saved successfully" for `201 Created`). If the wrong code is used, users see misleading feedback.

Recommendations for Clients: REST API clients should not directly trust status codes. Instead, clients should check documentation for potential API-dependent codes or API-defined behaviors. Similarly to testers, clients should also analyze response content and messages in-depth.

OAS as Baseline. We hypothesized that *REST API specifications perfectly reflect their implementations*, notably to assess the implications in practice. We acknowledge that REST APIs may behave differently in practice, which is not considered in the scope of this paper and is left for future work.

5 Conclusion and Future Work

In this work, we explored the prevalence of status code misuses in REST APIs. To do so, we developed SCOAS, a tool aimed at detecting status code misuses in OpenAPI specifications. The tool operates by comparing API responses against 24 status code usage rules derived from HTTP standards, and reports potential violations. Our evaluation showed that a total of 17,767 rule violations were detected across 60 specifications, highlighting the omnipresence of status code misuses in REST APIs. This led us to provide insights and relevant implications/recommendations for API testers and clients alike. For future work, we plan to add new status code usage rules (e.g., for the 3xx range) by analyzing the evolution of HTTP standards and REST APIs. We also plan to add automated rule fixes for OAS files in SCOAS, and expand the work for dynamic analysis.

Use of Generative AI. Generative AI was used for limited rephrasing purposes. The authors reviewed the content and take full responsibility for it.

Acknowledgments. Gilles Perrouin is an FNRS Research Associate.

Disclosure of Interests. The authors have no competing interests to declare that are relevant to the content of this article.

References

1. APTORI: OpenAPI conformance analyzer (2025). https://docs.aptori.dev/sift/analyzers/openapi-conformance
2. Bogner, J., Kotstein, S., Abajirov, D., Ernst, T., Merkel, M.: RESTRuler: towards automatically identifying violations of RESTful design rules in web APIs. In: 2024 IEEE 21st International Conference on Software Architecture (ICSA) (2024)
3. Bradburn, D.: OpenAPI conformance (2019). https://github.com/crunchr/openapi_conformance
4. Decrop, A.: SCOAS (2026). https://github.com/alixdecr/scoas
5. Decrop, A., Eraso, S., Devroey, X., Perrouin, G.: A public benchmark of REST APIs. In: 2025 IEEE/ACM 22nd International Conference on Mining Software Repositories (MSR), Los Alamitos, CA, USA, pp. 421–433. IEEE Computer Society (2025)
6. Di Meglio, S., Pontillo, V., Starace, L.L.L.: REST in pieces: RESTful design rule violations in student-built web apps. arXiv preprint arXiv:2507.11689 (2025)
7. Fielding, R., Nottingham, M., Reschke, J.: RFC 9110: HTTP semantics (2022). https://www.rfc-editor.org/rfc/rfc9110.html

8. Fielding, R.T.: Architectural styles and the design of network-based software architectures. University of California, Irvine (2000)
9. Golmohammadi, A., Zhang, M., Arcuri, A.: Testing RESTful APIs: a survey. ACM Trans. Softw. Eng. Methodol. **33**(1) (2023)
10. Massé, M.: REST API Design Rulebook. O'Reilly Media Inc. (2012)
11. Neumann, A., Laranjeiro, N., Bernardino, J.: An analysis of public REST web service APIs. IEEE Trans. Serv. Comput. **14**(4), 957–970 (2018)
12. Rodríguez, C., et al.: REST APIs: a large-scale analysis of compliance with principles and best practices. In: Bozzon, A., Cudre-Maroux, P., Pautasso, C. (eds.) ICWE 2016. LNCS, vol. 9671, pp. 21–39. Springer, Cham (2016). https://doi.org/10.1007/978-3-319-38791-8_2
13. SmartBear: OpenAPI specification (2026). https://swagger.io/specification
14. Specmantic: Specmantic (2026). https://github.com/specmatic/specmatic

PhD Symposium

Towards Governance-Aware Local and Hybrid AI Agents for Web Applications

Lucas Schröder and Martin Gaedke(✉)

Chemnitz University of Technology, Chemnitz, Germany
{lucas.schroeder,martin.gaedke}@informatik.tu-chemnitz.de

Abstract. Governance of AI systems is becoming a critical issue as both societal and regulatory circumstances demand requirements such as safe information handling, transparency, and explainability. This is complicated by the widespread use of third-party-operated LLMs, which limits organizations' control over the embedding and enforcement of governance and organizational policies directly within the agent. Consequently, users are required to exercise caution or are prevented from using these agents when interacting with web applications that contain potentially sensitive information or require transparent and explainable processing. We propose a framework and architecture for embedding governance and organizational policies for data handling and explainability within web agents based on local, tool-calling small language models. This core will be expanded with governance-aware hybrid routing to remote LLMs for non-critical tasks, balancing the high capabilities of large, third-party provided systems with the safe and transparent environment established through local processing.

Keywords: Governance · Web Agents · Human-AI Collaboration · Explainable AI · Small Language Models

1 Introduction

The field of artificial intelligence (AI) has seen enormous advancements in recent years, leading to a rapid adoption of the new technologies in almost every field of life. While initially using primarily reactive, chat-based interfaces, autonomous systems have emerged in the form of AI agents that can perform a variety of actions to solve tasks independently. For that, agents are often interacting with existing systems, including enterprise web applications such as knowledge, project, or customer relationship management tools [4,6,11,13].

As both the capabilities and adoption of these AI systems increase rapidly, governance over them is catching up slowly [6,7,13]. This makes the issue of ensuring the ethical, safe, and explainable use of AI increasingly relevant, as

A. Mauri et al. (Eds.): ICWE 2026, LNCS 16625, pp. 237–242, 2026.
https://doi.org/10.1007/978-3-032-29372-5_19

evident in the growing number of regulations, guidelines, and frameworks such as the OECD AI Principles[1], EU AI Act[2], 2024 PLD[3], or ISO/IEC 42001[4].

Two major points of interest in these frameworks are the involvement of data and the explainability of the agentic systems. Because of the established model of cloud-based processing using third-party-operated AI models, the autonomous access to large amounts of data, often including sensitive information, inherently includes risks regarding privacy and data protection [13,14]. At the same time, the agentic systems often act as a black box, making the agents' decision-making and actions non-transparent and unexplainable at times [6,8,13]. Both of these aspects are detrimental to the governance that users and organizations have over AI systems interacting with web applications, other agents, or other users.

Governance of AI systems generally concerns several aspects, including technical, ethical, and regulatory ones [1,7,8,11]. In the context of this work, the focus will be on technical operationalization, namely on enforcing policies about data access and data flows, in addition to transparency and explainability of the involved actions. This leads to our central research question:

How can AI agents that interact with web applications, other AI agents, and even other users be systematically designed to comply with governance or organizational policies, especially regarding data handling and explainable processing?

In this work, we propose exploring the use of locally running AI agents based on Small Language Models (SLMs) with governance-aware tool calls for interacting with web applications, other agents, or other users. This will be complemented through hybrid routing to either local SLMs, or, for non-critical tasks, external Large Language Models (LLMs). In this work, agents making use of such hybrid routing will be referred to as hybrid AI agents.

2 Problem Statement and Motivation

Embedding governance policies in AI agents interacting with web applications is particularly challenged by the prevalent cloud provider-based approach: By sending information for processing to what is essentially a third-party-operated black box, governance control over safe and explainable processing of potentially sensitive data is delegated to be handled by providers instead [10,13].

As a consequence, organizations do not generally have the ability to embed their own governance policies deep into the agent loop, which is especially relevant for organizations that require higher levels of governance than enabled by the provider [10]. Users who interact with such third-party-operated systems, therefore, first need to filter any data that is to be sent to the AI agent to avoid unintentionally exposing any sensitive information [4]. At the same time, they might be unable to use the agent at all for tasks that require auditability or explainability, because intermediate actions taken by the AI agents, such as tool

[1] https://www.oecd.org/en/topics/ai-principles.html.
[2] https://eur-lex.europa.eu/eli/reg/2024/1689/oj.
[3] https://eur-lex.europa.eu/eli/dir/2024/2853/oj.
[4] https://www.iso.org/standard/42001.

calls, are opaque to the user, unless the provider gives sufficient insight into the processing steps, for instance, by providing very detailed logs or traces.

These circumstances lead to users being unable to use these AI agents within their workflows or when interacting with existing web applications that either contain potentially sensitive information or require additional oversight or explainable processing. As a result, the usefulness of these agentic systems is reduced for affected users, as the additional effort to ensure compliance with their organizations' governance policies can outweigh the benefits of using the AI agent, if they can even be made compatible at all.

Both ethical and regulatory reasons demand that governance is applied to AI systems, including the safe handling of potentially sensitive information or the explainability of processing. As such, AI agents interacting with web applications or other agents on behalf of their users also need to be aware of these governance objectives and implement the applicable regulations. Consequently, there is a growing need to embed governance-awareness into these AI agents, allowing affected users to make full use of the capabilities of these agents [1,5,6,11].

3 Related Work

Agentic AI is increasingly employed to interact with web applications, including enterprise web applications, for example, through agentic web browsers. While initially relying on a mixture of DOM- or vision-based approaches for direct, human-like UI interactions in web applications, there are first approaches to translate MCP-like tool use to web applications, such as WebMCP [9,12,13]. While these approaches enable AI agents to interact with web applications on behalf of their users, comprehensive governance-aware architectures for these kinds of agents are still missing.

A growing body of work is focused on establishing governance for AI-based systems in the form of regulations, such as the EU AI Act, 2024 PLD, or frameworks and guidelines like ISO/IEC 42001 or the NIST AI RMF [8]. They consider governance aspects throughout the entire life-cycle of AI systems, from model training to the use of the deployed system, but often focus on principles, describing qualities that should be achieved or requirements that AI systems, or organizations using these systems, need to fulfill. However, these frameworks often do not yet consider how to operationalize these principles within tool-calling AI agents interacting with web applications, other agents, or human users [7].

Guardrail-based systems provide a first step in this direction by providing enforcement capabilities for automatic filtering of user inputs or agent outputs. While useful for implementing some governance principles, they are not yet fully developed to deal with more complex scenarios, such as access to sensitive information across multiple web applications and other systems [3].

A different aspect of the topic of governance of AI agents and the handling of potentially sensitive information is the topic of routing systems, such as Hybrid LLM [2], which combine local and remote processing. While often focusing on cost-saving or performance, systems such as PRISM [14] also consider sensitive information handling, routing calls depending on sensitivity to either a local/edge model or to a remote model. How to embed governance or organizational policies into such hybrid systems, specifically for AI agents interacting with web applications via tool calls, however, has not yet been explored in-depth.

This highlights a clear gap: Existing work on web-interacting agents, AI governance, and hybrid local/remote setups has not yet produced a comprehensive framework for embedding governance policies within the tool-calling and routing of AI agents interacting with web applications. In order to better analyze existing work and to gain a more comprehensive overview of the current state of the art, we plan to develop indicators to evaluate and compare prior work.

4 Objectives and Contributions

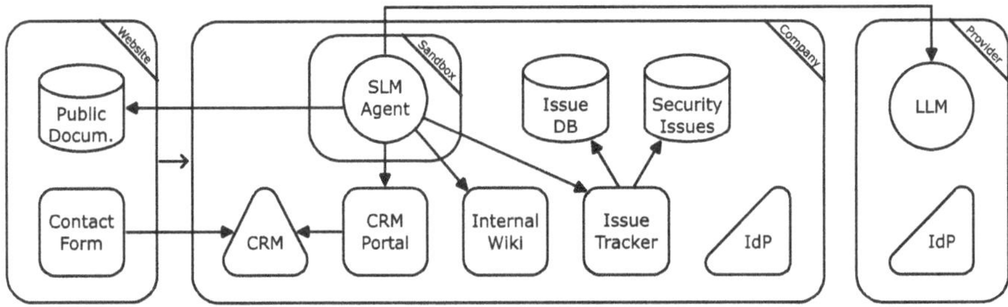

Fig. 1. An example of an agent integrated into the systems of a company. Access to multiple systems is necessary for its functionality, but poses governance issues, e.g., for data handling. This is combated through the use of a local, sandboxed SLM, governance-aware system interactions, and hybrid routing to the third-party LLM.

To better understand the objectives of this work, consider the following short scenario, which is also visualized in Fig. 1: A software company has deployed an agent to help customer support staff in handling incoming inquiries in a customer relationship management (CRM) application, acting as first-level support. To fulfill its tasks, the agent has access to the company's public product documentation, the internal wiki, and the development team's issue tracker. Naturally, there are several constraints for the agent's processing: Customer information requires local processing, vulnerabilities from the issue tracker should not be exposed, replies need to be accurate and harmless, and the agent's actions need to be explainable and auditable.

This scenario highlights how governance requirements affect agents and why their enforcement is critical. To solve this, we propose an architecture based on sandboxed local processing, governance-aware tools, and hybrid routing. Our main contributions will thus be represented by the following research objectives:

Sandboxed, Local Processing: Relying on third-party AI providers puts control over governance into the providers' hands, leading to potential compliance risks [10,13,14]. To prevent this and ensure reasonable control over and visibility into the agents' actions, we propose local processing using SLMs in a sandboxed environment. To maintain the required accuracy for tool calling, necessary optimizations need to be made to prompt and context management.

Enforcement of Governance Objectives in Prompts and Tool Calls: Operationalizing the governance objectives determined by relevant regulations and organizational policies requires enforcement through technical means [5–7]. Current approaches to operationalize governance requirements need to be expanded using both prompt- and guardrail-based approaches, in addition to logging and other measures enabling explainability and auditability.

Routing Decisions for Hybrid Systems: While local processing will be necessary sometimes, not every request will require it. As such, making use of the high capabilities of third-party operated models makes sense for some requests, demanding adequate, governance-based routing decisions [13,14]. Existing approaches for routing agent tasks in a hybrid local/remote system need to be expanded and integrated with the other techniques, forming a comprehensive framework for enforcing governance and organizational policies directly within the AI agent.

5 Current State and Conclusion

So far, this work is still in an early stage of conceptualization: We have identified the research gap of governance-awareness in AI agents interacting with web applications, reviewed core literature, and created an initial outline of the problem formulation and research objectives for closing the gap, as well as an early concept for a solution architecture. The next steps will be to further analyze the state of the art in the involved areas over the next few months, before refining the conceptual architecture by the beginning of next year. An implementation and evaluation of an initial, primarily local prototype of an AI agent for governance-aware interactions with web applications will follow and, after evaluation, be expanded with hybrid routing capabilities to remote LLMs. Concretely, this will involve the representation of governance policies, their enforcement and monitoring within the local agent, and governance-aware hybrid routing mechanisms between the local SLM and remote LLMs. Evaluation will combine policy-oriented metrics (e.g., policy violations in controlled scenarios) with task-level metrics (e.g., success rate or answer quality).

Governance of AI systems is an increasingly relevant topic, including technical, ethical, and regulatory aspects. Embedding enforcement of governance policies directly into the agent is critical to allow organizations to make full use of the capabilities provided by these agents. To tackle the issue of governance-awareness in AI agents interacting with web applications, we propose the use of local SLMs and lightweight tool calls for governance-aware interactions with web applications, while routing non-critical tasks to third-party operated LLMs.

Acknowledgments. This work is supported by the European Union's Erasmus+ Programme under grant agreement No 101177485, project Across (European University for Cross-Border Knowledge Sharing), and by the European Union's HORIZON Research and Innovation Programme under grant agreement No 101120657, project ENFIELD (European Lighthouse to Manifest Trustworthy and Green AI).

Disclosure of Interests. The authors have no competing interests to declare that are relevant to the content of this article.

References

1. Chaudhry, U., et al.: AI governance in practice report 2024. Tech. rep., June 2024
2. Ding, D., Mallick, A., Wang, C., et al.: Hybrid LLM: cost-efficient and quality-aware query routing, April 2024. https://doi.org/10.48550/arXiv.2404.14618
3. Dong, Y., et al.: Position: building guardrails for large language models requires systematic design. In: Proceedings of the 41st International Conference on Machine Learning, 21–27 July 2024, vol. 235, pp. 11375–11394. PMLR (2024)
4. Du, Y., Li, Z., Li, N., Ding, B.: Beyond data privacy: new privacy risks for large language models. TCDE Bull. **49**(4), 47–75 (2025)
5. Gaurav, S., Heikkonen, J., Chaudhary, J.: Governance-as-a-service: a multi-agent framework for AI system compliance and policy enforcement, August 2025. https://doi.org/10.48550/arXiv.2508.18765
6. Kraprayoon, J., Williams, Z., Fayyaz, R.: AI agent governance: A field guide, May 2025. https://doi.org/10.48550/arXiv.2505.21808
7. Lucaj, L., van der Smagt, P., Benbouzid, D.: AI regulation is (not) all you need. In: Proceedings of the 2023 ACM Conference on Fairness, Accountability, and Transparency, FAccT '23, pp. 1267–1279. ACM, New York, NY, USA (2023). https://doi.org/10.1145/3593013.3594079
8. National Institute of Standards and Technology: Artificial intelligence risk management framework: AI RMF 1.0. Tech. Rep. NIST AI 100-1, January 2023. https://doi.org/10.6028/NIST.AI.100-1
9. Ning, L., et al.: A survey of web-agents: towards next-generation AI agents for web automation with large foundation models. In: Proceedings of the 31st ACM SIGKDD Conference on Knowledge Discovery and Data Mining V.2, KDD '25, pp. 6140–6150. ACM, New York, NY, USA (2025). https://doi.org/10.1145/3711896.3736555
10. Petrin, M.: The impact of AI and new technologies on corporate governance and regulation. Singapore J. Leg. Stud., **90** (2024)
11. Tallam, K.: From autonomous agents to integrated systems, a new paradigm: orchestrated distributed intelligence, March 2025. https://doi.org/10.48550/arXiv.2503.13754
12. Walderman, B., Sagar, K., Farolino, D.: WebMCP. Tech. rep. (2026)
13. Xi, Z., et al.: The rise and potential of large language model based agents: a survey. SCIENCE CHINA Inf. Sci. **68**(2), 121101 (2025). https://doi.org/10.1007/s11432-024-4222-0
14. Zhan, J., Shen, H., Lin, Z., He, T.: PRISM: privacy-aware routing for adaptive cloud-edge LLM inference via semantic sketch collaboration, November 2025. https://doi.org/10.48550/arXiv.2511.22788

Toward Trustworthy, Teacher-Aligned Adaptive Learning on the Web

Jonas Gwozdz[1,2](✉) and Andreas Both[1]

[1] Web & Software Engineering (WSE) Research Group, Leipzig University of Applied Sciences (HTWK Leipzig), Leipzig, Germany
jonas.gwozdz@htwk-leipzig.de
[2] Netresearch DTT GmbH, Leipzig, Germany

Abstract. Large language models (LLMs) create new opportunities for scalable, personalized support in web-based education, but current systems often treat grading, feedback, tutoring, and deployment as separate problems. This PhD proposes a unified methodology for trustworthy, teacher-aligned adaptive learning loops on the web, integrating auditable grading automation, instructor steering, adaptive intervention, and scalable web deployment into one connected process. The research combines controlled classroom experiments, iterative web-architecture design, and production log analysis across enterprise and higher-education settings. Work completed in the first year includes one published and three submitted conference papers, classroom experiments with 132 students, and a production chatbot deployment, while the next phase targets cross-module transfer, broader higher-education rollout, and a systematic review.

Keywords. LLMs in education · adaptive assessment · automated grading · intelligent tutoring systems · human-in-the-loop · web engineering

1 Introduction and Problem Statement

Large language models (LLMs) offer new possibilities for scalable, personalized instruction in web-based educational settings [3,11]. Bloom's 2-sigma problem frames the underlying challenge: one-to-one tutoring substantially outperforms conventional instruction, but current intelligent tutoring systems (ITS) still require substantial authoring and operational effort [2,17]. Recent reviews suggest that LLMs lower these barriers for feedback, conversational support, and open-response assessment [3,11]. However, deployment in real-world courses remains challenging because grading criteria are course-specific, instructors need steering authority, and opaque model behavior complicates trust and governance [12,18]. Figure 1 summarizes the dissertation's four pillars.

A. Mauri et al. (Eds.): ICWE 2026, LNCS 16625, pp. 243–249, 2026.
https://doi.org/10.1007/978-3-032-29372-5_20

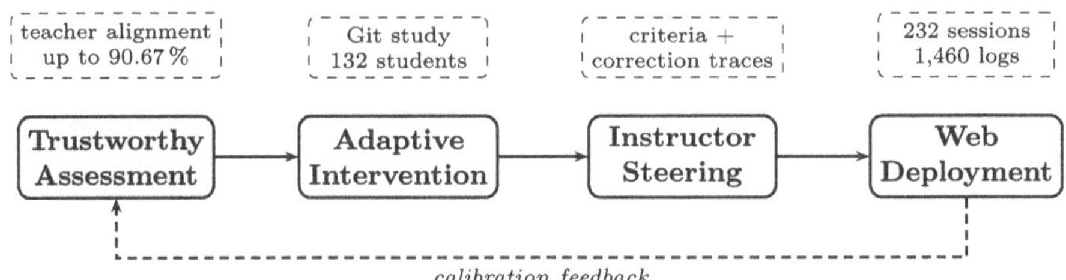

Fig. 1. Teacher-aligned adaptive learning loop framing of the dissertation.

Research Gap. Existing research typically studies automated grading, formative feedback, adaptive tutoring, and deployment architecture as separate concerns rather than as one connected learning process [4,12,16]. The field still lacks a unified methodology for teacher-aligned adaptive learning loops that connect diagnosis, intervention, instructor control, and web deployment across educational settings.

Thesis Statement. This PhD investigates how LLM-based web systems can support the full learning process in a way that is *trustworthy, teacher-aligned, and adaptive*, and validates this empirically across higher-education and enterprise settings. The scope covers short-answer assessment and tutoring in higher education and enterprise training; K-12 settings and essay-length response grading are excluded. The notion of trustworthiness aligns with three of the seven requirements of the EU High-Level Expert Group on Trustworthy AI [10]: *human agency and oversight* (teacher steering), *technical robustness* (confidence gating), and *transparency* (auditable grading traces); the remaining four requirements are acknowledged but not the primary focus.

The remainder surveys related work (Sect. 2), states research questions and methodology (Sect. 3), reports work done to date (Sect. 4), outlines the research plan (Sect. 5), and concludes (Sect. 6).

2 Related Work

Automated Short-Answer Grading (ASAG). ASAG research evolved from NLP pipelines toward foundation-model approaches [4]. Recent LLM-based pipelines achieve strong performance via few-shot prompting and rubrics [20]. Selective deferral reduces grading risk, but prior work does not yet model teacher alignment as a longitudinal process with governance checkpoints [14,18].

Formative Feedback and Adaptive Learning. Timely, criteria-based feedback is a key lever for learning and self-regulation [1,15,16], and adaptive learning translates learner traces into personalized routing [5]. However, these strands rarely connect teacher-defined criteria, adaptive follow-up, and session time constraints within one web-based learning loop.

ITS, LLMs, and web Architectures for Educational AI. ITS research showed that computer-aided tutoring can approximate key benefits of human tutoring, yet recent reviews note hallucination risks, weak pedagogical grounding, and a dominance of prototype evaluations with limited deployment evidence [3,11,12,17]. Retrieval-augmented generation and modular service decomposition provide standard patterns for grounding LLM components in web applications [13]. Systematic reviews confirm growing interest but note that most implementations remain isolated prototypes without deployment evidence [3,19]. Beyond generic LLM orchestration, educational AI deployments face domain-specific architectural challenges: teacher feedback must be captured and fed back into model calibration, grading confidence must be exposed through observable routing decisions, and governance boundaries must enforce who may override model outputs and under what conditions [12,18]. These concerns go beyond standard web service design and motivate a dedicated architectural contribution.

Positioning. Existing work addresses these dimensions in isolation. This PhD thesis aims to integrate them into a unified *controlled learning loop* in which each phase feeds the next: automated assessment produces diagnostic signals, which trigger adaptive intervention, whose outcomes inform instructor steering, which in turn recalibrates the assessment (Fig. 1). The web architecture is the substrate that closes this loop at deployment scale and enables personal context integration across applications in a federated knowledge base.

3 Research Questions and Methodology

Primary Research Question. How can LLM-based web systems support the full learning process in a way that is personalized, trustworthy, teacher-aligned, and adaptive? This question decomposes along four challenges identified in the research gap: (1) validating grading quality under real deployment conditions, (2) measuring the learning impact of adaptive LLM-based interventions, (3) scaling a teacher-aligned web architecture across courses and institutions, and (4) enabling instructor steering with minimal annotation effort.

RQ1 Under what conditions can LLM-based grading reliably replace human grading, and how should the transition be validated?

RQ2 How does LLM-generated adaptive feedback affect student learning outcomes and engagement compared to non-adaptive assessment?

RQ3 Can a web architecture for teacher-aligned assessment and tutoring scale across courses, institutions, and modalities?

RQ4 How can instructors steer LLM grading and content generation to reflect their pedagogical goals, and what correction effort is needed to reach stable teacher alignment?

Methodology. The dissertation follows a *mixed-methods, cumulative publication strategy*: controlled A/B/C classroom experiments (quasi-experimental), design-science prototype cycles for the web architecture and adaptive platform, production log analysis, and multi-model evaluation across multiple LLMs spanning Gemini, Claude, DeepSeek, Qwen, and Mistral model families. The approach also accommodates models released in the future.

4 Work Done to Date

Published Work. In [8] we introduced an RDF vocabulary for structured LLM evaluation, validated on a fire-safety domain experiment (28 questions, $n = 4$ LLMs), providing the evaluation layer that underpins quality assurance across the remaining pillar papers.

The Three-Paper Arc. In the paper [6], confidence gating and cross-model agreement operationalize RQ1 by showing how selective automation trades coverage against false-pass and false-fail risk.

In the submitted AIED paper [7], we move from assessment to intervention by mining weak-point signals from learner traces and routing students into adaptive microlearning rounds under fixed session limits, addressing RQ2.

In our ICWE paper [9], we abstract the grading workflow into a reusable web architecture with teacher feedback, observability, and governance boundaries as first-class components, reaching 90.67% teacher-aligned accuracy across five LLMs. This addresses RQ3 and lays the foundation for RQ4; direct empirical evidence for instructor steering is a primary target of the next phase.

Adaptive Learning Assistant Experiment. An A/B/C study ($n = 132$ students) compared adaptive-only and control conditions on a 25-item test regarding Git knowledge of computer science students; a gamification condition (participants could earn badges) was included as an experimental variable, but it is not a dissertation research focus. The process cycle repeatedly goes through two phases: a controlled performance assessment and automatically generated micro-learning tasks tailored to each student's specific knowledge gaps. A significant attrition difference emerged across groups (χ^2, $p = 0.0037$) despite a non-significant raw learning gain (ANOVA $p = 0.67$), suggesting that adaptive rounds improve *engagement* rather than test scores alone (addressing RQ2). A power-set analysis identified a 5-item early-stop screener that flags 87% of future failures while affecting only 32% of the cohort.

Software Engineering Assessment. Deployed on HTWK infrastructure, the experiment produced 548 wrong-attempt analyses and recurring misconception patterns that inform rubric refinement and the next grading-calibration cycle (addressing RQ1). This is one of three runs conducted in a controlled environment; this and one additional module run are still under analysis.

Slide-Context-Aware AI Chatbot. ScormIQ is a productive application embedded in SCORM courses for industrial training deployed at a large international company. Production analysis of 232 sessions and 1,460 log entries showed a median response latency of 3.71 s, 117/117 successful generations, and usage across eight languages, mainly for multilingual explanations and quiz coaching. The application rollout supports the deployment-at-scale pillar but has not yet matured into published evidence.

5 Planned Future Work

Multi-module Assessment and Cross-Module Transfer. Starting April 2026, we plan to replicate the current findings behind RQ1 and RQ2 across additional higher-education modules using biweekly low-stakes assessment and adaptive microlearning rounds, combining usage traces with learning-outcome data (RQ2, RQ3, RQ4). The central open hypothesis is that grading calibration from one module can transfer to a new module with ≥90% accuracy; we plan a transfer experiment in which prompts, rubrics, and thresholds are calibrated on one module and evaluated on a second before limited teacher correction.

Phase	Main milestones
2025	Infrastructure, ESWC paper, three classroom experiments, production deployment
2026	Conference papers, multi-module assessment, transfer experiment, systematic review
2027	Synthesis chapters, dissertation writing and submission

Dissertation Timeline

6 Conclusion

This PhD develops a methodology for trustworthy, teacher-aligned adaptive learning loops on the web, connecting grading validation (RQ1), adaptive intervention (RQ2), scalable web architecture (RQ3), and instructor steering (RQ4). For web engineering, the contribution is a reusable service architecture with observability, governance boundaries, and teacher steering for AI-supported learning. First-year evidence spans four papers, classroom experiments with 132 students, and one production deployment. Current limitations include the quasi-experimental design, a single-institution population, and the absence of direct steering evidence for RQ4. The next challenge is cross-module transfer of calibration and orchestration, demonstrating a reusable methodology rather than isolated systems.

Funding Information. This work was supported by the company Netresearch DTT GmbH and the Leipzig University of Applied Sciences through the project "Pro.Motion".

Generative AI Disclosure. Generative AI tools were used as objects of study in the reported systems and as drafting aids during manuscript preparation. All scientific claims, interpretations, and final manuscript decisions were verified by the authors.

References

1. Black, P., Wiliam, D.: Assessment and classroom learning. Assess. Educ.: Principles Policy Pract. **5**(1), 7–74 (1998)
2. Bloom, B.S.: The 2 sigma problem: the search for methods of group instruction as effective as one-to-one tutoring. Educ. Res. **13**(6), 4–16 (1984)
3. Bond, M., et al.: A meta-systematic review of artificial intelligence in higher education. Int. J. Educ. Technol. High. Educ. **21** (2024)
4. Burrows, S., Gurevych, I., Stein, B.: The eras and trends of automatic short answer grading. Int. J. Artif. Intell. Educ. **25**(1), 60–117 (2015)
5. Corbett, A.T., Anderson, J.R.: Knowledge tracing: modeling the acquisition of procedural knowledge. User Model. User-Adap. Inter. **4**(4), 253–278 (1994)
6. Gwozdz, J., Both, A.: Auditing LLM grading for short-answer responses: confidence gating and cross-model agreement. In: Proceedings of IEEE International Conference on Advanced Learning Technologies (ICALT) 2026 (2026)
7. Gwozdz, J., Both, A.: From assessment to learning: time-aware learning analytics for adaptive microlearning loops (2026). Submitted and under review
8. Gwozdz, J., Both, A.: RDF-based structured quality assessment representation of multilingual LLM evaluations. In: Curry, E., et al. (eds.) ESWC 2025. LNCS, vol. 15832, pp. 93–98. Springer, Heidelberg (2025). https://doi.org/10.1007/978-3-031-99554-5_17
9. Gwozdz, J., Both, A.: Toward reliable LLM-integrated web architectures for teacher-aligned automatic student grading. In: Proceedings of ICWE 2026 (2026)
10. High-Level Expert Group on AI: Ethics Guidelines for Trustworthy AI. Technical report, European Commission (2019)
11. Kasneci, E., et al.: ChatGPT for good? On opportunities and challenges of large language models for education. Learn. Individ. Differ. **103**, 102274 (2023)
12. Khalaily, A.: AI-powered intelligent tutoring systems in higher education: a review of current approaches, challenges, and future directions. In: 2025 International Conference on Smart Learning Courses (SCME), pp. 30–36 (2025)
13. Lewis, P. et al.: Retrieval-augmented generation for knowledge-intensive NLP tasks. In: Advances in Neural Information Processing Systems (NeurIPS), pp. 9459–9474 (2020)
14. Li, Z. et al.: Learning when to defer to humans for short answer grading. In: Wang, N., Rebolledo-Mendez, G., Matsuda, N., Santos, O.C., Dimitrova, V. (eds.) AIED 2023. LNCS, vol. 13916, pp. 414–425. Springer, Cham (2023). https://doi.org/10.1007/978-3-031-36272-9_34
15. Nicol, D.J., Macfarlane-Dick, D.: Formative assessment and self-regulated learning: a model and seven principles of good feedback practice. Stud. High. Educ. **31**(2), 199–218 (2006)
16. Shute, V.J.: Focus on formative feedback. Rev. Educ. Res. **78**(1), 153–189 (2008)

17. VanLehn, K.: The relative effectiveness of human tutoring, intelligent tutoring systems, and other tutoring systems. Educ. Psychol. **46**(4), 197–221 (2011)
18. Williamson, D.M., Xi, X., Breyer, F.J.: A framework for evaluation and use of automated scoring. Educ. Meas. Issues Pract. **31**(1), 2–13 (2012)
19. Zawacki-Richter, O., et al.: Systematic review of research on artificial intelligence applications in higher education. Int. J. Educ. Technol. High. Educ. **16**(1), 39 (2019)
20. Zhao, C., Silva, M., Poulsen, S.: Language models are few-shot graders. In: Cristea, A.I., Walker, E., Lu, Y., Santos, O.C., Isotani, S. (eds.) AIED 2025. LNCS, vol. 15880, pp. 3–16. Springer, Cham (2025). https://doi.org/10.1007/978-3-031-98459-4_1

Pipelined Simulation Using Cloud-Edge Computing for Safety in Autonomous Driving

Byeong-il Bae(✉) and In-Young Ko

School of Computing, Korea Advanced Institute of Science and Technology, Daejeon, Republic of Korea
bae.b.i@kaist.ac.kr , iko@kaist.ac.kr

Abstract. Simulation-based research has been widely conducted to ensure the safe operation of cyber-physical systems (CPS), such as autonomous vehicles. However, most simulation-based studies focus on the functionality of the ego vehicle during the development phase of the DevOps lifecycle. As a result, simulations performed during the development phase may differ subtly from real-world conditions and cannot cover all possible scenarios. Although simulations should also be conducted during the operations phase to ensure more rigorous safety assurance, significant challenges remain due to the limited computing resources of the ego vehicle and the virtually infinite number of possible driving scenarios. To address these challenges, this study proposes a simulation method that leverages a cloudâĂŞedge computing environment by partitioning the timeline, thereby overcoming the computational limitations of the ego vehicle. In addition, the proposed approach generates a comprehensive set of semantic trajectories—including illegal behaviors of non-player character (NPC) vehicles—using an ontology.

Keywords: Simulation-based Testing · Occlusion prediction · Cloud-edge computing

1 Introduction

Due to the rapid advancement of artificial intelligence (AI), traditional software systems, as well as cyber-physical systems (CPS) that integrate both hardware and software components, are increasingly adopting AI technologies [3]. However, because CPS operate in complex environments and interact with physical hardware, it is impossible to identify all potential faults before AI-enabled CPS are deployed. If faults occur during operation, the resulting failures may pose threats to human safety and lead to significant asset loss.

To mitigate these risks, developers perform system verification and testing. However, testing in real-world environments is often impractical due to safety concerns and high costs. Consequently, many existing studies adopt simulation-based testing to verify AI-enabled CPS. In the simulation, the ego vehicle refers

A. Mauri et al. (Eds.): ICWE 2026, LNCS 16625, pp. 250–255, 2026.
https://doi.org/10.1007/978-3-032-29372-5_21

to the vehicle equipped with an autonomous driving module that requires verification, while NPC vehicles refer to surrounding vehicles observed in the ego vehicle's environment. Most of these approaches focus on ego vehicle in the development phase of the DevOps lifecycle. In particular, scenarios generated during this phase often exclude unreasonable trajectories of NPC vehicles, as the primary objective is to evaluate AI behavior under normal conditions [4]. However, many real-world accidents are caused by unexpected or abnormal NPC behaviors (Fig. 1).

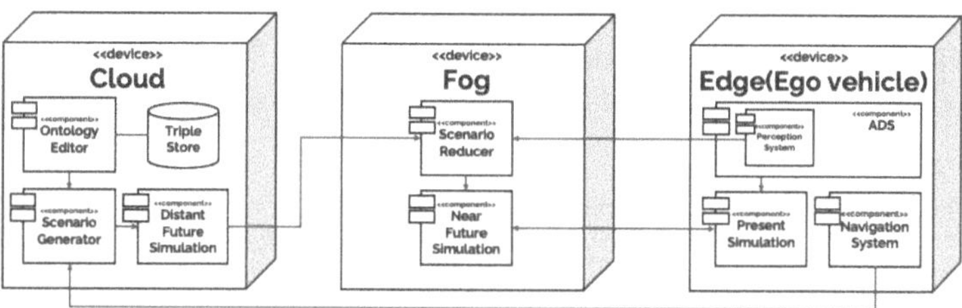

Fig. 1. Deployment view of the architecture for pipelined simulation. The system consists of cloud, fog, and edge computing nodes (the ego vehicle). Each node simulates the traffic environment, but the simulations are conducted at different time points and serve different roles.

Therefore, to ensure stronger safety guarantees, simulation-based testing should also be conducted during the operational phase [1], taking into account both the uncertainty inherent in AI systems and the discrepancies between simulated environments and real-world conditions. Runtime simulation should place greater emphasis on NPC behaviors than on the ego vehicle's actions to effectively prevent accidents. This is because, even if the ego vehicle operates flawlessly, unexpected or abnormal behaviors of NPC vehicles may still lead to accidents.

However, several challenges remain. First, the ego vehicle has limited computational resources and cannot generate and evaluate all possible trajectories within the available time. Second, predicted scenarios may deviate from actual real-world observations. To address these challenges, this study proposes a real-time simulation framework that operates in a virtual environment and enhances safety robustness through a cloudâĂŞedge computing architecture. The proposed framework partitions the future timeline and predicts possible NPC trajectories to prevent accidents.

The proposed method, referred to as *pipelined simulation*, divides the simulation process into three stages: the distant-future, the near-future, and the present. The distant-future stage generates diverse NPC trajectories, including abnormal behaviors such as illegal U-turns, traffic signal violations, and center-line crossings, and transmits these scenarios to the fog layer. The near-future stage reduces the scenario space based on currently perceived vehicles, thereby alleviating the computational burden on the ego vehicle (edge node). Finally, the present stage determines a safe driving trajectory by comparing the current scene with predicted scenarios received from the fog layer.

2 Research Issues

Predicting future traffic behavior is one of the most challenging tasks in autonomous driving systems. The distant-future simulation predicts potential trajectories of NPC vehicles that may appear along the ego vehicle's future driving path over the next few minutes. However, unknown future scenarios cannot be predicted accurately, and such scenarios cannot be directly applied to real-world decision-making. During the operations phase, there is insufficient time to generate a wide range of possible scenarios for numerous NPC vehicles.

2.1 Diverse Trajectory Generation

A large number of possible NPC vehicle trajectories can be anticipated. These vehicles may proceed straight or change lanes, and may also perform illegal U-turns or temporarily stop at the roadside. Furthermore, it is difficult to determine when and where these vehicles may change their behavior, and their behavior may vary depending on vehicle type. As a result, explicitly enumerating all possible scenarios becomes impractical. Moreover, in a cloud computing environment, computational resources should not be spent generating redundant or highly similar paths.

Diversity of NPC Scenario Starting Points Even if the predicted trajectories are similar to the actual trajectories of NPC vehicles, the perceived positions of NPC vehicles may differ from the predicted positions. For example, an NPC vehicle may be located at various positions within a lane along the future driving path at fine spatial resolutions, such as meter-level or even centimeter-level intervals. Therefore, predicted trajectories must be slightly adjusted according to the vehicle's actual speed, position, and heading.

Randomness in NPC Behavior Change Timing. A challenge in predicting NPC trajectories arises not only from the diversity of possible behaviors toward a destination, but also from uncertainty in the timing of behavioral changes. If behavior transitions are considered at every possible point, the number of scenarios increases rapidly, resulting in significant computational cost and processing time.

2.2 Simulating Diverse Trajectories Within a Short Time

The ego vehicle does not have sufficient time to simulate a large number of scenarios when it enters a future driving path for which distant-future simulations have predicted potential NPC trajectories. Therefore, the scenario set must be reduced based on priority criteria that reflect the likelihood of accidents.

3 Related Work

3.1 Occlusion

Occlusion research focuses on predicting unseen NPC vehicles in a given traffic scenario. It anticipates vehicles in the ego vehicle's blind spots and prepares for their potential sudden movements. Most existing approaches aim to accurately predict the behavior of vehicles in occluded regions. These methods infer the presence of NPC vehicles in unobserved road areas and generate safe driving strategies accordingly. For example, Yu et al. identify road segments to construct the centerline of potential NPC trajectories and employ mathematical formulations to derive probability distributions over these trajectories [6]. However, probabilistic models alone cannot effectively reduce the number of possible scenarios.

3.2 Simulation-Based Testing and Digital Twin

Many studies have been conducted on simulation and digital twins. Both research areas utilize virtual environments to simulate traffic evolution and monitor the state of the ego vehicle. For example, Kušić et al. used a digital twin to integrate real-time traffic information for microscopic motorway simulation [2]. In contrast, the proposed method aims to enhance driving safety by performing simulations across multiple temporal stages, namely the distant-future, the near-future, and the present.

3.3 Cloud-Edge Computing Environment

This study is related to the use of external computing resources to overcome the computational limitations of vehicles [5]. In our approach, to effectively handle future uncertainties, diverse scenarios are generated in the cloud layer, which has sufficient computational resources, and subsequently reduced at the fog layer by incorporating NPC information perceived by the ego vehicle (Fig. 2).

4 Research Plans

Our research question investigates how various valid scenario patterns generated for each lane in the cloud layer can be refined at the fog layer based on vehicles perceived by the edge layer, and how accurately the ego vehicle can assess the associated risk levels. Given a road environment, the system must rapidly generate valid movement patterns for each lane, including both legal and illegal behaviors. The proposed method constructs an ontology to represent vehicle maneuvers and their semantics, thereby enabling the efficient generation of a comprehensive set of possible behaviors within a given road environment.

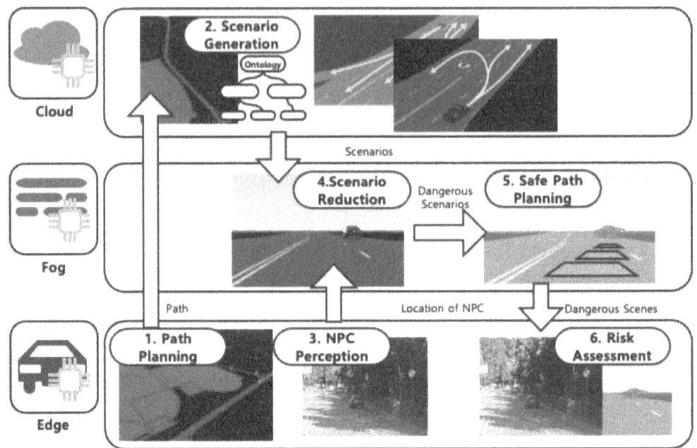

Fig. 2. Interaction among the cloud, fog, and edge layers in pipelined simulation. The cloud layer generates occlusion scenarios. The fog layer reduces the scenario set using the scenarios generated by the cloud and the locations of NPC vehicles perceived by the edge layer, and then identifies a safe route. The edge layer perceives NPC vehicle locations and assesses possible risks.

4.1 Practical Scenario Generation with an Ontology

Potential vehicle positions are assigned along each lane of a predicted future driving path to generate candidate routes for each lane. To efficiently extract semantically consistent paths within a short time, we propose a method that constructs an ontology representing vehicle movements and their associated semantics.

The proposed ontology incorporates several key components, including maneuver types, risky driving behaviors, traffic violations, and aggressive-driving taxonomies, thereby enabling the systematic generation of diverse driving scenarios. Based on this ontology, mutation techniques are applied to generate both legal and illegal trajectories that may arise in each lane.

Assigning Trajectories to NPC Vehicles. The possible future positions of vehicles to be perceived are virtually infinite. Therefore, during scenario generation in the cloud, NPC vehicle trajectories are generated from the moment they enter the ego vehicle's future path region until they exit it. The fog layer receives and stores these trajectories from the cloud layer and, upon detecting an NPC vehicle, assigns the trajectories corresponding to the lane it occupies.

Changing Behavior Based on the Ego Vehicle's Location. The behavior transition points of NPC vehicles are determined based on the ego vehicle's position. Using the ego vehicle's speed, behavioral changes are introduced at the minimum braking distance to generate critical scenarios. For example, an illegal U-turn performed far from the ego vehicle may pose low risk, whereas even a standard lane change within the ego vehicle's effective range can result in higher risk.

4.2 Scenario Reduction Based on Perceived NPC Vehicles

Before the ego vehicle enters a future driving path, the distant-future simulation generates potential NPC trajectories for each lane. If no vehicles are present in certain lanes along the future driving path, simulation at the fog layer is unnecessary. Furthermore, risk-critical scenarios generated in the cloud layer, based on safety metrics commonly used in autonomous driving, such as Minimum Safe Distance Factor (MSDF) and Time-to-Collision (TTC), are transmitted to the fog layer. By applying pre-generated trajectories only to nearby vehicles that can directly influence the ego vehicle, the number of scenarios can be effectively reduced.

5 Expected Contributions of the Ph.D. Research

In this study, we propose a distributed execution architecture for resource-constrained ego vehicles and extend simulation to the operational phase, thereby enabling simulation as a service. In addition, we employ a semantic model for scenario reduction and construct an ontology that models NPC vehicle behaviors as distinct knowledge entities.

Acknowledgments. This work was supported by Institute of Information & communications Technology Planning & Evaluation(IITP) grant funded by the Korea government(MSIT)(No. RS-2025-02218761 (50%), RS-2024-00406245 (50%))

References

1. Guissouma, H., Zink, M., Sax, E.: Continuous safety assessment of updated supervised learning models in shadow mode. In: 2023 IEEE 20th International Conference on Software Architecture Companion (ICSA-C), pp. 301–308. IEEE (2023)
2. Kušić, K., Schumann, R., Ivanjko, E.: A digital twin in transportation: real-time synergy of traffic data streams and simulation for virtualizing motorway dynamics. Adv. Eng. Inform. **55**, 101858 (2023)
3. Lamrani, I., Banerjee, A., Gupta, S.K.: Certification game for the safety analysis of AI-based CPS. In: International Conference on Computer Safety, Reliability, and Security, pp. 297–310. Springer (2021)
4. Lu, Y., Tian, Y., Wang, D., Chen, B., Peng, X.: DynNPC: finding more violations induced by ads in simulation testing through dynamic NPC behavior generation (2024). arXiv:2411.19567 arXiv preprint
5. Schafhalter, P., Kalra, S., Xu, L., Gonzalez, J.E., Stoica, I.: Leveraging cloud computing to make autonomous vehicles safer. In: 2023 IEEE/RSJ International Conference on Intelligent Robots and Systems (IROS), pp. 5559–5566. IEEE (2023)
6. Yu, M.Y., Vasudevan, R., Johnson-Roberson, M.: Occlusion-aware risk assessment for autonomous driving in urban environments. IEEE Robot. Autom. Lett. **4**(2), 2235–2241 (2019)

Deep Semantic Linking of Scientific Knowledge: An Agentic AI Framework for Knowledge Graph Construction

Sandra Schaftner(✉) and Martin Gaedke

Chemnitz University of Technology, Chemnitz, Germany
{sandra.schaftner,martin.gaedke}@informatik.tu-chemnitz.de

Abstract. The foundation of scientific research is the comprehensive analysis of existing literature. However, the exponential growth of published research leaves scientists increasingly overwhelmed, making it difficult to maintain a complete overview of the state-of-the-art or to discover hidden synergies between studies. The root of this problem lies in the traditional format of scholarly communication: crucial knowledge about applied methods, datasets, and metrics remains locked in semantically unlinked documents. While this format is optimal for human reading, it is highly inefficient for machine processing. Even modern AI research assistants frequently fail to provide complete, verifiable, and hallucination-free answers to complex research queries. To enable true machine-assisted exploration and verification, scholarly literature must be transformed from isolated documents into deeply interlinked, machine-readable structures. To achieve this, we introduce an agentic AI framework that automatically extracts key research entities, seamlessly interlinking the literature by mapping them to standard knowledge bases via unified URIs.

Keywords: Scientific Knowledge Graphs · Agentic AI · Large Language Models

1 Introduction

In daily digital life, graph-based representations are the invisible backbone of modern AI applications. Whether for Amazon product recommendations, Spotify playlists, or Google's semantic search, they rely on representing information as a machine-readable web of interlinked concepts.

In academia, this structured data foundation is missing. Scholarly communication relies on isolated documents, leaving valuable research knowledge – such as applied methods, metrics, or datasets – "frozen" in unstructured text. Relying on current AI tools for research causes three fundamental challenges: (1) a lack of verifiability, as the opaque nature of Large Language Models (LLMs) prevents reliable traceability to original sources and makes them prone to hallucinations;

M. Gaedke—PhD supervisor of the first author.

A. Mauri et al. (Eds.): ICWE 2026, LNCS 16625, pp. 256–262, 2026.
https://doi.org/10.1007/978-3-032-29372-5_22

(2) a lack of completeness, where complex aggregation queries (e.g., assessing method frequencies across thousands of papers) fail; and (3) a lack of interlinking, preventing the discovery of cross-disciplinary or -institutional synergies [17].

Bioinformatics demonstrates how structured knowledge representation overcomes these issues. The UniProt database exemplifies a highly precise Knowledge Graph (KG): protein knowledge is deep-semantically structured into triples, every fact links to its original paper (provenance), and entities seamlessly connect to external databases [15]. While other academic disciplines lag behind this ideal, replicating UniProt's manual expert curation is unfeasible given their sheer literature volume [15]. Automation is the only logical path forward, yet relying on uncontrolled LLMs fails to deliver the required scientific precision [7].

This dilemma leads to our central research question: *How can research knowledge, isolated in unstructured text documents, be scalably transformed into a machine-readable, semantically interoperable, and verifiable representation?*

To answer this, we conceptualize ALLMaC-SKG – Agentic LLM-augmented Construction of Scientific Knowledge Graphs (SKGs). This scalable framework establishes a verifiable data foundation required for advanced scientific discovery through (1) deep semantic mapping to standardized ontologies, (2) agentic workflow automation, and (3) federated exploration and interlinking.

2 Problem Statement and Motivation

Advanced scientific discovery is fundamentally hindered by a lack of deep semantic interlinking within published research. Persistent reliance on unstructured documents traps valuable research within isolated boundaries, severely limiting machine-actionability, resulting in poor input quality for modern LLMs, and impeding both automated extraction and manual exploration.

Limitations of Current AI Assistants. To address literature research challenges, current AI-powered assistants (e.g., Elicit, Consensus, SciSpace and Scite) leverage LLMs to synthesize answers. While they rely on underlying graphs, these are largely restricted to metadata – such as the Semantic Scholar Academic Graph (S2AG) – combined with stochastic text retrieval and vector embeddings [9]. While useful for basic discovery, these approaches inherently fail at precise quantitative aggregations or federated cross-repository retrieval. Current systems cannot reliably answer aggregation queries like: "How many papers in the last three years applied a Whisper model to the Common Voice dataset?" or "What unexploited research intersections exist between TU Chemnitz, the University of Udine, and the University of Girona?" To reliably answer such complex queries, AI requires structured graphs of explicit semantic facts, not just similarity-based vector embeddings.

Industry and Policy Needs for Structured Knowledge. Recognizing the limitations of purely text-based and shallow-structured approaches, both industry and

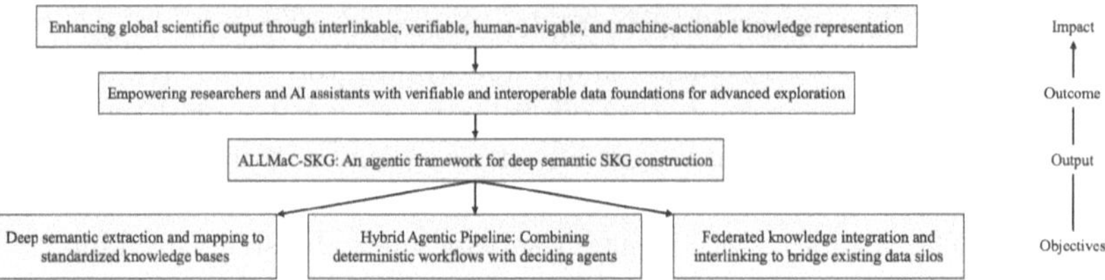

Fig. 1. The ALLMaC-SKG objectives tree, illustrating the path to overarching impact.

academia strongly push toward KGs for knowledge representation. In the enterprise sector, Gartner highlights that meeting high accuracy thresholds[1] makes it "crucial to bridge the gap between data and AI by using knowledge graphs"[2]. Parallel to industry, scientific initiatives – such as the Research Data Alliance (RDA), the European Open Science Cloud (EOSC), the Australian Research Data Commons (ARDC), and Germany's NFDI – aggressively pursue federated SKGs [2,14]. To achieve true FAIR compliance, these infrastructures rely on RDF and Linked Data principles. The overarching goal is to semantically interlink distributed knowledge via reusable standard ontologies and knowledge bases. Consequently, evaluating these systems requires strict adherence to FAIR principles, particularly semantic Interoperability (I) and Reusability (R). To effectively combat AI hallucinations, frameworks must further prioritize structural accuracy, semantic consistency, and provenance to the source document.

3 Related Work

The transition toward machine-actionable scholarly communication has driven the development of various SKGs [17]. However, achieving both deep semantic representation and high scalability remains an unsolved challenge. While LLMs are increasingly utilized, one of the latest paradigms of deploying them – Agentic AI – remains largely unexplored in the realm of KG construction (KGC).

Current Landscape of SKGs. Most existing SKGs model only shallow metadata (e.g., authorship, venues, citation networks), lacking detailed methodological content [17]. Apart from highly specialized domain KGs like UniProt [15], literature reports only two SKGs deeply model scientific claims: the Open Research Knowledge Graph (ORKG) [1] and the Computer Science Knowledge Graph (CS-KG) [6]. While UniProt excellently demonstrates deep semantics, scaling manually curated, niche-specific micro-graphs to every scientific domain is resource-wise unfeasible. However, existing broad-scope attempts face severe limitations. ORKG's reliance on manual crowdsourcing fails to scale and struggles with consistency [11]. CS-KG is criticized as sparse and incomplete [4].

[1] Gartner Report. https://www.gartner.com/en/documents/7444326.

[2] Gartner Press Release. https://www.gartner.com/en/newsroom/press-releases/2025-03-05-gartner-data-and-analytics-summit-2025-orlando-day-3-highlights.

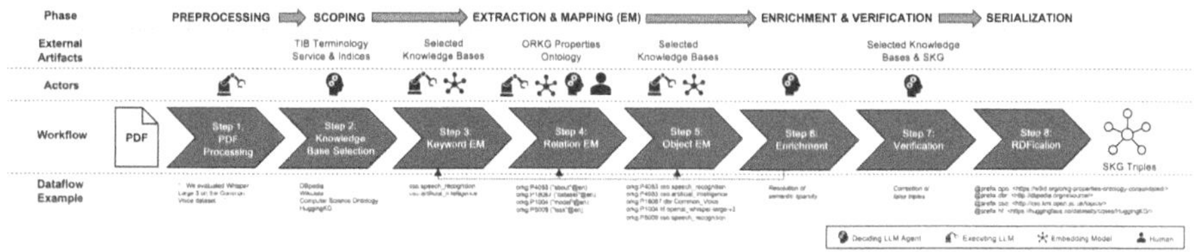

Fig. 2. The ALLMaC-SKG pipeline: Deterministic workflow with deciding agents.

Automated Construction and Agentic Workflows. To overcome manual bottlenecks, recent KGC pipelines increasingly leverage LLMs [3,17], yet rarely map entities to standardized vocabularies. Recently, KGC research has seen a surge in multi-agent frameworks [10]. However, many simply chain static LLM prompts together and label them as "agents," lacking the autonomous, dynamic plan-act-reflect loops defining true agentic systems [5]. One exception is Kaplunovich et al. [8], who apply a LangGraph KGC framework to the movie domain.

The Research Gap. There is currently no overarching automated framework for the deep semantic construction of SKGs from text. By fully exploiting advancements in agentic AI, this work proposes a concept and an architecture that entirely bridges the gap between high scalability through automation and deep semantic precision.

4 Objectives and Contributions

To fundamentally improve how researchers and AI systems interact with published literature, we introduce the ALLMaC-SKG framework. To realize the impact detailed in Fig. 1, this work is driven by three core objectives that constitute our main contributions:

Deep Semantic Mapping. Moving beyond superficial metadata, ALLMaC-SKG captures fine-grained entities like methods, datasets, and specific research properties. To answer complex multi-hop queries reliably, heterogeneous textual mentions must be resolved. The methodology robustly maps both extracted entities and properties to URIs via mapping agents utilizing vector search. Rather than creating redundant hierarchies, extractions are strictly linked to standard knowledge bases and ontologies like the ORKG Properties Ontology (OPO) [12,13], ensuring FAIR compliance and exploiting existing structural features.

Agentic Workflow Automation. ALLMaC-SKG utilizes a hybrid agentic pipeline, building on a deterministic workflow to guarantee consistent, sequential extraction routing, which is highly resource-efficient. According to LangGraph principles[3], workflows follow predetermined code paths, whereas true agents operate in

[3] LangChain AI: Workflows and Agents. https://docs.langchain.com/oss/python/langgraph/workflows-agents.

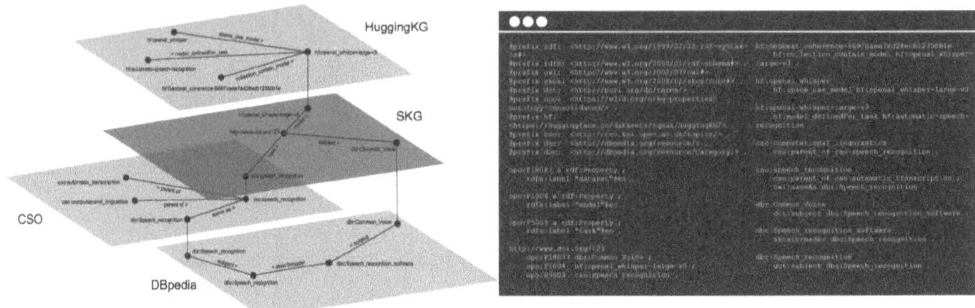

Fig. 3. Visualization of semantic snapping in ALLMaC-SKG. Dashed vertical lines represent the alignment of identical entities across the central SKG and external KGs.

dynamic feedback loops, directing their own actions. Such agents are employed at critical junctures requiring complex reasoning: (1) determining required domain-specific knowledge bases via search tools; (2) evaluating new relations for the OPO via Human-in-the-Loop review; (3) assessing semantic depth and deciding where iterative refinement is needed; and (4) conducting critical, tool-assisted verification before finalizing a paper. As seen in Fig. 2, other LLMs are utilized merely as processing tools within the deterministic path.

Federated Exploration and Semantic Snapping. To enable boundary-spanning knowledge discovery, isolated research must be placed into a global context. Mirroring bioinformatics initiatives [16], the methodology dynamically links publications with datasets, domain knowledge bases and global encyclopedic graphs like DBpedia. This envisions a meta-registry (similar to EOSC [14]) enabling "Semantic Snapping". Architecturally, ALLMaC-SKG can dock onto existing metadata foundations like S2AG [9], enriching them with deep semantic triples. Because all artifacts share global URIs, users can modularly combine KGs (e.g., institutional KGs + DBpedia + domain KGs), which semantically "snap" together at matching URI intersection nodes (cf. Fig. 3), dynamically interconnecting isolated knowledge spaces to uncover hidden research intersections.

5 Conclusion and Outlook

Constructing robust, semantically rich web-based knowledge architectures from unstructured text is a critical Web Engineering challenge. Even if future LLMs achieve near-perfect zero-shot extraction, the rigorous mapping of text to standard knowledge bases via deterministic agentic workflows remains a highly significant, FAIR-compliant blueprint transcending proprietary black-box products.

Toward this goal, initial efforts focused on foundational property extraction, resulting in the LOPE (LLM-driven Ontology-based Property Extraction) method and the OPO consolidation [12,13]. Future work will implement and rigorously evaluate the remaining ALLMaC-SKG modules against SOTA approaches. Finally, deploying the framework within the EU-funded Across Alliance[4] will assess its scalability, interoperability, and practical utility. This real-world application aims to overcome knowledge fragmentation, providing AI assistants and researchers with the data foundation demanded by modern research.

Acknowledgment. This work is supported by the European Union's Erasmus+ Programme under grant agreement No. 101177485, project Across (European University for Cross-Border Knowledge Sharing), and by the European Union's HORIZON Research and Innovation Programme under grant agreement No. 101120657, project ENFIELD (European Lighthouse to Manifest Trustworthy and Green AI).

Compliance with ethical standards

Disclosure of Interests. The authors have no competing interests to declare that are relevant to the content of this article.

References

1. Auer, S., et al.: Improving access to scientific literature with knowledge graphs. Bibl. Forsch. Prax. **44**(3), 516–529 (2020). https://doi.org/10.1515/bfp-2020-2042
2. Bernard, L., et al.: Base4NFDI - basic services for NFDI (2023). https://doi.org/10.5281/ZENODO.10245518
3. Bian, H., et al.: LLM-empowered knowledge graph construction: a survey (2025). https://doi.org/10.48550/arXiv.2510.20345
4. Borrego, A., et al.: Completing scientific facts in knowledge graphs of research concepts. IEEE Access **10**, 125867–125880 (2022). https://doi.org/10.1109/ACCESS.2022.3220241
5. Chand, B., et al.: Synergistic ai agents: Integrating knowledge graphs and large language models for scholarly communication. In: Open Conference Proceedings, vol. 8 (2026). https://doi.org/10.52825/ocp.v8i.3172
6. Dessì, D., et al.: SCICERO: a deep learning and NLP approach for generating scientific knowledge graphs. Knowl. Based Syst. **258**, 109945 (2022). https://doi.org/10.1016/j.knosys.2022.109945
7. Huang, L., et al.: A survey on hallucination in large language models: principles, taxonomy, challenges, and open questions. ACM Trans. Inf. Syst **43**(2) (2025). https://doi.org/10.1145/3703155
8. Kaplunovich, A.: LangGraph-orchestrated LLM agents for scalable movie knowledge graphs and question answering. In: Proceedings of the ICAIR 2025 (2025). https://doi.org/10.34190/icair.5.1.4142
9. Kinney, R., et al.: The semantic scholar open data platform (2025). https://doi.org/10.48550/ARXIV.2301.10140
10. Lu, Y.: KARMA: leveraging multi-agent LLMs for automated knowledge graph enrichment. arXiv arXiv:2502.06472 (2026)
11. Nechakhin, V., et al.: Evaluating LLMs for structured science summarization in the ORKG. Information **15**(6) (2024). https://doi.org/10.3390/info15060328

[4] Across Alliance. https://www.across-alliance.eu/.

12. Schaftner, S., Gaedke, M.: The LOPE method: improving consistent property extraction for scientific knowledge graphs using LLMs. In: WWW '26 Companion (2026). https://doi.org/10.1145/3774905.3795079
13. Schaftner, S., Gaedke, M.: ORKG properties ontology consolidated: LLM-driven refinement of crowdsourced knowledge for machine-actionability. In: WWW '26 Companion (2026). https://doi.org/10.1145/3774905.3795080
14. Schirrwagen, J., et al.: Data sources and persistent identifiers in the open science research graph of OpenAIRE. Int. J. Digit. Curation **15**, 5 (2020). https://doi.org/10.2218/ijdc.v15i1.722
15. The UniProt Consortium: UniProt: a worldwide hub of protein knowledge. Nucleic Acids Res. **47**(D1), D506–D515 (2018). https://doi.org/10.1093/nar/gky1049
16. Waagmeester, A., et al.: Wikidata as a knowledge graph for the life sciences. eLife **9**, e52614 (2020). https://doi.org/10.7554/eLife.52614
17. Zloch, M., et al.: Research knowledge graphs: the shifting paradigm of scholarly information representation. In: The Semantic Web, pp. 140–154 (2025). https://doi.org/10.1007/978-3-031-94578-6_9

SODPUB: A BPMN-Orchestrated Workflow-as-a-Service for Interoperability-Oriented Pre-Publication Quality Improvement in Open Government Data

Florian Hahn(✉) and Michael Martin

Chemnitz University of Technology, Chemnitz, Germany
{florian.hahn,michael.martin}@informatik.tu-chemnitz.de
https://www.tu-chemnitz.de/cs/dm/team/fh.php.en

Abstract. Open Government Data (OGD) publishing is often manual and locally heterogeneous, yielding inconsistent dataset quality and weak traceability of pre-publication decisions. SODPUB is a BPMN-orchestrated workflow-as-a-service that targets interoperability-oriented improvement before portal upload. Data providers submit CSV datasets via REST; the pipeline applies checks derived from W3C guidance, normalises tabular structure, generates CSV on the Web metadata, and produces DCAT-compatible catalog descriptions. Each proposed change is explained and versioned, and the workflow exports a machine-readable process trace aligned with PROV-O so that decisions remain auditable. The current implementation provides an executable BPMN skeleton, initial rule catalogue, and RDF trace generation; REST endpoints and portal connectors are under active development. Planned evaluation measures include acceptance rates of proposed fixes by portal staff, reduction of detectable structural and metadata issues, time per publication, and perceived transparency. The expected outcome is a reusable reference workflow that improves quality while preserving publisher release responsibility.

Keywords: Open Government Data · Dataset Publishing · REST · BPMN · Semantic Interoperability · DCAT · Provenance · CSVW

1 Motivation and Research Question

Open Government Data (OGD) portals have improved access to public-sector data, yet dataset quality and publication practices still vary substantially across publishers and administrative levels [4,11,14,26]. Many interventions focus on post-publication or metadata-only checks, although numerous issues originate earlier in the publishing process [1,21]. This work therefore investigates how best-practice recommendations can be operationalised as executable, reusable pre-publication services for existing portal environments.

A. Mauri et al. (Eds.): ICWE 2026, LNCS 16625, pp. 263–268, 2026.
https://doi.org/10.1007/978-3-032-29372-5_23

Research Question. To what extent can an executable BPMN-based workflow for pre-publication quality assurance, grounded in W3C best practices and machine-readable provenance, improve Open Government Data quality, process traceability, and decision accountability in portal publishing workflows?

2 Related Work and Background

2.1 OGD Publication Quality and Interoperability

Systematic analyses describe benefits and risks of OGD and repeatedly identify inconsistent formats, insufficient metadata, and lack of standardisation as barriers to reuse [4,5,14,24]. Evaluation and maturity models propose indicators and governance-oriented assessment dimensions [7,18]. The FAIR principles emphasise machine-actionable findability, interoperability, and reusability [25]. The 5-star scheme further motivates structured, machine-readable, and linkable publication practices. Recent European interoperability policy provides an additional motivation for cross-border, process-supported data flows [8].

2.2 Best Practices and Validation for Tabular and Catalog Metadata

For tabular data, the W3C CSV on the Web (CSVW) recommendations specify a data model and a JSON-based metadata vocabulary to describe and validate tabular datasets beyond loosely-defined CSV conventions [22,23]. For catalog metadata, DCAT is an RDF vocabulary designed to support interoperability between data catalogs published on the Web [2]. Provenance can be captured with PROV-O [15]. Constraint checking for RDF-based metadata and provenance graphs can be expressed with SHACL [13]. On the European data portal, metadata quality is operationalised via MQA indicators and dashboards, illustrating how metadata completeness and compliance can be measured [19,20].

2.3 Workflow Execution and Process Traceability

BPMN is a standard for modelling executable business processes [16]. In OGD contexts, BPMN has been proposed as a structuring mechanism for publication steps and responsibilities [11]. This PhD builds on an earlier prototype that maps Camunda-executed BPMN instances into RDF knowledge graphs via ontology-driven transformation, motivated by semantic completeness and querying [3,12]. Camunda provides a REST API for process and runtime interaction, enabling Web-based system integration [6].

3 Approach: Workflow-as-a-Service for Pre-publication Improvement

3.1 Goals

The approach pursues four goals: (i) pre-publication improvement before portal upload, (ii) operationalisation of CSVW and DCAT recommendations as executable checks and transformations, (iii) machine-readable explainability through PROV-O-aligned provenance, and (iv) compatibility with existing portals via a REST service rather than portal replacement.

3.2 System Overview

The system is designed as a service that receives a dataset and minimal contextual information such as publisher identity, license statement, and intended update frequency where available. A BPMN process orchestrates ingestion, file characterisation, tabular quality checks and normalisation, CSVW metadata generation, DCAT metadata generation, provenance export, and human-in-the-loop approval before upload. The service returns the improved dataset artefact, CSVW and DCAT metadata, and an explicit process trace, following the view that quality should emerge from repeatable publication processes rather than ad hoc interventions [1,21].

3.3 Rule Catalogue and Transformations

Rules are derived from CSVW for tabular metadata and schema constraints, DCAT for dataset and distribution descriptions, and SHACL for validating RDF outputs such as DCAT and PROV-O graphs [2,13,23]. The approach distinguishes between automatable structural checks and context-dependent decisions that remain with the publisher.

3.4 Security and Responsibility Boundaries

Because OGD publishing involves accountability and legal constraints (for example licensing statements), the system is explicitly designed as an assistance service. It proposes improvements and documents the performed steps. Publisher approval remains the final gate, and the service can be deployed with authenticated REST access to prevent unrestricted operations.

4 Work Completed and Planned Evaluation

4.1 Work Completed

Two foundations are already in place: (1) A BPMN-based model of an OGD publishing workflow and its role in standardisation was previously analysed and described [11]. (2) A prototype for ontology-driven transformation of Camunda BPMN instances into RDF knowledge graphs was developed to support semantic traceability and querying of process executions [3,12]. (3) A relevant investigation, if applying DCAT on Open Data Portal Software really improves the reusability and interoperability. [10] Furthermore, a survey paper on human-in-the-loop of Open Data portals, a relevant systematic review and a government related impact framework paper are currently under review.

The current PhD focus extends these foundations by shifting from post-hoc analysis to pre-publication improvement with concrete steps for the framework and its software. Additionally, this framework will be compared with no publication process and the current CKAN extension approach in a user study.

4.2 Evaluation Plan

The evaluation will address three dimensions, aligned with existing quality frameworks and portal practice:

1. **Quality impact**: Compare incoming datasets to improved candidates using measurable indicators, such as metadata completeness (DCAT fields), machine-readability improvements, and detection of structural issues [19,26].
2. **Process transparency**: Assess whether provenance answers common audit questions (what changed, which rule triggered, who approved) using PROV-O-aligned traces and SHACL validation reports [13,15].
3. **Operational feasibility**: Measure time-to-publish with and without the service, and record acceptance rates of proposed improvements by portal staff (human-in-the-loop) [1].

The empirical study design will use a controlled set of real portal datasets (CSV-focused) and compare baseline portal publication to workflow-supported publication. This scope matches prior observations that machine-readable formats and consistent structures are prerequisites for effective downstream use [9,26].

5 Expected Contribution

This research provides an executable, reusable reference workflow that integrates standards, automation, and traceability: (i) a BPMN workflow blueprint for pre-publication quality improvement, (ii) a standards-based rule catalogue grounded in W3C CSVW and DCAT, (iii) provenance-as-a-service for publication decisions using PROV-O, (iv) a portal-compatible REST interface aligned with common integration practices. This approach complements portal-side certification and metadata quality tooling such as ODI certificates and EU-level metadata quality dashboards [17,20], by moving improvements upstream in the publication pipeline.

6 Conclusion

This PhD project implements pre-publication quality improvement for OGD as a BPMN-orchestrated service that operationalises CSVW and DCAT and exports machine-readable provenance. Its expected contribution is a reusable, portal-compatible workflow that improves quality and traceability while preserving publisher approval as the final release step. Next steps are completing the

REST interface, formalising the rule catalogue, and evaluating quality impact, transparency, and operational feasibility in collaboration with portal operators.

Disclosure of Interests. The authors have no competing interests to declare that are relevant to the content of this article.

References

1. Abella, A., Ortiz-de Urbina-Criado, M., De-Pablos-Heredero, C.: The process of open data publication and reuse. J. Assoc. Inf. Sci. Technol. **70**(3), 296–300 (2019). https://doi.org/10.1002/asi.24116
2. Albertoni, R., Browning, D., Cox, S.J.D., Beltran, A.G., Perego, A., Winstanley, P.: Data catalog vocabulary (DCAT) - version 3. W3C Recommendation (2024). https://www.w3.org/TR/vocab-dcat-3/
3. Annane, A., Aussenac-Gilles, N., Kamel, M.: BBO: BPMN 2.0 based ontology for business process representation. In: 20th European Conference on Knowledge Management (ECKM 2019) (2019). https://hal.science/hal-02365012v1/document
4. Attard, J., Orlandi, F., Scerri, S., Auer, S.: A systematic review of open government data initiatives. Gov. Inf. Q. **32**(4), 399–418 (2015). https://doi.org/10.1016/j.giq.2015.07.006
5. Çaldağ, M.T., Gökalp, M.O., Gökalp, E.: Open government data: analysing benefits and challenges. In: 2019 1st International Informatics and Software Engineering Conference (UBMYK) (2019). https://doi.org/10.1109/UBMYK48245.2019.8965581
6. Camunda Services GmbH: Camunda platform 7 rest API reference. Camunda Documentation. https://docs.camunda.org/manual/latest/reference/rest/
7. Duarte, A.E., Bárbara, J., Machado, A., Burle, C., Meira, W., Alves, L.: Open data evaluation model in Brazilian governmental portals. In: Proceedings of the 24th Annual International Conference on Digital Government Research (2023). https://doi.org/10.1145/3598469.3598510
8. European Parliament and Council of the European Union: Regulation (EU) 2024/903 (interoperable Europe act). EUR-Lex (2024). https://eur-lex.europa.eu/eli/reg/2024/903/oj/eng. Accessed 13 Mar 2024
9. Fernández, J.D., Martínez-Prieto, M.A., Gutiérrez, C.: Publishing open statistical data: the Spanish census. In: Proceedings of the 1st International Conference on Semantic Data and its Applications, pp. 20–25 (2011). https://doi.org/10.1145/2037556.2037560
10. Hahn, F.: Geographical provenance of open government datasets: evaluating geospatial metadata in municipal open data portals. In: Proceedings of the International Conference on Dublin Core and Metadata Applications. Dublin Core Conference, vol. 2025. Dublin Core Metadata Initiative, Dublin (2025). https://doi.org/10.23106/dcmi.952512517. https://dcpapers-data.dublincore.org/articles/dcmi-2025/952512517/files/dcmi-952512517.pdf
11. Hahn, F.: Towards an standardized dataset publishing in open government data ecosystems. In: Curry, E., et al. (eds.) The Semantic Web: ESWC 2025 Satellite Events, pp. 205–214. Springer, Cham (2026). https://doi.org/10.1007/978-3-031-99554-5_35
12. Hahn, F., Todorovikj, S.: Ontology driven transformation of Camunda BPMN instances into RDF knowledge graphs (2025). https://doi.org/10.5281/zenodo.17702330

13. Knublauch, H., Kontokostas, D.: Shapes constraint language (SHACL). W3C Recommendation (2017). https://www.w3.org/TR/shacl/
14. Kucera, J., Chlapek, D.: Benefits and risks of open government data. J. Syst. Integr. **5**(1), 30–41 (2014). https://doi.org/10.20470/JSI.V5I1.185. https://www.researchgate.net/publication/289841566_Benefits_and_Risks_of_Open_Government_Data
15. Lebo, T., Sahoo, S., McGuinness, D.: PROV-O: The PROV ontology. W3C Recommendation (2013). https://www.w3.org/TR/prov-o/
16. Object Management Group: Business process model and notation (BPMN), version 2.0. Object Management Group (OMG) Specification (2010). https://www.omg.org/spec/BPMN/2.0/
17. Open Data Institute: ODI certificates. Open Data Institute. https://certificates.theodi.org/
18. Open Data Institute: Open data maturity model guide, edition 2.0. Open Data Institute (2025). https://theodi.org/documents/543/Open_Data_Maturity_Model_Guide_Edition_2.0.pdf
19. Publications Office of the European Union: Metadata quality assessment (MQA): Methodology. data.europa.eu. https://data.europa.eu/mqa/methodology
20. Publications Office of the European Union: Enhancing metadata quality across Europe: Introducing the MQA tool. data.europa.eu (2025). https://data.europa.eu/en/news-events/news/enhancing-metadata-quality-across-europe-introducing-mqa-tool
21. Sánchez-Nielsen, E., Morales, A., Mendo, O., Chavez Gutierrez, F.: SuDaMa: sustainable open government data management framework for long-term publishing and consumption. IEEE Access (2021). https://doi.org/10.1109/ACCESS.2021.3127472
22. Tennison, J.: CSV on the web: a primer. W3C Working Group Note (2016). https://www.w3.org/TR/tabular-data-primer/
23. Tennison, J., Kellogg, G., Herman, I.: Model for tabular data and metadata on the web (CSVW). W3C Recommendation (2015). https://www.w3.org/TR/tabular-data-model/
24. Wieczorkowski, J.: Barriers to using open government data. In: Proceedings of the 3rd International Conference on E-commerce, E-Business and E-Government (2019). https://doi.org/10.1145/3340017.3340022
25. Wilkinson, M.D., Dumontier, M., Aalbersberg, I.J.J., et al.: The fair guiding principles for scientific data management and stewardship. Sci. Data **3**, 160018 (2016). https://doi.org/10.1038/sdata.2016.18
26. Yi, M.: Exploring the quality of government open data: comparison study of the UK, the USA and Korea. Electron. Libr. **37**(1), 35–48 (2019). https://doi.org/10.1108/EL-06-2018-0124

Accessibility By Design

Salvatore Gatto(✉) and Ombretta Gaggi

University of Padua, Padua, Italy
{salvatore.gatto,gaggi}@math.unipd.it

Abstract. While digital accessibility is a fundamental human right, modern web systems often fail to meet legal standards due to inadequate developer tools and persistent barriers for users with visual impairments. This research proposes an **Accessibility by Design** framework that integrates accessibility considerations into both the development and consumption phases of web systems. The framework is composed of two complementary components: an AI-assisted development environment that leverages Large Language Models to support developers in auditing and generating accessible web components and a web-based multimodal system that translates visual STEM data into multisensory representations through sonification. The study evaluates how integrating accessibility considerations into product design enhances usability while ensuring equal access for all users regardless of their abilities.

Keywords: Web Accessibility · Sonification · LLM

1 Introduction

Digital accessibility is a fundamental human right, ensuring that all users can interact with technologies and services on equal terms. Although this principle is formally protected by the United Nations Convention on the Rights of Persons with Disabilities [8], practical implementation remains a challenge. According to a report of Web Accessibility in Mind (WebAIM), more than 95% of the world's top one million home pages still fail basic accessibility tests [12]. The major reason for this scenario is that accessibility is still often seen as an additional requirement rather than an integral part of the engineering process. However, as highlighted by the principle of Universal Design, designing for diverse user needs actually enhances usability for everyone, included search engines and AI agents [5]. From this perspective, accessibility should not be viewed merely as a matter of compliance, but as an opportunity to improve the overall quality of the web.

Developers often struggle to correctly interpret and implement current guidelines. Furthermore, even when digital content is available online, users with visual impairments still face significant barriers to accessing highly visual information, particularly in Science, Technology, Engineering, Mathematics (STEM) domains, where charts, graphs, and mathematical functions are central. Current tools usually address content creation and content consumption separately, without offering an integrated perspective that connects the two.

A. Mauri et al. (Eds.): ICWE 2026, LNCS 16625, pp. 269–275, 2026.
https://doi.org/10.1007/978-3-032-29372-5_24

This research addresses these challenges by proposing an **Accessibility By Design** framework to integrate accessibility into both the production and use of digital systems. The framework follows two complementary research directions. The first focuses on content creation, supporting developers with a tool based on Large Language Models (LLMs) to help them assess, fix, and generate web content that complies with current accessibility standards. The second focuses on content consumption, enabling end-users—particularly those with visual impairments—to access and interact with STEM content through alternative interaction modalities. The goal is to design a web-based mathematical suite that represents functions, bar charts, and pie charts through visual and auditory modalities, enabling users to access information in the way that best suits their needs. This research aims to make accessibility a core principle of web engineering rather than an afterthought or an extra constraint. The expected outcome is a unified framework that demonstrates the value of treating accessibility as a first-class requirement throughout the development process.

2 Research Questions

This research aims to investigate how an **Accessibility by Design** framework can reduce digital barriers by supporting both the creators and consumers of web content. The research is structured around three research questions:

RQ1: Supporting the production of accessible web content. How can LLMs be used to support developers in assessing, fixing, and generating web content that complies with current accessibility standards? In particular, how can techniques such as Retrieval-Augmented Generation (RAG) and fine-tuning improve the reliability of these systems in real development contexts?

RQ2: Supporting access to visual STEM content on the web. How can sonification approaches developed for mobile environments be extended to support web visual STEM content, e.g., mathematical functions, bar charts, and pie charts? Furthermore, how can these approaches be integrated into a unified web-based mathematical suite based on auditory feedback?

RQ3: Evaluation of the Integrated Framework. To what extent can the proposed Accessibility by Design framework, combining AI-driven developer support and multimodal web-native interfaces, improve accessibility across both content creation and content use compared to traditional approaches?

3 Background and Related Work

The W3C provides the technical foundations of web accessibility through the Web Content Accessibility Guidelines (WCAGs). WCAGs are organised in 4 core principles: Perceivable, Operable, Understandable, and Robust (POUR). Each principle contains a set of testable success criteria categorised into 3 levels (A, AA, and AAA) [10]. Despite this, their practical adoption remains challenging.

Several jurisdictions have introduced binding legal requirements. In the US, *Section 508 of the Rehabilitation Act* mandates accessibility for federal agencies' electronic and information technology, while in the EU, the *European Accessibility Act* (Directive 2019/882) defines common requirements for digital products and services across member states [2,9]. These regulations increase the need for tools that help developers correctly apply accessibility standards.

The adoption of these legal requirements led to the study of how LLMs can support activities such as generating descriptive alternative text and identifying accessibility issues that are difficult to detect through traditional analysis [7]. Prior work suggests that LLMs can provide better context-related feedback than traditional tools for the detection of rule-based violations [1,4].

Despite this potential, important reliability concerns remain: LLMs may hallucinate, identifying issues that are not in the source code or correcting snippets that do not present any violations. These limitations reduce trust in LLM-based accessibility support and highlight the need for approaches that can better ground model outputs in verified technical knowledge. This gap motivates investigating techniques such as RAG and fine-tuning to improve the reliability of AI-assisted accessibility support, as addressed in **RQ1**.

Accessibility in digital environments also depends on the presence of interaction modalities that make complex content perceivable to different users. This issue is particularly evident in STEM domains, where information is frequently conveyed through highly visual representations such as charts and mathematical functions [11]. Screen readers often provide limited support for communicating spatial relationships and structural properties in this type of content. In recent years, web-based interactive environments, such as Jupyter notebooks, have become widely adopted in STEM education, but they still present severe accessibility challenges for blind and visually impaired users [6], both in terms of content structure and accessibility of generated data representations.

To address these limitations, previous research has explored multimodal approaches based on sonification and haptic feedback. These techniques can provide alternative ways of representing complex visual information through sound and touch. In this context, the author's previous work, *GraficiAccessibili* [3], investigated the use of such techniques in a mobile environment for the study of mathematical functions. However, an open challenge remains in extending these solutions to a unified web-native environment that can support a broader range of STEM content. This gap motivates **RQ2**, which investigates how sonification approaches can be adapted for the web and integrated into a mathematical suite to enable accessible interaction with functions and statistical charts.

4 Proposed Methodology

This section describes the current research components—namely, the development of the *SviluppAbile* extension and the web-based evolution of *GraficiAccessibili*—and presents the unified framework that integrates them within the proposed Accessibility by Design core.

4.1 LLM-Based Accessibility Assistant

The first component of this research addresses the content creation dimension. *SviluppAbile* is a browser extension designed to support accessibility within the Web Engineering lifecycle. Unlike general-purpose AI models, *SviluppAbile* implements a RAG pipeline grounded in WCAGs 2.2 and W3C techniques. The goal is to improve the reliability of LLM outputs by grounding them in verified accessibility knowledge and making the generated feedback traceable to recognised standards. The tool operates in two complementary modes:

- **Assessment Mode:** analyses existing HTML, identifies potential accessibility violations, and provides explanations and remediation strategies linked to violations identified by traditional tools.
- **Develop Mode:** supports generation of code compliant with the standards and explanations of best practices to follow for developers.

We also investigates fine-tuning techniques as a complementary strategy to further improve the reliability and accuracy of model outputs. A comparative evaluation will be conducted to assess how RAG, fine-tuning, and their combination influence the quality of accessibility feedback generated by *SviluppAbile*.

This component addresses **RQ1** by investigating how LLM-based systems can support developers to assess and generate accessible web content.

4.2 GraficiAccessibili on Web

The second component addresses the content consumption, through the web-native evolution of *GraficiAccessibili* [3] to generalise the sonification engine beyond mathematical functions and extend it to bar charts and pie charts, completing the development of the mathematical suite introduced in Sect. 1.

This component addresses **RQ2** by investigating how multimodal access to visual STEM content can be integrated into a web-native environment.

4.3 The Integrated Accessibility By Design Framework

The synthesis of these two components forms the proposed **Accessibility by Design** framework (Fig. 1). The framework connects accessibility at the level of content creation with accessibility at the level of content consumption, thus reflecting the two complementary dimensions of the research.

On the developer side, *SviluppAbile* supports the production of accessible web content by combining standards-based knowledge, contextual explanations, and AI-assisted guidance. On the end-user side, *GraficiAccessibili* supports access to visual STEM information through sonification and other multisensory interaction channels. Taken together, these two components operationalise the Accessibility by Design vision by addressing accessibility across both content creation and content consumption.

To investigate these research directions, the methodology combines system development with comparative evaluation. For **RQ1**, *SviluppAbile* will be

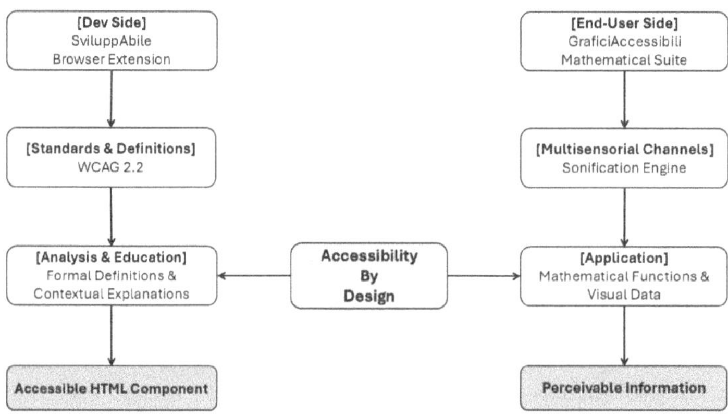

Fig. 1. The proposed Accessibility by Design framework.

assessed in terms of its ability to identify, explain, and generate accessible web content in alignment with WCAG requirements. For **RQ2**, the web-based evolution of *GraficiAccessibili* will be evaluated with respect to its support for auditory interaction with mathematical functions and statistical charts. For **RQ3**, the integrated framework will be examined as a unified accessibility approach spanning both content creation and consumption, compared with traditional reactive workflows.

From a Web Engineering perspective, integrating accessibility requirements into the development process improves the quality of web systems for all users. Web solutions compliant with WCAGs include features that benefit the broader user base, such as adequate color contrast, semantic markup that improves both readability and maintainability, and clearly structured content. Similarly, a mathematical suite designed to make STEM content accessible to users with visual impairments becomes a more effective educational tool for all students.

5 Conclusion and Future Work

This paper presented an **Accessibility by Design** research framework aimed at integrating accessibility into both the production and use of digital systems. The proposed study is structured around two complementary research directions: supporting developers in the creation of accessible web content, and enabling multimodal access to visual STEM information for end users. Together, these directions aim to position accessibility as a core principle of Web Engineering rather than as a reactive adaptation. The current stage of the research includes the development of the *SviluppAbile* browser extension and the web-based evolution of *GraficiAccessibili*. These two components provide the foundation for investigating how accessibility can be addressed across both content creation and content consumption within a unified framework. Future work will focus on completing the development of these tools and evaluating their effectiveness.

On the developer side, *SviluppAbile* will be assessed on its ability to identify accessibility violations, explain them clearly, and generate web content that complies with WCAG requirements. To support this evaluation, we plan to develop a web-based dataset of content-specific accessibility violations and compare the system's performance with that of traditional accessibility tools.

On the end-user side, *GraficiAccessibili* will be extended to support bar and pie charts, with effectiveness evaluated through controlled listening tasks involving both sighted users and users with visual impairments. These tasks will assess information perception via sonification. Moreover, we aim to collaborate with schools to identify features and support the suite's adoption.

Finally, the integrated framework will be examined as a whole to explore its potential to improve accessibility practices across both content creation and use, compared with traditional approaches.

References

1. Duarte, C., Costa, M., Seixas Pereira, L., Guerreiro, J.A.: Expanding automated accessibility evaluations: leveraging large language models for heading-related barriers. In: Companion Proceedings of the 30th International Conference on Intelligent User Interfaces, IUI 2025 Companion, pp. 39–42. Association for Computing Machinery, New York (2025). https://doi.org/10.1145/3708557.3716329
2. EU Parliament and Council of the EU Union: Directive 2019/882 of the EU Parliament and Council of 17-04-2019 on the accessibility requirements for products and services (2019). Journal of the EU Union, L 151, 7-06-2019, pp. 70–115
3. Gatto, S., Gaggi, O., Grosset, L., Fovino, L.G.N.: Accessible mathematics: representation of functions through sound and touch. IEEE Access **12**, 121552–121569 (2024). https://doi.org/10.1109/ACCESS.2024.3448509
4. López-Gil, J.M., Pereira, J.: Turning manual web accessibility success criteria into automatic: an LLM-based approach. Univ. Access Inf. Soc. **24**, 837–852 (2025). https://doi.org/10.1007/s10209-024-01108-z
5. Mace, R.L.: What is universal design? The Center for Universal Design, NC State University (1997). https://design.ncsu.edu/research/center-for-universal-design/
6. Potluri, V., Singanamalla, S., Tieanklin, N., Mankoff, J.: Notably inaccessible — data driven understanding of data science notebook (in)accessibility. In: Proceedings of the 25th International ACM SIGACCESS Conference on Computers and Accessibility (2023). https://doi.org/10.1145/3597638.3608417
7. Singh, N., Wang, L.L., Bragg, J.: Figura11y: AI assistance for writing scientific alt text. In: Proceedings of the 29th International Conference on Intelligent User Interfaces, IUI 2024, pp. 886–906. Association for Computing Machinery, New York (2024). https://doi.org/10.1145/3640543.3645212
8. UN: Convention on the rights of persons with disabilities and optional protocol (2006). https://www.un.org/disabilities/documents/convention/convoptprot-e.pdf
9. U.S. General Services Administration: Section 508 law and related laws and policies. https://www.section508.gov/manage/laws-and-policies/section-508-law/
10. W3C Web Accessibility Initiative: Web content accessibility guidelines overview. https://www.w3.org/WAI/standards-guidelines/wcag/

11. Wandy, A.: STEM for Students with Blindness and Visual Impairments: Tenets of an Inclusive Classroom. Master's thesis, State University of New York College at Brockport, New York, USA (2020). https://soar.suny.edu/handle/20.500.12648/4876
12. Web Accessibility In Mind: The WebAIM million the 2026 report on the accessibility of the top 1,000,000 home pages (2026). https://webaim.org/projects/million/

Early Detection of Cognitive Decline in Aging Adults Throught AI-Driven IoT/IoMT

Daniel Mocinha-Sanchez(✉), Javier Romero-Alvarez, Jose Garcia-Alonso, and Juan M. Murillo

Escuela Politécnica, Quercus Software Engineering Group, University of Extremadura, Av. de la Universidad, S/N, 10003 Cáceres, Spain
{dmocinhas,jromero,jgaralo,juanmamu}@unex.es

Abstract. The quality of life of aging adults has improved over time through the incorporation of technological innovations in their homes, such as voice assistants or monitoring systems. However, current systems do not detect certain patterns that indicate dementia or mild cognitive decline due to limitations in the level of detail of the collected data or in the interpretability of the information already available. In this context, IoT and IoMT devices can be used to collect information that allows automatic detection of possible patterns or alterations. Integration of collected data with artificial intelligence models can improve the interpretability of the data and the detection of behavior patterns that indicate cognitive decline. This thesis aims to design an architecture that uses data from IoT/IoMT devices to identify behavior patterns using artificial intelligence models, with the aim of preventing dementia or mild cognitive decline in aging people through early detection and monitoring strategies.

Keywords: Web services · Cognitive decline · Artificial Intelligence

1 Introduction and Motivation

Cognitive decline [14] is the state between changes associated with normal aging and certain alterations in dementia, manifested by amnesia, memory loss, and other cognitive afflictions that affect the performance of daily living. This type of decline, considered "mild cognitive decline", can represent an early stage of dementia [4], currently accounting for between 1 and 6% of cases of cognitive decline. Around 15% may be treatable [13], but not all cases are present in the same way, as its manifestation varies from person to person. It usually presents with recurrent memory problems. However, it may also involve symptoms or cognitive alterations that affect other domains such as visuospatial function, attention, language, and orientation [6,15].

These symptoms may occur in conjunction with mood changes or psychological disorders such as anxiety or depression [3,9]. These are reflected in small

A. Mauri et al. (Eds.): ICWE 2026, LNCS 16625, pp. 276–281, 2026.
https://doi.org/10.1007/978-3-032-29372-5_25

actions that gradually disrupt the living environment and daily routine, such as repeatedly forgetting to close the refrigerator door for a long time, forgetting to turn off electronic devices, or forgetting to take their daily medication. Cognitive decline is also preceded by other physical and cognitive factors considered significant risk factors, which may form part of possible behavioral patterns for those who have already been diagnosed. Among the most important risk factors are lack of physical activity and hypertension [12].

The main problem is the challenge of detecting anomalies in an individual's daily routine through the identification of patterns associated with cognitive decline. Although these factors are relatively easy to identify, data collection can be a complex task in which the specialist conducting the assessment plays a crucial role in monitoring the performed actions by the individual in their daily life. If the collected data has insufficient quality, the interpretability of the information is compromised, making the subsequent detection of anomalous patterns that can indicate cognitive decline in aging adults more difficult. Although tools currently facilitate data collection through IoT or IoMT devices [11] or the application of Artificial Intelligence (AI) models [17], their implementation can be highly demanding and may not necessarily be successful.

However, technological advances have led to a paradigm shift in the management of aging adults' health and well-being, enabling the implementation of new methodologies. Knowing that technology has greatly benefited the health and well-being of aging people through IoT and IoMT devices to facilitate their daily routine [5]. This Ph.D. thesis aims to address these challenges by proposing a solution based on methodologies and techniques that allows to collect data and to monitor aging people's behavior through using IoT and IoMT sensors [7], to process data in order to complete and make sense of their medical history, and to interpret data to search possible anomalous behavior patterns by applying AI-Driven models.

The rest of this work is structured as follows. Section 2 presents the related work. Section 3 defines the scope and objectives of the project, describing the problems the project intends to address. Section 4 describes the research methodology to be followed. Finally, Sect. 5 presents the main findings of the investigation.

2 Related Work

There are many areas of research and development related to cognitive decline. Through the application of new technologies, intelligent monitoring systems can be implemented to track aging people's biometric data in real time. AI-Driven models can be applied to rapidly detect behavioral patterns and interpret potential outcomes [1]. These technological advances have driven the digitalization of the sector, enabling innovative solutions for the care and treatment of aging people, facilitating the automation of many previously manual and repetitive processes. Among the existing contributions in this line of research, the following proposals are particularly noteworthy.

- Real-Time Elderly Healthcare Monitoring Expert System Using Wireless Sensor Network [2]. This proposal presents a healthcare expert system focused on the care and needs of aging people. The proposal seeks to develop an integrated and multidisciplinary approach that addresses their actual healthcare needs.
- MNA-net: Multimodal Neuroimaging Attention-Based Architecture for Cognitive Decline Prediction [16]. This proposal defines an attention-based multimodal neuroimaging model designed to predict the progression of cognitive decline in individuals over a ten-year period.
- Human microservices: A framework for turning humans into service providers [10]. This work treats people as connectors between services and other users by collecting data from their phones and turning them into service providers.

Regarding the relevance of this proposal to existing work, this Ph.D. thesis involves the design and development of a web-based architecture capable of integrating data collected from IoT/IoMT devices and processing it through AI-driven models. This includes the implementation of data management mechanisms, web services for data communication, and interactive web interfaces that allow healthcare professionals to monitor behavioral patterns and interpret the results provided by explainable AI models. Therefore, this Ph.D. thesis contributes to supporting the detection and analysis of cognitive decline in aging adults.

3 Aims and Objectives

This thesis proposal involves the development and research of a solution focused on monitoring aging people who have, or may develop, mild cognitive decline, providing a temporary overview of their functional and cognitive evolution. The objective is to facilitate the detection of behavior patterns by applying AI-Driven models capable of identifying signs of deterioration and supporting the selection of treatments or interventions better suited to the person's condition. In addition, some research questions and objectives have been established as the main scientific contributions of this thesis.

- *How can data on an aging person's daily routine be collected?* A wide range of IoT and IoMT devices are currently available to gather large volumes of data related to key indicators associated with cognitive decline. These devices can be orchestrated to enable centralized data retrieval through an API.
- *How can abnormal behavior patterns be detected in aging people?* Existing studies in this field identify potential risk factors for cognitive decline. By applying artificial intelligence models, such patterns can be characterized and, based on processed data, individuals at risk of developing mild cognitive decline can be identified.
- *How is the information reported to specialists?* The information generated by AI models must be shown and interpreted in some way to specialists. Techniques such as Explainable AI are increasingly being used to explain the

results produced by the models. This information must be offered to support clinical decisions about patients.

4 Research Methodology

To achieve the objectives of this Ph.D. thesis, the Design Science research methodology [8] is used. Design Science is a research methodology composed of two paradigms that seek to develop and verify theories that explain human behavior and extend knowledge through the creation and innovation. This methodology is widely applied in engineering disciplines and is applicable to fields such as web engineering and artificial intelligence (AI). Following the methodology and its phases, an initial research plan is proposed, as shown in Fig. 1.

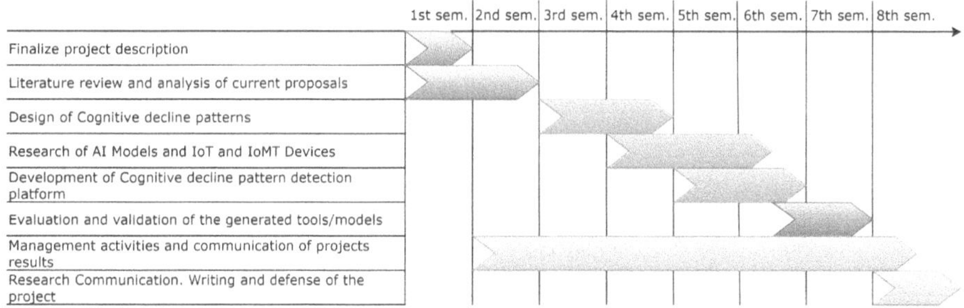

Fig. 1. Architecture and workflow of the proposal

The proposed architecture follows a phased workflow, as defined in Fig. 2. First, data will be collected and compiled using interconnected IoT and IoMT devices.

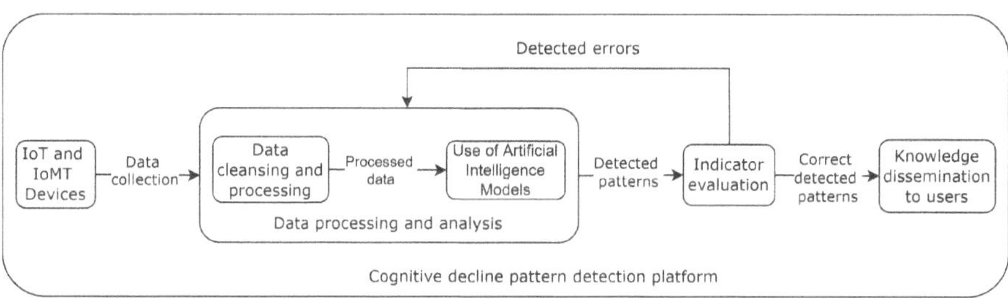

Fig. 2. Proposed system architecture

This data will then be processed and analyzed using machine learning models to detect possible behavior patterns and build a routine profile for each person. After data analysis is performed, the extracted results must be interpreted considering the indicators or risk factors defined for the pattern. Finally, this information is displayed to the rest of the platform users.

5 Conclusion

The main contribution of this thesis would be to provide a solution that facilitates the monitoring of patients with early or moderate cognitive decline, or who may have any other type of problem that could lead to progressive cognitive decline through the use of an AI-Driven model and the integration of IoT and IoMT devices. It would provide healthcare professionals and specialists with information on the progression of each aging person over time, facilitating prioritization according to any signs of deterioration they may present and the adaptation of any interventions that may be carried out. By proposing possible improvements, the architecture could be extended to the rest of the population, not just limited to use by aging people. In this way, any person could be monitored, tracking the evolution of personal parameters and allowing for effective monitoring.

Acknowledgments. This work has been partially funded by the European Union 'Next Generation EU/PRTR', by the Ministry of Science, Innovation and Universities (PDC2025-165096-C31). It also has the support of the ATHENA project (PID2024-155693NB-C41), funded by MICIU/AEI/10.13039/501100011033; and 85% co-funded by the European Union, European Regional Development Fund, and the Regional Government of Extremadura. Managing Authority: Ministry of Finance, Grant GR24099; and by the Operational Programme of the European Regional Development Fund (ERDF) of Extremadura, Grant EE25021.

References

1. Ali, H.: AI in neurodegenerative disease research: early detection, cognitive decline prediction, and brain imaging biomarker identification. Int. J. Eng. Technol. Res. Manag. **6**(10), 71 (2022). https://doi.org/10.5281/zenodo.14890442
2. Almarashdeh, I., et al.: Real-time elderly healthcare monitoring expert system using wireless sensor network (2019). arXiv:1908.03518
3. Botto, R., Callai, N., Cermelli, A., Causarano, L., Rainero, I.: Anxiety and depression in Alzheimer's disease: a systematic review of pathogenetic mechanisms and relation to cognitive decline. Neurol. Sci. **43**(7), 4107–4124 (2022). https://doi.org/10.1007/s10072-022-06068-x
4. Deary, I.J., et al.: Age-associated cognitive decline. Br. Med. Bull. **92**(1), 135–152 (2009). https://doi.org/10.1093/bmb/ldp033
5. Flores-Martin, D., Laso, S., Berrocal, J., Canal, C., Murillo, J.M.: Allowing IoT devices collaboration to help elderly in their daily lives. In: García-Alonso, J., Fonseca, C. (eds.) IWoG 2019. CCIS, vol. 1185, pp. 111–122. Springer, Cham (2020). https://doi.org/10.1007/978-3-030-41494-8_11

6. Goes, M., et al.: The quality of life of older individuals following the world health organization assessment criteria. Geriatrics **5**(4), 102 (2020). https://doi.org/10.3390/geriatrics5040102
7. Gorelova, A., Meliá, S., Gadzhimusieva, D., Parichenko, A.: Applying discrete event simulation on patient flow scenarios with health monitoring systems. In: International Conference on Web Engineering, pp. 101–108. Springer (2023). https://doi.org/10.1007/978-3-031-34444-2_8
8. Hevner, A.R., March, S.T., Park, J., Ram, S.: Design science in information systems research. Manag. Inf. Syst. Q. **28**(1), 6 (2008). https://aisel.aisnet.org/misq/vol28/iss1/6/
9. Jesús-Azabal, M., Mariano, L., García-Alonso, J., Galán-Jiménez, J.: Distributed sustainable IoT architecture for detecting loneliness in isolated rural areas. In: García-Alonso, J., Fonseca, C. (eds.) IWoG 2021. LNB, pp. 42–54. Springer, Cham (2022). https://doi.org/10.1007/978-3-030-97524-1_5
10. Laso, S., Berrocal, J., García-Alonso, J., Canal, C., Manuel Murillo, J.: Human microservices: a framework for turning humans into service providers. Softw. Pract. Exp. **51**(9), 1910–1935 (2021)
11. Mäkitalo, N., Flores-Martin, D., Berrocal, J., Murillo, J.M., Mikkonen, T.: Human data model: an approach for IoT applications development for elderly healthcare. In: García-Alonso, J., Fonseca, C. (eds.) IWoG 2020. LNB, pp. 111–120. Springer, Cham (2021). https://doi.org/10.1007/978-3-030-72567-9_11
12. Pacholko, A.G., Iadecola, C.: Hypertension, neurodegeneration, and cognitive decline. Hypertension **81**, 991–1007 (2024). https://api.semanticscholar.org/CorpusID:268083842
13. Parfenov, V.A., Zakharov, V.V., Kabaeva, A.R., Vakhnina, N.V.: Subjective cognitive decline as a predictor of future cognitive decline: a systematic review. Dementia Neuropsychologia **14**(03), 248–257 (2020). https://doi.org/10.1590/1980-57642020dn14-030007
14. Park, H.L., O'Connell, J.E., Thomson, R.G.: A systematic review of cognitive decline in the general elderly population. Int. J. Geriatr. Psychiatry **18**(12), 1121–1134 (2003). https://doi.org/10.1002/gps.1023
15. Steffens, D.C., et al.: Perspectives on depression, mild cognitive impairment, and cognitive decline. Arch. Gen. Psychiatry **63**(2), 130–138 (2006). https://doi.org/10.1001/archpsyc.63.2.130
16. Vo, J., Sharif, N., Hassan, G.M.: MNA-Net: multimodal neuroimaging attention-based architecture for cognitive decline prediction. In: PRIME@MICCAI (2024). https://api.semanticscholar.org/CorpusID:273706212
17. Vu Nguyen Hai, D., Gaedke, M.: Applying predictive analytics on research information to enhance funding discovery and strengthen collaboration in project proposals. In: Brambilla, M., Chbeir, R., Frasincar, F., Manolescu, I. (eds.) ICWE 2021. LNCS, vol. 12706, pp. 490–495. Springer, Cham (2021). https://doi.org/10.1007/978-3-030-74296-6_37

A Web Engineering Method for AI-Assisted Knowledge Graph Construction in Industrial Domains

Maheshika Hansamalee Walpola(✉), Sheeba Samuel, and Martin Gaedke

Chemnitz University of Technology, Chemnitz, Germany
{maheshika.walpola,sheeba.samuel,martin.gaedke}@informatik.tu-chemnitz.de

Abstract. Predictive maintenance systems rely on machine learning (ML) to anticipate equipment failures, but domain engineers often cannot explain why a prediction was made, limiting trust and adoption. Knowledge graphs (KGs) can connect predictions with structured domain knowledge, but building industrial KGs requires semantic web expertise domain engineers lack. This proposal addresses three problems: ML predictions lack human-readable explanations, KG construction has no reproducible method with formal validation, and no web-based approach enables non-technical users to build and query KGs. The proposed Web Engineering method integrates large language model (LLM) assistance across the KG lifecycle, from ontology elicitation and data validation to natural language querying and explanation generation. The method is realised through a web portal following End-User Development (EUD) principles, enabling domain engineers to construct ontologies, ingest data, query the KG, and inspect prediction explanations. Evaluation uses CMP semiconductor manufacturing, with a second use case planned in wind turbine monitoring.

Keywords: Knowledge Graphs · Web Engineering · AI Prediction Explanation · Ontology Engineering · Predictive Maintenance · End-User Development · Industry 5.0

1 Introduction

Predictive maintenance systems powered by machine learning (ML) can detect early signs of equipment failure from sensor data [1], and KGs can make those predictions traceable by linking them to structured domain knowledge [2,3], though building such systems for industrial use remains an open challenge [5].

Industry 5.0 calls for human-centred manufacturing where domain engineers, such as process and maintenance engineers, not only IT specialists, take part in shaping AI-driven processes [13]. At present, no method enables these engineers to construct and use knowledge structures independently. This PhD proposal presents a Web Engineering method because web-based delivery requires no software installation, reaches any device through a browser, and enables guided

A. Mauri et al. (Eds.): ICWE 2026, LNCS 16625, pp. 282–288, 2026.
https://doi.org/10.1007/978-3-032-29372-5_26

workflows that shield users from underlying semantic technologies. The method uses AI-assisted ontology construction, SHACL-based validation (Shapes Constraint Language, a W3C standard for validating RDF data) defined collaboratively by knowledge engineers and domain experts, and a web portal that enables domain engineers to construct, query, and obtain explanations from industrial KGs through a browser.

1.1 Problem Statement and Motivation

Three problems limit the adoption of KG-based explanation systems in industrial predictive maintenance. **ML predictions are not interpretable for domain engineers.** When a predictive maintenance system warns that a machine is likely to fail, the engineer needs to understand *why* before acting [2]. Existing KG approaches can link predictions to process context [2], but are built by knowledge engineers rather than the domain experts who need them; vocabulary must be elicited through repeated interviews and iterative review cycles slow construction significantly. **Industrial KG construction lacks reproducible methods.** Building industrial KGs has typically taken months of specialised effort, and neither reproducible construction methods nor formal sensor data validation have been established [5]. Although LLMs can now assist across the KG construction lifecycle [12], existing LLM-assisted approaches [6,7] have not been applied in industrial sensor domains with formal quality checks, unlike rule-based tools which lack semantic inference. Industrial sensor data poses distinct challenges: process-specific terminology is sparse in general-purpose training corpora, sensor schemas impose strict datatype and unit constraints, and safety-critical contexts require formal validation rather than approximate extraction. **No web-based method exists for non-technical users.** Current KG tools, such as Protégé require knowledge of OWL, SPARQL, and RDF, which manufacturing and process engineers typically do not have [10]. To our knowledge, no existing work addresses all three problems within a single reproducible method combining LLM-assisted ontology construction, SHACL-enforced validation, and a web-based EUD portal.

1.2 Research Aims and Objectives

This research is guided by the following overarching question: *How should a Web Engineering method be designed to support AI-assisted construction, quality assurance, and explanation of industrial KGs within a single reproducible process accessible to domain engineers?*

The research addresses this gap through four objectives. **OBJ 1:** To develop and evaluate an LLM-assisted pipeline for industrial ontology construction, benchmarked against manual construction in coverage, correctness, and time. **OBJ 2:** To construct and validate RDF-based industrial KGs through automated sensor data mapping with SHACL constraints, measuring conformance rates on real sensor datasets. **OBJ 3:** To design and evaluate a web portal following EUD principles that enables domain engineers to perform all method stages and inspect prediction explanations through a browser. **OBJ 4:** To assess cross-domain generalisability by replicating the method in a structurally different industrial domain. The research is supported by the WiProFlex industry project[1], with CMP semiconductor manufacturing as the primary evaluation domain. A second case study in wind turbine condition monitoring will test generalisability. Wind turbines differ from CMP in sensor types, failure modes, and maintenance workflows, and an existing KG baseline (XAI4Wind [4]) allows direct comparison.

2 Related Work

Structured domain knowledge can ground ML outputs in human-understandable concepts [2], and a survey establishes that KGs can serve as explanation tools across ML systems [3]. In industrial maintenance, the XAI4Wind system demonstrated a multimodal KG for explainable wind turbine decision support [4], and a review examined KG applications across production environments [5]. These works demonstrate the value of KG-based explanations, but all required extensive manual effort by knowledge engineers, none presented a reusable construction method, and none evaluated explanation quality with domain experts.

A recent roadmap shows that LLMs can assist across the full KG construction lifecycle, including ontology engineering, knowledge extraction, graph completion, and question answering [12]. More specifically, LLM-assisted pipelines have produced ontologies with accuracy approaching that of human experts [6], and LLMs can perform ontology learning tasks such as term typing and taxonomy discovery [7]. These efforts focus on general knowledge engineering and have not been tested with SHACL-enforced validation or human-in-the-loop review in industrial sensor domains. A SHACL-based web-form generator has been shown to support KG editing by non-specialist users [8], though it does not cover ontology construction, LLM assistance, or ML prediction explanation.

End-User Development research investigates how people without programming skills can build and extend software systems [9]. Recent work on accelerating ontology engineering with LLMs indicates that these tasks still require significant expert labour and calls for approaches that lower the barrier for non-specialists [10], which motivates the portal design proposed here. Unlike existing LLM-assisted approaches, which target general-domain knowledge extraction without formal quality assurance, the method proposed here integrates SHACL-enforced validation and domain expert review at each stage.

3 Research Methodology

3.1 Overall Approach

The research follows Design Science Research [11] and produces a reusable method comprising four stages, visualised in Fig. 1 and linked to the objectives from Sect. 1.2.

[1] https://www.tu-chemnitz.de/wiproflex/index.html.en.

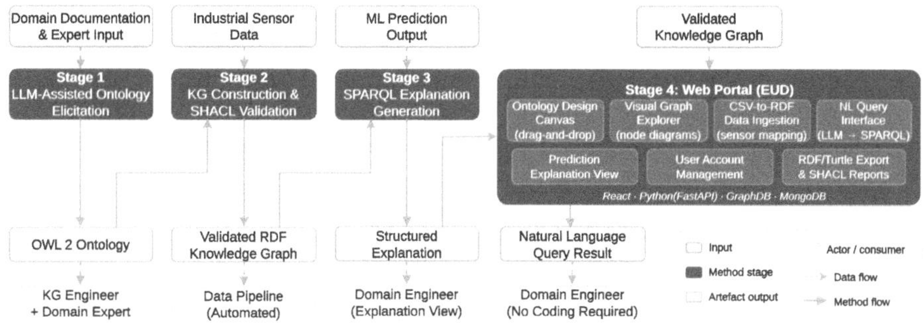

Fig. 1. Overview of the four-stage method.

As shown in Fig. 1, in the first stage (OBJ 1), the knowledge engineer and domain expert extract domain knowledge with LLM assistance. The knowledge engineer is involved once at setup to configure the LLM prompting environment and review the initial ontology structure; thereafter, domain engineers drive the process independently through the portal without requiring semantic web expertise. Documentation such as sensor manuals, equipment specifications, and maintenance logs is processed by the LLM using structured prompts that guide the extraction of OWL 2 class hierarchies, properties, and relationships. The LLM presents each proposed element in plain-language descriptions that the domain expert can accept or reject without requiring OWL expertise.

In the second stage (OBJ 2), the knowledge graph is constructed and validated. First, the knowledge engineer and domain expert define SHACL constraint sets that match the ontology from Stage 1. An automated pipeline then maps industrial sensor data to the OWL 2 classes defined in Stage 1 and stores the readings as RDF triples with provenance metadata, producing the KG, noting that column names are often ambiguous and standard ETL tools omit the provenance links RDF requires. Before the graph is used, SHACL validation checks for property violations, datatype mismatches, and missing values.

The third stage (OBJ 3) uses the validated knowledge graph to generate explanations for ML predictions. When the ML model flags a prediction, the system selects a parameterised SPARQL query template matching the prediction type (e.g., tool wear, slurry degradation) and retrieves a subgraph of related process steps, sensor readings, and failure patterns. The LLM then summarises the retrieved subgraph into a plain-language explanation grounded in the KG, ensuring the output reflects factual graph content rather than unconstrained generation.

The fourth stage brings all previous stages together in a web portal built on a component-based frontend, a REST API layer, and an RDF triplestore (see Fig. 1, Stage 4). Through a standard browser, practitioners can edit ontologies, ingest sensor data via CSV-to-RDF upload, query the graph using natural language, inspect prediction explanations, and explore the graph visually.

3.2 Evaluation Design

The primary evaluation uses CMP manufacturing data from the WiProFlex project, with real sensor data and direct access to domain engineers. For OBJ 1, a controlled experiment compares AI-assisted ontology construction against manual construction in Protégé, measuring time, coverage, and correctness. For OBJ 2, SHACL conformance rates are measured on the CMP sensor dataset. For OBJ 3, a usability study with domain engineers will evaluate the portal in terms of usability, trust, and overall user experience, combining qualitative and quantitative measures as appropriate. For OBJ 4, the method is replicated in the wind turbine domain and compared against XAI4Wind.

4 Preliminary Results

The core method components are under development and initial testing.

CMP Process Ontology (OBJ 1). A CMP Process Ontology (CMPO) is being constructed with domain experts and currently comprises 57 OWL 2 classes, 32 object properties, and 33 data properties covering process stages, sensor types, polishing parameters, slurry chemistry, wafer properties, and failure modes. A systematic literature review established that no dedicated CMP process ontology existed prior to this work.

RDF Pipeline and SHACL Validation (OBJ 2). A data pipeline currently maps 28 CMP sensor columns to CMPO classes and stores readings as RDF triples with provenance metadata. An initial SHACL validation run found violations in three property categories; these were resolved through schema alignment with the domain expert, bringing conformance to an acceptable level. Further constraint coverage is being extended as part of Phase 2.

KG Web Portal (OBJ 3). An early version of the portal supports the core method stages through a standard browser, including ontology editing, data ingestion, natural language querying, prediction explanation, and graph exploration.[2]

5 Research Plan and Contributions

Research Plan. Phase 1 (in progress, OBJ 1 & OBJ 3): literature review, CMPO construction, and portal development. Phase 2 (Q3 2026, OBJ 2): full SHACL coverage and explanation module. Phase 3 (Q1 2027, OBJ 1 & OBJ 3): usability study and controlled ontology construction experiment. Phase 4 (Q2 2027, OBJ 4): replication in wind turbine monitoring.

Contributions to Web Engineering. **(a)** A reusable Web Engineering method for AI-assisted industrial KG construction with documented stages,

[2] Portal prototype: https://github.com/MaheshikaWalpola/KGPortal.

roles, and artefacts; **(b)** a validated evaluation framework combining controlled experiments, SHACL-based quality metrics, and usability studies; **(c)** an EUD web portal enabling practitioners to construct, validate, query, and obtain explanations from industrial KGs; and **(d)** cross-domain empirical evidence from CMP and wind turbine domains. Method artefacts, prompt templates, and SHACL patterns are available in the project repository. The method connects ML-driven predictions and human understanding through the web, with results targeting Web Engineering and Semantic Web venues.

Acknowledgments. This work was funded by the European Social Fund Plus (ESF+) and by funding of the Free State of Saxony of the Federal Republic of Germany under grant number 100693458 (WiProFlex).

Disclosure of Interests. The authors have no competing interests to declare that are relevant to the content of this article.

References

1. Carvalho, T.P., et al.: A systematic literature review of machine learning methods applied to predictive maintenance. Comput. Ind. Eng. (2019). https://doi.org/10.1016/j.cie.2019.106024
2. Lécué, F.: On the role of knowledge graphs in explainable AI. Semant. Web. 41–51 (2020). https://doi.org/10.3233/SW-190374
3. Tiddi, I., et al.: Knowledge graphs as tools for explainable machine learning: a survey. Artif. Intell. (2022). https://doi.org/10.1016/j.artint.2021.103627
4. Chatterjee, J., et al.: XAI4Wind: a multimodal knowledge graph database for explainable decision support in operations & maintenance of wind turbines. arXiv preprint arXiv:2012.10489 (2020). https://doi.org/10.48550/arXiv.2012.10489
5. Buchgeher, G., et al.: Knowledge graphs in manufacturing and production: a systematic literature review. IEEE Access (2021). https://doi.org/10.1109/ACCESS.2021.3070395
6. Kommineni, V.K., et al.: From human experts to machines: an LLM supported approach to ontology and knowledge graph construction. arXiv preprint arXiv:2403.08345 (2024). https://doi.org/10.48550/arXiv.2403.08345
7. Giglou, H.B., et al.: LLMs4OL: large language models for ontology learning. In: Payne, T.R., et al. (eds.) ISWC 2023, pp. 408–427 (2023). https://doi.org/10.1007/978-3-031-47240-4_22
8. Wright, J., et al.: Schímatos: a SHACL-based web-form generator for knowledge graph editing. In: Pan, J.Z., et al. (eds.) ISWC 2020, pp. 65–80 (2020). https://doi.org/10.1007/978-3-030-62466-8_5
9. Fischer, G.: End-user development: empowering stakeholders with artificial intelligence, meta-design, and cultures of participation. In: IS-EUD 2021, pp. 1–16 (2021). https://doi.org/10.1007/978-3-030-79840-6_1
10. Shimizu, C., et al.: Accelerating knowledge graph and ontology engineering with large language models. J. Web Semant. (2025). https://doi.org/10.1016/j.websem.2025.100862
11. Hevner, A.R., et al.: Design science in information systems research. MIS Q. 75–105 (2004). https://doi.org/10.2307/25148625

12. Pan, S., et al.: Unifying large language models and knowledge graphs: a roadmap. IEEE Trans. Knowl. Data Eng. 3580–3599 (2024). https://doi.org/10.1109/TKDE.2024.3352100
13. Breque, M., et al.: Industry 5.0: towards a sustainable, human-centric and resilient European industry. Technical Report, European Commission (2021). https://doi.org/10.2777/308407

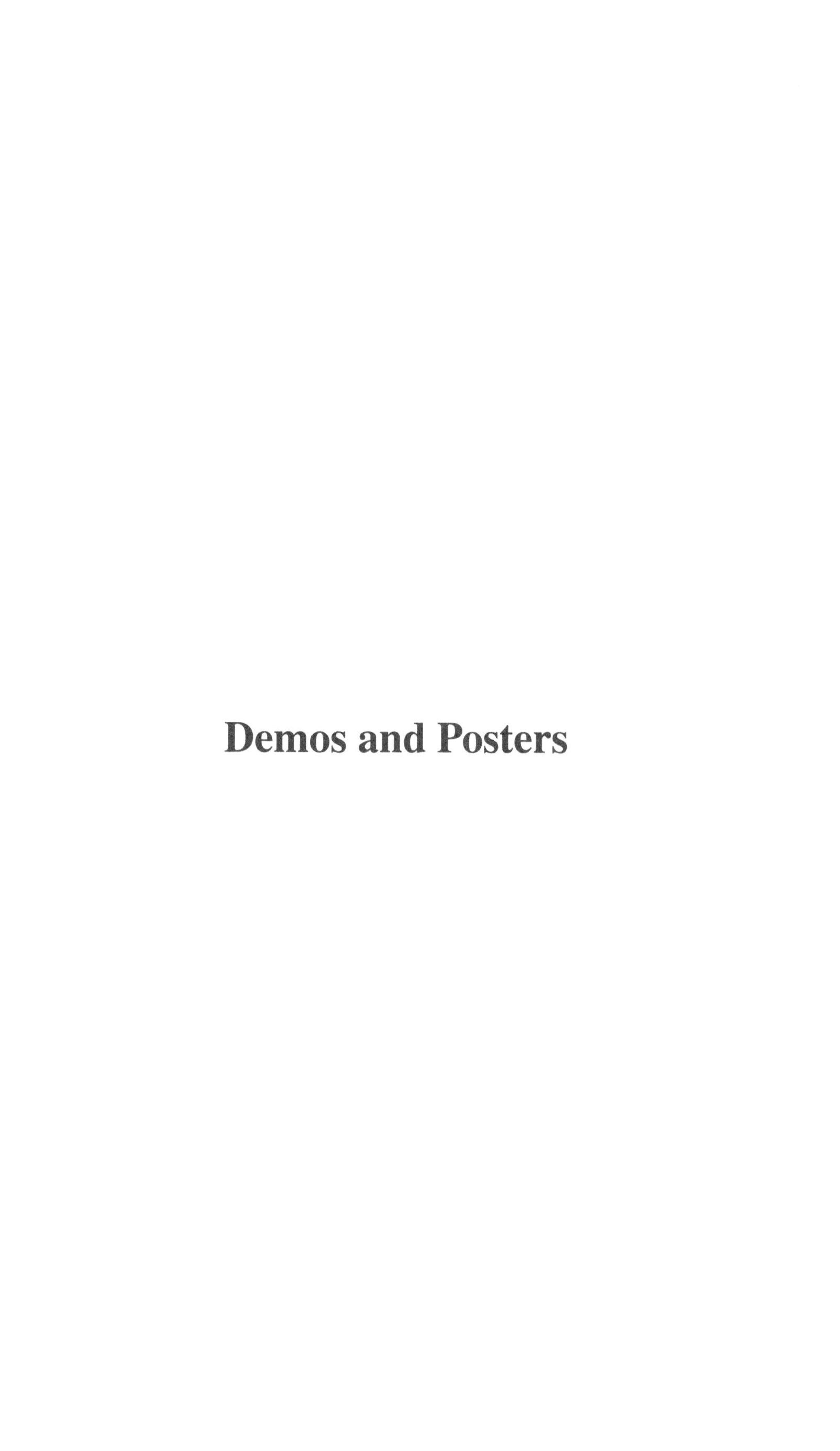

Demos and Posters

DynBench Generator: A Web-Based Platform for On-Demand KGQA Benchmark Creation

Aleksandr Gashkov[1(✉)], Maria Eltsova[1,2], and Andreas Both[1]

[1] Web and Software Engineering (WSE) Research Group, Leipzig University of Applied Sciences (HTWK Leipzig), Leipzig, Germany
alexander.gashkov@gmail.com
[2] CBZ München GmbH, Heilbronn, Germany

Abstract. Evaluating Knowledge Graph Question Answering (KGQA) systems is increasingly unreliable due to static benchmarks, evolving Knowledge Graphs (KG), and memorization effects in Large Language Models (LLM). We present DynBench Generator, a web frontend for automatically generating new KGQA benchmark datasets that both preserve the original question and query complexity and are resistant to LLM memorization. In this demo, we showcase an interactive platform that enables on-demand generation and inspection of memorization-resistant question-query pair for fair and reproducible KGQA evaluation.

Keywords: KGQA Benchmarks · Dataset Generator · LLM application

1 Introduction

Knowledge Graph Question Answering (KGQA) enables users to query Knowledge Graphs (KGs) using natural language (NL) by translating questions into SPARQL queries. KGQA systems rely heavily on benchmark datasets for development and evaluation. However, KGs evolve continuously while benchmarks *remain fixed* and gradually *become outdated* whereas their creation *requires extensive manual effort*. Recently appeared, Large Language Models (LLMs) are increasingly used in the field of KGQA and show strong performance across many NL processing tasks. As these models are adopted in both research and practice in KGQA, trustworthy evaluation becomes essential because benchmark scores are often used to compare approaches and guide system selection. At the same time, many public benchmarks are likely included in LLM training corpora, which creates *memorization effects* and can make evaluation scores reflect recall of seen examples (cf. [3]) rather than genuine generalization. *This all* makes the quality and freshness of benchmark datasets a central concern, especially in domains where models must generate formal queries from a NL. As a result, *KGQA datasets become unsuitable* as benchmarks since data encountered during training cannot be reused in testing or validation.

A. Mauri et al. (Eds.): ICWE 2026, LNCS 16625, pp. 291–295, 2026.
https://doi.org/10.1007/978-3-032-29372-5_27

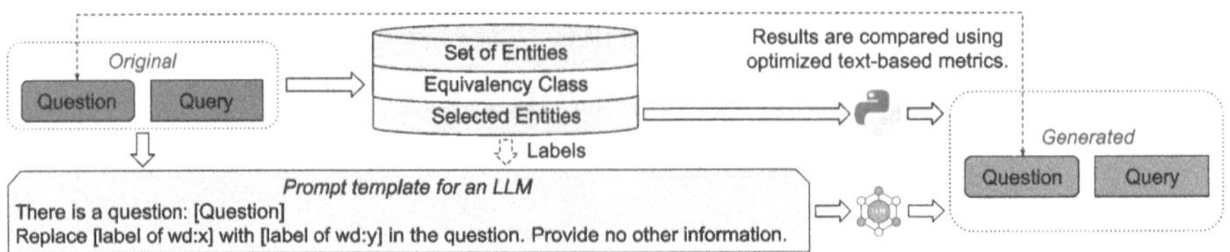

Fig. 1. DynBench's workflow.

DynBench addresses this problem – a fully automated framework that dynamically generates new KGQA benchmark datasets from existing ones while preserving linguistic and structural complexity [1,2]. Instead of manually crafting new datasets, DynBench produces semantically consistent questionâĂŞquery (QQ) pairs through controlled entity and property substitution within the same KG. We introduce the DynBench demonstrator enabling researchers to generate and validate new pairs for KGQA benchmarks interactively and gain insights.

2 DynBench Demonstrator

DynBench functions as a two-component system: (1) *Backend Service* (originally discussed in [2], cf. Fig. 1): FastAPI-based REST API that handles the core transformation logic and (2) *Frontend Application*: Streamlit-based web interface for interactive exploration and feedback collection when operating on existing KGQA datasets consisting of NL questions paired with SPARQL queries. The system extracts entities and relations from the SPARQL query, retrieves equivalent entities from the KG, rewrites the SPARQL query using a Python function *Replace*, updates the NL question using an LLM, and automatically validates the generated pair. Therefore, this pipeline enables the continuous creation of new benchmark versions without a manual annotation.

The central mechanism of DynBench is the construction of equivalence classes. For each entity in a query, DynBench retrieves alternatives from the KG that share the same semantic type using the Wikidata taxonomy, in particular, using the properties `instance of` (P31) and `subclass of` (P279).

By restricting replacements to entities with matching types, DynBench preserves semantic validity and prevents trivial or nonsensical substitutions. For example, the given question: *Was Sigmund Freud married?* might be transformed automatically into *Was Minna Planer married?*. The corresponding SPARQL query is transformed accordingly while maintaining structure and complexity.

DynBench introduces a back-transformation validation method. After the generated question is transformed back (i.e., to the question with the original entity), the original and back-transformed questions are compared while a similarity metric is computed. Among many tested metrics, the *Levenshtein distance* proved the most reliable, reaching up to 0.96 precision and showing the strongest correlation with human evaluation [1]. The DynBench approach was applied to two multilingual datasets: QALD-9-plus [4] and RuBQ 2.0 [5]. Human

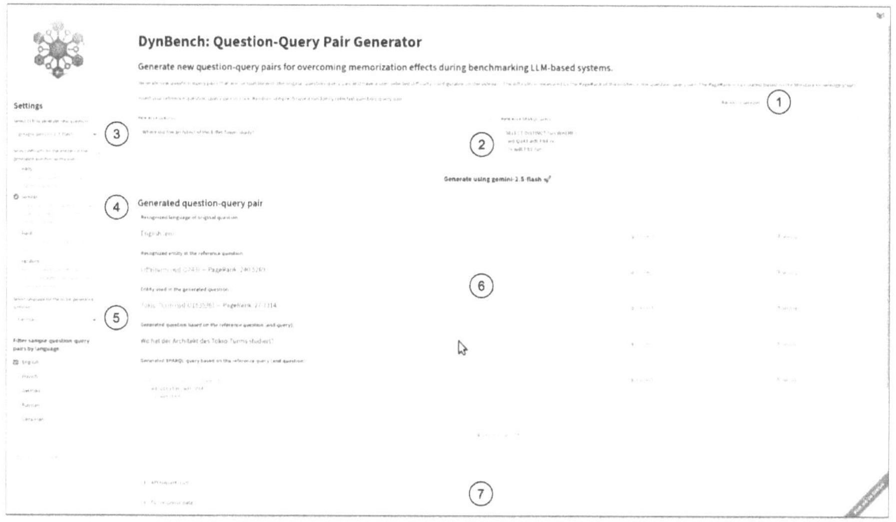

Fig. 2. DynBench UI (available at https://wse-research.org/dynbench/)

evaluation showed up to 92% correct transformations for QALD-9-plus and 98% for RuBQ 2.0[1]. These results demonstrate that DynBench can reliably produce high-quality, non-memorized benchmark datasets. However, in this demo, filtering or correcting the candidates is disabled; we leave it to the user to decide which results are correct (still available to the users in the UI).

3 Demo Experience

DynBench provides an intuitive web-based interface for generating semantically equivalent QQ pairs with configurable difficulty levels. Users can use a QQ pair ① (cf. Fig. 2) from the predefined set (we used the well-known benchmark from [4]) or freely enter a SPARQL query and thereafter generate a new QQ pair ② from the given data. To enable users to customize the generated data, they can configure the to-be-used LLM ③; what kind of type-equivalent entities should be retrieved from Wikidata and be used in the generated question ④; the selection defines how well-known the picked entity should be, e.g., having a "similar" PageRank implies that the selected entity is as well-known as the one in the original question; hence, the question should have similar difficulty ("easy", "hard", "random" have a corresponding meaning). The demonstrator also enables cross-language QQ pair generation, where ⑤ shows the currently 20 supported target language options. Additionally, the UI integrates feedback options ⑥ for the most important aspect of the transformation process (question, query, used entities). Finally, additional information is shown to provide knowledge about

[1] Evaluation data is available at https://anonymous.4open.science/r/robust-benchmark-generator-8660.

the integrated API to help users automate their process and, for the sake of transparency, also shows all additional data from the backend process ⑦ (e.g., the Levenshtein distance). The DynBench demonstrator is provided as an MIT-licensed open-source web application[2].

4 Conclusion and Future Work

This paper addresses a crucial problem in the field of AI-driven systems: How to trust a model when benchmark datasets are also publicly available. We present the DynBench Demonstrator, which is able to interactively generate multilingual, scalable, repeatable, and memorization-resistant datasets by preserving both the NL surface forms and the structural complexity of the original SPARQL queries from a given KGQA benchmark. Our demonstrator enables users to configure the transformation to match their domain-specific aspects regarding the comparability and multilinguality. Additionally, multiple feedback functionalities are integrated to enable domain-specific self-optimization of the generator in future work. This is particularly important for researchers and practitioners who need new benchmark instances that are not already known to modern LLMs while still remaining comparable to established benchmarks in terms of linguistic formulation and query complexity. Such comparability is essential for fair evaluation because it allows the community to reduce memorization effects without fragmenting the benchmarking landscape. Beyond dataset generation itself, the system also supports process automation through its easy-to-use API, whose functionality is directly exposed in the frontend. This makes DynBench not only a research prototype but also a practical tool that can be integrated into evaluation workflows for on-demand benchmark generation and validation.

Looking forward, we target further multilingual expansion to both high- and low-resource languages. Moreover, we are going to refine the multi-entity and relation substitution that requires the mechanisms to reduce semantic drift and handle more complex question-query pairs.

References

1. Gashkov, A., Perevalov, A., Eltsova, M., Both, A.: Automated robust dynamic generation of KGQA benchmark datasets. In: ICSC. IEEE (2026)
2. Gashkov, A., Perevalov, A., Eltsova, M., Both, A.: Towards dynamically generated KGQA benchmark datasets for memorization-resistant evaluations. In: Knowledge Graphs and Semantic Web, pp. 25–40. Springer (2026)
3. Gashkov, A., Perevalov, A., Eltsova, M., Both, A.: SPARQL query generation with LLMs: measuring the impact of training data memorization and knowledge injection. In: Web Engineering: 25th International Conference, ICWE 2025 (2025)

[2] https://github.com/WSE-research/DynBench-Frontend/.

4. Perevalov, A., Diefenbach, D., Usbeck, R., Both, A.: QALD-9-plus: a multilingual dataset for question answering over DBpedia and wikidata translated by native speakers. In: International Conference Semantic Computing (ICSC), pp. 229–234 (2022)
5. Rybin, I., Korablinov, V., Efimov, P., Braslavski, P.: RuBQ 2.0: an innovated Russian question answering dataset. In: ESWC, pp. 532–547 (2021)

AugmentAble: Teaming Web Augmentation and LLMs for Instant Accessibility Improvements

Sarah Mayrhofer(✉), Stefan Klikovits, and Manuel Wimmer

Johannes Kepler University, Linz, Austria
k12126245@students.jku.at, {stefan.klikovits,manuel.wimmer}@jku.at

Abstract. Various reports reveal that Web Accessibility remains one of the major concerns that still requires additional awareness. In addition to providing development support in IDEs for creating Web pages, post-development support can also be provided by using Web augmentation techniques. However, the scripts for augmenting Web pages to improve such aspects must currently be developed manually and may require continuous adaptation to the evolving Web sites. In this work, we tackle these challenges by integrating LLMs into the Web augmentation process to improve accessibility concerns on the client side. In particular, our approach first performs an LLM-based accessibility evaluation of Web pages, and based on this feedback, the LLM is instrumented to resolve reported issues.

Keywords: Web Accessibility · Web Augmentation · LLMs

1 Introduction

Web accessibility remains a persistent challenge in modern Web engineering. Despite established guidelines such as the Web Content Accessibility Guidelines (WCAG) [9], many Web sites still exhibit issues such as missing alternative texts, insufficient contrast, and unlabeled form elements [8]. These problems significantly affect users who rely on assistive technologies (such as screen readers) and persist even in professionally developed systems.

Existing approaches primarily focus on improving accessibility during development, e.g., through IDE support, static analyzers, or testing tools. However, these solutions require access to the source code. In contrast, Web augmentation enables runtime modifications of Web pages directly in the browser. Prior work has demonstrated that such techniques can improve accessibility [3–5]. Nevertheless, traditional augmentation scripts must be manually developed and continuously maintained as Web pages evolve.

Recent advances in Large Language Models (LLMs) enable automated reasoning over HTML structures and contextual content, including the generation

A. Mauri et al. (Eds.): ICWE 2026, LNCS 16625, pp. 296–300, 2026.
https://doi.org/10.1007/978-3-032-29372-5_28

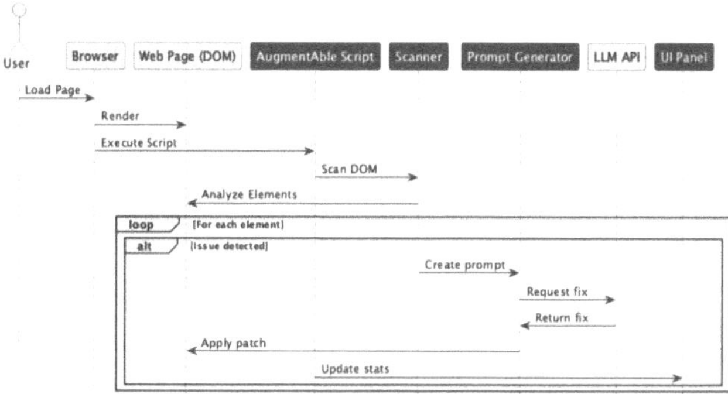

Fig. 1. AugmentAble remediation process overview, showing the interaction between the AugmentAble script logic, DOM, and LLM.

of semantic descriptions and accessibility annotations. This creates new opportunities to dynamically generate accessibility improvements during runtime. Correcting HTML during development is often insufficient, as many Web sites integrate third-party content, legacy systems, and dynamic Document Object Model (DOM) trees, such that the final page state is only known at runtime. Our approach overcomes this by treating a Web page as a "black box", ensuring accessibility even when the original source code is inaccessible or unchangeable [7].

In this work, we present *AugmentAble*, a browser-based Web augmentation tool that leverages LLMs to automatically detect and repair accessibility issues at runtime. The system analyzes the DOM, generates context-aware fixes via an LLM, and applies them directly within the browser without modifying the underlying Web application source code.

Our approach extends the recent applications of LLMs for improving the accessibility of Web pages. *AccessGuru* [1], for instance, employs LLMs to detect and repair syntactic, semantic, and layout violations in Web pages during development. Similarly, [6] evaluates the use of ChatGPT for the automatic fixing of non-accessible Web sites and [2] presents a modular framework to improve the accessibility of static sites and Angular single-page applications.

In contrast to existing approaches, AugmentAble focuses on the accessibility improvements in the client-side browser, such that it can be applied without the Web page developer/owner's involvement. In particular, our work contributes (*i*) an LLM-based methodology for automated accessibility improvement of existing Web pages; and (*ii*) an openly available proof-of-concept implementation.

2 Approach

The proposed approach, AugmentAble[1], follows a non-invasive Web augmentation strategy to improve accessibility at runtime. It operates as a client-side Web

[1] Vibe-coded proof-of-concept: https://doi.org/10.5281/zenodo.19558289.

augmentation script using the TamperMonkey browser plugin, which intercepts the DOM and alters it without requiring access to the application's sources.

As displayed in AugmentAble's interaction process (Fig. 1), the operation pipeline is initiated after the page is rendered in the browser.

To minimize latency, the system employs a two-layered fix strategy. A Heuristic Layer performs immediate, rule-based checks and corrections for common WCAG violations, such as enforcing contrast ratios and injecting metadata-based ARIA attributes (`Analyze Elements` phase).

Elements requiring contextual reasoning, e.g., images lacking alt-text, are handled by a second layer. This pipeline transmits detected violations to external Multimodal LLMs (e.g., Qwen-VL, Aya-Vision) for semantic description generation (cf. Fig. 1, `LLM API`). The generated fix is then applied as a DOM patch.

All structural or semantic DOM modifications are dynamically applied in real-time. To maintain transparency, the system includes an Audit Interface in the UI panel (`UI Panel`). This categorization allows users to validate the improvements. The Audit Interface also logs structural violations, e.g., non-sequential heading hierarchies.

Fig. 2. AugmentAble application. Colored boxes highlight enhanced elements.

3 Demonstration

Figure 2 presents the application of AugmentAble on Web pages with common accessibility issues. Typical improvements include images without alternative text, interactive elements lacking descriptive labels, and form inputs without associated annotations. Our system detects such issues, generates fixes using the LLM, and applies them in real time. Figure 2 shows the "after"-view (below), with colored boxes indicating accessibility enhancements.

The resulting improvements enable assistive technologies, such as screen readers, to better interpret the content. All applied fixes are visualized through the interface panel, which summarizes detected issues and applied modifications, allowing for a transparent audit of the LLM's interventions.

We point the reader to https://www.youtube.com/watch?v=Tqp58vtmrV4 for a video demonstration of AugmentAble.

4 Discussion and Future Work

Our work on AugmentAble describes a novel approach to the enhancement of accessibility in Web browsers using client-side techniques. Our current state of research builds on public LLMs hosted on HuggingFace. We note that in the current state, no information is cached, and therefore, the LLM has to be repeatedly consulted on every page visit. As future work, we therefore plan to introduce a caching mechanism that allows the application of accessibility fixes without the need to re-trigger the LLM queries.

Moreover, we aim to extend our work in several ways: First, as accessibility is a highly sensitive topic, we aim to explore the integration of locally hosted LLMs (e.g., via Ollama), ensuring that sensitive data never leaves the user's machine, by comparing AugmentAble's performance across different model sizes.

Further, at the moment, AugmentAble generically executes all possible accessibility augmentations. Since accessibility is, however, a highly individual aspect, we plan to implement user-centric profiles which allow users to customize AugmentAble to their specific needs, such as adjusting individual contrast preferences, focus-indicator styles, or keyboard navigation (tab order). This will transition AugmentAble from a general one-size-fits-all tool to a personalized accessibility assistant that adapts any Web site to each user's requirements.

Finally, to evaluate the impact and suitability of AugmentAble for the needs of our tool's target audience, we will perform an extensive usability evaluation.

Acknowledgments. We thank the Blindenverein Oberösterreich and the JKU Institute for Integrational Studies for their enthusiastic cooperation.

References

1. Fathallah, N., Hernández, D., Staab, S.: AccessGuru: leveraging LLMs to detect and correct web accessibility violations in HTML Code. In: Proceedings of the Computers and Accessibility. ASSETS, ACM (2025). https://doi.org/10.1145/3663547.3746360
2. Fernández-Navarro, C., Chicano, F.: Automated LLM-based accessibility remediation: from conventional websites to angular single-page applications (2026). https://arxiv.org/abs/2602.17887
3. Firmenich, S., Garrido, A., Paternò, F., Rossi, G.: User interface adaptation for accessibility. In: Yesilada, Y., Harper, S. (eds.) Web Accessibility. HIS, pp. 547–568. Springer, London (2019). https://doi.org/10.1007/978-1-4471-7440-0_29
4. Garrido, A., Rossi, G., Medina-Medina, N., Grigera, J., Firmenich, S.: Improving accessibility of web interfaces: refactoring to the rescue. Univers. Access Inf. Soc. **13**(4), 387–399 (2014). https://doi.org/10.1007/S10209-013-0323-2
5. González-Mora, C., Garrigós, I., Casteleyn, S., Firmenich, S.: Augmenting websites with voice commands: an approach focused on accessibility. J. Web Eng. **24**(2), 163–198 (2025). https://doi.org/10.13052/JWE1540-9589.2421
6. Othman, A., others Amira Dhouib, Al Jabor, A.N.: Fostering websites accessibility: a case study on the use of the large language models ChatGPT for automatic remediation. In: PETRA. ACM (2023). https://doi.org/10.1145/3594806.3596542

7. Paternò, F., Vinci, M., Manca, M., Iannuzzi, N.: How an LLM can improve automatic web accessibility validation? In: 16th Biannual Conf. of the Italian SIGCHI Chapter, ACM (2025). https://doi.org/10.1145/3750069.3750310
8. WebAIM: the WebAIM million: the 2025 report on the accessibility of the top 1,000,000 home pages (2025). https://webaim.org/projects/million/
9. World Wide Web Consortium (W3C): Web Content Accessibility Guidelines (WCAG) 2.2 (2024). https://www.w3.org/TR/WCAG22/

SmartScrape: A Neuro-Symbolic Web Information Extraction

Ganjali Imanov(✉) and Radek Burget

Faculty of Information Technology, Brno University of Technology, Božetěchova 2, 61200 Brno, Czechia
{iimanov,burgetr}@fit.vut.cz

Abstract. We introduce SmartScrape, a neuro-symbolic framework for extracting structured information from the web. The task addressed is to extract records that follow a predefined schema from semi-structured sources, such as product web pages. The system integrates a Graph Neural Network (GNN) that scores content elements with an Integer Linear Programming (ILP) constraint solver, which guarantees schema consistency, uniqueness, and additional logical and presentation constraints. We illustrate the method on a basic (product, price) extraction scenario. The implemented system outputs visual proof-carrying justifications, supports drift detection using the stability metric $\sigma(P)$, and we also include an ablation study contrasting ILP-based and greedy reasoning modes. On a set of 100 pages, SmartScrape attains 97% field-level accuracy with no constraint violations.

Keywords: Web information extraction · GNN · ILP · Constraint solving · Drift detection · FitLayout

1 Introduction

Web information extraction (WIE) supports applications such as price monitoring and large-scale data collection from web pages. We address structured record extraction, where exactly one value must be assigned to each field of a target schema (e.g., `title, price`). Unlike flat node classification, valid outputs must satisfy global structural constraints.

We propose SmartScrape, a neuro-symbolic method combining GNN node scoring with Integer Linear Programming (ILP) inference that globally optimises field assignments under schema, layout, and format constraints. Integrated with FitLayout [1], SmartScrape produces constraint-valid, proof-carrying extraction records.

2 Related Work

Early wrapper induction systems, such as *Stalker* and *IEPAD*, inferred extraction rules directly from the HTML structure. While highly accurate on known

A. Mauri et al. (Eds.): ICWE 2026, LNCS 16625, pp. 301–305, 2026.
https://doi.org/10.1007/978-3-032-29372-5_29

templates, these wrappers were brittle: even minor DOM changes could invalidate the learned rules. To improve robustness, later work adopted machine learning approaches that treat extraction as node classification over document representations derived from the DOM. Recent state-of-the-art methods employ Graph Neural Networks (GNNs) to model structural relationships between nodes [5], and in some cases incorporate visual layout information [3]. More recently, transformer-based models have also been applied for representing web documents [2,4].

While these models improve generalization, they typically predict fields independently for each node, which can lead to structurally inconsistent data records. SmartScrape complements such approaches by introducing a constraint-guided inference layer: neural models provide node-level scores, and an Integer Linear Programming (ILP) solver selects field assignments that maximize these scores while enforcing schema, layout, and format constraints.

3 System Overview

The SmartScrape pipeline comprises five phases. Figure 1 illustrates the data flow, showing the input and output of each stage.

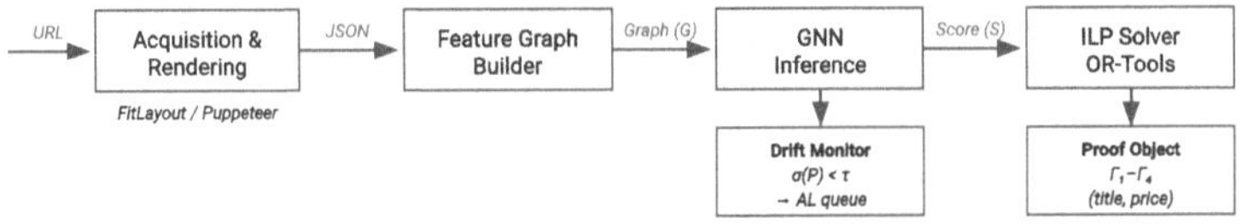

Fig. 1. SmartScrape pipeline. Boxes show processing stages. The Drift Monitor runs in parallel on every page and feeds uncertain pages into an active-learning queue.

Acquisition and Rendering. FitLayout renders the target URL in headless Chromium via Puppeteer and returns a JSON layout model containing precise bounding boxes, reading order, and segmentation blocks for all DOM nodes. *Input:* URL. *Output:* JSON layout model.

Feature Graph Builder. Each DOM node is encoded into a 147-dimensional feature vector: a 128-dim character n-gram hash (text semantics), a 4-dim normalized bounding box (visual geometry), and a 15-dim one-hot tag embedding. A heterogeneous graph is constructed by adding KNN edges ($k = 3$) based on vertical position proximity. *Input:* JSON layout model. *Output:* attributed graph G.

GNN Inference. A two-layer Graph Convolutional Network (GCN, hidden dimensions $64 \rightarrow 32$) produces per-node class probabilities over {price, title, other}. Heuristic priors (currency-pattern match, y-zone indicator, stop-word list) are injected into the score matrix before the ILP stage. *Input:* graph G. *Output:* score matrix $S \in [0, 1]^{N \times 3}$.

Constraint Solver (ILP). OR-Tools SCIP solves the integer program

$$\max \sum_{i,f} s(i,f) \cdot x_i^f \quad \text{subject to constraints } \Gamma \tag{1}$$

where $x_i^f \in \{0,1\}$ indicates whether node i is assigned to field f. A greedy fallback (select the highest-scoring node per field, independently) is available as an ablation baseline. *Input:* score matrix S. *Output:* binary assignment + proof object.

Drift Monitor. The stability metric $\sigma(P)$ measures the average GNN margin gap across all nodes on page P:

$$\sigma(P) = \overline{|p_1(n) - p_2(n)|}_{n \in P} \tag{2}$$

where $p_1(n)$ and $p_2(n)$ are the top-two class probabilities for node n. A high margin gap indicates that the model is confident; a low $\sigma(P)$ signals that the GNN is uncertain about the page layout, which typically happens after template drift Δ. Pages with $\sigma(P) < \tau = 0.6$ are automatically queued for active-learning re-annotation, without any human trigger. *Input:* score matrix S. *Output:* drift flag + annotation queue entry.

4 Example Formal Constraints

Table 1. Active constraint set Γ enforced by the ILP solver.

ID	Constraint
Γ_1	**Uniqueness:** $\sum_i x[i, \text{Price}] \leq 1$; $\sum_i x[i, \text{Title}] \leq 1$
Γ_2	**Footer trap:** $y(n) > 0.8 \times \text{PageHeight} \Rightarrow x[n, \text{Title}] = x[n, \text{Price}] = 0$
Γ_3	**Product zone:** $y(n) > 500\,\text{px} \Rightarrow x[n, \text{Title}] = x[n, \text{Price}] = 0$
Γ_4	**Format:** $x[n, \text{Price}] = 1 \Rightarrow \text{HasCurrency}(n) \wedge \text{IsNumeric}(n)$

Table 2. Ablation study: ILP vs. Greedy on 30 held-out pages.

Method	Title Acc.	Price Acc.	Both Correct	Violations
Greedy (no Γ)	83%	80%	77%	4
SmartScrape ILP (Γ)	**97%**	**97%**	**93%**	**0**

The constraint set Γ enforces four properties on every extracted record. The constraint used in our sample application of (title, price) pair extraction are formally listed in Table 1. They combine logical and presentation constraints to be considered: Γ_1 *Uniqueness:* A product record has one title and one price. Γ_2 *Footer trap:* Nodes whose vertical center exceeds $0.8 \times \text{PageHeight}$ are classified as footer nodes and excluded from assignment. The threshold 0.8 was determined empirically. Γ_3 *Product zone:* On the target site, the main product block lies within the first 450–480 px of the rendered page. This threshold is site-specific and is exposed as a configurable parameter. Γ_4 *Format:* A node is only mapped to Price if it both matches the currency-symbol regular expression and includes at least one numeric token.

In the implemented SmartScrape framework, each extracted record is accompanied by a proof object listing the active constraints and their status, enabling downstream auditing without re-running the pipeline.

5 Evaluation and Conclusions

We implemented SmartScrape in Python using PyTorch for GNN implementation and Google OR-Tools for implementing the LP solver. Our implementation is available at GitHub[1] and it also includes an annotation tool.

For preliminary evaluation, we manually annotated 100 product pages from a fictional online bookstore[2]. The GNN was trained for 100 epochs on 40 pages with early stopping on a validation set of 11 pages, reaching validation accuracy of 98.8%. Table 2 reports field-level accuracy on 30 held-out pages under two reasoning modes. The ILP solver improves both accuracy (+14 pp title, +17 pp price) and eliminates all constraint violations versus the greedy baseline. The $\sigma(P)$ metric correctly flags low-confidence pages for re-annotation.

SmartScrape shows that augmenting GNN-based web extraction with an ILP inference layer and formal constraints improves the reliability of structured record extraction while preserving low latency. By combining learned node representations with constraint-guided optimization, the system produces schema-consistent extraction results without ad-hoc post-processing.

Future work will extend the evaluation to additional extraction domains and explore retrieval-augmented LLM validation to handle ambiguous or previously unseen page structures.

Acknowledgements. This work was supported by the project Application of advanced techniques for cybersecurity and efficient processing of heterogeneous data, FIT-S-26-9019, funded by Brno University of Technology.

References

1. Burget, R.: Scraping data from web pages using SPARQL queries. In: Web Engineering, pp. 293–300. Springer Nature Switzerland, Cham (2023)

[1] https://github.com/Ganjali717/smart_scrape.
[2] https://books.toscrape.com/.

2. Deng, X., Shiralkar, P., Lockard, C., Huang, B., Sun, H.: DOM-LM: Learning generalizable representations for HTML documents, (2022). arXiv:2201.10608 arXiv preprint
3. Hotti, A., Risuleo, R.S., Magureanu, S., Moradi, A., Lagergren, J.: Graph neural networks for nomination and representation learning of web elements, (2021)
4. Li, J., Xu, Y., Cui, L., Wei, F.: MarkupLM: Pre-training of text and markup language for visually-rich document understanding. In: Proceedings of ACL, pp. 5043–5051. (2022)
5. Lin, B.Y., Sheng, Y., Vo, N., Tata, S.: FreeDOM: A transferable neural architecture for structured information extraction on web documents. In: KDD '20. p. 1092–1102. ACM, New York, NY, USA (2020)

AISA: A Web-Based Platform for Evaluating the Literature Search Capabilities of LLMs

Abbas Rahimi(✉), Manuel Wimmer, and Michael Gusenbauer

Johannes Kepler University, Linz, Austria
{abbas.rahimi,manuel.wimmer,michael.gusenbauer}@jku.at

Abstract. The huge amount of academic data is challenging for research processes, but a rigorous review of prior studies remains a must for scientific progress. While Large Language Models (LLMs) are seen in several studies as potential help, it is evident that they have limitations, including the generation of fake references and misclassifications of research. Existing ways to test LLMs, such as manual checks or text comparisons, are tedious and costly. Therefore, automation support to systematically assess them for this particular context is needed.

To shed more light on this area, this paper presents a methodology and a Web-based platform for assessing LLM-based literature search. The methodology starts by using human-composed systematic literature reviews (SLRs) as a benchmark. The platform provides search prompt templates, sends instantiations of them to LLMs, and then systematically validates if the generated references actually exist in authoritative databases. Subsequently, the platform compares the LLM's findings with the set of included studies in the benchmark SLRs we use as ground truth. We specifically measure three metrics: how often LLMs generate fake references (existence check), how relevant the reported papers are compared to the ground truth (precision), and how well the LLMs have found all the important papers (recall). Ultimately, this work provides a flexible methodology, a practical platform, and reliable benchmarks to determine the current status of LLMs for academic literature search.

Keywords: Literature search · Large language model · Testing

1 Introduction

Given the sheer volume of scientific discoveries, SLRs have become indispensable for synthesizing evidence. However, the overwhelming labor involved in traditional SLRs has prompted the academic world to investigate LLMs as a means to automate literature search. While LLMs offer automation potential, they suffer from hallucinations which generate so-called ghost references [1]. Studies show a hallucination rate of 30–50% in the medical domain [2]. Current evaluation relies on unscalable manual checks or flawed metrics such as basic

A. Mauri et al. (Eds.): ICWE 2026, LNCS 16625, pp. 306–310, 2026.
https://doi.org/10.1007/978-3-032-29372-5_30

accuracy, which ignore the high scientific cost of "Lost Evidence" [3]. Moreover, they may produce different results each time they are run, making it hard to achieve consistent, reproducible outcomes, which is essential in SLRs.

To address this need, we have developed the AI Search Audit (AISA) methodology, which allows for complete automation of checking LLM-generated references against authoritative databases and human-composed seed SLRs.

2 AISA Approach

The methodology is conceptually grounded in information retrieval evaluation protocols and is operationalized through a Web-based platform.

2.1 Assessment Methodology

Testing an LLM's ability to conduct literature surveys requires an objective, verifiable standard. Our evaluation methodology achieves this through a structured, five-step process:

1. **Data Preparation and Establishing Ground Truth:** The process begins by identifying seed SLRs. These are high-quality SLRs from various academic fields that have clear search methodologies and precisely defined lists of included studies. The latter serves as our Ground Truth (GT).
2. **Standardized Prompting:** Adaptable prompt templates are constructed to embed the research questions and the specific inclusion/exclusion criteria derived from the seed SLRs. The target LLMs are explicitly instructed to return their retrieved references in a structured format.
3. **Existence Check:** To efficiently identify fabricated references, AISA automatically analyzes the output generated by the LLMs and checks each reference against authoritative bibliographic databases. This verification process confirms the existence of the DOI, matches titles to DOIs, and validates author lists to classify each reference as either verified real or hallucinated.
4. **Relevance Check:** Next, the verified real papers are compared against the human-curated GT. A multi-tier matching method is employed to identify matches.
5. **Metric Calculation:** In the final step, we evaluate the LLM's retrieval performance by using well-established metrics to assess the level of correctness and completeness.

2.2 AISA Platform (Tooling)

To execute the presented methodology at scale, we implemented AISA as a Web-based platform. The system architecture separates workflow management, AI orchestration, and data persistence into distinct engineering modules (Fig. 1):

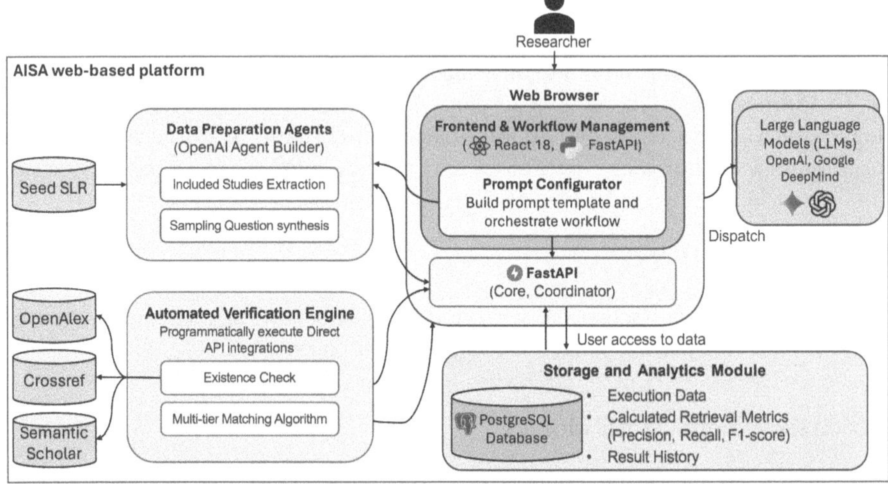

Fig. 1. AISA Platform Architecture

1. **Frontend and Workflow Management:** We developed the front-end using React 18 and the underlying system that manages the execution workflow via FastAPI. This provides researchers with a convenient Prompt Configurator. It is designed to simplify the preparation of prompts and the submission of requests to LLMs.
2. **Data Preparation Agents:** The extraction of seed SLRs' sampling scope is automated by the OpenAI Agent Builder. To make sure the generated sampling scope accurately reflected the original SRL, we leveraged the powerful text-summarization abilities of LLMs [4] and used a precise, carefully designed structured prompt. Finally, we empirically confirmed the semantic accuracy of the output through human-in-the-loop expert validation.
3. **Automated Verification Engine:** Our backend system performs existence validation checks by connecting to authoritative databases such as OpenAlex and Crossref. This module also checks the relevance to the ground truth using a multi-tier relevance matching algorithm.
4. **Storage and Analytics Module:** All information from the executions, including metrics such as precision and recall, along with result histories, is managed by the FastAPI backend. This data is finally stored in a database.

3 Demonstration

For demonstration, we will present the AISA Web application, which comprises a modular Python architecture. We plan the following demonstration workflow:

- **Setting Up the Input:** We present selected cases of SLRs across computer science, medicine, and social sciences. We plan to showcase how different LLMs are evaluated using our standardized prompt templates.
- **Execution:** We will proceed with running API requests to the selected LLMs for the generation of potential bibliographies expressed in JSON format.
- **Verification:** We will demonstrate how the Verification Engine automatically checks the generated reference list against authoritative literature databases and distinguishes between fabricated ghost references and actual, verifiable publications.
- **Result Dashboard:** Finally, the dashboard will illustrate the key evaluation metrics such as existence checks (measuring errors in reference existence), precision (assessing the relevance of identified papers against the GT), and recall (indicating how many relevant papers have been found).

4 Conclusion and Future Work

AISA is a Web-based tool that offers researchers an automated and scalable way to assess how well LLM models generate correct and relevant references in the context of systematic literature searching. In a preliminary trial on 55 different LLM-based literature search tools involving 275 runs of a social science SLR, our tool detected "ghost references" by identifying 90.8% of the 11,583 generated citations as valid. Notably, the LLMs' ability to discover relevant citations was much weaker, with a relevance precision of only 11.4% and a recall rate of 7.6%.

There are several future research lines to be investigated. We plan an evaluation of AISA by including a larger number of LLM-based literature search systems with a larger set of seed SLRs from different scientific disciplines. Additionally, to mitigate the effect of the "stochastic" nature of LLMs, we intend to repeat the runs several times. Furthermore, we plan to integrate further metrics to the platform, such as the Weighted Matthews Correlation Coefficient (WMCC) to provide a metric that is robust on imbalanced datasets as suggested in [3].

Acknowledgements. This work is partially funded by the Linz Institute of Technology (LIT), the State of Upper Austria, and the Federal Ministry of Education, Science and Research.

References

1. Suppadungsuk, S., et al.: Examining the validity of ChatGPT in identifying relevant nephrology literature: findings and implications. J. Clin. Med. **12**(17), 5550 (2023). https://doi.org/10.3390/jcm12175550
2. Chelli, M., et al.: Hallucination rates and reference accuracy of ChatGPT and bard for systematic reviews: comparative analysis. J. Med. Internet Res. **26**, e53164 (2024). https://doi.org/10.2196/53164

3. Madeyski, L., Kitchenham, B., Shepperd, M.: LLM4SCREENLIT: recommendations on assessing the performance of large language models for screening literature in systematic reviews. arXiv preprint arXiv:2511.12635 (2025)
4. Glickman, M., Zhang, Y.: AI and generative AI for research discovery and summarization. Harvard Data Sci. Rev. **6**(2) (2024). https://doi.org/10.1162/99608f92.7f9220ff

GNN-Based Token Reduction for LLM Semantic Element Detection in E-Commerce Product Pages

Hamza Salem(✉) and Radek Burget

Faculty of Information Technology, Brno University of Technology, Božetěchova 2, 61200 Brno, Czechia
{xsalem00,burgetr}@fit.vut.cz

Abstract. Applying Large Language Models (LLMs) to whole-page semantic element detection in e-commerce is prohibitively expensive: typical product pages contain hundreds to thousands of DOM elements, and LLM costs scale linearly with input tokens. We propose a hybrid approach that uses a Graph Neural Network (GraphSAGE) as a pre-filter to reduce the candidate set before LLM processing. Our preliminary results on the Klarna Product Page Dataset show approximately **90% reduction** in elements sent to the LLM (from hundreds to 5–10 per page) while maintaining **94.5% nomination accuracy**. This position paper presents the core idea, motivates the token-saving focus, and reports preliminary results to solicit feedback before thorough experimental evaluation in an extended journal submission.

Keywords: Graph Neural Networks · Large Language Models · Token Reduction · Semantic Element Detection · E-Commerce · Web Automation

1 Introduction

Semantic element detection in e-commerce product pages—identifying titles, prices, cart buttons, images, and similar elements—is essential for web automation, price monitoring, and autonomous shopping assistants. Large Language Models (LLMs) excel at semantic understanding and can classify such elements from their text and context. However, processing entire web pages with LLMs faces a fundamental cost barrier: **token consumption**. Commercial LLM APIs charge per token, and a typical e-commerce page can have 500–4,000 DOM elements. Sending full page content or even per-element HTML to an LLM becomes expensive at scale.

Graph Neural Networks (GNNs) offer a complementary strength: they efficiently operate on graph-structured data and can reason over spatial and structural relationships without token-based costs. Web pages naturally form graphs through DOM hierarchy and spatial layout. The key insight of our approach

A. Mauri et al. (Eds.): ICWE 2026, LNCS 16625, pp. 311–314, 2026.
https://doi.org/10.1007/978-3-032-29372-5_31

is to **combine both**: use a GNN to filter elements down to a small candidate set, then apply an LLM only to those candidates for fine-grained classification. This achieves semantic accuracy while **saving tokens**. Under tight API budgets, that matters for large-scale monitoring, catalog comparison, and agentic checkout (e.g., nominating only title, price, and "add to cart" avoids LLM calls over hundreds of irrelevant nodes).

This paper presents our preliminary work on this token-saving angle and seeks community feedback; a journal submission will give full methodology and experiments.

2 Related Work and Motivation

A comprehensive survey by Zhu et al. [1] reviews how LLMs are applied across IR components: query rewriters, retrievers, rerankers, readers, and search agents. These methods typically feed documents or passages directly to LLMs for relevance judgment, summarization, or answer generation—often without pre-filtering to reduce input size. The survey notes that LLM-based rerankers and readers face efficiency challenges due to large model parameters and API costs; retrievers require fast response while LLMs incur high latency. Our setting—semantic element detection on e-commerce pages—shares these concerns: pages contain hundreds to thousands of elements, and processing all of them with an LLM would be prohibitively expensive.

The Klarna Product Page Dataset [2] benchmarks web element nomination using GNNs and LLMs. Their GCN-Mean+GPT-4 pipeline achieves strong accuracy by passing top-10 candidates per class to GPT-4 for final nomination. However, they do not emphasize token savings or cost analysis. In contrast, some approaches apply LLMs directly to web content without pre-filtering: Sancheti et al. [3] use ChatGPT for end-to-end web profile extraction, feeding web content to the LLM for Named Entity Extraction and revalidation. Such "brute force" usage incurs high token costs when processing many elements.

Our contribution is to explicitly frame the hybrid GNN-LLM architecture as a **token-saving strategy**: the GNN stage reduces the number of elements that ever reach the LLM, directly lowering token consumption and cost.

3 Approach

3.1 Two-Stage Hybrid Architecture

We use a two-stage pipeline:

Stage 1 (GNN Filtering): A GraphSAGE model performs *binary* classification on each page element: important vs. unimportant. Elements predicted as important form the candidate set. We build spatial-relational graphs (emphasizing visual layout over pure DOM hierarchy) and use 23 multi-modal features (position, size, text, visual properties). GraphSAGE's inductive learning enables generalization to unseen page layouts. *Implementation (summary):* three layers, mean aggregation [4], width 128, Adam with class-weighted loss, minibatches, merchant-level train/test split.

Stage 2 (LLM Classification): Only the candidates (typically 5–10 per page) are passed to an open-source LLM for fine-grained classification into semantic categories: Title, Price, Add to Cart, Cart, Image.

The GNN thus acts as a **token-saving filter**: instead of sending hundreds of elements to the LLM, we send only the small subset that the GNN deems important.

3.2 Token-Saving Mechanism

Let n be the number of elements on a page. Without filtering, an LLM-based approach would need to process $O(n)$ elements. With our GNN filter, we process only $k \ll n$ candidates. On the Klarna dataset, n ranges from hundreds to thousands per page, while k is typically 5–10. This yields roughly 90% reduction in the number of elements (and thus tokens) sent to the LLM.

4 Preliminary Results

We evaluate on a subset of 1,000 pages from the Klarna Product Page Dataset. Table 1 summarizes our preliminary findings.

Table 1. Preliminary results on Klarna Product Page Dataset (1,000 pages).

Metric	Value
Baselines (Klarna et al.)	
GCN-Mean nomination accuracy	∼78–81%
GCN-Mean+GPT-4 nomination accuracy	∼95%
Our approach	
GNN binary classification accuracy	95.4%
Nomination accuracy (GNN + LLM)	94.5%
Reduction in elements sent to LLM	∼90%
Typical candidates per page	5–10

Our 94.5% nomination accuracy is close to Klarna et al.'s GCN-Mean+GPT-4 (∼95%) while using open-source LLMs; the ∼90% cut in elements processed as LLM input lowers tokens and, at typical pay-per-token rates, cost roughly in proportion (e.g., ∼10 vs. 500+ elements per page).

Limitations. These are preliminary results. We have not yet conducted rigorous ablation studies, full cross-validation, or detailed token/cost analysis. A comprehensive evaluation is planned for the journal submission.

5 Discussion and Future Work

We propose the hybrid GNN-LLM architecture as a practical approach to semantic element detection that addresses LLM cost and token limitations. The token-saving angle is our main differentiator from prior work.

Feedback Sought. We welcome views on the token-saving framing, experiments that would most strengthen the work, and applications (e.g., agents, accessibility).

Future Work. We will pursue stronger token/cost evaluation, baselines beyond our current filter, integration with agentic stacks (e.g., MCP), and finer-grained GNN outputs (multi-class or multi-label heads) that could further cut LLM use compared with binary pre-filtering alone.

6 Conclusion

We presented a hybrid GNN-LLM approach for semantic element detection, with a specific focus on **saving tokens** by using a GraphSAGE model to pre-filter page elements before LLM classification. Preliminary results show 90% reduction in LLM processing while maintaining 94.5% nomination accuracy. We invite feedback to refine the approach before a more comprehensive journal submission.

Acknowledgements. This work was supported by the project Application of advanced techniques for cybersecurity and efficient processing of heterogeneous data, FIT-S-26-9019, funded by Brno University of Technology.

References

1. Zhu, Y., Yuan, H., Wang, S., et al.: Large language models for information retrieval: a survey. ACM Trans. Inf. Syst. **44**(1), 54 (2025). Art. 12. https://doi.org/10.1145/3748304
2. Hotti, A.: The Klarna Product Page Dataset: Web Element Nomination with Graph Neural Networks and Large Language Models (2023). arXiv preprint arXiv:2111.02168
3. Sancheti, P., Karlapalem, K., Vemuri, K.: LLM driven web profile extraction for identical names. In: Companion Proceedings ACM Web Conference 2024 (WWW 2024), pp. 1616–1625. ACM (2024). https://doi.org/10.1145/3589335.3651946
4. Hamilton, W.L., Ying, R., Leskovec, J.: Inductive representation learning on large graphs. In: NeurIPS, pp. 1025–1035 (2017)
5. Wu, Z., et al.: A comprehensive survey on graph neural networks. IEEE Trans. Neural Netw. Learn. Syst. **32**(1), 4–24 (2021)
6. Zhou, J., et al.: Graph neural networks: a review of methods and applications. AI Open **1**, 57–81 (2020)
7. Kipf, T.N., Welling, M.: Semi-supervised classification with graph convolutional networks. In: ICLR (2017)

Low-Code and No-Code with BESSER to Create and Deploy Smart Web Applications

Iván Alfonso[1(✉)], Armen Sulejmani[1], Aaron Conrardy[1,2], and Jordi Cabot[1,2]

[1] Luxembourg Institute of Science and Technology, Esch-sur-Alzette, Luxembourg
{ivan.alfonso,armen.sulejmani,aaron.conrardy,jordi.cabot}@list.lu
[2] University of Luxembourg, Esch-sur-Alzette, Luxembourg

Abstract. The increasing demand for web applications containing AI-agents, seen as smart web applications, has prompted the need for new techniques to facilitate their creation. Low-code has risen as an approach that reduces the amount of handwritten code by focusing on the abstraction of components in the form of models combined with automated generators to produce applications. Existing low-code platforms are commercial, leading to drawbacks such as the risk of vendor lock-in, limited extensibility, and more. We present the open-source BESSER low-code framework, which allows users to design, generate and deploy their application via a freely accessible web-based editor, while guaranteeing transparency and extensibility.

1 Introduction

The increasing demand for better software in recent years has created a need for advanced strategies to improve developer productivity. Low-code development, the latest reincarnation of model-driven engineering approaches, addresses this demand but introduces challenges related to the growing complexity of modern software requirements, such as AI-powered agents. Low-code development platforms (LCDPs) aim to accelerate software development by relying on high-level models and automated code generation, reducing manual programming effort.

However, while these platforms are effective for building conventional applications and even improved their support for smart components, the most popular and complete ones are usually the commercial ones [1]. This leads to drawbacks such as limited support for interoperability, vendor lock-in, limited choice for technological stack for external components or deployment, limited to no extensibility, and limited to no access to generated code.

On the other hand, applying model-driven approaches supported by graphical notations to the development of web and mobile user interfaces (UIs) is nothing new. Languages such as IFML [3], OOWS [4], or UWE [5] are often seen as foundational for the development of traditional UIs. Yet, these do not cover the definition of smart components, and provide limited or fragmented tool support for the complete creation and deployment pipeline.

A. Mauri et al. (Eds.): ICWE 2026, LNCS 16625, pp. 315–319, 2026.
https://doi.org/10.1007/978-3-032-29372-5_32

In this paper, we present a demo of the open-source low-code platform BESSER [2], which aims to address the challenges described above. Specifically, BESSER offers a freely available web-based modeling editor[1] for design and deployment of smart web applications following a low-code and no-code approach.

2 Demonstration

Figure 1 presents the part of BESSER's pipeline for developing smart web applications used in the demonstration. The demonstration contains the example of a web application of a library, with a conversational agent responding to frequently asked questions. During the demo, this scenario is specified through three models: a class diagram, a graphical user interface (GUI), and an agent model. These models are provided as a template on the BESSER platform (https://editor.besser-pearl.org), allowing attendees to load them and then generate and deploy the application. The only additional requirement to complete the demo is a free account on GitHub[2] and Render[3], the former being used for hosting the models and generated code, and the latter for running frontend and backend servers. A video demonstration of the presented scenario is available[4].

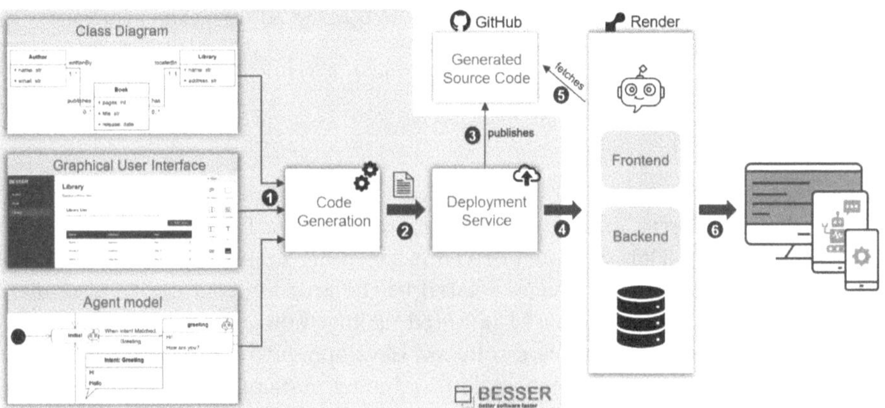

Fig. 1. BESSER pipeline for smart web applications

[1] https://github.com/BESSER-PEARL.
[2] https://github.com/.
[3] https://render.com/.
[4] https://besser.readthedocs.io/en/latest/examples/smart_web.html.

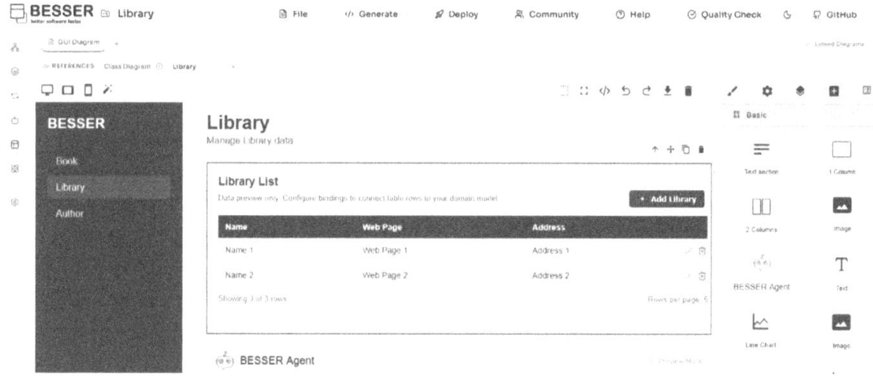

Fig. 2. GUI editor in BESSER

3 Modeling, Generating and Deploying Smart Web Applications with BESSER

BESSER provides the B-UML (BESSER-UML) language, which enables the modeling of smart web applications via three complementary but still interrelated perspectives: *structural*, *agent*, and *GUI* perspectives.

The **structural** perspective specifies the static aspects of the web application through class diagrams, including classes, attributes, methods, relationships, and other elements, reusing core UML [6] concepts for this perspective while extending and simplifying selected aspects of the specification for smart web applications. For example, meta-attributes such as `description`, `URI`, and `icon` are added to classes to capture platform-specific information. The **agent** perspective enables explicit modeling of autonomous agents using an extended state-machine language. Agents are defined in terms of states, transitions, intents, and actions executed in each state. These actions may include textual responses (e.g., for chat interactions), calls to Python methods (e.g., to invoke external APIs), or operations driven by Large Language Model (LLM) outputs, combining the controlled output from state machines with the openness of LLMs.

From the **GUI** perspective, the editor provides a no-code interface that allows users to drag and drop UI components onto a blank page (Fig. 2), which are immediately rendered. The designed page is internally parsed into the GUI part of B-UML, inspired by IFML [3] and extended with constructs for rich view components (e.g., charts and chat interfaces) and styling properties (e.g., colors and layout). The GUI can link to the structural and agent models, consolidating all models into a smart web application.

The generation pipeline orchestrates specialized sub-generators, each responsible for a distinct technology layer, producing a deployment-ready project from the modeled smart web application.

The **backend generator** transforms the structural model into three interconnected Python modules: *Pydantic classes* for data validation, *SQLAlchemy* *models* for database schema and ORM, and a *FastAPI REST API* exposing comprehensive CRUD endpoints for all entities and relationships. The **frontend generator** interprets the GUI model to produce a React-based application with TypeScript. View components are mapped to React components including data tables, interactive forms, method invocation buttons, and chart visualizations. When an **agent model** is provided, **BESSER**'s **Agentic Framework (BAF) generator** generates the agent backend as executable Python scripts. The generated backend exposes a WebSocket endpoint, and the frontend embeds a chat widget that connects to this service to exchange messages and display responses.

BESSER streamlines cloud deployment by integrating with GitHub and Render for one-click deployment. Users authenticate via GitHub OAuth and trigger deployment from the editor. The backend generates the application, creates a GitHub repository, and pushes the codebase with a `render.yaml` configuration defining free-tier services: FastAPI backend, React frontend, and optional agent service. Render automatically detects this configuration, provisions services, installs dependencies, and deploys all components. The platform provides live URLs with SSL certificates and manages cold-start behavior. This workflow enables users to go from model edits to a publicly accessible web application typically within a few minutes with no manual infrastructure configuration.

4 Conclusion

In this paper, we showcase how BESSER enables the design, generation and deployment of a smart web application following a low-code / no-code approach through a web-based editor. We described the architecture and components relevant to the demonstration, chosen to enable extensibility. The generated code can be deployed as is or act as a prototype that can be manually extended. For the future, we plan to explore how perspectives can be integrated within the creation of smart web applications, such as the integration of personalization via user profiles or recommendation components using neural networks.

Acknowledgement. This work is supported by the Luxembourg National Research Fund (FNR) PEARL program, grant agreement 16544475.

References

1. Alfonso, I., Conrardy, A., Cabot, J.: Towards the interoperability of low-code platforms. In: Intelligent Information Systems, pp. 3–11. Springer Nature Switzerland, Cham (2025)
2. Alfonso, I., et al.: Building BESSER: an open-source low-code platform. In: International Conference on Business Process Modeling, Development and Support, pp. 203–212. Springer (2024)
3. Brambilla, M., Fraternali, P.: Interaction Flow Modeling Language: Model-Driven UI Engineering of Web and Mobile Apps with IFML. Morgan Kaufmann (2014)

4. Fons, J., Pelechano, V., Pastor, O., Valderas, P., Torres, V.: Applying the Oows model-driven approach for developing web applications. The internet movie database case study, pp. 65–108. Springer (2008)
5. Hennicker, R., Koch, N.: A UML-based methodology for hypermedia design. In: Evans, A., Kent, S., Selic, B. (eds.) UML 2000. LNCS, vol. 1939, pp. 410–424. Springer, Heidelberg (2000). https://doi.org/10.1007/3-540-40011-7_30
6. Object Management Group: OMG unified modeling language (OMG UML), version 2.5.1 (2017). Object Management Group (OMG) Standard

Implementing Liquid Software with WebAssembly

Henri Kärkkäinen(✉), Viljami Järvinen, Pyry Kotilainen, and Tommi Mikkonen

University of Jyväskylä, Jyväskylä, Finland
{henri.k.karkkainen,viljami.a.e.jarvinen,pyry.kotilainen, tommi.j.mikkonen}@jyu.fi

Abstract. In this paper, we introduce a demonstration of a prototype orchestration system utilizing a WebAssembly interpreter that allows the creation of snapshots of the WebAssembly modules under execution. With this, a liquid software IoT system is achieved, where software and their runtime environments can flow from one device to another. The demonstration hardware consists of two Raspberry Pi IoT devices and a computer acting as the orchestrator. The audience can interact with the orchestrator through a web interface to deploy different software configurations to the devices, pause and resume module execution, or move the snapshot to another device and resume execution, as well as observe the program flow from device to device.

Keywords: WebAssembly · Internet of Things · IoT · Liquid Software · Snapshot

1 Introduction

Liquid software refers to an approach in which applications and data can flow seamlessly from one device to another [3,9]. Such applications can take full advantage of the computing, storage, and communication resources available on all devices owned by the end user. Liquid software has the ability to flow from one device to another following user's attention and usage context. Liquid software may also help resolve a typical multi device ownership issue in which the user becomes bound to the device and software of a certain manufacturer [4].

In this demo, we aim to demonstrate how snapshots of WebAssembly (Wasm) modules can be used to move state and execution of programs from one device to another using an example system of a couple of IoT devices and an orchestrator. The project is available as a GitHub repository, which contains the web interface, the orchestrator, and the supervisor capable of taking snapshots of the Wasm modules. [2].

A. Mauri et al. (Eds.): ICWE 2026, LNCS 16625, pp. 320–324, 2026.
https://doi.org/10.1007/978-3-032-29372-5_33

2 Background and Motivation

Wasm has been studied as an enabling technology for software isomorphism and liquid software [5]. Isomorphic programs can be executed on a heterogeneous set of devices without the need to make changes to the program [3]. In previous work, a liquid IoT system has been developed in which the orchestrator can deploy Wasm modules for execution to different node devices of the system, presented in ICWE 2024 [6].

Although the system can deploy Wasm modules on different node devices of the system, the execution of programs cannot flow from one device to another without a full restart in the new environment. The motivation behind our revised system is to enable full software liquidity where programs and their state can flow from one device to another, being able to continue from where the execution stopped at the previous environment. This is accomplished by the use of snapshots that save the state of the Wasm module's runtime environment, which required expanding the capabilities of existing Wasm interpreters. Compared to existing techniques, which usually save the state of the operating system or user process, our Wasm interpreter saves only the state of the Wasm module's runtime environment. This has the benefit of being less dependent on the underlying software and hardware that is used in the liquid IoT system.

A Wain Wasm interpreter [8] was modified using design science research as a method to create and implement an artifact in a masters thesis study. [7]. The main goal of the study was to find out if freezing and saving the state of a Wasm module is possible. As a result of the study, it was found that it is possible to take a snapshot of the Wasm module in execution and move the execution to another device using the created snapshot. The creation of a snapshot and resuming execution were found to be fast operations, both causing only a minor regression to the interpreter's performance. Performance was evaluated by benchmarking the changes against the original interpreter, including measurements in the liquid software context of snapshot size and overhead during migration between devices [7].

3 System Overview

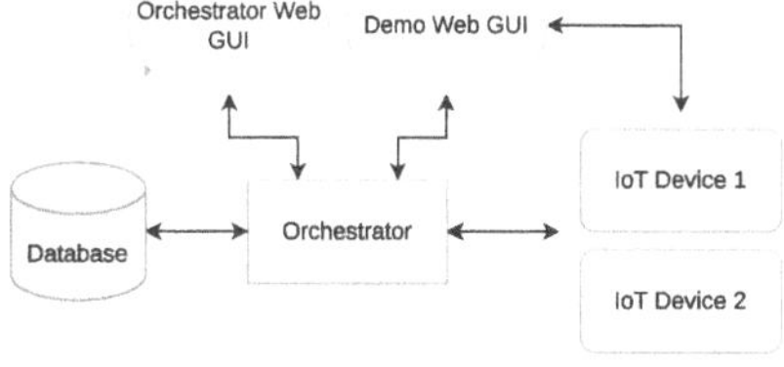

Fig. 1. Demo system diagram.

The system consists of an orchestrator and a variable number of heterogeneous node devices in the same local area network, shown in Fig. 1. The user or another system that interacts with our system can control the system through the orchestrator. The orchestrator can deploy Wasm modules to the devices and change these configurations. The supervisor can be used on the node devices to execute Wasm modules. The supervisor communicates with the orchestrator and uses our modified Wasm interpreter to run the Wasm modules. If a snapshot is requested, the supervisor can communicate with the Wasm interpreter to stop the execution and ask for the bytes of the created snapshot.

To implement snapshot functionality and the ability to resume the execution of a Wasm module from a snapshot, the Wasm interpreter used with the supervisor was changed from Wasmtime [1] to a modified version of Wain [8]. Saving Wasm module's state to a snapshot was made possible by observing a signal to take a snapshot between instructions and by serializing the contents of the Wasm module's runtime into a buffer if a snapshot was signaled. The buffer is shared between the interpreter and the supervisor threads. The runtime was extended by additional fields that store information about the number of instructions executed in the module and its function bodies.

4 Demo Setup and Experience

The aim is to demonstrate the system's ability to relocate execution of Wasm modules along with their execution state from one device to another using Wasm module snapshots. The demonstration allows the audience to use the orchestration system to move the execution of Wasm modules and their state between devices and to observe how the software flows and adapts in the system. The demo system consists of two Raspberry Pi computers acting as IoT devices and a laptop acting as the orchestrator, all connected to the same local area network.

A special Web GUI was developed for the demonstration that enables the control of snapshots and moving execution from device to device, as well as observing the execution. This GUI is also run by the laptop.

During the demonstration, the audience can interact with the system through the web GUI and change the execution environment of the Wasm modules to observe how software flows between devices. The GUI offers the following functionality:

- Execute WebAssembly modules on the devices
- Visually follow the progress and state of the WebAssembly module
- Take a snapshot of the WebAssembly module and its state
- Resume execution from snapshot on a desired device and follow its progress and state

Figure 2 shows the demo web GUI in a simplified use case. The output windows of both IoT devices, their log output, and the drop down menus to select the applications to deploy are displayed. At the bottom are buttons to deploy and run the application, and to take snapshots. The figure presents the results of the deployment of a program that visualizes the mandelbrot fractal. The Wasm module of the program is first in execution on device 1. Then, a snapshot is taken and the execution is moved to device 2 which completes the execution of the Wasm module. The intermediate and final results of the task will be shown to the audience in the GUI.

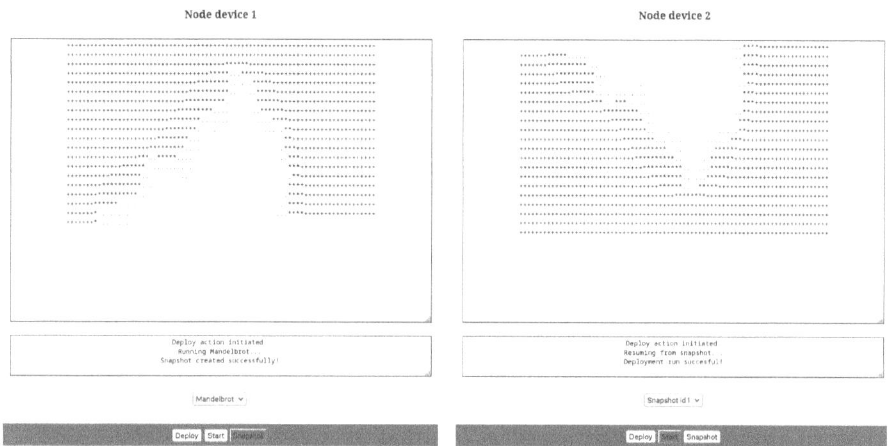

Fig. 2. Web GUI depicting results of a program flow between devices.

References

1. Bytecode alliance: Wasmtime. https://wasmtime.dev/. Accessed 12 Mar 2026
2. Demo code repository: https://github.com/LiquidAI-project/ICWE-2026. Accessed 08 Apr 2026
3. Gallidabino, A., et al.: On the architecture of liquid software: technology alternatives and design space. In: Institute of Electrical and Electronics Engineers Inc. **13**(Proceedings - 2016 13th Working IEEE/IFIP Conference on Software Architecture, WICSA 2016), pp. 122–127 (2016). https://doi.org/10.1109/WICSA.2016.14
4. Gallidabino, A., et al.: architecting liquid software. J. Web Eng. **16**(5–6), 433–470 (2017). https://journals.riverpublishers.com/index.php/JWE/article/view/3271
5. Kotilainen, P.: Orchestrating Isomorphic IoT Systems. Ph.D. thesis, University of Jyväskylä (2025)
6. Kotilainen, P., Järvinen, V., Autto, T., Rathnayaka, L., Mikkonen, T.: Demonstrating liquid software in iot using webassembly. In: Stefanidis, K., Systä, K., Matera, M., Heil, S., Kondylakis, H., Quintarelli, E. (eds.) Web Engineering, pp. 381–384. Springer Nature Switzerland, Cham (2024)
7. Kärkkäinen, H.: Liquid Software -paradigman tukeminen tilannekuvat mahdollistavalla WebAssembly-tulkilla. Master's thesis, University of Jyväskylä (2026)
8. Rhysd: Wain. https://github.com/rhysd/wain. Accessed 12 Mar 2026

9. Taivalsaari, A., Mikkonen, T., Systä, K.: Liquid software manifesto: the era of multiple device ownership and its implications for software architecture. In: Proceedings of the 2014 IEEE 38th Annual Computer Software and Applications Conference, COMPSAC 2014, pp. 338–343. IEEE Computer Society, USA (2014). https://doi.org/10.1109/COMPSAC.2014.56

Rankless: Data-Specific Compilation for Real-Time Citation Network Exploration

Endre M. Borza(✉)

Center for Collective Learning, CIAS, Corvinus University, Budapest, Hungary
endre.borza@uni-corvinus.hu

Abstract. Interactive exploration of the global scholarly citation network – hundreds of millions of papers, billions of edges – is a highly challenging task: databases are too slow for deep hierarchical breakdowns, while full precomputation is infeasible across millions of queryable entities. We present Rankless, a publicly deployed platform built on *data-specific compilation*, a build-time pipeline that compiles dataset structure into Rust source code and typed binary layouts, eliminating runtime query parsing, planning, and type dispatch, while increasing caching efficiency. In a controlled comparison of 792 hierarchical queries across 5 entity types, Rankless responds 65.3× faster and uses 3.4× less peak memory than a PostgreSQL + Flask baseline. The live system at `rankless.org` serves interactive visualizations based on this technology from a single commodity server.

Keywords: Data visualization · Scholarly data · Low-latency web systems · Metaprogramming · Graph analytics

1 Introduction

Exploring how a university's impact distributes across countries, or which subfields drive an author's citations, requires navigating hundreds of millions of papers connected by billions of edges. Existing platforms provide search and retrieval [1,2], require offline data preparation [3,4], or reduce complex profiles to ordinal rankings [5] – none deliver real-time, multi-level hierarchical breakdowns at full dataset scale.

We present Rankless [8], demonstrating that large, mostly-static datasets are more efficiently served by compiling dataset knowledge into the binary than by querying a database at runtime – a web architecture pattern we term *data-specific compilation*. A build-time pipeline generates typed Rust code and binary layouts from the dataset's structure, the serving layer executes queries over arrays with no query planner, no type dispatch, and no SQL layer – sub-second interactive exploration from a single commodity server, directly addressing ICWE 2026's focus on performant and sustainable web systems.

A. Mauri et al. (Eds.): ICWE 2026, LNCS 16625, pp. 325–328, 2026.
https://doi.org/10.1007/978-3-032-29372-5_34

Table 1. Performance comparison over 792 hierarchical breakdown queries.

Metric	PostgreSQL + Flask	Rankless (Rust)	Ratio
Total query time	6 402.3 s	98.0 s	65.3×
Peak memory	4 222 MiB	1 225 MiB	3.4×

2 System Architecture

2.1 Data-Specific Compilation Pipeline

The pipeline ingests OpenAlex [1] JSON dumps and SCImago [6] journal rankings through sequential Rust steps. Each step reads predecessors' outputs, writes binary data, and generates Rust source via the `dmove_macro` metaprogramming crate – producing entity type definitions, attribute accessors, and link iterators whose types match actual data dimensions. The serving binary encodes every byte layout at compile time; the run phase is a stateless HTTP server.

2.2 Serving Layer

The Axum HTTP server loads binary data. A Unicode-normalized trie provides sub-millisecond entity search. A thread-pooled tree engine builds multi-level breakdowns on the fly – e.g., impact by field → subfield → country – surfacing the most-cited paper per branch. Entities with >100k citations are proactively cached. The Svelte frontend renders visualizations as hand-written SVG, with Cytoscape.js [7] for co-authorship layout - the sole dependency.

3 Performance Evaluation

We compare Rankless against a PostgreSQL + Flask baseline serving the same OpenAlex data in a normalized, indexed schema. Both systems run in Docker containers on the same machine over 792 hierarchical queries spanning 5 entity types and 32 breakdown configurations with 1–4 hierarchy levels (Table 1). A full benchmark description is available in the project repository.[1]

Rankless completes the full query set in 98.0 s – averaging ∼124 ms per query – versus 6 402.3 s for the baseline PostgreSQL. The baseline uses standard best practices (indexes, foreign keys, normalized schema), without query-specific denormalization. Beyond eliminating joins and query planning, the generated code produces functions simple enough to avoid pressure on the L1 instruction cache, and typed layouts use narrow integer widths, reducing data cache pressure. Correctness was validated by comparing breakdown trees from both systems: 20/32 configurations achieve Pearson $r > 0.99$ with mean relative error

[1] https://github.com/endremborza/rankless/blob/rankless-main/docs/benchmarking.

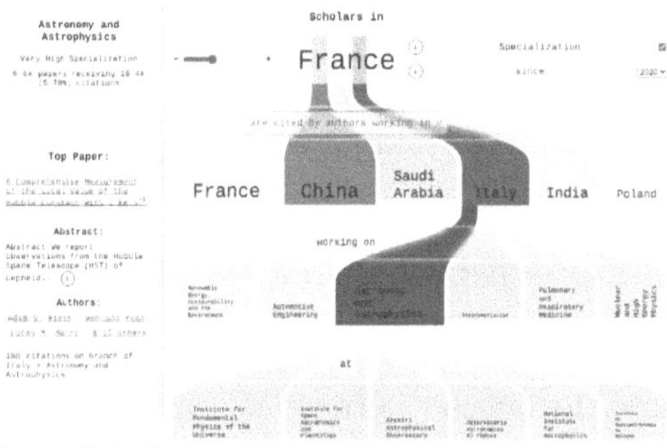

Fig. 1. Hierarchical breakdown of papers by scholars in France since 2020, grouped by citing country, field, and institution – with the most-cited paper surfaced per branch.

below 1%. The remaining configurations primarily involve journal-level matching, where Rankless applies additional journal-quality adjustments, leading to small, systematic deviations. As detailed in the online benchmarking report, these deviations are minor and do not affect the overall performance comparison.

4 Demonstration Scenario

Attendees interact directly with the live system[2] using a browser. Each cycle lasts under two minutes and can be repeated for multiple participants:

1. **Personal discovery.** Attendees search for their own institution or themselves as an author – autocomplete responds in under 10 ms – and immediately see a research profile.
2. **Hierarchical exploration.** The interactive tree (Fig. 1) reveals how impact distributes across fields, countries, and institutions: an attendee can discover, for example, which subfield at their university attracts the most international citations.
3. **Live reconfiguration.** Toggling between *production* and *impact*, applying year filters, and switching breakdown axes trigger instant recomputation – demonstrating compiled data access in practice.
4. **Network views.** Research-space networks, geographical citation flows, co-authorship graphs, and author peer heatmaps provide complementary perspectives on any entity.

This dataset covers 1.7B citations, 80M works, 4M authors, and 33k institutions from the OpenAlex snapshot, entities with sufficient citation activity for meaningful breakdowns.

[2] https://rankless.org.

5 Related Work

Semantic Scholar [2] and OpenAlex [1] provide search and API access but optimize for retrieval, not interactive multi-level analytics. VOSviewer [3] and CiteSpace [4] offer powerful bibliometric visualizations but require users to download and prepare data subsets offline, limiting scale. Graph databases and OLAP engines support flexible analytical queries but incur runtime query-planning overhead that grows with hierarchy depth. Rankless trades the flexibility of general-purpose query engines for speed and efficiency by compiling dataset structure directly into the binary – a trade-off viable when data is large, mostly static, and queried along known hierarchical dimensions.

6 Conclusion

Data-specific compilation – generating typed code and binaries from dataset characteristics – enables interactive exploration of billion-edge graphs from a single commodity server at 65.3× the throughput of a database baseline. The pattern applies wherever large, mostly-static data is queried along known dimensions: biological interaction networks, knowledge graphs, or web-scale recommendation systems. By replacing a database cluster with a compiled binary, data-specific compilation also offers a concrete, lower-energy web architecture. Future work will focus on structured APIs for autonomous scholarly agents.

Acknowledgments. Supported by the Learn Data ERA Chair from the European Research Executive Agency, funded by the European Union under Horizon Europe Grant Agreement 101086712.

Use of Generative AI. The author used generative AI for stylistic editing of the manuscript.

Disclosure of Interests. The author has no competing interests to declare that are relevant to the content of this article.

References

1. Priem, J., Piwowar, H., Orr, R.: OpenAlex: a fully-open index of scholarly works, authors, venues, institutions, and concepts. arXiv:2205.01833 (2022)
2. Kinney, R., et al.: The semantic scholar open data platform. arXiv:2301.10140 (2023)
3. Van Eck, N., Waltman, L.: Software survey: VOSviewer, a computer program for bibliometric mapping. Scientometrics **84**(2), 523–538 (2010)
4. Chen, C.: CiteSpace II: detecting and visualizing emerging trends and transient patterns in scientific literature. JASIST **57**(3), 359–377 (2006)
5. Waltman, L., et al.: The Leiden ranking 2011/2012: data collection, indicators, and interpretation. JASIST **63**(12), 2419–2432 (2012)
6. SCImago Journal Rank (2026). https://www.scimagojr.com
7. Shannon, P., et al.: Cytoscape: a software environment for integrated models of biomolecular interaction networks. Genome Res. **13**(11), 2498–2504 (2003)
8. Borza, E.M.: Rankless (2026). https://github.com/endremborza/rankless

A Web-Based Demonstrator for Quantum Circuit Programming Education

Bernhard Schenkenfelder[1(✉)], Raphael Zefferer[1], and Manuel Wimmer[2]

[1] Software Competence Center Hagenberg GmbH, Hagenberg, Austria
{Bernhard.Schenkenfelder,Raphael.Zefferer}@scch.at
[2] Johannes Kepler University Linz, Linz, Austria
manuel.wimmer@jku.at

Abstract. Advances in quantum computing have raised public awareness, however, learning the fundamentals of programming quantum computers remains challenging. Quantum circuits are the most widely used programming model for quantum computing. Existing graphical quantum circuit simulators allow users to design quantum circuits and observe the outcomes of executing them. While these tools can be used for educational purposes, they only address simulation and do not help novice quantum circuit programmers understand how to improve circuits or explore interesting circuit patterns. To better support such scenarios, we introduce the Virtual Quantum Table, a Web-based demonstrator that facilitates quantum circuit synthesis, optimization, and discovery with LLMs. It allows users to explore quantum circuit programming interactively from different angles. Synthesis involves reverse engineering circuits from expected results, optimization focuses on producing efficient circuits, and discovery allows to explore interesting circuit patterns.

Keywords: Quantum Circuits · Web-Based Programming · Education

1 Introduction

Advances in quantum computing have increased the attention from the general public [6]. It opens up new possibilities in certain fields and improves others, e.g., cryptography[1] and database searches [5]. However, the core concepts of quantum computing are not intuitive, making them inaccessible to those without the necessary mathematical/physical background [2]. As a result, visual quantum circuit modeling tools and simulators have been developed to lower the entry barrier. They allow users to combine quantum gates into quantum circuits, execute them, and observe the outcome probability states. Examples include the IBM Quantum Composer[2] and Quirk[3], both are Web-based and use a drag-and-drop interface with immediate feedback. We contribute to these efforts by

[1] https://awards.acm.org/about/2025-turing.
[2] https://quantum.cloud.ibm.com/composer.
[3] https://github.com/Strilanc/Quirk.

A. Mauri et al. (Eds.): ICWE 2026, LNCS 16625, pp. 329–332, 2026.
https://doi.org/10.1007/978-3-032-29372-5_35

introducing a demonstrator that goes beyond quantum circuit simulation. The *Virtual Quantum Table* enables users to explore circuits interactively from multiple angles by synthesizing, optimizing, and discovering them. Synthesis generates circuits from probability states, deepening the causal understanding of quantum gates and probability states. Optimization helps to develop an understanding of efficiency, and discovery introduces interesting circuit patterns. The goal of adding these functions is to improve the learning experience by offering a more comprehensive approach to understanding the main components of quantum circuits and their connections. The *Virtual Quantum Table* is available at https://quantumtable.scch.at, and its sources are in a public repository [4].

2 Cyber-Physical Quantum Table

The *Virtual Quantum Table* was inspired by its cyber-physical counterpart, the *Quantum Table* (Fig. 1). Designed as a tabletop collaborative workbench, the *Quantum Table* facilitates the simulation of quantum circuits through tangible interaction, i.e., quantum gates that can be placed on a circuit grid [1]. We transformed the *Quantum Table* into a Web app and added experimental features for educational purposes, which may be transferred back to the *Quantum Table*.

Fig. 1. The *Quantum Table* allows to simulate quantum circuits by tangible interaction.

3 Demonstration Scenarios

The demonstrator has four main functions: manual quantum circuit simulation as well as LLM-based circuit synthesis, optimization, and discovery (Table 1).

User Interface and Interaction. The *Virtual Quantum Table* consists of quantum gates, a circuit grid, probability states, buttons, and status messages (Fig. 2). The quantum gates are arranged in a circle. They can be dragged onto the circuit grid and selected for LLM prompting by clicking on them. The gates on the 3-by-6 circuit grid are colored in two ways. Green gates represent the current circuit, while blue gates indicate the previous circuit (e.g., the optimization result and the circuit to be optimized). The bars and numbers representing the probability states can also be green or blue.

Table 1. The main functions, their inputs and outputs, and learning objectives.

Function	Input	Output	Learning Objective
Simulation	Circuit	Probability States	Causal Understanding
Synthesis	Gates, Probability States	Circuit	Causal Understanding
Optimization	Gates, Circuit	Circuit	Efficiency
Discovery	Gates	Circuit, Description	Circuit Patterns

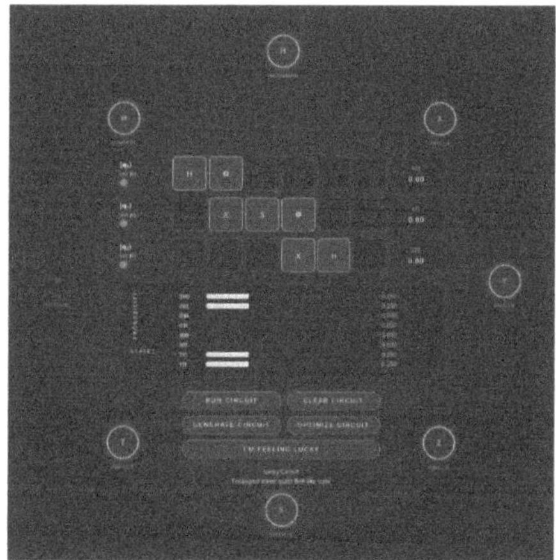
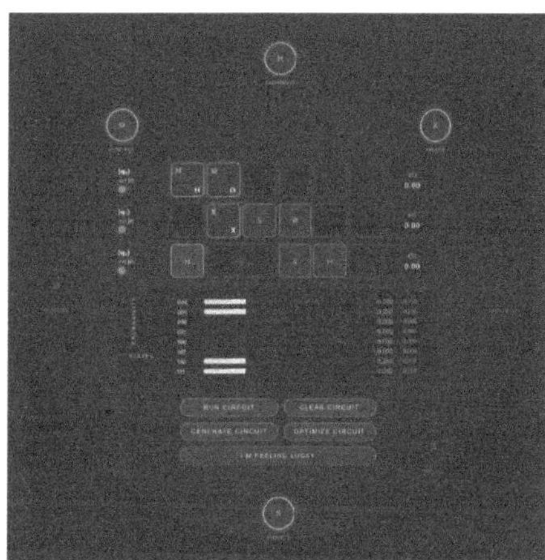

Fig. 2. The *Discovery* function was used to generate an example circuit (Bell state) to demonstrate entanglement (left). The circuit was simplified using the *Optimization* function (right).

Synthesis. This function uses the desired outcome probability states as input. These states are passed to the LLM, instructing it to generate a quantum circuit approximating the probability states. The prompt also specifies constraints, including the number of qubits and layers in the circuit grid, and allowed quantum gates. The LLM is prompted to return the circuit as a two-dimensional array, where each cell contains either a valid gate identifier or `null`. Finally, the output needs to be returned as valid JSON, containing a single key named `grid`. The generated circuit is displayed in the grid and simulated, i.e., the probability states are computed. This allows users to compare the resulting probability distribution (green) to the originally specified target distribution (blue).

Optimization. The optimization process takes the current circuit as input. The LLM is prompted to find a simpler, equivalent circuit. The result is displayed in a way that makes it easy to identify the changes made by the LLM. Quantum gates that have been removed are highlighted in blue, and those that have been added are highlighted in green. If a gate is modified or kept in a certain grid slot, the interface displays the original and new gates with a blue-green gradient.

Discovery. This feature randomly generates interesting quantum circuit patterns to showcase quantum phenomena, encouraging exploration and discovery. The LLM is also instructed to provide a brief description of the pattern or effect demonstrated by the circuit to support the learning process.
Vibe-Coding. Remarkably, only a single image of the *Quantum Table* and a brief prompt [4] were required to vibe-code the first version of the *Virtual Quantum Table*. All subsequent modifications, including new features, issue resolution, LLM interaction via an API, and containerization, were also vibe-coded.

4 Future Work

To ensure that the results are reliable and match those of the physical *Quantum Table*, the vibe-coded logic of the simulation function should be replaced with Qiskit[4] as back-end in the future. As part of our larger effort on low-code development [3], we will study the potential of LLMs for quantum circuit generation and evaluation.

Acknowledgement. The *Virtual Quantum Table* has been developed using vibe-coding. The research reported in this paper has been funded by BMIMI, BMWET, and the State of Upper Austria in the frame of the SCCH competence center INTEGRATE (FFG grant no. 892418) part of the FFG COMET Competence Centers for Excellent Technologies Programme.

References

1. Hillmich, S., Zefferer, R., Gartner, M., Schenkenfelder, B., Bruckner, S., Brandstätter, U.: Quantum table: a tangible quantum circuit demonstrator. OASIcs, Volume 134, Programming 2025 **134**, 18:1–18:3 (2025)
2. Liu, J., Franklin, D.: Introduction to quantum computing for everyone: experience report. In: Proceedigns of the 54th ACM Technical Symposium on Computer Science Education, pp. 1157–1163. ACM, Toronto ON Canada (2023)
3. Schenkenfelder, B.: LLM-based generation of low-code development platforms. In: Proceedigns of the ACM/IEEE 28th International Conference on Model Driven Engineering Languages and Systems Companion (MODELS-C), pp. 59–64. IEEE (2025)
4. Schenkenfelder, B., Zefferer, R., Wimmer, M.: Virtual quantum table (2026). https://doi.org/10.5281/zenodo.19483347
5. Seegerer, S., Michaeli, T., Romeike, R.: Quantum computing as a topic in computer science education. In: Proceedigns of the 16th Workshop in Primary and Secondary Computing Education, pp. 1–6. ACM (2021)
6. Suter, V., Ma, C., Pöhlmann, G.M., Meckel, M.: Narratives on quantum technologies: a cross-domain analysis of media, business, and policy discourses. Data Policy **8** (2026)

[4] https://www.ibm.com/quantum/qiskit.

MLProvLens: Exploring End-to-End Provenance in ML Pipelines with a W3C PROV-Aligned Framework

Ahmad Qadeib Alban(✉), Khalid Belhajjame, and Daniela Grigori

Université Paris Dauphine-PSL, LAMSADE, Paris, France
{ahmad.qadeib-alban,kbelhajj,daniela.grigori}@dauphine.psl.eu

Abstract. Once specified and enacted, end-to-end machine learning (ML) pipelines, together with contextual information about how artifacts are consumed and produced during execution, constitute valuable assets that can be shared or published for reuse. Indeed, ML pipelines involve multiple repetitive data transformation steps before, during, and after model training. Evaluating alternative configurations at each stage requires continuous monitoring of the workflow, particularly to support informed model selection for deployment. Although existing monitoring solutions record metrics and configurations, these logs are typically expressed using ad hoc data models, and lack support for tracing complete derivation paths from training data to deployed models. To overcome such limitation, we introduced in a previous work a unified, W3C PROV-compatible meta-model for capturing end- to-end provenance of ML pipelines. In this demonstration, we present an interactive system that operationalizes this meta-model through a lightweight provenance exploration interface. The graphical user interface allows user to load a provenance graph, search for nodes of interest, render provenance subgraphs, inspect node metadata and relationships, and execute predefined end-to-end provenance queries over the full pipeline.

Keywords: Provenance · ML pipelines · W3C PROV · Interactive GUI

1 Introduction

The development of machine-learning (ML) models is inherently exploratory and iterative, spanning data ingestion, preprocessing, feature engineering, model design, training, and optimisation. Because predictive performance relies heavily on upstream data transformations and training configurations, understanding an ML pipeline requires reasoning over its end-to-end flow rather than isolated steps.

Provenance provides a formal record of the origin, context, and derivation history of data products and artifacts. In complex ML pipelines, effective provenance tracking must cover the entire lifecycle while handling heterogeneous arti-

A. Mauri et al. (Eds.): ICWE 2026, LNCS 16625, pp. 333–337, 2026.
https://doi.org/10.1007/978-3-032-29372-5_36

fact granularities. Existing approaches, however, address only parts of this problem. Fine-grained frameworks capture preprocessing provenance at the level of records and individual values, but remain limited to the preprocessing phase [2]. In contrast, MLflow2PROV tracks runs, parameters, models, and related experiment artifacts, yet lacks a unified view of upstream data transformations [3].

Our system bridges the gap between these disparate tracking tools by integrating fine-grained data-preparation provenance with coarse-grained experiment tracking into a unified graph. Through an interactive GUI, users can explore provenance graphs, inspect artifact metadata, and execute end-to-end queries that trace model evaluation metrics back to their originating data transformations.

2 System Architecture

Our demonstration system operationalizes the provenance meta model introduced in our previous work [1], for capturing end-to-end provenance in ML pipelines. The model distinguishes between prospective lineage, which describes the intended pipeline structure at design time, and retrospective lineage, which captures the actual execution history. This separation enables unified representation that connects the planned workflow with its execution, providing complete traceability of how data, models, and results are used and generated through the ML lifecycle. A detailed description of our meta-model is presented in [1].

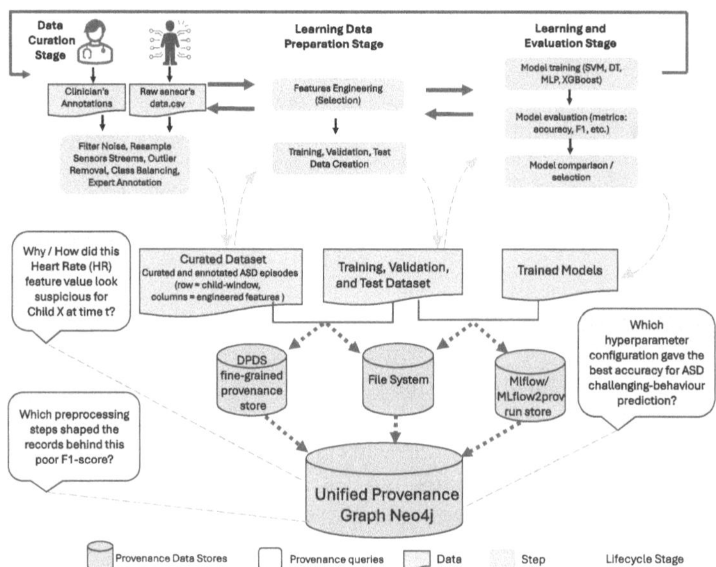

Fig. 1. End-to-end ML pipeline lifecycle and provenance integration.

ML pipelines are designed to be centered around three stages: Data Curation, Learning Data Preparation, and Learning. As depicted in Fig. 1, the Data Curation stage transforms raw inputs through operations such as filtering, resampling, outlier removal, and annotation. The learning data preparation stage refines the curated data through feature engineering and splitting. Finally, the Learning Stage iteratively perform model comparison and selection, producing optimized trained models and performance metrics. The figure also highlights how provenance queries can trace model outputs back to their originating data transformations.

To capture provenance across these stages, our system integrates two complementary provenance solutions: DPDS for fine-grained preprocessing provenance [2], and MLflow2PROV for experiment and model lifecycle provenance [3]. These are unified into a single provenance graph.

To support interactive exploration, the system provides a modular GUI architecture. The unified graph is exported into nodes.csv and rels.csv, and indexed in a local SQLite database for efficient querying. The data-access layer executes provenance queries over this index database, while the control layer, implemented using Gradio, manages user interaction. Finally, the visualization layer, based in Plotly and NetworkX, renders the interactive provenance graph and associated charts.

3 Demonstration Scenarios

Initially, the user loads the provenance graph by providing the `nodes.csv` and `rels.csv` files generated by the provenance meta-model implementation. Once loaded, the system initializes (or reuses) the SQLite index and displays a statistical summary of the graph structure, including the counts of nodes and relationships. The demonstrator then proceeds with the following two scenarios.

Graph Exploration: In this scenario, the user (e.g., a clinician) explores a provenance fragment centered on a pipeline element of interest. As shown in Fig. 2 (1), the user enters a keyword in the search field, optionally filters by node type, and retrieves matching nodes. After selecting a node, the user configures traversal depth and direction, and renders the corresponding subgraph (Fig. 2 (2)). Upstream traversal reveals lineage, downstream traversal shows impact, and bidirectional traversal exposes the local neighborhood. To ensure interactive rendering, the user may limit the number of displayed nodes. Figure 2 illustrates an example centered on the training step `train_xgb`. Additional metadata and adjacent relationships for the selected node are displayed in the inspection panel (Fig. 2 (3)).

End-to-End Query Execution: The GUI also provides a second tab, End-To-End Query, where the user selects a query from a predefined list of 15 provenance queries introduced in our previous work [1]. These queries cover data curation, data-to-model integration, and learning/configuration analysis. After selecting a query and providing the required input parameters, the system executes the corresponding provenance traversal over the unified graph. Results are presented

Fig. 2. Screenshot of part of the demonstrator. (1) The user searches for a provenance node and selects a matching result. (2) The user configures traversal parameters and renders the corresponding subgraph. (3) The system displays detailed metadata and adjacent relationships for the selected node.

both as a textual explanation and as a highlighted subgraph. For example, a user may trace a poor F1-score back to the preprocessing steps and records that influenced the training data.

For demonstration purposes, the GUI operates on a reduced provenance graph to ensure readability and responsiveness during live interaction. The underlying meta-model and implementation, however, have been evaluated on real datasets as reported in our previous work[1].

4 Conclusions and Future Work

This demonstration complements our previous provenance meta-model by providing an interactive system for exploring and querying end-to-end provenance in ML pipelines. While the meta-model integrates fine-grained preprocessing provenance with experiment-level model provenance, the system enables users to move seamlessly from raw and curated data artifacts to model runs, trained models, and evaluation outcomes. This makes the demo particularly relevant for provenance-driven debugging, model selection, and inspection of complex ML workflows ongoing work focuses on applying and assessing the demonstrator on a broader range of pipelines, as well as extending the query capabilities.

[1] The source code is available at https://github.com/aq1992dauphine/End_To_End_Provenance_Meta_Model. A video walkthrough illustrating the complete demonstration scenarios, along with a technical report are available at: https://drive.google.com/drive/folders/1rIVZiESOV18ayOkfXXWm7ytVBcdC_KZj?usp=sharing.

References

1. Alban, A.Q., Belhajjame, K., Grigori, D.: A w3c prov-aligned metamodel for tracing end-to-end provenance in ml pipelines. In: RCIS 2026. To appear
2. Chapman, A., Lauro, L.: Supporting better insights of data science pipelines with fine-grained provenance. ACM Trans. Database Syst. **49**(2), 6:1–6:42 (2024)
3. Schlegel, M., Sattler, K.: Capturing end-to-end provenance for machine learning pipelines. Inf. Syst. (2025)

Client-Driven Offline-First RDF 1.2 Using OR-Sets

Jitse De Smet(✉) and Ruben Taelman

IDLab, Department of Electronics and Information Systems, Ghent University – imec, Ghent, Belgium
{jitse.desmet,ruben.taelman}@ugent.be

Abstract. As autonomous agents increasingly write to shared RDF knowledge graphs concurrently, especially in the context of decentralized data ecosystems, principled conflict resolution becomes critical. Existing RDF CRDT approaches either require dedicated infrastructure or introduce consistency boundary problems when storing bookkeeping across multiple resources. We instantiate the state-based OR-Set over RDF 1.2 triple terms - unlike prior work, retaining all bookkeeping within a single dataset without additional infrastructure - and demonstrate a proof-of-concept datastore wrapper to use in query engines, enabling agents to query and update a conflict-free knowledge graph via standard SPARQL, unaware of the underlying merge machinery. Future work will investigate constraint-aware merge semantics for RDF CRDTs. **npm package**: https://www.npmjs.com/package/orset-rdf-store **poster**: https://orset-rdf.poster.jitsedesmet.be/.

Keywords: Conflict-free Replicated Data Types · OR-Set · RDF 1.2 · Decentralized Web · Offline-First · SPARQL

1 Introduction

Knowledge graphs expressed in RDF are a central pillar of neuro-symbolic AI: techniques such as GraphRAG [6], GRASP [14], and the Model Context Protocol (MCP) [4] make it increasingly common for multiple agents to read from and write to the same RDF knowledge graph simultaneously - one agent enriches the graph while another reasons over it, and a third corrects errors it discovers.

In decentralized data ecosystems - such as Solid [13], IDSA [2], and Gaia-X [1] - each participant governs their own data without relying on a central authority. A critical challenge is concurrent offline editing: when two agents independently modify the same resource while offline, their updates collide once connection is restored. Asking an agent to resolve such conflicts manually is not always desirable - an agent that has been offline may struggle to grasp how much has changed. Conflict-free Replicated Data Types (CRDTs) [10] offer a principled solution, guaranteeing that any two replicas converge to the same state through well-defined merge algorithms, with no coordination required.

A. Mauri et al. (Eds.): ICWE 2026, LNCS 16625, pp. 338–341, 2026.
https://doi.org/10.1007/978-3-032-29372-5_37

Solutions have been proposed for RDF-based CRDTs [9] and even CRDTs in Solid [7], but the introduction of RDF 1.2 [8] opens new possibilities. RDF 1.2's triple terms - where the object of a triple can itself be a triple - enable efficient, first-class modelling of state-based CRDTs directly within RDF datasets, without any external bookkeeping.

In this paper, we present a**state-based add-wins set CRDT** modelled entirely in RDF 1.2. All bookkeeping stays within the same dataset, enabling atomic updates on the resource without server intervention, and allowing both **CRDT-aware and CRDT-unaware clients** to coexist without friction. By plugging a CRDT-aware datastore into a query engine, conflict resolution becomes fully transparent to both agents and query engines - as demonstrated by our PoC implementation. Agents can then query and update a conflict-free knowledge graph through standard SPARQL interfaces, without any awareness of the underlying CRDT machinery.

2 Related Work

Decentralized Data Ecosystems and Interface Heterogeneity. Decentralized data ecosystems consist of self-governed data stores, each individually positioned in the continuous *Consistency Availability Partition-tolerance* (CAP) space and exposed through heterogeneous interfaces [11] - their only shared infrastructure being the Web itself. Our CRDT is designed to work across such ecosystems by depending only on what every participant already has: the ability to store and exchange RDF data over the Web, plus **ETag support** to avoid mid-air collisions.

CRDTs. Existing RDF CRDT approaches require more infrastructure than the Web alone. The m-ld project [3] provides a JavaScript CRDT engine for RDF with a similar eventual-consistency goal, but requires a dedicated m-ld domain server. Gruss et al. [7] store the latest RDF state alongside a binary CRDT representation from a user-chosen library (e.g. Yjs or Automerge), plus a hypermedia description of supported operations. While this lets non-CRDT-aware clients consume the data, it relies on a separate binary blob outside the RDF dataset, introducing a consistency boundary problem where a standard HTTP server cannot atomically update multiple resources. Braid-HTTP [12] proposes adding merge-type headers to HTTP, which is complementary to our approach and could replace our custom patch encoding in a future iteration.

Since we abstract at the RDF dataset level - where only set-based operations exist - we limit ourselves to set CRDTs. The SU-Set [9] extends the OR-Set [10] for RDF using an operation-based approach, whereas we adopt the state-based OR-Set formalization of Bieniusa et al. [5], which aligns naturally with HTTP's Representational State Transfer (REST) semantics - exchanging full dataset state rather than individual operations. Where Bieniusa et al. optimize tombstone removal using causal delivery and a known replica set, we instead exploit NTP time drift bounds - an approach better suited to open decentralized ecosystems where replica sets are unknown.

3 State-Based Add-Wins CRDT-RDF

The OR-Set [5] is a replicated set where each element carries a set of unique add-tags; removing an element moves its tags to a tombstone set rather than deleting them outright, ensuring that a concurrent add always wins over a concurrent remove. We instantiate this over RDF 1.2, setting elements as RDF 1.2 triples and unique tags as UUDv4 identifiers. RDF 1.2 triple terms allow a triple to appear in the object position of another triple, enabling statements to be made about triples directly. We use this to link each tracked triple, its add-tags, and its tombstones through an identifying node, as shown in Fig. 1. A triple is considered present when it has at least one add-tag not in its tombstone set. On merge, multiple identifying nodes for the same triple are consolidated into one.

```
<> a crdt:container .
[] crdt:tags <<( <> a crdt:container )>> ;
   crdt:add "be2f95dd-8ca9-416c-b1d0-81dc45ba54c8"^^crdt:uuid .
:me a :human .
[] crdt:tags <<( :me a :human )>> ;
   crdt:add "96d482e5-3ce7-4f24-a21b-a9d0506ff5b0"^^crdt:uuid ;
   crdt:remove "77c01067-1594-475e-8c64-76f9c4ec4402"^^crdt:uuid .
[] crdt:tags <<( :me a :man )>> ;
   crdt:remove
"216ac011-c2ba-4ff0-825c-7f9cf1efa4ff--2025-03-13T14:00:00Z"^^crdt:stamp-uuid .
```

Fig. 1. RDF 1.2 representation of a state-based OR-Set with two triples present: '<> a crdt:container' and ':me a :human'. The latter has one add-tag not in its tombstone set, so it remains present. Since ':me a :man' has no add-tags, it is not present.

NTP Tombstone Optimization. Without garbage collection, tombstones accumulate indefinitely - a fundamental challenge for all state-based CRDTs. Bieniusa et al.'s solution requires causal delivery and a known replica set, assumptions that do not hold in open decentralized ecosystems. We instead exploit NTP synchronization: since NTP enters panic mode after a drift exceeding 1000s, any two synchronized clients differ by at most 2000s. By stamping each tag with its creation or tombstone time using 'crdt:stamp-uuid' - formatted as {`uuid`}{`xsd:dateTime`} - a CRDT dataset can declare a synchronization interval d, after which stale metadata is pruned: 1. an add-tag may be dropped if a newer one exists and all replicas have seen it; 2. a tombstone may be dropped once all replicas have seen it; and 3. the identifying blank node may be dropped if no other triple references it. A tag is universally seen once its timestamp is older than $d + 4000$s - a bound derived from the worst-case NTP drift between any two synchronized replicas.

4 Conclusion

We presented a state-based add-wins set CRDT modelled entirely in RDF 1.2, requiring no infrastructure beyond RDF-over-HTTP with ETag support - something most modern Web servers already provide. All bookkeeping stays within the dataset itself, eliminating the consistency boundary problem. An NTP-based tombstone pruning mechanism keeps the CRDT manageable without requiring a known replica set. By abstracting at the quad-store level, the CRDT can be plugged into existing query engines, making conflict resolution fully transparent to both agents and SPARQL clients alike. A current limitation is the lack of constraint-aware merge: two individually valid states can merge into a state that violates domain constraints, a problem we plan to address in future work.

acknowledgement. Jitse De Smet is a predoctoral fellow of the Research Foundation Flanders (FWO) (1SB8525N). The described research activities were supported by SolidLab Vlaanderen (Flemish Government, EWI, and RRF project VV023/10). Ruben Taelman is a postdoctoral fellow of the Research Foundation Flanders (FWO) (1202124N).

References

1. Gaia-x. https://gaia-x.eu/
2. International data spaces association. https://internationaldataspaces.org/
3. m-ld. https://www.m-ld.org/
4. Model context protocol (2026). https://modelcontextprotocol.io/
5. Bieniusa, A., et al.: An optimized conflict-free replicated set. CoRR (2012)
6. Edge, D., Trinh, H., Cheng, N.: From local to global: a graph rag approach to query-focused summarization (2024). arXiv:2404.16130 arXiv preprint
7. Gruss, J., Ciortea, A., Salvaneschi, G., Mayer, S.: Real-time collaboration in linked data systems. In: Proceedings of the ISWC 2023 Posters, Demos and Industry Tracks. CEUR Workshop Proceedings, vol. 3632. CEUR-WS.org (2023)
8. Hartig, O., Champin, P.A., Kellogg, G., Seaborne, A.: SPARQL 1.2 query language. Tech. rep. (2025). https://www.w3.org/TR/rdf12-concepts/
9. Ibáñez, L., Skaf-Molli, H., Molli, P., Corby, O.: Synchronizing semantic stores with commutative replicated data types. In: Proceedings of the 21st World Wide Web Conference, WWW 2012. ACM (2012)
10. Shapiro, M., Preguiça, N., Baquero, C., Zawirski, M.: A comprehensive study of Convergent and Commutative Replicated Data Types. Research Report RR-7506, Inria – Centre Paris-Rocquencourt ; INRIA (2011)
11. Smet, J.D.: Optimizing write performance in decentralized data ecosystems. In: The Semantic Web: ESWC 2025 Satellite Events - Portoroz, Slovenia, June 1-5, 2025, Proceedings. Springer (2025)
12. Toomim, M., Little, G., Walker, R., Bellomy, B., Gentle, S.: Braid-HTTP: Synchronization for HTTP. Internet-Draft draft-toomim-httpbis-braid-http-04, Internet Engineering Task Force (2023). https://datatracker.ietf.org/doc/draft-toomim-httpbis-braid-http/04/, work in Progress
13. Verborgh, R.: Linking the World's Information - Essays on Tim Berners-Lee's Invention of the World Wide Web. In: Seneviratne, O., Hendler, J.A. (eds.) ACM Books, ACM (2023). Re-decentralizing the web, for good this time
14. Walter, S., Bast, H.: GRASP: Generic reasoning and SPARQL generation across knowledge graphs. In: International Semantic Web Conference, pp. 271–289. Springer (2025)

Exploring ML Model Card Metadata Granularities for Enhanced Discovery and Insights through Knowledge Graphs

Muhammad Asif Suryani(✉), Kanishka Silva, Benjamin Zapilko, and Brigitte Mathiak

Knowledge Technologies for the Social Sciences, GESIS-Leibniz-Institut für Sozialwissenschaften, Köln, Germany
{asif.suryani,kanishka.silva,benjamin.zapilko,brigitte.mathiak}@gesis.org

Abstract. Hugging Face models are on the rise currently nearly touching 3 million mark. This substantial increase has brought numerous challenges such as relevant model card discovery focusing tasks, architecture and license. For example, text classification as filtering criterion brings 112,077 models, and the user may select other filters to reduce that number[1]. Moreover, current Hugging Face searching mechanism does not support certain metadata granularities i.e., base-model, dataset, and publications. This practically overlooks the relevant model discovery process considering these interconnections among models. In this demo paper, we exploit the Hugging Face model card metadata features and showcase i) valuable insights, ii) interconnections across heterogeneous metadata features as knowledge graph instance based on schema.org mappings, and iii) user queryable mechanism. Hence, these aspects support granular, metadata-driven model card discovery across research communities.

Keywords: Metadata Granularities · Knowledge Graphs · Model Discovery · Hugging Face

1 Introduction

[1] Research artifacts such as Machine Learning (ML) models, publications, and datasets are an essential element in the scholarly ecosystem. Numerous open repositories host them collectively or individually. ML models have been on the rise and are available at Hugging Face, one of the prominent repositories. However, an increase in the number of ML models brings various challenges at the repository level and affects the model discovery process. Hugging Face provides a keyword-based searching mechanism, but unable to exploit more granular features. An efficient model discovery process would assist users in finding the relevant model(s) inline with their needs. As ML models are expansive considering

[1] Accessed date:19 March 2026

A. Mauri et al. (Eds.): ICWE 2026, LNCS 16625, pp. 342–346, 2026.
https://doi.org/10.1007/978-3-032-29372-5_38

computation resources, a system exploiting meta-information from Hugging Face will be helpful. ML models are capable of generating heterogeneous metadata features to assist in the discovery process [4,6].

Hugging Face model cards generate heterogeneous metadata features such as tasks, architecture, dataset, publications, and base-models. These features collectively assist the users in finding relevant models targeting more granular configuration such as models with datasets, models with publications, and models with base-models. It will be helpful for researchers to get first-hand information focusing technical insights, which may save efforts and time [1,2,7].

In this paper, we demonstrate our system that exploits the heterogeneous metadata features of Hugging Face model cards. The system is capable of presenting repository-level insights, knowledge graph (KG) based enhanced discovery targeting interconnection among metadata features, also providing a queryable interface to allow users more flexibility in the model discovery process.

2 Related Work

ML models are facilitating various downstream tasks. Recently, a study targeting Hugging Face model card metadata presented key insights that approximately half of the total models receive downloads every month and also indicates statistics considering metadata completeness [7]. Another survey investigated metadata variations in research repositories and emphasized the formulation of a unified schema to facilitate the harmonization and provenance of research artifacts [3]. KGs provide queryable interfaces that target research artifacts, entities, and respective relationships. Numerous initiatives are already serving research communities [5], such as ORKG[2] and GESIS KG[3].

3 System Overview

The overall approach involves two steps: metadata extraction and KG construction. In metadata extraction, raw metadata is gathered from Hugging Face API and pre-processed into a structured format by resolving nested fields and handling missing values. For KG construction, structured metadata is mapped to the schema.org vocabulary to create RDF triples. Each model card becomes a *schema:SoftwareSourceCode* node, capturing its name, URL, task, license, and popularity as literal properties. The user or organization, datasets, base-models, and publications are linked as typed nodes through *schema:creator*, *schema:dataset*, *schema:isBasedOn* and *schema:citation* respectively.

Dataset. The demonstration uses a snapshot of the Hugging Face model card metadata of March 2026 available at Zenodo [8].

Applying the above mappings results in approximately 1.8 million RDF triples across five node types: *Model*, *Creator*, *Dataset*, *Paper*, *BaseModel*.

---

2 https://orkg.org.

3 https://data.gesis.org/gesiskg/site/.

System Architecture. The system is deployed as three containerized services using Docker Compose, as illustrated in Figure 1. The FastAPI server reads CSV data in chunks, constructs RDF triples, and streams them to the triple store in 2000-triple batches using the SPARQL 1.1 Graph Store Protocol. Apache Jena Fuseki 4 acts as the SPARQL 1.1 endpoint, supported by TDB2 persistent on-disk storage to prevent re-uploads during subsequent runs. The React 18 frontend is compiled and served by nginx, communicating with FastAPI via a REST API and SPARQL proxy API.

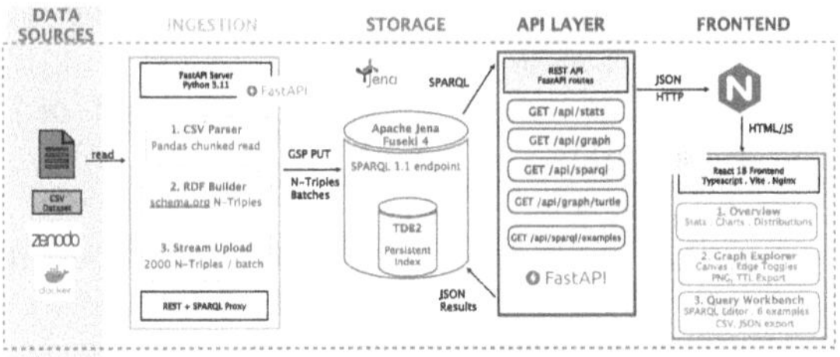

Fig. 1. System Architecture Diagram.

4 Demonstration

Interface Overview. The system interface is organized as shown in Figure 2. **Overview** tab presents repository-level statistics from the loaded KG, including KPI cards, task and license distributions and top-10 rankings by downloads, datasets and base models. **Graph Explorer** tab visualizes the KG on a canvas with four edge-type toggles (Creator, Dataset, Paper, and Base Model), and supports PNG and Turtle RDF export. **Query Workbench** tab exposes Fuseki SPARQL 1.1 endpoint with six pre-built queries and a live editor. Results are paginated with linked URIs and exportable as CSV or JSON.

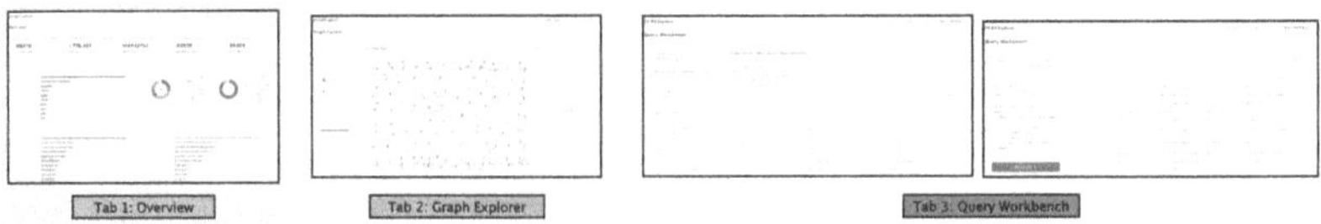

Fig. 2. User Interface with 3-Tabs Layout.

Use Case: Finding Fine-Tuned Qwen Models with Link to Papers. To select a fine-tuned model, researchers often need to know about its origin and link to papers. In Hugging Face metadata, base-model and publication links are stored separately with no way to query them together. Our system resolves this via a single SPARQL traversal over the KG shown in Figure 33, joining *schema:isBasedOn* and *schema:citation* to return all Qwen-derived models with their paper links in one citation-backed list.

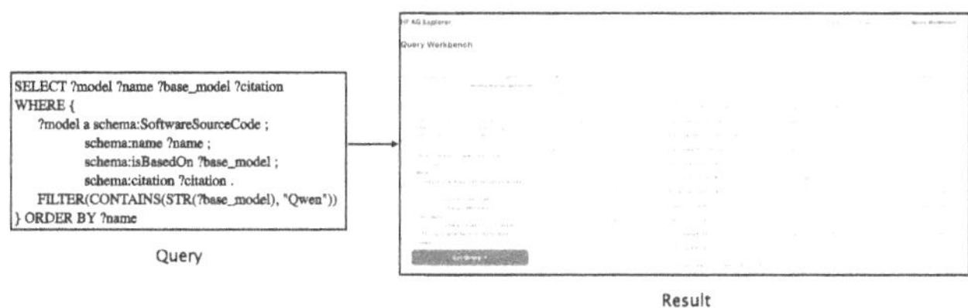

Fig. 3. Use Case Overview.

5 Conclusion

This demo paper showcases how the granular metadata features of Hugging Face models in knowledge graph settings can support enhanced model discovery. For future directions, a Hugging Face Knowledge Graph (HFKG) covering heterogeneous features and link to external repositories seems is work in progress. However, provenance of model cards will be an exciting direction, besides grouping models considering size of models, type of models, similar loss functions, and learning rate would be interesting.

AI Declaration. In this study, the grammar check and proofreading were carried out by AppleâĂŹs Artificial Intelligence tool. Further, Claude (Anthropic) was used for coding assistance during the User Interface development.

Acknowledgement. This work has been partially funded by Deutsche Forschungsgemeinschaft (DFG), NFDI4DataScience (Grant no. 460234259). Authors also acknowledge Hugging Face as data source and thank the individuals involved in this research.

References

1. Castaño, J., Martínez-Fernández, S., Franch, X., Bogner, J.: Analyzing the evolution and maintenance of ML models on hugging face. In: Proceedings of the 21st International Conference on Mining Software Repositories, pp. 607–618 (2024)
2. Face, H.: Hugging face APIS. https://huggingface.co (2026). Accessed 20 Feb 2026
3. Gesese, G.A., et al.: A survey on metadata for machine learning models and datasets: standards, practices, and harmonization challenges. In: International Workshop on Scientific Knowledge-Representation 2025 (2025). Discovery, and Assessment
4. Indamutsa, A., Di Rocco, J., Almonte, L., Di Ruscio, D., Pierantonio, A.: Advanced discovery mechanisms in model repositories. Softw. Pract. Exper. **54**(11), 2214–2248 (2024)
5. Silva, K., et al.: Research knowledge graphs in NFDI4datascience: key activities, achievements, and future directions. In: 55. Jahrestagung der Gesellschaft für Informatik, INFORMATIK 2025, pp. 1183–1193 (2025). https://doi.org/10.18420/INF2025_102
6. Suryani, M.A., Burwicz-Galerne, E., Mathiak, B., Wallmann, K., Renz, M.: Extracting and modeling tabular data from marine geology publications into a heterogeneous information network. ICPRAM, pp. 453–460 (2025)

7. Suryani, M.A., Karmakar, S., Mathiak, B., Mayr, P.: Model card metadata collection from hugging face to foster multidisciplinary ai research: a dataset. In: Proceedings of the 14th International Conference on Data Science, Technology and Applications, pp. 583–590. (2025)
8. Suryani, M.A., Karmakar, S., Mathiak, B., Mutschke, P., Mayr, P.: Hugging face model cards metadata dataset (2025). https://doi.org/10.5281/zenodo.16030672

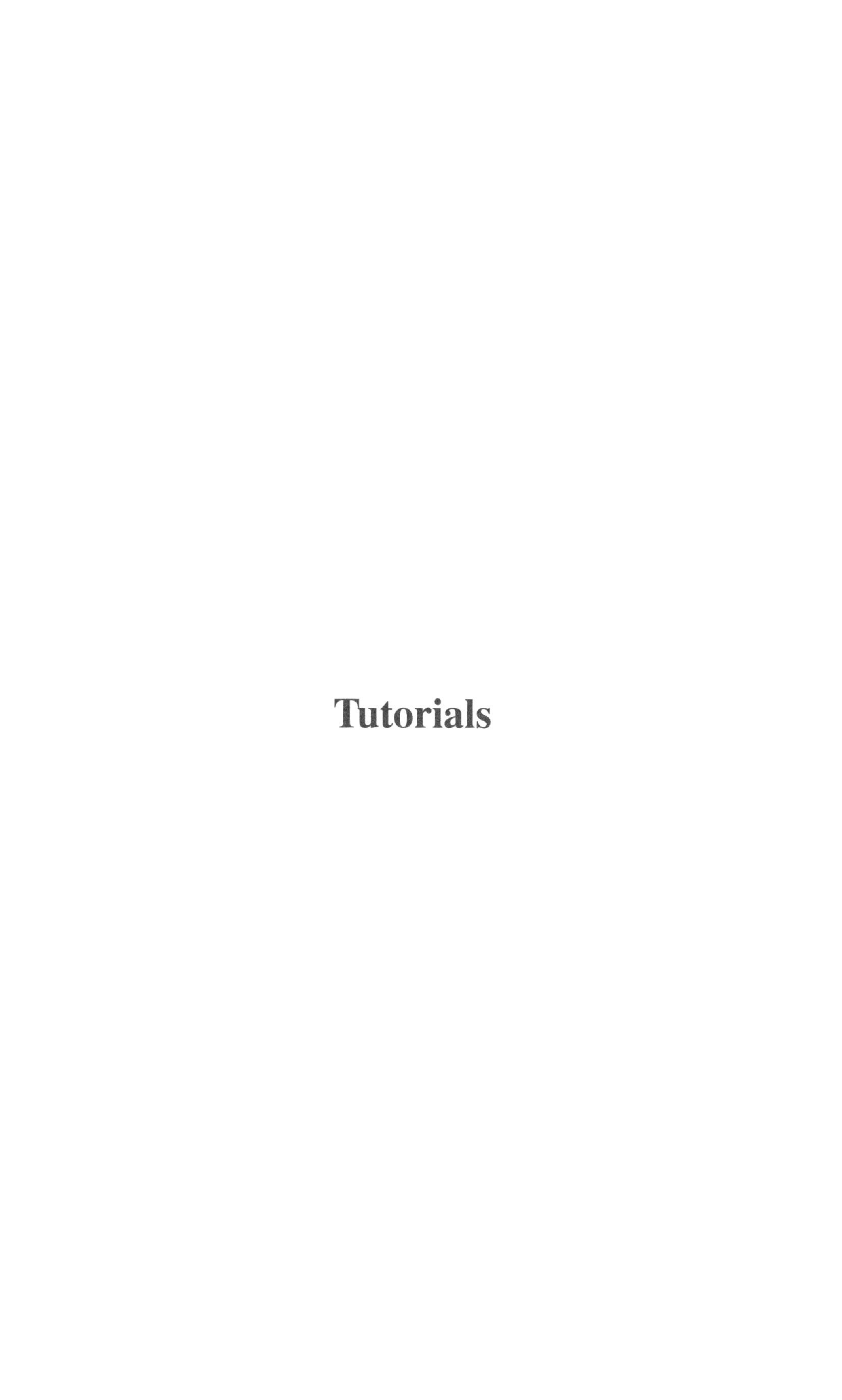

Tutorials

Exploring Design Alternatives for Automated Web GUI Generation from Discourse Models

Hermann Kaindl(✉)

WU, Wien, Vienna, Austria
hermann.kaindl@wu.ac.at

Abstract. *Interaction design* is considered important for achieving usable Web user interfaces. *Communicative acts* as abstractions from speech acts can model basic building blocks ('atoms') of communication, like a question or an answer. When, e.g., a question and an answer are glued together as a so-called adjacency pair, a simple 'molecule' of a dialogue is modeled. Deliberately complex discourse structures can be modeled using relations from Rhetorical Structure Theory (RST). The content of a communicative act can refer to *ontologies* of the domain of discourse. Taking all this together, we created a new discourse metamodel that specifies what discourse models may look like. Such discourse models can specify an interaction design.

This tutorial demonstrates how such an interaction design can be used for *automated Web user-interface generation.* Based on AI optimization techniques, the graphical user interfaces (GUIs) are automatically generated and tailored to a device such as a smartphone according to a given device specification. Our approach, in contrast to others, can explore *alternatives* in the design space of GUIs. We present a user story about this theme using our approach, which also includes employing unique *customization techniques* to address usability.

Keywords: Interaction design · discourse models · automated Web GUI generation · customization · design alternatives

1 Intended Audience and Assumed Background

The target audience is interaction designers, Web designers, or project managers. Also educators can benefit from this tutorial.

The assumed attendee background is some familiarity with scenarios/use cases as well as interest in interaction design. There are no pre-requisites such as knowledge about Human-Computer Interaction in general.

2 Tutorial Structure and List of Topics Covered

This tutorial is a mix of lectures, group discussions and exercises.

In order to provide a common basis for participants with different background, this tutorial starts with an overview of background material. An overview of discourse-based

A. Mauri et al. (Eds.): ICWE 2026, LNCS 16625, pp. 349–353, 2026.
https://doi.org/10.1007/978-3-032-29372-5_39

modeling follows, which will be brief but sufficient for understanding the generation and customization of GUIs.

Based on that, this tutorial shows how GUIs can be generated automatically and, in this course tailored to different devices (as specified).

This tutorial also presents a user story with this approach, with its focus on alternatives in the course of generating Web GUIs. This includes specific customization techniques of our approach.

Last but not least, this tutorial contrasts such a model-driven approach with recent LLM-based approaches.

2.1 Summary of Topics Covered

- *Background*
  - Interaction design
  - Speech acts
  - Conversation Analysis
  - Model-driven transformation
- *Interaction design based on discourse modeling*
  - Discourse example
  - Communicative Acts
  - Adjacency Pair
  - RST relations
  - Exercise: Understand given model
- *GUI Generation*
  - Process of user-interface generation
  - Generation of Structural UI Model
  - Generation of Behavioral UI Model
  - Weaving of structural and behavioral models
  - Optimization for tailoring to device
  - Examples of generated user interfaces
  - Unified Communication Platform
- *User story*
  - Design alternatives
  - Customization
- *LLM-based approaches*
  - Exercise: Try to generate a GUI using an LLM-based approach
  - Contrasting model-based with generative AI

  - Pros and cons

- *Conclusion*

3 Learning Objectives and Outcomes

In this tutorial, participants will learn about an approach to GUI generation from models at the highest level of the Cameleon Reference Framework, i.e., the Tasks & Concepts Level. These models focus on the specification of (classes of) dialogues for modeling activities that can be performed by the user or the application (system). Participants will get an overview of both automatically generating and customizing Web GUIs, and how this approach can be used for exploring design alternatives. Participants will also understand the inherent difference between such a model-driven approach and recent LLM-based approaches.

References

1. Bogdan, C., et al.: Generating an abstract user interface from a discourse model inspired by human communication. In: Proceedings of the 41st Hawaii International Conference on System Sciences (HICSS'08), IEEE, Waikoloa, Big Island, Hawaii (2008)
2. Bogdan, C., Kaindl, H., Falb, J., Popp, R.: Modeling of interaction design by end users through discourse modeling. In: Proceedings of the 2008 ACM International Conference on Intelligent User Interfaces (IUI'08). ACM Press, Maspalomas, Gran Canaria, Spain (2008)
3. Falb, J., Kaindl, H., Horacek, H., Bogdan, C., Popp, R., Arnautovic, E.: A discourse model for interaction design based on theories of human communication. In: CHI'06 Extended Abstracts on Human Factors in Computing Systems, ACM Press, pp. 754–759 (2006)
4. Falb, J., Kavaldjian, S., Popp, R., Raneburger, D., Arnautovic, E., Kaindl, H.: Fully automatic user interface generation from discourse models. In: Proceedings of the 2009 ACM International Conference on Intelligent User Interfaces (IUI'09), ACM Press. Tool demo paper (2009)
5. Kaindl, H., Popp, R., Raneburger, D.: Exploring design alternatives for automated web GUI generation. In: Krems, J.F., da Silva, H.P., Cipresso, P. (eds.) Computer-Human Interaction Research and Applications. CHIRA 2025. Communications in Computer and Information Science, vol. 2836. Springer (2026)
6. Falb, J., Popp, R., Röck, T., Jelinek, H., Arnautovic, E., Kaindl, H.: Using communicative acts in interface design specifications for automated synthesis of user interfaces. In: Proceedings of the 21st IEEE/ACM International Conference on Automated Software Engineering (ASE'06), pp. 261–264 (2006)
7. J. Falb, R. Popp, R., Röck, T., Jelinek, H., Arnautovic, E., Kaindl, H.: UI prototyping for multiple devices through specifying interaction design. In: Proceedings of the 11th IFIP TC 13 International Conference on Human-Computer Interaction (INTERACT 2007), Rio de Janeiro, Brazil. Springer, pp. 136–149 (2007)
8. Kaindl, H., Popp, R., Raneburger, D.: Alternative interaction design patterns for automated GUI generation from discourse-based communication models. In: Proceedings of the 2014 IEEE International Conference on Systems, Man and Cybernetics (SMC'14). San Diego, CA, USA. IEEE (2014)

9. Kavaldjian, S., Bogdan, C., Falb, J., Kaindl, H.: Transforming Discourse Models to Structural User Interface Models, Models in Software Engineering, MoDELS 2007 Workshops, LNCS 5002, pp. 77–88. Springer-Verlag, Berlin-Heidelberg (invited) (2008)
10. Kavaldjian, S., Falb, J., Kaindl, H.: Generating content presentation according to purpose. In: Proceedings of the 2009 IEEE International Conference on Systems, Man and Cybernetics (SMC 2009). San Antonio, TX, USA. IEEE (2009)
11. Popp, R., Falb, J., Raneburger, D., Kaindl, H.: A transformation engine for model-driven UI generation. In: Proceedings of the 4th ACM SIGCHI Symposium on Engineering Interactive Computing Systems (EICS´12), Copenhagen, Denmark (2012)
12. Popp, R., Kaindl, H., Badalians Gholi Kandi, S., Raneburger, D., Paterno, F.: Duality of task- and discourse-based interaction design for GUI generation. In: Proceedings of the 2014 IEEE International Conference on Systems, Man, and Cybernetics (SMC'14), pp. 3323–3328 (2014)
13. Popp, R., Kaindl, H., Raneburger, D.: Connecting interaction models and application logic for model-driven generation of web-based graphical user interfaces. In: Proceedings of the 20th Asia-Pacific Software Engineering Conference (APSEC'13). ACM (2013)
14. Popp, R., Raneburger, D., Kaindl, H.: Tool support for automated multi-device GUI generation from discourse-based communication models. In: Proceedings of the ACM SIGCHI Symposium on Engineering Interactive Computing Systems (EICS'13) (2013)
15. Raneburger, D., Alonso-Ríos, D., Popp, R., Kaindl, H., Falb J.: A user study with GUIs tailored for smartphones. In: Human-Computer Interaction – INTERACT 2013 (Heidelberg) (Lecture Notes in Computer Science), Vol. 8118, pp. 505–512. Springer (2013)
16. Raneburger, D., Kaindl, H., Popp, R.: Strategies for automated GUI tailoring for multiple devices. In: Proceedings of the 48st Annual Hawaii International Conference on System Sciences (HICSS-48) (2015)
17. Raneburger, D., Kaindl, H., Popp, R.: Model transformation rules for customization of multi-device graphical user interfaces. In: Proceedings of the 7th ACM SIGCHI Symposium on Engineering Interactive Computing Systems (EICS'15), pp. 100–109 (2015)
18. Raneburger, D., Kaindl, H., Popp, R., Šajatovic, V., Armbruster, A.: A process for facilitating interaction design through automated GUI generation. In: Proceedings of the 29th ACM/SIGAPP Symposium on Applied Computing (SAC'14) (2014)
19. Raneburger, D., Popp, R., Kaindl, H.: Model-driven transformation for optimizing PSMs: a case study of rule design for multi-device GUI generation. In: Proceedings of the 8th International Joint Conference on Software Technologies (ICSOFT'13). SciTePress (2013)
20. Raneburger, D., Popp, R., Kaindl, H.: A user study to evaluate the customization of automatically generated GUIs. In: Proceedings of the 21st Congress of the International Ergonomics Association (IEA 2021), Lecture Notes in Networks and Systems, pp. 683–690. Springer, Cham (2021)
21. Raneburger, D., Popp, R., Kaindl, H., Armbruster, A., Šajatović, V.: An iterative and incremental process for interaction design through automated GUI generation. In Human-Computer Interaction. Theories, Methods, and Tools. HCI 2014. Lecture Notes in Computer Science, vol. 8510. Springer, Cham (2014)
22. Raneburger, D., Popp, R., Kaindl, H., Falb, J.: Automated WIMP-UI behavior generation: parallelism and granularity of communication units. In: Proceedings of the 2011 IEEE International Conference on Systems, Man and Cybernetics (SMC'11), pp. 2816–2821 (2011)
23. Raneburger, D., Popp, R., Kaindl, H., Falb, J., Ertl, D.: Automated generation of device-specific WIMP-UIs: weaving of structural and behavioral models. In: Proceedings of the 2011 SIGCHI Symposium on Engineering Interactive Computing Systems (EICS'11) (2011)
24. Rathfux, T., Popp, R., Kaindl, H.: Adding custom widgets to model-driven GUI generation. In: Proceedings of the 8th ACM SIGCHI Symposium on Engineering Interactive Computing Systems (EICS'16), Brussels, Belgium (2016)

25. Rathfux, T., Thöner, J., Kaindl, H., Popp, R.: Combining design-time generation of web-pages with responsive design for improving low-vision accessibility. In: Proceedings of the ACM SIGCHI Symposium on Engineering Interactive Computing Systems (EICS'18), Paris (2018)

Author Index

A. Mauri et al. (Eds.): ICWE 2026, LNCS 16625, pp. 355–356, 2026.
https://doi.org/10.1007/978-3-032-29372-5

Zeitfracht Medien GmbH
Ferdinand-Jühlke-Straße 7
99095 Erfurt, Deutschland
produktsicherheit@kolibri360.de